CompTIA Linux+ Certification Guide

A comprehensive guide to achieving LX0-103 and LX0-104 certifications with mock exams

Philip Inshanally

BIRMINGHAM - MUMBAI

CompTIA Linux+ Certification Guide

Commissioning Editor: Vijin Boricha
Acquisition Editor: Rohit Rajkumar
Content Development Editor: Ronn Kurien
Technical Editor: Prachi Sawant
Copy Editor: Safis Editing
Project Coordinator: Jagdish Prabhu
Proofreader: Safis Editing
Indexer: Pratik Shirodkar
Graphics: Tom Scaria
Production Coordinator: Shantanu Zagade

First published: September 2018

Production reference: 2180419

Published by Packt Publishing Ltd.
Livery Place
35 Livery Street
Birmingham
B3 2PB, UK.

ISBN 978-1-78934-449-3

www.packtpub.com

`mapt.io`

Mapt is an online digital library that gives you full access to over 5,000 books and videos, as well as industry leading tools to help you plan your personal development and advance your career. For more information, please visit our website.

Why subscribe?

- Spend less time learning and more time coding with practical eBooks and Videos from over 4,000 industry professionals

- Improve your learning with Skill Plans built especially for you

- Get a free eBook or video every month

- Mapt is fully searchable

- Copy and paste, print, and bookmark content

Packt.com

Did you know that Packt offers eBook versions of every book published, with PDF and ePub files available? You can upgrade to the eBook version at `www.packt.com` and as a print book customer, you are entitled to a discount on the eBook copy. Get in touch with us at `customercare@packtpub.com` for more details.

At `www.packt.com`, you can also read a collection of free technical articles, sign up for a range of free newsletters, and receive exclusive discounts and offers on Packt books and eBooks.

Contributors

About the author

Philip Inshanally has been in the IT industry for over 17 years. He has extensively worked in various platforms. Philip has his own consulting firm which provides local and remote support around the world; focusing towards designing, planning, implementing and documenting to name a few. As an industry professional, he has the competitive edge due to his ongoing development. He has acquired excellent skills, and this has helped him in dealing with individuals both locally and internationally. He is a father of one; Matthew Zach Inshanally.

He has experience in routing, switching, OTT, and various Linux distributions. Also, other vendor-specific technologies such as Cisco, Extreme, Juniper, Microsoft, Sandvine, Zhone, and so on.

First and foremost, I would like to thank my creator for blessing me with the ability to produce such a remarkable book. Also, I would like to thank a number of persons who have been close to me and supported me throughout the entire process; namely, my mom, dad, sister and my son Matthew.

About the reviewer

Sreecharan Gaddam has finished bachelors in computer science from the University of Sathyabama, Chennai, India. He started working on cloud technologies in various platforms also he completed the masters of science from the University northwestern polytechnic with major in computer science. He was an intern in Viotalk and moved to the senior positions as a developer. He is exploring Continuous delivery and Continuous deployment tools areas like Jenkins, Chef, and puppet. He has four years of experience in Linux environment. He worked on SSL, Encrypting the links, Virtual Private Cloud, Route 53, NAT Gateways, and subnets. He also worked on languages like Python, Ruby, Go and Java for scripting and developing the applications.

Packt is searching for authors like you

If you're interested in becoming an author for Packt, please visit `authors.packtpub.com` and apply today. We have worked with thousands of developers and tech professionals, just like you, to help them share their insight with the global tech community. You can make a general application, apply for a specific hot topic that we are recruiting an author for, or submit your own idea.

Table of Contents

Preface

Linux+ certification demonstrates technical competency and provides a broad awareness of Linux operating systems. Professionals who have achieved the Linux+ certification exhibit all-important knowledge of installation, operation, administration, and troubleshooting services.

The CompTIA Linux+ Certification Guide is an overview of the certification that gives you insights into the system architecture. You'll understand how to install and uninstall Linux distribution, followed by working with various package managers. Once you've grasped all this, you'll move on to manipulating files and processes at command-line interface (CLI) and creating, monitoring, killing, restarting, and modifying processes. As you progress, you'll be equipped to work with display managers and learn how to create, modify, and remove user accounts and groups, as well as understand how to automate tasks. The last set of chapters helps you configure dates and set up local and remote system logging. In addition to this, you'll explore different internet protocols, along with discovering network configuration, security administration, Shell scripting and SQL management.

By the end of this book, you'll not only have gotten to grips with all the modules using practice questions and mock exams, but you'll also be well prepared to achieve the LX0-103 and LX0-104 certification exams.

Who this book is for

The CompTIA Linux+ Certification Guide is for you if you want to gain the CompTIA Linux+ certificate. This guide is also for system administrators and rookie Linux professionals interested in enhancing their Linux and Shell scripting skills. No prior knowledge of Linux is needed, although some understanding of Shell scripting would be helpful.

What this book covers

Chapter 1, *Configuring the Hardware Settings*, this chapter focuses on viewing interrupts, looking at /proc/interrupts, CPU info viewing the /proc/cpuinfo, raid status viewing /proc/mdstat, the devices directory /dev, the /proc virtual directory, the lsmod command and usage, the modprobe command and usage, the lspci command command and usage.

Chapter 2, *Booting the System*, this chapter focuses on the process of booting the system, looking at the GRUB and GRUB2 configuration file, focusing on the timer, default boot entry, passing argument at the GRUB/GRUB2 boot menu, the chkconfig command, the systemctl, the dmesg command, the various start/stop scripts0.

Chapter 3, *Changing Runlevels and Boot Targets*, this chapter focuses on the introduction of runlevels and boot targets, the types of runlevels and boot targets available in the LINUX distributions, the differences between runlevels and boot targets, working with runlevels at the CLI, also working with boot targets at the CLI.

Chapter 4, *Designing a Hard Disk Layout*, this chapter focuses on creating partitions/segmenting a physical hard disk at the CLI, emphasis on the usage of the fdisk utility, the parted utility, the steps to create, remove, define the partition type, format the hard disk with the various mkfs commands.

Chapter 5, *Installing a Linux Distribution*, this chapter focuses on installing a Linux Distribution, particularly the Red Hat flavour of CentOS and the Debian flavour of Ubuntu, the reader will be exposed to installing a Linux distro using a well-known method of a Live CD.

Chapter 6, *Using Debian Package Management*, in Linux, software is added, removed in a number of ways. Here the focus is on the way we add software in a Debian distribution, particularly using the dpkg, apt-get, aptitude commands from the CLI, synaptic from a GUI, and the reader learns how to add, remove, update, erase a software in a Debian distribution listed.

Chapter 7, *Using YUM Package Management*, in this chapter, we focus on adding software in a Red Hat distribution, particularly using the yum, dnf, rpm commands from the CLI, yumex from a GUI, the reader learn to add, remove, update, and erase software in a Red Hat environment.

Chapter 8, *Performing File Management*, in this chapter, the reader learns about the various commands that Linux provides which are common distributions to manipulate files, process(s), at the CLI. These commands can be classified into several categories: file system navigation, file manipulation, directory manipulation, and file location, and file examination, CPU hardware identity, process priority, manipulating CPU priority for process.

Chapter 9, *Creating, Monitoring, Killing, and Restarting Processes*, in Linux, a process is more or less synonymous with a running program. init / systemd, the first process run by the kernel when it boots. This chapter focuses on how we create a process, monitor hardware usages for existing processes, terminate / kill a process or restart a process at the CLI.

Chapter 10, *Modifying Process Execution,* there may be times when you'll want to give priority to important programs over other programs, also, sending some programs to the background allowing the user to continue using the shell or bring some programs to the foreground. This chapter focuses on the methods of accomplishing just that, using the nice and renice, fg, bg commands.

Chapter 11, *Display Managers,* this chapter focuses on the various display managers available in Linux distros, such as X Display Manager (XDM), KDE Display Manager (KDM), Gnome Display Manager (GDM), Light Display Manager (LightDM) which is used To handle GUI logins, they all use the XDMCP - X Display Manager Control Protocol which starts the local computer's X server.

Chapter 12, *Managing User and Group Accounts,* this chapter focuses on user and group management, covering from user account creation, modifying existing user account(s), removing user account(s), group creation, modifying groups of users, removing group(s), as well as best practices to consider when managing users and groups. Focus is placed on using commands such as useradd, usermod, userdel, groupadd, groupmod, groupdel, who, w, change, passwd, last, whoami, configuration files such as /etc/passwd, /etc/shadow, /etc/group, /etc/skel file.

Chapter 13, *Automating Tasks,* this chapter focuses on automating common administration task(s) in a Linux environment as well as commonly used methods to consider when setting up automation for a given task. Focus is placed on using commands such as crontab, at, atq, atrm, anacron, configuration files such as /etc/at.deny, /etc/at.allow, /etc/cron. {daily,hourly,monthly,weekly}, /etc/cron.allow, /etc/anacrontab.

Chapter 14, *Maintaining System Time and Logging,* this chapter focuses on configuring the date and time along with the setting the time zone. Also, the steps to set to logging locally using rsyslog, logrotate in a Linux distribution and configuring logging to be sent to a remote syslog server for management. Commands covered includes the tzselect, tzconfig, date, journalctl, directories include the / etc/timezone, /etc/localtime, /usr/share/zoneinfo, /etc/logrotate.conf, /etc/logrotate.d/, /etc/systemd/journald.conf, / var/log/, /var/log/journal/, /etc/rsyslog.conf.

Chapter 15, *Fundamentals of Internet Protocol,* this chapter focuses on the basic principles surrounding how a network such as the Internet works, by breaking down how two computers communicate with each other, we delve into Internet Protocol (IP) addressing, particularly IPv4, the various classes of IPv4 such as the ClassA, ClassB, ClassC, CIDR notation, then we look at subnetting. Next we take a look at IPv6, the format of an IPv6 address, the well-known IPv6 address, ways to cut down on the lengthy IPv6 address.

Finally, we look at the differences between some well-known protocols such as UDP, TCP and ICMP and their port numbers

Chapter 16, *Network configuration and troubleshooting*, this chapter focuses on the basic network configuration in a Linux environment, looking at configuring an IPv4 address, subnet mask, default gateway. Next we look at configuring an IPv6 address, default gateway, Then we focus on configuring client side DNS, Finally we focus on network troubleshooting. Commands such as `ifup`, `ifdown`, `ifconfig`, `ip`, `ip link`, `ip route`, `route`, `ping`, `ping6`, `netstat`, `traceroute`, `traceroute6`, `tracepath`, `tracepath6`, `dig`, `host`, `hostname`.

Chapter 17, *Performing Security Administrative Tasks*, this chapter focuses on the performing security administrative tasks in a Linux environment, focusing on setting up host security, granting user(s) special permissions with sudoers, date encryption. Commands covered are the `sudo`, `ssh-keygen`, `ssh-agent`, `ssh-add`, `gpg`, configuration files covered includes `/etc/sudoers`, `/etc/hosts.allow`, `/etc/hosts.deny`, `~/.ssh/id_rsa`, `~/.ssh/id_rsa.pub`, `/etc/ssh/ssh_host_rsa_key`, `~/.ssh/authorized_keys`, `/etc/ssh_known_hosts`.

Chapter 18, *Shell Scripting and SQL Data Management*, this chapter focuses on introducing Shell scripting and SQL data management in a Linux environment. First we look at the basic format when writing scripts, identifying the interpreter for the script, configuring the script to be executable, using `for`, `while` loop, `if` statements. Then we focus our attention to SQL data management, we cover basic SQL commands such as `insert`, `update`, `select`, `delete`, `from`, `where`, `group by`, `order by`, `join`.

Chapter 19, *Mock Exam - 1*, this mock exam will compile of realistic exam questions and answers. You'll gain the insight of examples drawn from real-world scenarios, with detailed guidance and authoritative coverage of key topics. Realistic exam questions from recent tests to bring you the best method of preparing for the CompTIA LX0-103/LX0-104 exam.

Chapter 20, *Mock Exam - 2*, this mock exam will compile of realistic exam questions and answers. You'll gain the insight of examples drawn from real-world scenarios, with detailed guidance and authoritative coverage of key topics. Realistic exam questions from recent tests to bring you the best method of preparing for the CompTIA LX0-103/LX0-104 exam.

To get the most out of this book

It is assumed that some readers may have limited or no knowledge about Linux operating systems. It is also assumed that some readers are Linux users but may need a bit of a refresher on interfacing with a Linux environment.

The key to reinforcing each chapter to memory is by grabbing copies of various Linux distributions; namely CentOS, Fedora, and Ubuntu. Then install the various Operating Systems in a virtual environment such as VMware or VirtualBox. Next, follow along each chapters (the chapters are independent of each other so you can choose any given chapter to study/practice) by practicing inside the various Linux distributions in order to better grasp each chapter. After practicing the various chapters, you will become more productive within a Linux environment; this will empower you to be better equipped in mixed environments where there are both Windows and Linux Operating Systems.

You can follow the along the tutorials presented in `Chapter 5`, *Installing a Linux Distribution* of this book for getting started with installation.

Download the color images

We also provide a PDF file that has color images of the screenshots/diagrams used in this book. You can download it here: `https://www.packtpub.com/sites/default/files/downloads/9781789344493_ColorImages.pdf`.

Conventions used

There are a number of text conventions used throughout this book.

`CodeInText`: Indicates code words in text, database table names, folder names, filenames, file extensions, pathnames, dummy URLs, user input, and Twitter handles. Here is an example: "To see the runlevel at the shell in real time, we can use the `runlevel` command."

A block of code is set as follows:

```
while <condition>
do
        <command1>
        <command2
```

Any command-line input or output is written as follows:

```
$[philip@localhost Desktop]$ who -r
run-level 5 2018-06-20 08:20 last=S
[philip@localhost Desktop]$
```

Bold: Indicates a new term, an important word, or words that you see onscreen. For example, words in menus or dialog boxes appear in the text like this. Here is an example: "Select **System info** from the **Administration** panel."

Warnings or important notes appear like this.

 Tips and tricks appear like this.

Get in touch

Feedback from our readers is always welcome.

General feedback: If you have questions about any aspect of this book, mention the book title in the subject of your message and email us at customercare@packtpub.com.

Errata: Although we have taken every care to ensure the accuracy of our content, mistakes do happen. If you have found a mistake in this book, we would be grateful if you would report this to us. Please visit www.packt.com/submit-errata, selecting your book, clicking on the Errata Submission Form link, and entering the details.

Piracy: If you come across any illegal copies of our works in any form on the Internet, we would be grateful if you would provide us with the location address or website name. Please contact us at copyright@packt.com with a link to the material.

If you are interested in becoming an author: If there is a topic that you have expertise in and you are interested in either writing or contributing to a book, please visit authors.packtpub.com.

Reviews

Please leave a review. Once you have read and used this book, why not leave a review on the site that you purchased it from? Potential readers can then see and use your unbiased opinion to make purchase decisions, we at Packt can understand what you think about our products, and our authors can see your feedback on their book. Thank you!

For more information about Packt, please visit packt.com.

1
Configuring the Hardware Settings

This chapter covers viewing interrupts. It focuses on `/proc/interrupts`, CPU info viewing (`/proc/cpuinfo`), and viewing the physical memory installed. It also looks at `/proc/meminfo`, the `free` command, viewing swap memory, and adding and removing additional swap memory using the `dd`, `mkswap`, `swapon`, and `swapoff` commands. The raid status (viewing `/proc/mdstat`) is outlined, as is the `/dev` devices directory, the `/proc` virtual directory, the `lsmod` command and its usage, the `modprobe` command and its usage, and the `lspci` command and its usage. The `/proc` directory is a virtual filesystem that is created upon boot up, which stores various items of hardware information about a system.

Navigating through the various directories and using these commands is very informative, and allows you to retrieve hardware information in a Linux environment.

We will cover the following topics in this chapter:

- Viewing CPU, RAM, and swap info
- Interrupts and devices
- Modules

Viewing CPU, RAM, and swap info

Let's take a look at how we can view CPU, RAM, and swap info on a Linux system.

First, we will focus our attention on gaining information on a CPU, so we will look at the `/proc/cpuinfo` file. We can garner detailed information about the CPU, ranging from the vendor ID, the CPU family, the model name, the CPU rate in MHZ, its cache size, and the number of cores, to name a few. Here is an excerpt from running the `cat` command alongside `/proc/cpuinfo`:

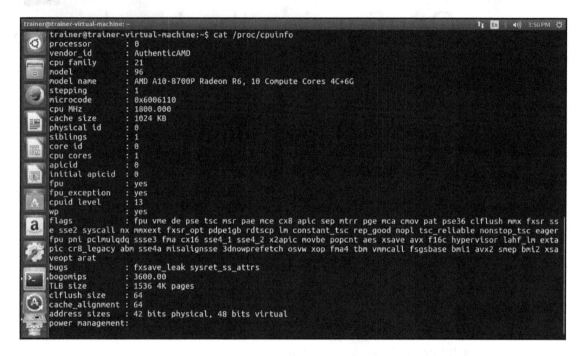

Some more information is given here about the CPU:

```
trainer@trainer-virtual-machine: ~                                     ↑↓ En  ◀)) 3:51 PM ⏻
processor       : 0
vendor_id       : AuthenticAMD
cpu family      : 21
model           : 96
model name      : AMD A10-8700P Radeon R6, 10 Compute Cores 4C+6G
stepping        : 1
microcode       : 0x6006110
cpu MHz         : 1800.000
cache size      : 1024 KB
physical id     : 0
siblings        : 1
core id         : 0
cpu cores       : 1
apicid          : 0
initial apicid  : 0
fpu             : yes
fpu_exception   : yes
cpuid level     : 13
wp              : yes
flags           : fpu vme de pse tsc msr pae mce cx8 apic sep mtrr pge mca cmov pat pse36 clflush mmx fxsr ss
e sse2 syscall nx mmxext fxsr_opt pdpe1gb rdtscp lm constant_tsc rep_good nopl tsc_reliable nonstop_tsc eager
fpu pni pclmulqdq ssse3 fma cx16 sse4_1 sse4_2 x2apic movbe popcnt aes xsave avx f16c hypervisor lahf_lm exta
pic cr8_legacy abm sse4a misalignsse 3dnowprefetch osvw xop fma4 tbm vmmcall fsgsbase bmi1 avx2 smep bmi2 xsa
veopt arat
bugs            : fxsave_leak sysret_ss_attrs
bogomips        : 3600.00
TLB size        : 1536 4K pages
clflush size    : 64
cache_alignment : 64
address sizes   : 42 bits physical, 48 bits virtual
power management:

trainer@trainer-virtual-machine:~$ ▮
```

From the preceding output, we can see detailed information pertaining to the CPU that we ran the `cat /proc/cpuinfo` command against.

Next, let's take a look at how we can gather information on the amount of physical memory, the **Random Access Memory (RAM)**, installed in a system. We will focus on two commands: the `cat /proc/meminfo` and the `free` commands.

Using the Linux system for demonstration once again, we will look at the output of the `cat /proc/meminfo` command:

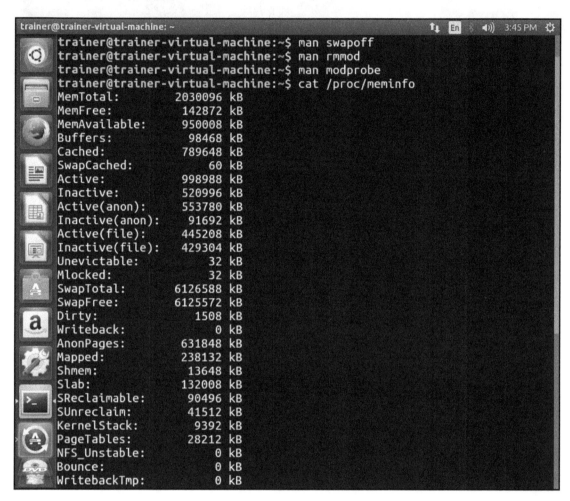

Some more memory usage information is shown in the following screenshot:

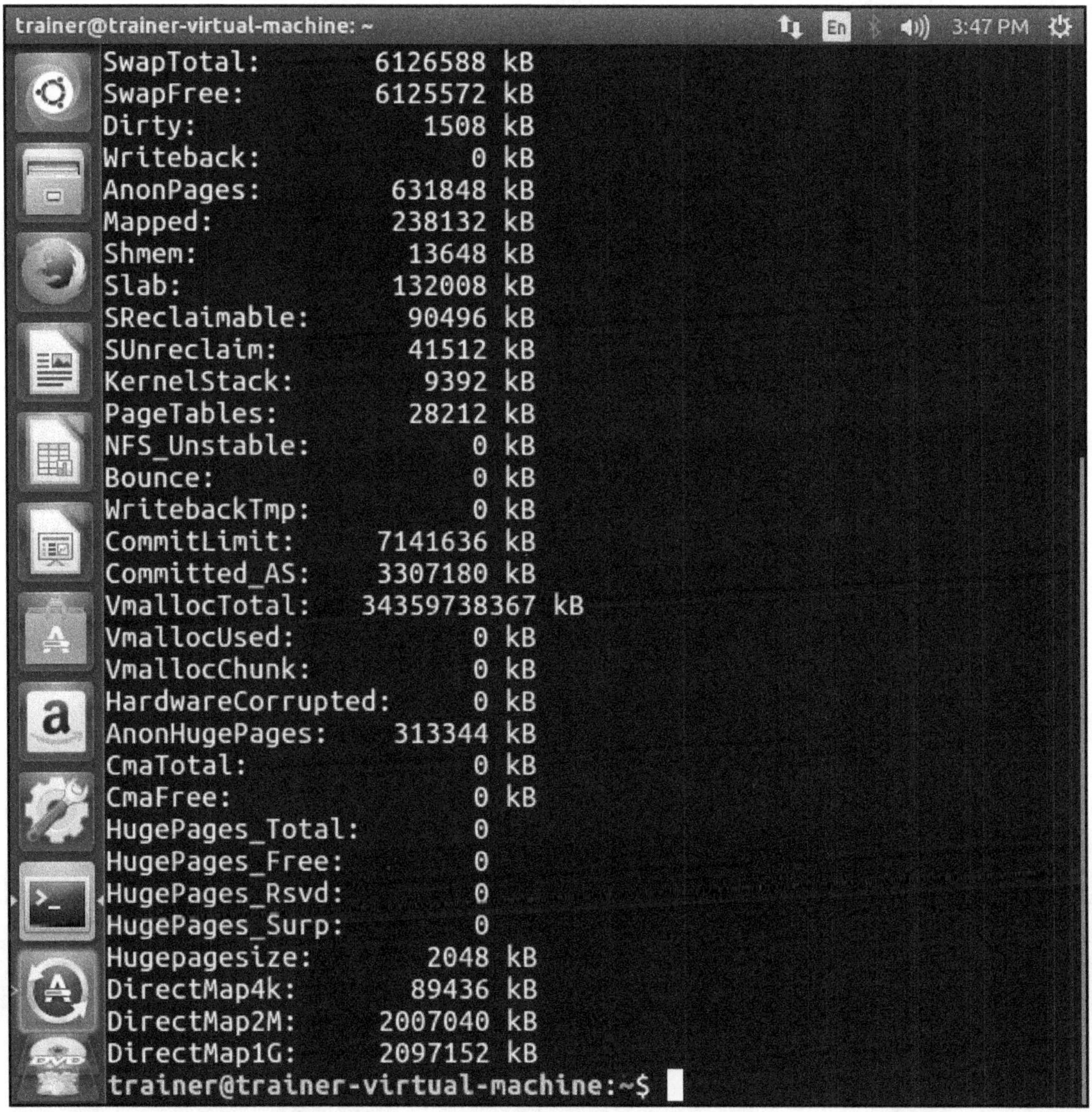

From the preceding output, we can see some important fields, namely the first three fields (MemTotal, MemFree, and MemAvailable), which reflect the current status of our physical memory (RAM).

Now let's look at another command, the free command. This command will give us the memory information in a more human-readable format. Using our test Linux system, we will run the free command:

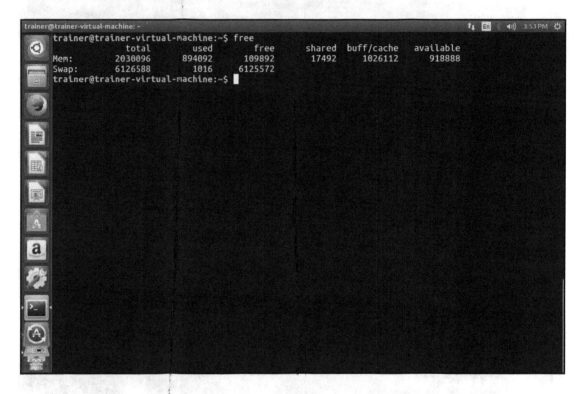

Running the `free` command on its own yields the preceding results in kilobytes. We can tag some options onto the `free` command to be even more explicit. Here is a list of options that we can use with the `free` command, using an Ubuntu distro:

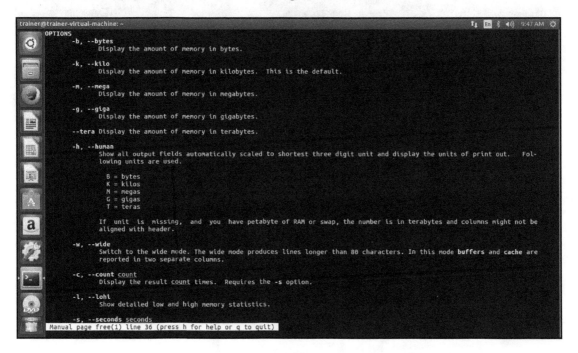

These are some more options that we can pass with the `free` command on an Ubuntu distro:

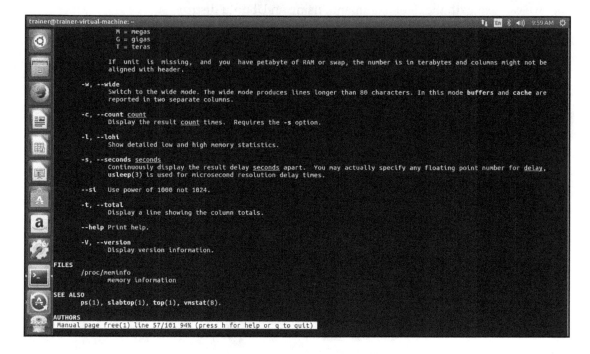

Similarly, if we take a look at the main page of the `free` command on a CentOS 7 distribution, we can see similar options:

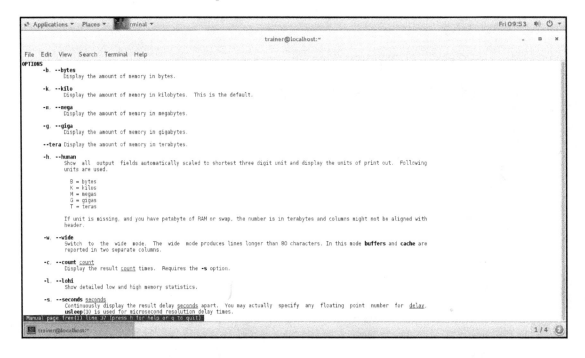

Some more options that we can pass with the `free` command on a CentOS 7 distro are shown in the following screenshot:

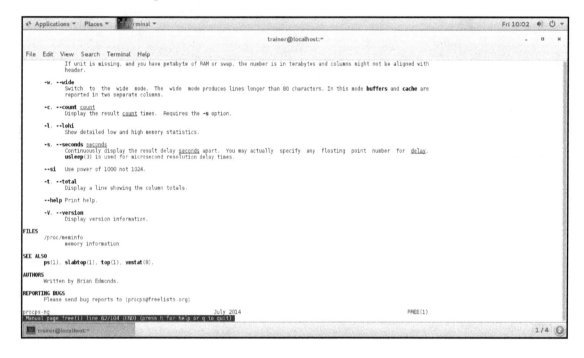

Let's try a few of the options with the `free` command:

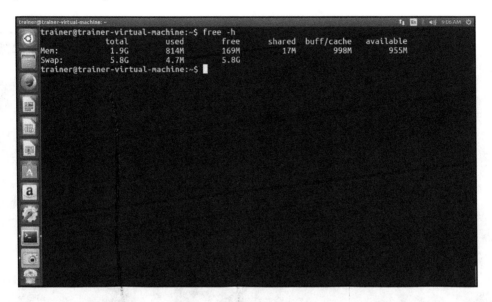

The preceding output is by far one of the most commonly used options (-h) with the `free` command. We can even take it a step further by tagging on the (-g) option to display the total amount of physical memory in gigabytes:

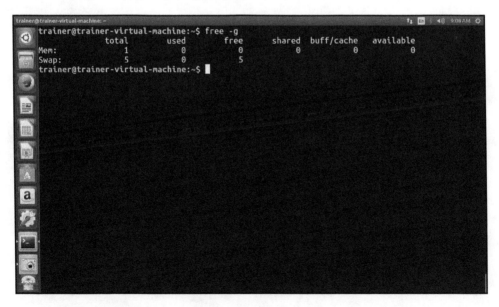

We can even see the low and high memory statistics by using yet another fantastic option, the (−l) option:

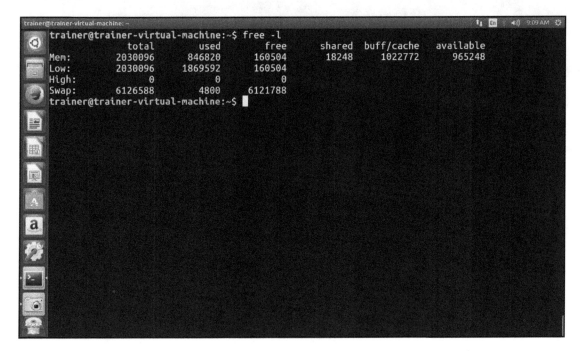

In the preceding screenshot, we are not just shown the RAM information, but also our swap memory. This is displayed in the last row. We can use another command if we prefer to see only the swap memory. Here, we can use the swapon command:

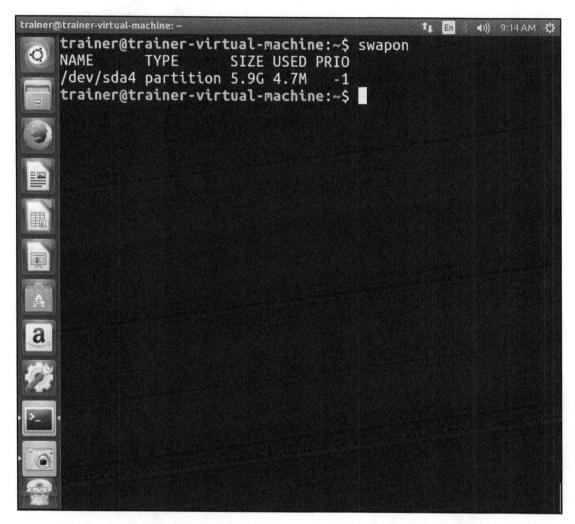

Here are some options that can be used with the `swapon` command from the main page of `swapon` on an Ubuntu distro:

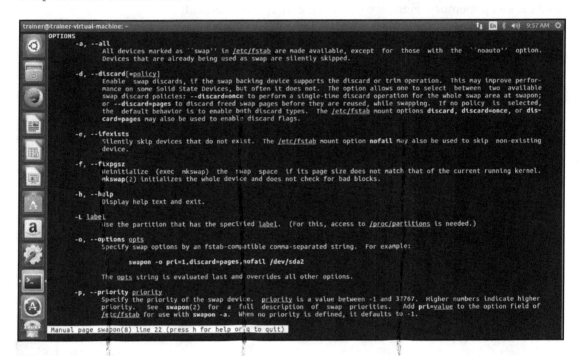

Some more options that can be passed with the swapon command on an Ubuntu distro are shown in the following screenshot:

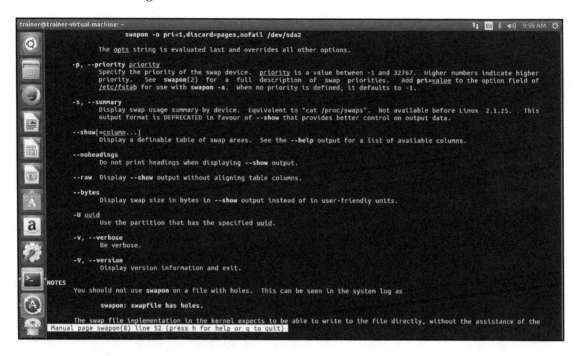

Here are some options that can be used with the `swapon` command from the main page of `swapon` on a CentOS 7 distro:

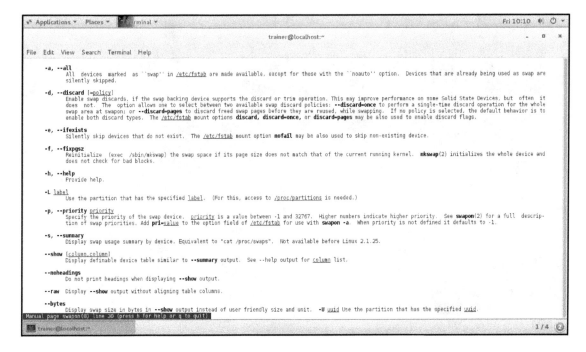

Some more options that can be passed with the `swapon` command on a CentOS 7 distro are shown in the following screenshot:

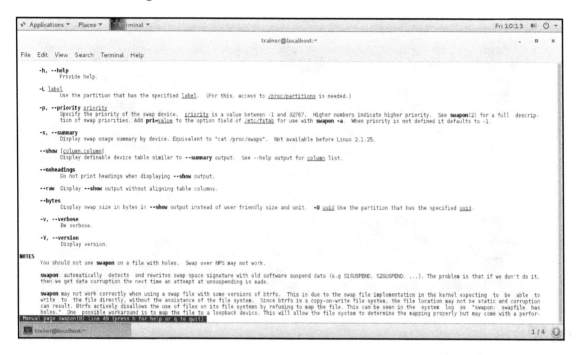

We can also see swap information from within the `/proc` directory, specifically in `/proc/swaps`:

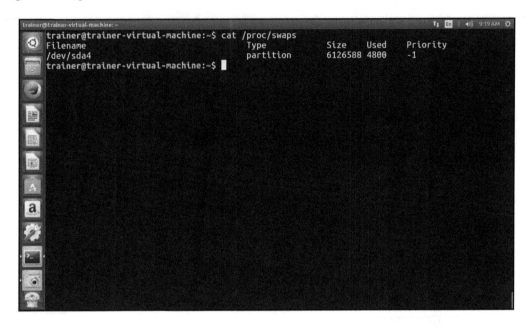

From the preceding output, we can see that the swap space is using the `/dev/sda4` partition. Now, if for some reason we run out of physical memory and we have maxed out our swap space, then we can either add more physical memory or add more swap space. So, let's focus on the steps to add more swap space.

We will need to create a blank file using the `dd` command. Note that you need root access to run this command at the shell:

```
trainer@trainer-virtual-machine:~$ dd if=/dev/zero of=/root/myswapfile
bs=1M count=1024
dd: failed to open '/root/myswapfile': Permission denied
trainer@trainer-virtual-machine:~$
```

From the preceding output, we can see that we got a `Permission denied` message, so let's switch to the root and try to rerun that command:

```
root@trainer-virtual-machine:/home/trainer# dd if=/dev/zero
of=/root/myswapfile bs=1M count=1024
1024+0 records in
1024+0 records out
1073741824 bytes (1.1 GB, 1.0 GiB) copied, 17.0137 s, 63.1 MB/s
root@trainer-virtual-machine:/home/trainer#
```

There we go; we've just created a `swap` file using the name `myswapfile`. Now we need to run the `mkswap` command and call the `swap` file that we just created at the shell:

```
root@trainer-virtual-machine:~# mkswap myswapfile
Setting up swapspace version 1, size = 1024 MiB (1073737728 bytes)
no label, UUID=e3b8cc8f-ad94-4df9-8608-c9679e6946bb
root@trainer-virtual-machine:~#
```

Now, the last step is to turn on the `swap` file so that the system uses it as needed:

```
root@trainer-virtual-machine:~# swapon myswapfile
swapon: /root/myswapfile: insecure permissions 0644, 0600 suggested.
root@trainer-virtual-machine:~#
```

We've got that warning message telling us about insecure permissions. We will discuss permissions in a later chapter. For now, we will continue to use the existing permissions. The last step is to verify that the `swap` file is indeed available to our system:

```
root@trainer-virtual-machine:~# swapon
NAME              TYPE       SIZE    USED   PRIO
/dev/sda4         partition  5.9G    960K   -1
/root/myswapfile  file       1024M   0B     -2
root@trainer-virtual-machine:~#
```

And, voila, we now have the newly created `swap` file at our system's disposal. We can also run the `free` command, and we will now find that the swap memory has increased by one gigabyte:

```
root@trainer-virtual-machine:~# free -h
      total   used   free   shared  buff/cache   available
Mem:  1.9G    848M   72M    13M     1.0G         924M
Swap: 6.8G    960K   6.8G
root@trainer-virtual-machine:~#
```

 In order for the changes to be safe upon reboot, you will need to add an entry in `/etc/fstab`.

Should we no longer want to use a `swap` file, we can use the `swapoff` command to remove `myswapfile` from the swap memory. Here is how we would accomplish this at the shell:

```
root@trainer-virtual-machine:~# swapoff myswapfile
root@trainer-virtual-machine:~#
```

Now let's rerun the `swapon` command followed by the `free` command to verify that `myswapfile` is indeed removed from swap usage:

```
root@trainer-virtual-machine:~# swapon
NAME          TYPE        SIZE    USED    PRIO
/dev/sda4 partition   5.9G    1.6M    -1
root@trainer-virtual-machine:~# free -h
        total     used     free     shared   buff/cache   available
Mem:     1.9G     931M     133M     17M        917M          845M
Swap:    5.8G     1.6M     5.8G
root@trainer-virtual-machine:~#
```

As we can see, `myswapfile` is no longer available for use as swap memory. Here are the options we can use with the `swapoff` command on an Ubuntu distro:

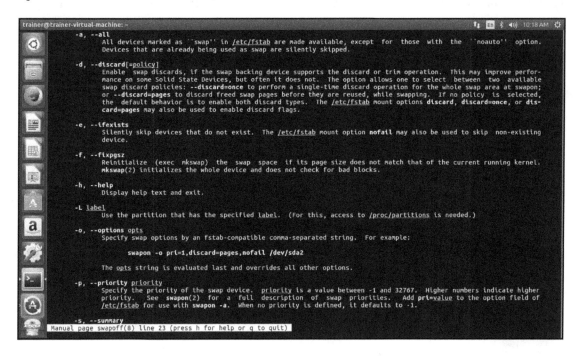

Some more options that can be passed with the `swapoff` command are shown in the following screenshot:

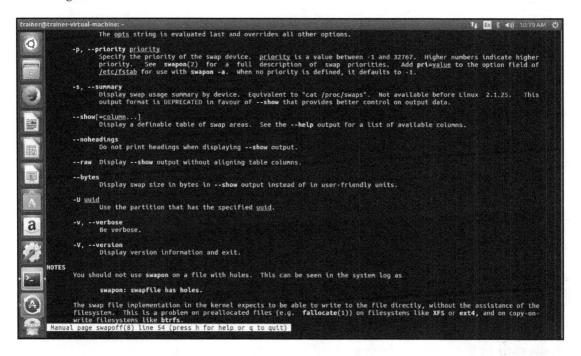

Here are the options we can use with the `swapoff` command on a CentOS 7 distro:

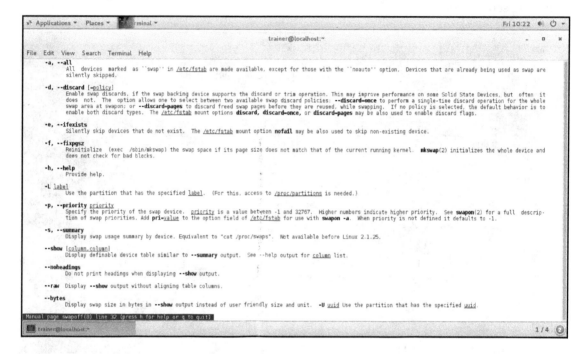

Some more options that can be passed with the `swapoff` command are shown in the following screenshot:

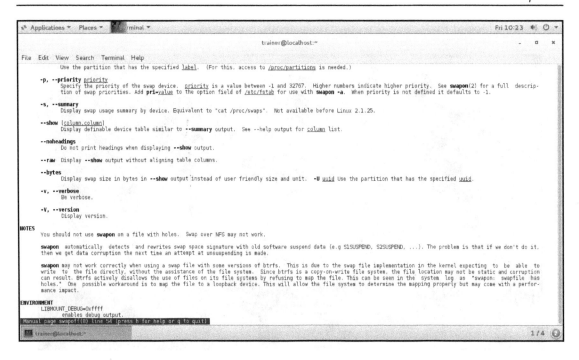

Use the partition that has the specified label. (For this, access to /proc/partitions is needed.)

-p, --priority priority
    Specify the priority of the swap device. priority is a value between -1 and 32767. Higher numbers indicate higher priority. See **swapon**(2) for a full descrip-
    tion of swap priorities. Add **pri**-value to the option field of /etc/fstab for use with **swapon -a**. When priority is not defined it defaults to -1.

-s, --summary
    Display swap usage summary by device. Equivalent to "cat /proc/swaps". Not available before Linux 2.1.25.

--show [column,column]
    Display definable device table similar to **--summary** output. See --help output for column list.

--noheadings
    Do not print headings when displaying **--show** output.

--raw Display **--show** output without aligning table columns.

--bytes
    Display swap size in bytes in **--show** output instead of user friendly size and unit. **-U** uuid Use the partition that has the specified uuid.

-v, --verbose
    Be verbose.

-V, --version
    Display version.

NOTES
    You should not use **swapon** on a file with holes. Swap over NFS may not work.

    swapon automatically detects and rewrites swap space signature with old software suspend data (e.g S1SUSPEND, S2SUSPEND, ...). The problem is that if we don't do it,
    then we get data corruption the next time an attempt at unsuspending is made.

    swapon may not work correctly when using a swap file with some versions of btrfs. This is due to the swap file implementation in the kernel expecting to be able to
    write to the file directly, without the assistance of the file system. Since btrfs is a copy-on-write file system, the file location may not be static and corruption
    can result. Btrfs actively disallows the use of files on its file systems by refusing to map the file. This can be seen in the system log as "swapon: swapfile has
    holes." One possible workaround is to map the file to a loopback device. This will allow the file system to determine the mapping properly but may come with a perfor-
    mance impact.

ENVIRONMENT
    LIBMOUNT_DEBUG=0xffff
        enables debug output.
Manual page swapoff(8) line 54 (press h for help or q to quit)

Interrupts and devices

Now let's switch gears and look at the **Interrupt Requests** (**IRQs**) and devices that are
available in our Linux system. You can think of an interrupt as a service hotline that we
would use whenever we need a particular item. We would ring a service hotline. The
theory remains the same for devices within a Linux system; whenever it requires the CPU's
attention, it sends out signals via interrupts. Traditional 32-bit architectures support up to
16 interrupts (0-15, as shown in the following screenshot). Newer architectures support far
more than 16 interrupts.

Let's take a look at the `/proc` directory once again, honing in on `/proc/interrupts`:

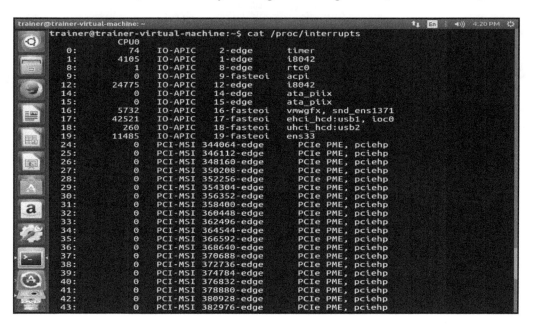

More interrupts are shown in the following screenshot:

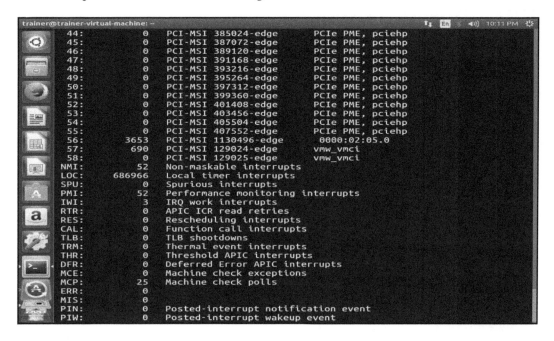

Some more interrupts are shown in the following screenshot:

From the preceding output, we can see that there are far more interrupts available. The output is read from left to right, where left represents the interrupt number, and moving to the right indicates the devices or services that are using the interrupts. We can see that the timer is using interrupt 0.

Now, let's turn our attention to devices. When we work with devices in a Linux system, the devices are represented by files. This enables us to communicate with the actual hardware in the system. There are some commonly used devices, such as hard disks, DVDs, and USBs, to name a few. Hard disks are represented as sd(n). For example: /dev/sda, /dev/sdb, /dev/sdc, and so on. Hard disk partitions are represented in the form of sd(n). For example: /dev/sda1, /dev/sda2, /dev/sdb1, and so on. Similarly, floppy disks are represented as fd. There are some special use-case files, such as /dev/null, /dev/zero, and /dev/tty*. You would use /dev/null when you want to send output from another command and the output is not needed. This is known as redirecting. /dev/zero is used in conjunction with the dd command that we covered earlier for creating blank files. /dev/tty* is used for remote logins. Let's take a look at how devices are shown in the Linux environment.

We will take a look at `/proc/devices` using our test Linux system:

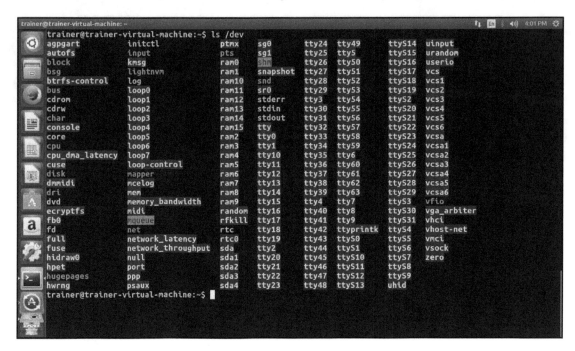

From the preceding output, the hard disk and partition are represented in the format of `/dev/sdXY`, where X represents the hard disk and Y represents the partition. We can tell the `ls` command to filter the output to only the hard disk and partition information as follows:

```
root@trainer-virtual-machine:~# ls /dev/sd*
/dev/sda   /dev/sda1   /dev/sda2   /dev/sda3   /dev/sda4
root@trainer-virtual-machine:~#
```

Modules

Have you ever wondered what happened to the term *drivers* in a Linux environment? Well, wonder no more. Most people coming from a Microsoft Windows background are accustomed to interacting with hardware through the use of drivers. In Linux, we refer to drivers as modules. This isn't as scary as it sounds. We load and unload modules whenever we are working with a piece of hardware. For example, when we plug in a USB drive, a module is loaded into the backend and is unloaded automatically when we remove the USB drive. It's that flexible.

Let's take a look at how we can view the modules that are installed in the Linux system using the lsmod command:

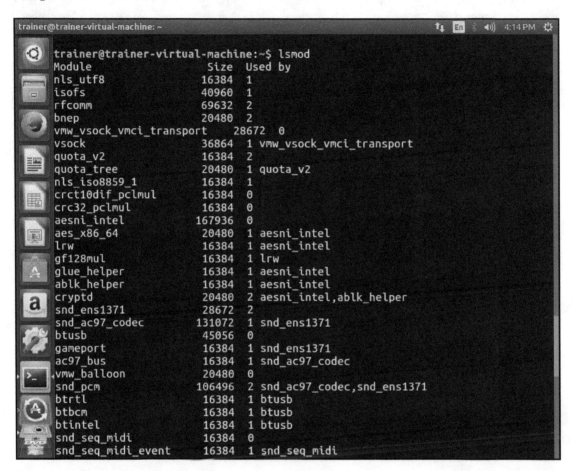

More modules that are available for use are shown in the following screenshot:

```
trainer@trainer-virtual-machine: ~                                    ↑↓ En ┆ ◀)) 4:17 PM ⚙
nfit                    32768  0
8250_fintek             16384  0
shpchp                  36864  0
i2c_piix4               24576  0
vmw_vmci                65536  2 vmw_vsock_vmci_transport,vmw_balloon
mac_hid                 16384  0
parport_pc              32768  0
ppdev                   20480  0
lp                      20480  0
parport                 49152  3 lp,ppdev,parport_pc
autofs4                 40960  2
hid_generic             16384  0
usbhid                  49152  0
hid                    118784  2 hid_generic,usbhid
vmwgfx                 237568  3
ttm                     98304  1 vmwgfx
psmouse                126976  0
drm_kms_helper         147456  1 vmwgfx
syscopyarea             16384  1 drm_kms_helper
sysfillrect             16384  1 drm_kms_helper
sysimgblt               16384  1 drm_kms_helper
fb_sys_fops             16384  1 drm_kms_helper
mptspi                  24576  4
mptscsih                40960  1 mptspi
mptbase                102400  2 mptspi,mptscsih
ahci                    36864  1
libahci                 32768  1 ahci
drm                    360448  6 ttm,drm_kms_helper,vmwgfx
e1000                  135168  0
scsi_transport_spi      32768  1 mptspi
pata_acpi               16384  0
fjes                    28672  0
trainer@trainer-virtual-machine:~$ ▊
```

From the preceding output, we can see that a number of modules are available for use in this Linux system. We read the output from left to right. Wherever we see a 0 value under the Used by column, it means that the module is not currently in use.

Now let's look at the process to remove a module using the rmmod command. We will remove the usbhid module, since it's not currently in use. We can quickly verify this is not in use by using lsmod | grep usbhid:

```
root@trainer-virtual-machine:~# lsmod | grep usbhid
usbhid                  49152  0
```

Great! Let's go ahead and remove that module using the `rmmod` command:

```
root@trainer-virtual-machine:~# rmmod usbhid
root@trainer-virtual-machine:~#
root@trainer-virtual-machine:~# lsmod | grep usbhid
root@trainer-virtual-machine:~#
```

There we go; the `usbhid` module is no longer loaded in the Linux system. It still resides there, however, because it was compiled in the kernel. There are only a few options to pass with `rmmod`. Here, they are on an Ubuntu distro:

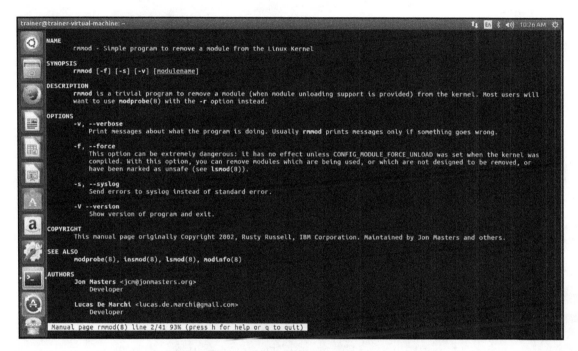

Similarly, here are the options to pass with the rmmod on a CentOS 7 distro:

In order for us to reinstall this usbhid module, we will use another popular command: insmod. Let's see how insmod works at the shell:

```
root@trainer-virtual-machine:~# insmod usbhid
insmod: ERROR: could not load module usbhid: No such file or directory
root@trainer-virtual-machine:~#
```

Now, based on the preceding output, it may seem to be contradictory that the insmod command is unable to find the usbhid module. Don't worry, this module is compiled in the kernel. That being said, we can use yet another helpful command, modprobe. This, by far, is more popular than insmod, as modprobe actually calls insmod in the backend whenever we add a module using modprobe. Interestingly enough, modprobe can be used to remove module(s) too. It does this by calling rmmod in the backend.

> We can use insmod itself to install the usbhid module. The only catch is that you have to specify the absolute path to the module. modprobe, on the other hand, uses the modules directory (namely /lib/modules/$(KERNEL_RELEASE)/) for modules, and loads modules based on the rules defined in the /etc/modprobe.d/ directory.

So, let's use `modprobe` to install the `usbhid` module at the shell.

```
root@trainer-virtual-machine:~# modprobe -v usbhid
insmod /lib/modules/4.4.0-24-generic/kernel/drivers/hid/usbhid/usbhid.ko
root@trainer-virtual-machine:~#
```

We used the (-v) option with `modprobe` because, by default, it will not show what is happening in the background. As you can see, `modprobe` is indeed calling `insmod` in the backend. Now we can remove this `usbhid` module using `modprobe`, and we will see that it is calling `rmmod` in the backend:

```
root@trainer-virtual-machine:~# modprobe -r -v usbhid
rmmod usbhid
root@trainer-virtual-machine:~#
```

From the preceding output, it is evident that `modprobe` is calling `rmmod` to remove a module.

Here are some options that can be used with the `modprobe` command on an Ubuntu distro:

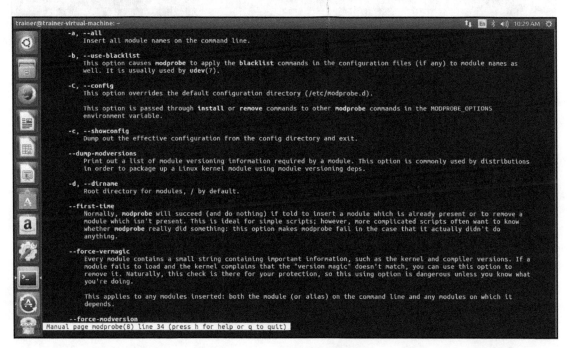

More options that can be passed with the `modprobe` command are shown in the following screenshot:

Some more options that can be passed with the `modprobe` command are shown in the following screenshot:

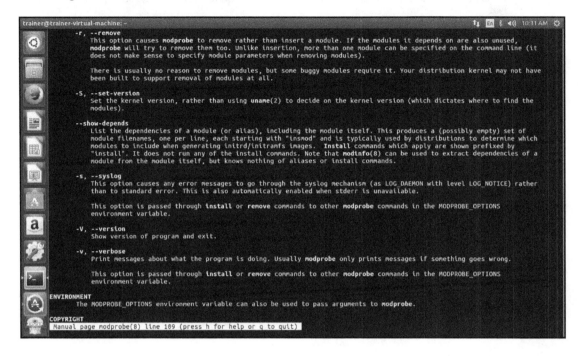

Here are some options that can be used with the `modprobe` command on a CentOS 7 distro:

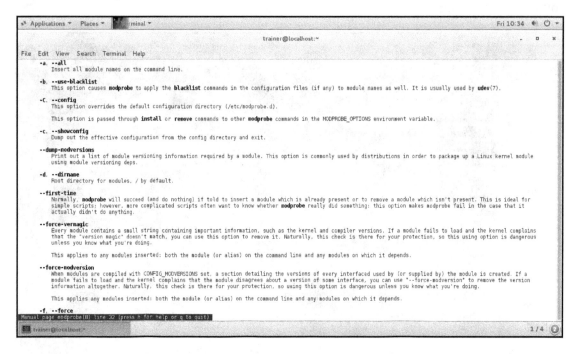

Some more options that can be passed with the `modprobe` command are shown in the following screenshot:

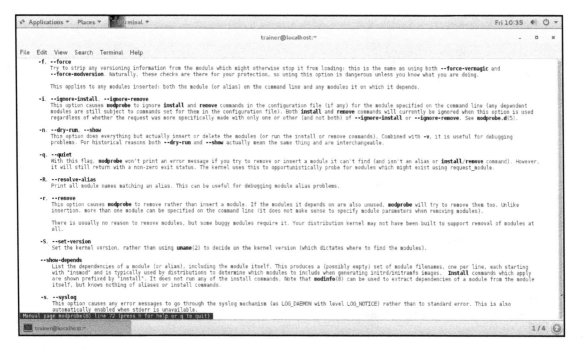

More options that can be passed with the `modprobe` command are shown in the following screenshot:

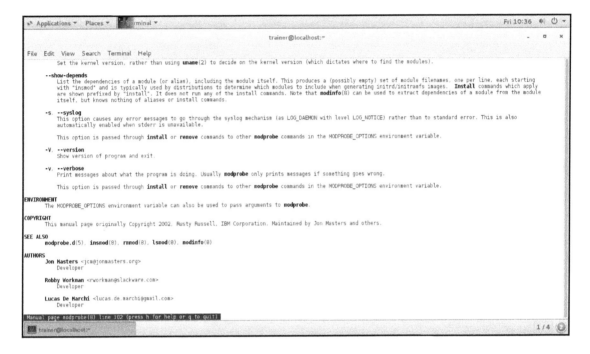

Summary

In this chapter, we focused on hardware settings, looking at the CPU, RAM, and swap information in the various directories. We used a variety of commands. Also, we touched on IRQs and the various interrupts available in a Linux system. We then looked at devices, in the context of files. Finally, we worked with modules. We saw the various modules currently available in a Linux system, and learned the steps to install and remove a module.

In the next chapter, we will focus on the process of booting the system. Moreover, the various boot managers will be covered. This is another critical aspect for every Linux engineer to get to grips with. Simply put, without a boot manager, the system won't be able to boot unless we boot off some form of media. Gaining the knowledge will put you, as a Linux engineer, ahead of other so-called engineers. You will be at a greater advantage regarding certification after completing the next chapter.

Questions

1. Which directory is created as a virtual file system?

   A. /dev
   B. /lib
   C. /proc
   D. None of the above

2. What is the command to view the CPU info?

   A. less /proc
   B. more /proc
   C. cat /proc
   D. cat /proc/cpuinfo

3. What is the command to view the RAM inside the /proc directory?

   A. tail /proc/free
   B. less /proc/free
   C. cat /proc/meminfo
   D. cat /proc/RAM

4. Which option is used with the free command to display the memory info in a friendly format?

   A. free -F
   B. free -L
   C. free -h
   D. free -free

5. Which command is used to tell the system that a file is a swap file?

   A. doswap
   B. format swap
   C. mkswap
   D. swap

6. Which command is used to activate a `swap` file?

    A. `Swap`
    B. `onSwap`
    C. `swap`
    D. `swapon`

7. Which command is used to display the swap-partition info?

    A. `mkswap`
    B. `swapon`
    C. `swap`
    D. `swapoff`

8. Which device file can redirect messages to be sent for discard?

    A. `/dev/discard`
    B. `/dev/null`
    C. `/dev/redirect`
    D. `None of the above`

9. Which command is used to display the currently available modules in a Linux system?

    A. `insmod`
    B. `depmod`
    C. `rmmod`
    D. `lsmod`

10. Which command is used to install a module without having to specify the absolute path?

    A. `rmmod`
    B. `modules`
    C. `modrm`
    D. `modprobe`

Further reading

- This website will give you all of the necessary information about the current CompTIA Linux+ certification: `https://www.comptia.org/`
- This website will give you details relating to LPI exams, specifically the LPIC-1 that you earn by passing both CompTIA Linux+ exams: `http://www.lpi.org/`
- This last website gives you details about the various Linux kernels available: `https://www.kernel.org/`

2
Booting the System

In the previous chapter, we covered the common hardware settings we manage on a daily basis. We touched on some commands that can be used to identify the hardware within a Linux system. This chapter continues from there and takes a step further, this time focusing on the process of booting the system. This looks at the GRUB and GRUB2 configuration files, focusing on the timer, default boot entry, and passing arguments to the GRUB/GRUB2 boot menu. It also covers the `chkconfig`, `pstree`, `ps`, `systemctl`, and `dmeg` commands, as well as the various start/stop scripts.

We will cover the following topics in this chapter:

- The boot process explained
- Understanding GRUB and GRUB2
- Working with GRUB
- Working with GRUB2

The boot process explained

In Linux, during boot up, the system looks for the boot sector on the hard disk. Once it finds the boot sector, it then searches for a boot loader. In turn, the boot loader loads the boot manager. In Linux, this will usually be either GRUB or GRUB2. After this stage, the user is presented with a boot menu. Finally, the user is given the opportunity to either select an operating system to load or edit an existing entry. The options available are usually going to be different versions of the Linux kernel. Sometimes, it might be an entirely different Linux distribution. However, in mixed environments, you may come into contact with another operating system, such as Microsoft Windows.

After the user selects a Linux kernel, depending on the Linux distribution release, a single process is started, known as `init`, which stands for *initialization*. `init` is often referred to as *System V init* or *SysV* because System V was the first commercial Unix operating system. Most early Linux distributions were identical to the System V operating system. The other daemon used to manage a Linux distribution is known as `systemd`, which stands for System Management Daemon. The following is a simple flow for the process that we just discussed:

Boot Sector > Boot Loader > Boot Menu => OS loads

In Linux, you may come across the term **daemon**. Rest assured, that's simply referring to a process.

Before we go deeper, let's keep in mind one of the biggest differences between `init` and `systemd`: `init` starts scripts one at a time, whereas `systemd` starts multiple scripts parallel to each other. That being said, here is the output from the `pstree` command on a CentOS 5 system that uses `init`:

```
[root@localhost philip]# pstree
init─┬─ManagementAgent───2*[{ManagementAgen}]
     ├─NetworkManager─┬─dhclient
     │                └─{NetworkManager}
     ├─VGAuthService
     ├─abrtd
     ├─acpid
     ├─atd
     ├─auditd───{auditd}
     ├─bonobo-activati───{bonobo-activat}
     ├─clock-applet
     ├─console-kit-dae───63*[{console-kit-da}]
     ├─crond
     ├─cupsd
     ├─2*[dbus-daemon───{dbus-daemon}]
     ├─dbus-launch
     ├─devkit-power-da
     ├─dnsmasq
     ├─gconfd-2
     ├─gdm-user-switch
```

From the preceding output, we can see all of the processes originating from init; hence, they are considered child processes.

Another command we can leverage to see the actual process number being used by init is the ps command in our CentOS 5 system:

```
[philip@localhost Desktop]$ ps -aux
 Warning: bad syntax, perhaps a bogus '-'? See
/usr/share/doc/procps-3.2.8/FAQ
 USER PID %CPU   %MEM  VSZ RSS TTY STAT START TIME COMMAND
 root   1   0.3   0.1  19364 1524 ? Ss  05:48   0:01 /sbin/init
 root   2   0.0   0.0  0     0    ? S   05:48   0:00 [kthreadd]
 root   3   0.0   0.0  0     0    ? S   05:48   0:00 [migration/0]
 root   4   0.0   0.0  0     0    ? S   05:48   0:00 [ksoftirqd/0]
 root   5   0.0   0.0  0     0    ? S   05:48   0:00 [migration/0]
 root   6   0.0   0.0  0     0    ? S   05:48   0:00 [watchdog/0]
 root   7   0.2   0.0  0     0    ? S   05:48   0:00 [events/0]
 root   8   0.0   0.0  0     0    ? S   05:48   0:00 [cgroup]
 root   9   0.0   0.0  0     0    ? S   05:48   0:00 [khelper]
 root  10   0.0   0.0  0     0    ? S   05:48   0:00 [netns]
 root  11   0.0   0.0  0     0    ? S   05:48   0:00 [async/mgr]
 root  12   0.0   0.0  0     0    ? S   05:48   0:00 [pm]
 root  13   0.0   0.0  0     0    ? S   05:48   0:00 [sync_supers]
 root  14   0.0   0.0  0     0    ? S   05:48   0:00 [bdi-default]
 root  15   0.0   0.0  0     0    ? S   05:48   0:00 [kintegrityd/]
 root  16   0.5   0.0  0     0    ? S   05:48   0:01 [kblockd/0]
```

From the preceding output, we can see that the first process started is PID 1, and it is indeed the init process.

Here are some options that we can use with the ps command:

```
[philip@localhost Desktop]$ ps --help
******** simple selection ******** ******** selection by list ********
-A all processes -C by command name
-N negate selection -G by real group ID (supports names)
-a all w/ tty except session leaders -U by real user ID (supports names)
-d all except session leaders -g by session OR by effective group name
-e all processes -p by process ID
T all processes on this terminal -s processes in the sessions given
a all w/ tty, including other users -t by tty
g OBSOLETE -- DO NOT USE -u by effective user ID (supports names)
r only running processes U processes for specified users
x processes w/o controlling ttys t by tty
********** output format ********** ********** long options **********
-o,o user-defined -f full --Group --User --pid --cols --ppid
-j,j job control s signal --group --user --sid --rows --info
```

```
-O,O preloaded -o v virtual memory --cumulative --format --deselect
-l,l long u user-oriented --sort --tty --forest --version
-F extra full X registers --heading --no-heading --context
********* misc options *********
-V,V show version L list format codes f ASCII art forest
-m,m,-L,-T,H threads S children in sum -y change -l format
-M,Z security data c true command name -c scheduling class
-w,w wide output n numeric WCHAN,UID -H process hierarchy
[philip@localhost Desktop]$
```

Now, let's turn our attention to systemd. We will run the pstree command on our Linux system:

```
philip@philip-virtual-machine:~$ pstree
systemd─┬─ModemManager───2*[{ModemManager}]
        ├─NetworkManager───2*[{NetworkManager}]
        ├─VGAuthService
        ├─accounts-daemon───2*[{accounts-daemon}]
        ├─acpid
        ├─avahi-daemon───avahi-daemon
        ├─boltd───2*[{boltd}]
        ├─colord───2*[{colord}]
        ├─cron
        ├─cups-browsed───2*[{cups-browsed}]
        ├─cupsd
        ├─dbus-daemon
        ├─firefox─┬─Web Content───19*[{Web Content}]
        │         ├─Web Content───20*[{Web Content}]
        │         └─52*[{firefox}]
        ├─fwupd───4*[{fwupd}]
        ├─gdm3─┬─gdm-session-wor───gdm-wayland-ses───gnome-session-b───gnome-shell─┬─Xwayland
        │                                                                          ├─ibus-daemon─┬─ibus-dconf───3*[{ibus-dconf}+
        │                                                                          │             ├─ibus-engine-sim───2*[{ibus-e+
        │                                                                          │             └─2*[{ibus-daemon}]
        │                                                                          └─9*[{gnome-shell}]
```

From the preceding output, we can see all other processes being spawned by the system. These are known as child processes.

We can also run the `pstree` command on the CentOS 7 distro, and see similar results:

```
[philip@localhost ~]$ pstree
 systemd─┬─ModemManager───2*[{ModemManager}]
   ├─NetworkManager─┬─dhclient
   │   └─3*[{NetworkManager}]
   ├─VGAuthService
   ├─abrt-watch-log
   ├─abrtd
   ├─accounts-daemon───2*[{accounts-daemon}]
   ├─alsactl
   ├─anacron
   ├─at-spi-bus-laun─┬─dbus-daemon───{dbus-daemon}
   │   └─3*[{at-spi-bus-laun}]
   ├─at-spi2-registr───2*[{at-spi2-registr}]
   ├─atd
   ├─auditd─┬─audispd─┬─sedispatch
   │   │   └─{audispd}
   │   └─{auditd}
   ├─avahi-daemon───avahi-daemon
   ├─chronyd
   ├─colord───2*[{colord}]
   ├─crond
   ├─cupsd
   ├─2*[dbus-daemon───{dbus-daemon}]
   ├─dbus-launch
   ├─dconf-service───2*[{dconf-service}]
   ├─dnsmasq───dnsmasq
```

 On almost all newer Linux distributions, `systemd` has replaced `init`.

Now, let's check which process number `systemd` is using on the Linux system by using the `ps` command:

```
root@ubuntu:/home/philip# ps -aux
 USER PID %CPU %MEM VSZ RSS TTY STAT START TIME COMMAND
 root 1 0.0 0.5 185620 4996 ? Ss Jun19 0:05 /lib/systemd/systemd --system -
-d
 root 2 0.0 0.0 0 0 ? S Jun19 0:00 [kthreadd]
 root 3 0.0 0.0 0 0 ? S Jun19 0:06 [ksoftirqd/0]
 root 5 0.0 0.0 0 0 ? S< Jun19 0:00 [kworker/0:0H]
 root 7 0.0 0.0 0 0 ? S Jun19 0:06 [rcu_sched]
 root 8 0.0 0.0 0 0 ? S Jun19 0:00 [rcu_bh]
 root 9 0.0 0.0 0 0 ? S Jun19 0:00 [migration/0]
```

```
root 10 0.0 0.0 0 0 ? S Jun19 0:00 [watchdog/0]
root 11 0.0 0.0 0 0 ? S Jun19 0:00 [kdevtmpfs]
root 12 0.0 0.0 0 0 ? S< Jun19 0:00 [netns]
root 13 0.0 0.0 0 0 ? S< Jun19 0:00 [perf]
root 14 0.0 0.0 0 0 ? S Jun19 0:00 [khungtaskd]
root 15 0.0 0.0 0 0 ? S< Jun19 0:00 [writeback]
root 16 0.0 0.0 0 0 ? SN Jun19 0:00 [ksmd]
root 17 0.0 0.0 0 0 ? SN Jun19 0:01 [khugepaged]
root 18 0.0 0.0 0 0 ? S< Jun19 0:00 [crypto]
root 19 0.0 0.0 0 0 ? S< Jun19 0:00 [kintegrityd]
root 20 0.0 0.0 0 0 ? S< Jun19 0:00 [bioset]
root 21 0.0 0.0 0 0 ? S< Jun19 0:00 [kblockd]
root 22 0.0 0.0 0 0 ? S< Jun19 0:00 [ata_sff]
root 23 0.0 0.0 0 0 ? S< Jun19 0:00 [md]
root 24 0.0 0.0 0 0 ? S< Jun19 0:00 [devfreq_wq]
```

Some output is omitted for the sake of brevity.

From the preceding output, we can clearly see that the system is indeed listed as the first process started.

 systemd emulates init. For example, we can start/stop daemon(s) with the service command.

Now, in order for us to see the processes that have been started on the Linux distribution, we can run the chkconfig command on our CentOS 7 distribution:

```
[philip@localhost Desktop]$ chkconfig
NetworkManager 0:off 1:off 2:on 3:on 4:on 5:on 6:off
abrt-ccpp 0:off 1:off 2:off 3:on 4:off 5:on 6:off
abrtd 0:off 1:off 2:off 3:on 4:off 5:on 6:off
acpid 0:off 1:off 2:on 3:on 4:on 5:on 6:off
atd 0:off 1:off 2:off 3:on 4:on 5:on 6:off
auditd 0:off 1:off 2:on 3:on 4:on 5:on 6:off
blk-availability 0:off 1:on 2:on 3:on 4:on 5:on 6:off
bluetooth 0:off 1:off 2:off 3:on 4:on 5:on 6:off
cpuspeed 0:off 1:on 2:on 3:on 4:on 5:on 6:off
crond 0:off 1:off 2:on 3:on 4:on 5:on 6:off
cups 0:off 1:off 2:on 3:on 4:on 5:on 6:off
dnsmasq 0:off 1:off 2:off 3:off 4:off 5:off 6:off
firstboot 0:off 1:off 2:off 3:on 4:off 5:on 6:off
haldaemon 0:off 1:off 2:off 3:on 4:on 5:on 6:off
htcacheclean 0:off 1:off 2:off 3:off 4:off 5:off 6:off
httpd 0:off 1:off 2:off 3:off 4:off 5:off 6:off
ip6tables 0:off 1:off 2:on 3:on 4:on 5:on 6:off
```

```
iptables 0:off 1:off 2:on 3:on 4:on 5:on 6:off
irqbalance 0:off 1:off 2:off 3:on 4:on 5:on 6:off
kdump 0:off 1:off 2:off 3:on 4:on 5:on 6:off
lvm2-monitor 0:off 1:on 2:on 3:on 4:on 5:on 6:off
mdmonitor 0:off 1:off 2:on 3:on 4:on 5:on 6:off
messagebus 0:off 1:off 2:on 3:on 4:on 5:on 6:off
netconsole 0:off 1:off 2:off 3:off 4:off 5:off 6:off
netfs 0:off 1:off 2:off 3:on 4:on 5:on 6:off
network 0:off 1:off 2:on 3:on 4:on 5:on 6:off
```

Some of the previous output is omitted for the sake of brevity.

In the preceding output, we are only shown daemons that use init. This is useful on systems running native init, such as earlier Linux distributions.

Here are the most commonly used options that can be passed with the chkconfig command for older Linux distributions that use init:

--level levels	Specifies the runlevels an operation should pertain to. It is given as a string of numbers from 0 to 6. For example, --level 35 specifies runlevels 3 and 5.
--add name	This option adds a new service for management by chkconfig. When a new service is added, chkconfig ensures that the service has either a start or a kill entry in every runlevel. If any runlevel is missing such an entry, chkconfig creates the appropriate entry, as specified by the default values in the init script. Note that default entries in LSB-delimited INIT INFO sections take precedence over the default runlevels in the initscript; if any required-start or required-stop entries are present, the start and stop priorities of the script will be adjusted to account for these dependencies.
--del name	The service is removed from chkconfig management, and any symbolic links in /etc/rc[0-6].d that pertain to it are removed. Note that future package installs for this service may run chkconfig --add, which will re-add such links. To disable a service, run chkconfig name off.
--override name	If the service name is configured exactly as it would be if the --add option had been specified with no override file in /etc/chkconfig.d/name, and if /etc/chkconfig.d/name now exists and is specified differently from the base initscript, this changes the configuration for the service name to follow the overrides instead of the base configuration.
--list name	This option lists all of the services that chkconfig knows about, and whether they are stopped or started in each runlevel. If a name is specified, information is only displayed with regards to the service name.

To see the daemons started in newer Linux distributions, we will use the `systemctl` command:

```
[philip@localhost ~]$ systemctl
 add-requires hybrid-sleep reload-or-restart
 add-wants is-active reload-or-try-restart
 cancel is-enabled rescue
 cat is-failed reset-failed
 condreload isolate restart
 condrestart is-system-running set-default
 condstop kexec set-environment
 daemon-reexec kill set-property
 daemon-reload link show
 default list-dependencies show-environment
 delete list-jobs snapshot
 disable list-sockets start
 edit list-timers status
 emergency list-unit-files stop
 enable list-units suspend
 exit mask switch-root
 force-reload poweroff try-restart
 get-default preset unmask
 halt reboot unset-environment
 help reenable
 hibernate reload
[philip@localhost ~]$
```

From the preceding output, we can see a variety of options that can be passed with the `systemctl` command; we will use the `list-unit-files` option with `systemctl`:

```
[philip@localhost ~]$ systemctl list-unit-files
UNIT FILE                              STATE
proc-sys-fs-binfmt_misc.automount      static
dev-hugepages.mount                    static
dev-mqueue.mount                       static
proc-fs-nfsd.mount                     static
proc-sys-fs-binfmt_misc.mount          static
sys-fs-fuse-connections.mount          static
sys-kernel-config.mount                static
sys-kernel-debug.mount                 static
tmp.mount                              disabled
var-lib-nfs-rpc_pipefs.mount           static
brandbot.path                          disabled
cups.path                              enabled
systemd-ask-password-console.path      static
systemd-ask-password-plymouth.path     static
systemd-ask-password-wall.path         static
```

Some of the following output is omitted for the sake of brevity:

```
umount.target                        static
virt-guest-shutdown.target           static
chrony-dnssrv@.timer                 disabled
fstrim.timer                         disabled
mdadm-last-resort@.timer             static
systemd-readahead-done.timer         indirect
systemd-tmpfiles-clean.timer         static
392 unit files listed.
```

From the preceding output, we can see that 392 units are listed. We can be more specific and look for only the services that are enabled/running:

```
[philip@localhost ~]$ systemctl list-unit-files | grep enabled
cups.path                                    enabled
abrt-ccpp.service                            enabled
abrt-oops.service                            enabled
abrt-vmcore.service                          enabled
abrt-xorg.service                            enabled
abrtd.service                                enabled
accounts-daemon.service                      enabled
atd.service                                  enabled
auditd.service                               enabled
autovt@.service                              enabled
avahi-daemon.service                         enabled
bluetooth.service                            enabled
chronyd.service                              enabled
crond.service                                enabled
cups.service                                 enabled
dbus-org.bluez.service                       enabled
dbus-org.fedoraproject.FirewallD1.service    enabled
dbus-org.freedesktop.Avahi.service           enabled
dbus-org.freedesktop.ModemManager1.service   enabled
dbus-org.freedesktop.NetworkManager.service  enabled
dbus-org.freedesktop.nm-dispatcher.service   enabled
display-manager.service                      enabled
dmraid-activation.service                    enabled
firewalld.service                            enabled
```

Some of the preceding output is omitted for the sake of brevity.

We can also see the status, the directory from where the daemon is being executed, and the **Process ID (PID)** for a daemon with the `systemctl` command. We will use the `status` option as follows:

```
[philip@localhost ~]$ systemctl status sshd.service
 ● sshd.service - OpenSSH server daemon
   Loaded: loaded (/usr/lib/systemd/system/sshd.service; enabled; vendor
preset: enabled)
   Active: active (running) since Wed 2018-06-20 09:35:31 PDT; 1h 43min ago
     Docs: man:sshd(8)
           man:sshd_config(5)
 Main PID: 1072 (sshd)
   CGroup: /system.slice/sshd.service
           └─1072 /usr/sbin/sshd -D
[philip@localhost ~]$
```

We can also stop, start, restart, enable, and disable a daemon with the `systemctl` command. Let's say we want to stop the `sshd` service using the `systemctl` command. In this case, we would simply do this:

```
[philip@localhost ~]$ systemctl stop sshd
```

Now, as soon as we press *Enter* on the CentOS 7 system, we will get an authentication prompt because we are attempting to stop the `sshd` service as a standard user:

sshd is considered to be a system service. Also, a unit in the context of systemd is a service, and vice versa.

Now we'll enter the root password:

And now the sshd service has been stopped:

```
[philip@localhost ~]$ systemctl stop sshd
[philip@localhost ~]$
```

Now let's recheck the status of the sshd service to confirm it has indeed stopped. We can do this using the systemctl command:

```
[philip@localhost ~]$ systemctl status sshd.service
● sshd.service - OpenSSH server daemon
   Loaded: loaded (/usr/lib/systemd/system/sshd.service; enabled; vendor
preset: enabled)
   Active: inactive (dead) since Wed 2018-06-20 11:20:16 PDT; 21min ago
     Docs: man:sshd(8)
           man:sshd_config(5)
 Main PID: 1072 (code=exited, status=0/SUCCESS)
[philip@localhost ~]$
```

From the preceding code, we can conclude that the sshd service has been stopped.

DMESG

Now, when the system is booting, there are a number of messages relating to various aspects of our system, ranging from hardware to services that fly across the screen quickly. It would be useful to be able to view those messages while troubleshooting. It's always useful to gather as much information as possible to aid troubleshooting.

We can leverage yet another powerful command, the dmesg command:

```
philip@ubuntu:~$ dmesg
[ 0.000000] Initializing cgroup subsys cpuset
[ 0.000000] Initializing cgroup subsys cpu
[ 0.000000] Initializing cgroup subsys cpuacct
[ 0.000000] Linux version 4.4.0-128-generic (buildd@lcy01-amd64-019) (gcc
version 5.4.0 20160609 (Ubuntu 5.4.0-6ubuntu1~16.04.9) ) #154-Ubuntu SMP
Fri May 25 14:15:18 UTC 2018 (Ubuntu 4.4.0-128.154-generic 4.4.131)
[ 0.000000] Command line: BOOT_IMAGE=/boot/vmlinuz-4.4.0-128-generic
root=UUID=adb5d090-3400-4411-aee2-dd871c39db38 ro find_preseed=/preseed.cfg
auto noprompt priority=critical locale=en_US quiet
```

Some of the following output is omitted for the sake of brevity:

```
[ 13.001702] audit: type=1400 audit(1529517046.911:8): apparmor="STATUS"
operation="profile_load" profile="unconfined" name="/usr/bin/evince"
pid=645 comm="apparmor_parser"
[ 19.155619] e1000: ens33 NIC Link is Up 1000 Mbps Full Duplex, Flow
Control: None
[ 19.156584] IPv6: ADDRCONF(NETDEV_CHANGE): ens33: link becomes ready
[ 105.095992] do_trap: 33 callbacks suppressed
[ 105.095996] traps: pool[2056] trap int3 ip:7f778e83c9eb sp:7f776b1eb6f0
error:0
philip@ubuntu:~$
```

From the preceding output, we can see various pieces of information, including CPU detection, PCI drivers, and Ethernet, to name a few.

GRUB and GRUB2

Now we'll switch gears and discuss the boot managers whose jobs are to present the boot menu, from which the user has the options to select which operating system/Linux kernel to load or edit. First, we will focus on GRUB and then move on to GRUB2.

GRUB

GRUB stands for **Grand Unified Bootloader**. GRUB is primarily used for booting Linux distributions. However, GRUB can work with other boot loaders. A common use-case scenario is for dual booting with a Microsoft operating system: it does this by doing a hand-off to the Windows bootloader for Microsoft operating systems.

GRUB uses the `/boot/grub/grub.conf` file. Sometimes you will see `/boot/grub/menu.1st`, but this file is simply a symbolic link to `/boot/grub/grub.conf`. Using the CentOS 6.5 distro, run the following command:

```
[root@localhost ~]# ls -l /boot/grub
total 274
-rw-r--r--. 1 root  root    63 Jun 20 01:47    device.map
-rw-r--r--. 1 root  root 13380 Jun 20 01:47 e2fs_stage1_5
-rw-r--r--. 1 root  root 12620 Jun 20 01:47 fat_stage1_5
-rw-r--r--. 1 root  root 11748 Jun 20 01:47 ffs_stage1_5
-rw-------. 1 root  root   769 Jun 20 01:48    grub.conf
-rw-r--r--. 1 root  root 11756 Jun 20 01:47 iso9660_stage1_5
-rw-r--r--. 1 root  root 13268 Jun 20 01:47 jfs_stage1_5
lrwxrwxrwx. 1 root  root    11 Jun 20 01:47    menu.1st -> ./grub.conf
-rw-r--r--. 1 root  root 11956 Jun 20 01:47 minix_stage1_5
-rw-r--r--. 1 root  root 14412 Jun 20 01:47 reiserfs_stage1_5
-rw-r--r--. 1 root  root  1341 Nov 14 2010    splash.xpm.gz
-rw-r--r--. 1 root  root   512 Jun 20 01:47    stage1
-rw-r--r--. 1 root  root 126100 Jun 20 01:47 stage2
-rw-r--r--. 1 root  root 12024 Jun 20 01:47  ufs2_stage1_5
-rw-r--r--. 1 root  root 11364 Jun 20 01:47  vstafs_stage1_5
-rw-r--r--. 1 root  root 13964 Jun 20 01:47  xfs_stage1_5
[root@localhost ~]#
```

From the preceding output, we can see `/boot/grub/grub.conf` and also the symbolic link `/boot/grub/menu.1st`.

We can view the actual `/boot/grub/grub.conf` file as follows:

```
[root@localhost ~]# cat /boot/grub/grub.conf
# grub.conf generated by anaconda
#
# Note that you do not have to rerun grub after making changes to this
file
# NOTICE:  You have a /boot partition.  This means that
# all kernel and initrd paths are relative to /boot/, eg.
# root (hd0,0)
# kernel /vmlinuz-version ro root=/dev/sda2
# initrd /initrd-[generic-]version.img
#boot=/dev/sda
```

```
default=0
timeout=5
splashimage=(hd0,0)/grub/splash.xpm.gz
hiddenmenu
title CentOS (2.6.32-431.el6.x86_64)
root (hd0,0)
kernel /vmlinuz-2.6.32-431.el6.x86_64 ro root=UUID=05527d71-25b6-4931-
a3bb-8fe505f3fa64 rd_NO_LUKS rd_NO_LVM LANG=en_US.UTF-8 rd_NO_MD
SYSFONT=latarcyrheb-sun16 crashkernel=auto KEYBOARDTYPE=pc KEYTABLE=us
rd_NO_DM rhgb quiet
initrd /initramfs-2.6.32-431.el6.x86_64.img
[root@localhost ~]#
```

From the preceding output, the common options would be as follows:

- default=0: This means it is the first entry to boot from the menu.
- timeout=5: This gives the amount of seconds (5, in this case) that the menu will be displayed for before the Linux kernel is booted or the Windows boot loader gets a hand-off from GRUB.
- splashimage=(hd0,0)/grub/splash.xpm.gz: This is the background image of the boot menu.
- root (hd0,0): This refers to the first hard disk and the first partition on the first hard disk.

GRUB2

GRUB2 uses a more programmatic approach in the way the menu is presented. At first glance, GRUB2 may look intimidating, but rest assured that it's not as complicated as it appears to be. The syntax is similar to a programming language, with lots of *if...then* statements. Here is what /boot/grub/grub.cfg looks like on a CentOS 7 system:

```
[root@localhost ~]# cat /boot/grub2/grub.cfg
#
# DO NOT EDIT THIS FILE
#
# It is automatically generated by grub2-mkconfig using templates
# from /etc/grub.d and settings from /etc/default/grub
#
### BEGIN /etc/grub.d/00_header ###
set pager=1
if [ -s $prefix/grubenv ]; then
load_env
fi
```

```
if [ "${next_entry}" ] ; then
set default="${next_entry}"
set next_entry=
save_env next_entry
set boot_once=true
else
set default="${saved_entry}"
fi
```

Some of the following output is omitted for the sake of brevity in /boot/grub/grub.cfg:

```
### BEGIN /etc/grub.d/10_linux ###
 menuentry 'CentOS Linux (3.10.0-693.el7.x86_64) 7 (Core)' --class centos -
-class gnu-linux --class gnu --class os --unrestricted $menuentry_id_option
'gnulinux-3.10.0-693.el7.x86_64-advanced-16e2de7b-
b679-4a12-888e-55081af4dad8' {
 load_video
 set gfxpayload=keep
 insmod gzio
 insmod part_msdos
 insmod xfs
 set root='hd0,msdos1'
 if [ x$feature_platform_search_hint = xy ]; then
 search --no-floppy --fs-uuid --set=root --hint-bios=hd0,msdos1 --hint-
efi=hd0,msdos1 --hint-baremetal=ahci0,msdos1 --hint='hd0,msdos1'
40c7c63f-1c93-438a-971a-5331e265419b
 else
 search --no-floppy --fs-uuid --set=root
40c7c63f-1c93-438a-971a-5331e265419b
 fi
 linux16 /vmlinuz-3.10.0-693.el7.x86_64 root=UUID=16e2de7b-
b679-4a12-888e-55081af4dad8 ro crashkernel=auto rhgb quiet LANG=en_US.UTF-8
 initrd16 /initramfs-3.10.0-693.el7.x86_64.img
 }
### END /etc/grub.d/10_linux ###
```

So, to interpret the /boot/grub/grub.cfg file, we look for lines that start with
menuentry. These lines start the actual menu entry for an operating system, such as a
Linux distribution or a Windows OS.

Entries are enclosed within curly braces {}.

Working with GRUB

Now we're going to interact with GRUB. We will add a custom boot entry. This will be presented upon reboot.

 Before you work with GRUB, always make a backup copy of your /boot/grub/grub.conf.

We will use the vi command, which will open /boot/grub/grub.conf in the visual editor:

```
[root@localhost ~]# cat /boot/grub/grub.conf
 # grub.conf generated by anaconda
 #
 # Note that you do not have to rerun grub after making changes to this
file
 # NOTICE: You have a /boot partition. This means that
 # all kernel and initrd paths are relative to /boot/, eg.
 # root (hd0,0)
 # kernel /vmlinuz-version ro root=/dev/sda2
 # initrd /initrd-[generic-]version.img
#boot=/dev/sda
default=0
timeout=5
splashimage=(hd0,0)/grub/splash.xpm.gz
hiddenmenu
 title CentOS (2.6.32-431.el6.x86_64)
 root (hd0,0)
 kernel /vmlinuz-2.6.32-431.el6.x86_64 ro root=UUID=05527d71-25b6-4931-
a3bb-8fe505f3fa64 rd_NO_LUKS rd_NO_LVM LANG=en_US.UTF-8 rd_NO_MD
SYSFONT=latarcyrheb-sun16 crashkernel=auto KEYBOARDTYPE=pc KEYTABLE=us
rd_NO_DM rhgb quiet
 initrd /initramfs-2.6.32-431.el6.x86_64.img
 [root@localhost ~]# vi /boot/grub/grub.conf
```

Now we're inside vi, we will press *I* on the keyboard to enter the insert mode, scroll down using the down-arrow key until we reach the last line, and then press *Enter* to go to a new line:

```
# grub.conf generated by anaconda
 #
 # Note that you do not have to rerun grub after making changes to this
file
 # NOTICE: You have a /boot partition. This means that
```

```
# all kernel and initrd paths are relative to /boot/, eg.
# root (hd0,0)
# kernel /vmlinuz-version ro root=/dev/sda2
# initrd /initrd-[generic-]version.img
#boot=/dev/sda
default=0
timeout=5
splashimage=(hd0,0)/grub/splash.xpm.gz
hiddenmenu
title CentOS (2.6.32-431.el6.x86_64)
root (hd0,0)
kernel /vmlinuz-2.6.32-431.el6.x86_64 ro root=UUID=05527d71-25b6-4931-
a3bb-8fe505f3fa64 rd_NO_LUKS rd_NO_LVM LANG=en_US.UTF-8 rd_NO_MD
SYSFONT=latarcyrheb-sun16 crashkernel=auto KEYBOARDTYPE=pc KEYTABLE=us
rd_NO_DM rhgb quiet
initrd /initramfs-2.6.32-431.el6.x86_64.img
~
  ~
  ~
-- INSERT --
```

Next, we will start our entry using the following keywords: `title`, `root`, `kernel`, and `initrd`. We will insert our own custom values, as shown here:

```
# grub.conf generated by anaconda
#
# Note that you do not have to rerun grub after making changes to this
file
# NOTICE: You have a /boot partition. This means that
# all kernel and initrd paths are relative to /boot/, eg.
# root (hd0,0)
# kernel /vmlinuz-version ro root=/dev/sda2
# initrd /initrd-[generic-]version.img
#boot=/dev/sda
default=0
timeout=5
splashimage=(hd0,0)/grub/splash.xpm.gz
hiddenmenu
title CentOS (2.6.32-431.el6.x86_64)
root (hd0,0)
kernel /vmlinuz-2.6.32-431.el6.x86_64 ro root=UUID=05527d71-25b6-4931-
a3bb-8fe505f3fa64 rd_NO_LUKS rd_NO_LVM LANG=en_US.UTF-8 rd_NO_MD
SYSFONT=latarcyrheb-sun16 crashkernel=auto KEYBOARDTYPE=pc KEYTABLE=us
rd_NO_DM rhgb quiet
initrd /initramfs-2.6.32-431.el6.x86_64.img
title CompTIA Linux+ (Our.Custom.Entry)
root (hd0,0)
kernel /vmlinuz-2.6.32-431.el6.x86 ro
```

```
initrd /initramfs-2.6.32-431.el6.x86_64.img
-- INSERT --
```

Now we will save and exit `vi`. We use `:wq` to save our change(s) and exit `vi`:

```
title CompTIA Linux+ (Our.Custom.Entry)
root (hd0,0)
kernel /vmlinuz-2.6.32-431.el6.x86 ro
initrd /initramfs-2.6.32-431.el6.x86_64.img
:wq
```

Based on the preceding output, here is a breakdown of our custom entry:

- The `title` defines our customer boot entry.
- `root (hd0,0)` tells it to search for the first hard disk and the first partition on the first hard disk.
- The `kernel /vmlinuz-2.6.32-431.el6.x86 ro` tells GRUB to look for the location of the Linux kernel. In this case, it's `vmlinuz-2.6.32-431.el6.x86 ro` (ro means it loads the kernel as read-only).
- `inidrd /initramfs-2.6.32-431.el6.x86_64.img` specifies the initial RAM disk file to use (this aids the system boot up).

The last step is to reboot our CentOS system and be presented with the GRUB boot menu:

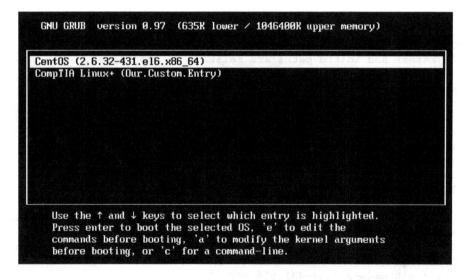

From the preceding output, we can see that our new custom boot entry is displayed in GRUB, which is awesome. We can interact in real time at the GRUB menu. Let's say we wanted to tag on or remove an option from one of these entries. To do this, we would simply press the *E* key, as shown here:

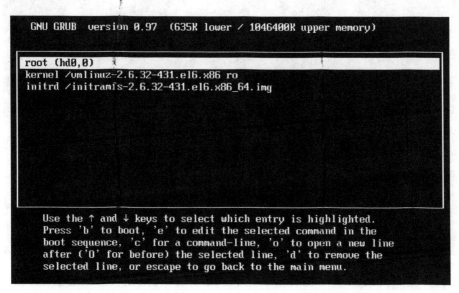

Now we can press the *E* key once again to edit the entry. Let's say we want to specify that the root filesystem resides in /dev/; we would do this as shown in the following screenshot:

Now, we can press the *Enter* key, which will save our changes, and the *Esc* key to return to the previous screen. Through this, we will see the new option added:

```
   GNU GRUB  version 0.97  (635K lower / 1046400K upper memory)

 ┌──────────────────────────────────────────────────────────────────┐
 │ root (hd0,0)                                                      │
 │ kernel /vmlinuz-2.6.32-431.el6.x86 ro root=/dev/Our_Entry        │
 │ initrd /initramfs-2.6.32-431.el6.x86_64.img                      │
 │                                                                  │
 │                                                                  │
 │                                                                  │
 │                                                                  │
 │                                                                  │
 │                                                                  │
 │                                                                  │
 │                                                                  │
 └──────────────────────────────────────────────────────────────────┘
      Use the ↑ and ↓ keys to select which entry is highlighted.
      Press 'b' to boot, 'e' to edit the selected command in the
      boot sequence, 'c' for a command-line, 'o' to open a new line
      after ('O' for before) the selected line, 'd' to remove the
      selected line, or escape to go back to the main menu.
```

From the preceding output, we can see how easy it is to work in real-time at the GRUB boot menu and also how to add a custom boot entry in GRUB.

In GRUB, the first hard disk and the first partition are identified as (hd0, 0), whereas in the Linux shell, the first hard disk and first partition is identified as (sda1).

Working with GRUB2

We add a custom boot entry in GRUB2 in a slightly different way from GRUB. In GRUB2, instead of editing the actual /boot/grub/grub.cfg, we work with /etc/default/grub and /etc/grub.d. Let's do a listing of /etc/grub.d to see all of the available files:

```
philip@ubuntu:~$ ls -l /etc/grub.d/
total 76
-rwxr-xr-x 1 root root 9791 Apr 15 2016 00_header
-rwxr-xr-x 1 root root 6258 Mar 15 2016 05_debian_theme
-rwxr-xr-x 1 root root 12261 Apr 15 2016 10_linux
-rwxr-xr-x 1 root root 11082 Apr 15 2016 20_linux_xen
-rwxr-xr-x 1 root root 1992 Jan 28 2016 20_memtest86+
```

```
-rwxr-xr-x 1 root root 11692 Apr 15 2016 30_os-prober
-rwxr-xr-x 1 root root 1418 Apr 15 2016 30_uefi-firmware
-rwxr-xr-x 1 root root 214 Apr 15 2016 40_custom
-rwxr-xr-x 1 root root 216 Apr 15 2016 41_custom
-rw-r--r-- 1 root root 483 Apr 15 2016 README
philip@ubuntu:~$
```

 Before you work with GRUB2, always make a backup copy of your
/boot/grub/grub.cfg.

From the preceding output, we can see a number of files. Their names start with a number, and the numbers are read in sequential order. Let's say we want to add a custom boot entry in GRUB2. We are going to create a custom entry and name it /etc/grub/40_custom. We will see the following code in vi:

```
#!/bin/sh
exec tail -n +3 $0
# This file provides an easy way to add custom menu entries. Simply type the
# menu entries you want to add after this comment. Be careful not to change
# the 'exec tail' line above.
echo "Test Entry"
cat << EOF
menuentry "CompTIA_LINUX+" {
set root ='hd0,0'
}
EOF
```

From the preceding output, we can see that the syntax is a bit similar to programming. In GRUB2, it's an entire programming language. The next step is to save our changes, then run grub-mkconfig (the name implies we're talking about legacy GRUB, but we're actually referring to GRUB2). This depends on the Linux distribution. In CentOS 7, you will see commands that start with grub2:

```
root@ubuntu:/home/philip# grub-mkconfig
Generating grub configuration file ...
#
# DO NOT EDIT THIS FILE
#
# It is automatically generated by grub-mkconfig using templates
# from /etc/grub.d and settings from /etc/default/grub
#
### BEGIN /etc/grub.d/00_header ###
```

```
if [ -s $prefix/grubenv ]; then
set have_grubenv=true
load_env
fi
```

Some of the following output is omitted for the sake of brevity:

```
### BEGIN /etc/grub.d/40_custom ###
# This file provides an easy way to add custom menu entries. Simply type
the
# menu entries you want to add after this comment. Be careful not to
change
# the 'exec tail' line above.
echo "Test Entry"
cat << EOF
menuentry "CompTIA_LINUX+" {
set root ='hd0,0'
}
EOF
```

When we run this command, the grub-mkconfig command finds the custom entry. This then generates a new boot menu. Upon the next reboot of the system, we will see the new boot menu. We can also change options in /etc/default/grub, including options such as the default OS, the timer, and so on. Here is the content of /etc/default/grub:

```
root@ubuntu:/home/philip# cat /etc/default/grub
# If you change this file, run 'update-grub' afterwards to update
# /boot/grub/grub.cfg.
# For full documentation of the options in this file, see:
# info -f grub -n 'Simple configuration'
GRUB_DEFAULT=0
GRUB_HIDDEN_TIMEOUT=0
GRUB_HIDDEN_TIMEOUT_QUIET=true
GRUB_TIMEOUT=10
GRUB_DISTRIBUTOR=`lsb_release -i -s 2> /dev/null || echo Debian`
GRUB_CMDLINE_LINUX_DEFAULT="quiet"
GRUB_CMDLINE_LINUX="find_preseed=/preseed.cfg auto noprompt
priority=critical locale=en_US"
```

Based on the preceding output, the timer value is set to `10`. Also, note that there is a default value of `0`. Continuing down the configuration file, we see the following code:

```
# Uncomment to enable BadRAM filtering, modify to suit your needs
# This works with Linux (no patch required) and with any kernel that
obtains
# the memory map information from GRUB (GNU Mach, kernel of FreeBSD ...)
#GRUB_BADRAM="0x01234567,0xfefefefe,0x89abcdef,0xefefefef"
# Uncomment to disable graphical terminal (grub-pc only)
#GRUB_TERMINAL=console
# The resolution used on graphical terminal
# note that you can use only modes which your graphic card supports via VBE
# you can see them in real GRUB with the command `vbeinfo'
#GRUB_GFXMODE=640x480
# Uncomment if you don't want GRUB to pass "root=UUID=xxx" parameter to
Linux
#GRUB_DISABLE_LINUX_UUID=true
# Uncomment to disable generation of recovery mode menu entries
#GRUB_DISABLE_RECOVERY="true"
# Uncomment to get a beep at grub start
#GRUB_INIT_TUNE="480 440 1"
```

Now, let's reboot our Ubuntu system and check out the GRUB2 boot menu:

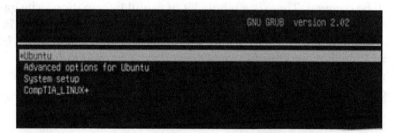

From the preceding screenshot, we can now see our custom menu option in GRUB2. We can even scroll through the entries and edit them by pressing the *E* key.

In GRUB2, the first hard disk starts with `0` and the first partition starts with `1`, unlike in legacy GRUB.

Summary

In this chapter, we took a look at the boot process. We then discussed `init` and `systemd`. We used the `pstree` command and saw the first process that is loaded. We also used the `ps` command to identify the process number. We then looked at the boot messages that would normally scroll across the screen using the `dmesg` command. The messages displayed offer us hints as to what was loaded upon boot up. Furthermore, we can use the messages displayed to assist us whilst troubleshooting. Next, we covered GRUB and GRUB2, looking at the structure of GRUB, particularly `/boot/grub/grub/conf`. We looked at adding a custom menu entry in GRUB. We then explored interacting with GRUB in real time at the boot menu. After that, we looked at GRUB2, focusing on the structure of `/boot/grub/grub.cfg`. In addition, we looked into the other locations that play a role in the GRUB2 configuration: the `/etc/default/grub/` and the `/etc/grub.d/` directories. We then added a custom menu entry inside `/etc/grub.d/` using the `/etc/grub.d/40_custom` file. After that, we updated GRUB2 with `grub-mkconfig` (Ubuntu distribution). Finally, we interacted in real time with the GRUB2 boot menu.

In the next chapter, we will focus on runlevels and boot targets. These are critical topics that we need to fully understand as Linux engineers. We will manage the system using various methods at the command line. Commands such as `runlevel`, `init`, and `systemctl`, to name a few, will be covered. There is a whole lot of useful information to be gained in the next chapter. It's essential to understand how runlevels work. Adding to this is the concept of boot targets. On most newer distributions, you will come into contact with boot targets. This will aid you in managing your Linux systems from a command-line environment. Your skill set will continue to grow as you work throughout the next chapter. This will further take you closer to success in your quest for certification.

Questions

1. Where is the boot loader located on the hard disk?

   A. The boot sector
   B. The secondary partition
   C. The logical partition
   D. None of the above

2. Which was the first commercial Unix operating system?

      A. systemd
      B. upstart
      C. System X
      D. System V

3. Which command displays the processes, starting with the parent process followed by the child processes?

      A. `dnf`
      B. `systemctl`
      C. `pstree`
      D. `ps`

4. Which is the first process that is started on a CentOS 5 system?

      A. `systemd`
      B. `init`
      C. `kickstart`
      D. `upstart`

5. What has replaced `init` in newer releases of the Linux kernel?

      A. `telinit`
      B. `systemctl`
      C. `systemb`
      D. `systemd`

6. Which command lists the processes that are running on a CentOS 7 distribution?

      A. `systemd list-unit-files`
      B. `systemX list-unit-files`
      C. `systemctl list-unit-files`
      D. `service status unit-files`

7. Which command lists the hardware drivers that are loaded during system boot?

      A. `cat /var/log/messages`
      B. `tail -f /var/log/startup`
      C. `head /var/messages`
      D. `dmesg`

8. In which directory is the GRUB configuration file located in a CentOS 5 distribution?

    A. `/boot/`
    B. `/grub/boot/`
    C. `/boot/grub/`
    D. `/grub/grub-config/`

9. What starts a custom menu entry when adding an entry in GRUB?

    A. `title`
    B. `menu entry`
    C. `Operating System`
    D. `default =0`

10. What starts a custom menu entry when adding an entry in GRUB2?

    A. `title`
    B. `root = /vmlinuz/`
    C. `menuentry`
    D. `menu entry`

11. Which letter key is used to edit an entry in real-time at the GRUB boot menu?

    A. C
    B. E
    C. B
    D. A

Further reading

- You can get more information about the CentOS distributions, such as installing, configuration best practices, and so on, at `https://www.centos.org`.
- The following website gives you a lot of useful tips and best practices from users in the Linux community, particularly for the Debian distributions, such as Ubuntu: `https://askubuntu.com`.
- This following link gives you information that relates to various commands that work on both CentOS and Ubuntu. You can post your questions there and other community members will respond: `https://www.linuxquestions.org`.

3
Changing Runlevels and Boot Targets

In the previous chapter, we focused on the booting process. Afterward, the focus was switched to the various boot managers available in Linux distributions. In particular, we worked with GRUB and GRUB2, which are by far the most popular boot managers available. We looked at their respective configuration files, focusing on the timer, default boot entry, and passing arguments at the GRUB/GRUB2 boot menu. Finally, separate illustrations were created in order to add a customer boot entry in the boot menu for both GRUB and GRUB2. This chapter focuses on the introduction of runlevels and boot targets, the types of runlevels and boot targets available in the Linux distributions, and the differences between runlevels and boot targets. We will also look at working with runlevels and boot targets at the CLI.

In this chapter, we will cover the following topics:

- Introduction to runlevels
- Introduction to boot targets
- Working with runlevels
- Working with boot targets

Introduction to runlevels

The concept of runlevels goes back to the SysV days of, runlevel for a purpose. Different tasks require various daemons to be running upon system boot. This is particularly useful in server environments, where we try to minimize as much overhead as possible in our servers. We are usually going dedicate a role to a server. In doing so, we cut down on the amount of applications that are required to be installed on a given server. For instance, a web server would usually have an application that serves up content to users and a database used for lookup(s).

Another typical use case is a print server. This is usually only used for managing print jobs. That being said, from the perspective of runlevels, we would usually scale down on the amount of services that are running inside a given server. For those coming from a Windows background, think about Safe Mode. Usually, we would boot in to Safe Mode to minimize the programs and drivers that are loaded. Runlevels take that idea further, whereby we can tell a Linux distribution what we would like to start/stop in a given runlevel. The cool part is that we have a number of runlevels that we can use in a Linux distribution. You will find runlevels in Linux distributions that use SysV init.

Take a look the following table:

Runlevel	0	1	2	3	4	5	6
Daemon	off	on	on	on	on	on	off

Based on the preceding table, whenever a daemon is **off**, it means that the daemon is not going to run in that runlevel. Similarly, whenever a daemon is **on**, it is configured to run in the particular runlevel(s).

A daemon and a service are typically used interchangeably.

Runlevels usually have various start/stop scripts that are run whenever a runlevel has been selected in a Linux distribution that supports init. We can take a look at a CentOS 6.5 system to see which runlevel is in use. We will look at the /etc/inittab configuration file:

```
[philip@localhost Desktop]$ cat /etc/inittab
 # inittab is only used by upstart for the default runlevel.
 #
 # ADDING OTHER CONFIGURATION HERE WILL HAVE NO EFFECT ON YOUR SYSTEM.
 #
 # System initialization is started by /etc/init/rcS.conf
 #
 # Individual runlevels are started by /etc/init/rc.conf
 #
 # Ctrl-Alt-Delete is handled by /etc/init/control-alt-delete.conf
 #
 # Terminal gettys are handled by /etc/init/tty.conf and
/etc/init/serial.conf,
 # with configuration in /etc/sysconfig/init.
 #
 # For information on how to write upstart event handlers, or how
 # upstart works, see init(5), init(8), and initctl(8).
 #
 # Default runlevel. The runlevels used are:
 # 0 - halt (Do NOT set initdefault to this)
 # 1 - Single user mode
 # 2 - Multiuser, without NFS (The same as 3, if you do not have
networking)
 # 3 - Full multiuser mode
 # 4 - unused
 # 5 - X11
 # 6 - reboot (Do NOT set initdefault to this)
 #
 id:5:initdefault:
[philip@localhost Desktop]$
```

From the preceding output, there are seven runlevels supported on the CentOS distribution. In particular, runlevel 5 is the runlevel that presents a graphical user interface to the user.

The other popular runlevels are 0 for halting or shutting down the system, 1 for single user mode (often used for recovery) and 6 for rebooting the system. The line that says id:5:initdefault: is the line that tells CentOS which runlevel to use upon system boot.

Now let's take a look at /etc/inittab on an Ubuntu 6.06 distribution that supports init:

```
                            ubuntu@ubuntu: ~
File  Edit  View  Terminal  Tabs  Help
ubuntu@ubuntu:~$
ubuntu@ubuntu:~$ cat /etc/inittab
# /etc/inittab: init(8) configuration.
# $Id: inittab,v 1.91 2002/01/25 13:35:21 miquels Exp $

# The default runlevel.
id:2:initdefault:

# Boot-time system configuration/initialization script.
# This is run first except when booting in emergency (-b) mode.
si::sysinit:/etc/init.d/rcS

# What to do in single-user mode.
~~:S:wait:/sbin/sulogin

# /etc/init.d executes the S and K scripts upon change
# of runlevel.
#
# Runlevel 0 is halt.
# Runlevel 1 is single-user.
# Runlevels 2-5 are multi-user.
# Runlevel 6 is reboot.

l0:0:wait:/etc/init.d/rc 0
l1:1:wait:/etc/init.d/rc 1
l2:2:wait:/etc/init.d/rc 2
l3:3:wait:/etc/init.d/rc 3
l4:4:wait:/etc/init.d/rc 4
```

From the preceding output, we can focus on the line that says id:2:initdefault:. The 2 tells the Linux kernel to use runlevel 2 upon system boot. Ubuntu 6.06 is using runlevel 2, by default. In fact, in Ubuntu, runlevels 2-5 are considered to be multi-users; there is no distinction between runlevels 2-5.

In CentOS 6.5, we can check which daemons are running in the various runlevels by using the chkconfig command; this will give a nice summary of the various services:

```
[philip@localhost Desktop]$ chkconfig
NetworkManager 0:off 1:off 2:on 3:on 4:on 5:on 6:off
abrt-ccpp 0:off 1:off 2:off 3:on 4:off 5:on 6:off
abrtd 0:off 1:off 2:off 3:on 4:off 5:on 6:off
acpid 0:off 1:off 2:on 3:on 4:on 5:on 6:off
atd 0:off 1:off 2:off 3:on 4:on 5:on 6:off
auditd 0:off 1:off 2:on 3:on 4:on 5:on 6:off
blk-availability 0:off 1:on 2:on 3:on 4:on 5:on 6:off
bluetooth 0:off 1:off 2:off 3:on 4:on 5:on 6:off
cpuspeed 0:off 1:on 2:on 3:on 4:on 5:on 6:off
crond 0:off 1:off 2:on 3:on 4:on 5:on 6:off
cups 0:off 1:off 2:on 3:on 4:on 5:on 6:off
dnsmasq 0:off 1:off 2:off 3:off 4:off 5:off 6:off
firstboot 0:off 1:off 2:off 3:on 4:off 5:on 6:off
haldaemon 0:off 1:off 2:off 3:on 4:on 5:on 6:off
htcacheclean 0:off 1:off 2:off 3:off 4:off 5:off 6:off
httpd 0:off 1:off 2:off 3:off 4:off 5:off 6:off
ip6tables 0:off 1:off 2:on 3:on 4:on 5:on 6:off
iptables 0:off 1:off 2:on 3:on 4:on 5:on 6:off
irqbalance 0:off 1:off 2:off 3:on 4:on 5:on 6:off
kdump 0:off 1:off 2:off 3:on 4:on 5:on 6:off
lvm2-monitor 0:off 1:on 2:on 3:on 4:on 5:on 6:off
mdmonitor 0:off 1:off 2:on 3:on 4:on 5:on 6:off
messagebus 0:off 1:off 2:on 3:on 4:on 5:on 6:off
netconsole 0:off 1:off 2:off 3:off 4:off 5:off 6:off
netfs 0:off 1:off 2:off 3:on 4:on 5:on 6:off
network 0:off 1:off 2:on 3:on 4:on 5:on 6:off
ntpd 0:off 1:off 2:off 3:off 4:off 5:off 6:off
ntpdate 0:off 1:off 2:off 3:off 4:off 5:off 6:off
portreserve 0:off 1:off 2:on 3:on 4:on 5:on 6:off
postfix 0:off 1:off 2:on 3:on 4:on 5:on 6:off
psacct 0:off 1:off 2:off 3:off 4:off 5:off 6:off
quota_nld 0:off 1:off 2:off 3:off 4:off 5:off 6:off
rdisc 0:off 1:off 2:off 3:off 4:off 5:off 6:off
restorecond 0:off 1:off 2:off 3:off 4:off 5:off 6:off
rngd 0:off 1:off 2:off 3:off 4:off 5:off 6:off
rsyslog 0:off 1:off 2:on 3:on 4:on 5:on 6:off
saslauthd 0:off 1:off 2:off 3:off 4:off 5:off 6:off
smartd 0:off 1:off 2:off 3:off 4:off 5:off 6:off
snmpd 0:off 1:off 2:off 3:off 4:off 5:off 6:off
snmptrapd 0:off 1:off 2:off 3:off 4:off 5:off 6:off
spice-vdagentd 0:off 1:off 2:off 3:off 4:off 5:on 6:off
sshd 0:off 1:off 2:on 3:on 4:on 5:on 6:off
sysstat 0:off 1:on 2:on 3:on 4:on 5:on 6:off
udev-post 0:off 1:on 2:on 3:on 4:on 5:on 6:off
```

```
vmware-tools 0:off 1:off 2:on 3:on 4:on 5:on 6:off
vmware-tools-thinprint 0:off 1:off 2:on 3:on 4:on 5:on 6:off
wdaemon 0:off 1:off 2:off 3:off 4:off 5:off 6:off
winbind 0:off 1:off 2:off 3:off 4:off 5:off 6:off
wpa_supplicant 0:off 1:off 2:off 3:off 4:off 5:off 6:off
[philip@localhost Desktop]$
```

From the preceding output, we can see a variety of services. Some are running in multiple runlevels, while some are turned off entirely. Take, for example, the network service; it is set to `0:off 1:off 2:on 3:on 4:on 5:on 6:off`. This tells the system to start the network service in runlevels 2-5, leaving the network service off on runlevels 0-1 and 6. Most of the services are set to run only in runlevels 2-5.

We can look inside the `/etc/rc.d/` to see the various scripts that are set up to either start/stop:

```
[philip@localhost Desktop]$ ls -l /etc/rc.d
total 60
drwxr-xr-x. 2 root root 4096 Jun 20 01:49 init.d
-rwxr-xr-x. 1 root root 2617 Nov 22 2013 rc
drwxr-xr-x. 2 root root 4096 Jun 20 01:49 rc0.d
drwxr-xr-x. 2 root root 4096 Jun 20 01:49 rc1.d
drwxr-xr-x. 2 root root 4096 Jun 20 01:49 rc2.d
drwxr-xr-x. 2 root root 4096 Jun 20 01:49 rc3.d
drwxr-xr-x. 2 root root 4096 Jun 20 01:49 rc4.d
drwxr-xr-x. 2 root root 4096 Jun 20 01:49 rc5.d
drwxr-xr-x. 2 root root 4096 Jun 20 01:49 rc6.d
-rwxr-xr-x. 1 root root 220 Jun 20 01:48 rc.local
-rwxr-xr-x. 1 root root 19688 Nov 22 2013 rc.sysinit
[philip@localhost Desktop]$
```

Based on the preceding output, there are various directories for each of the respective runlevels, 0-6. Additionally, we can go even further down the filesystem hierarchy and expose the child directories. Let's pick `/etc/rc.d/rc5.d` and expose its content:

```
[philip@localhost Desktop]$ ls -l /etc/rc.d/rc5.d/
total 0
lrwxrwxrwx. 1 root root 16 Jun 20 01:44 K01smartd -> ../init.d/smartd
lrwxrwxrwx. 1 root root 17 Jun 20 01:44 K05wdaemon -> ../init.d/wdaemon
lrwxrwxrwx. 1 root root 16 Jun 20 01:44 K10psacct -> ../init.d/psacct
lrwxrwxrwx. 1 root root 19 Jun 20 01:41 K10saslauthd ->
../init.d/saslauthd
lrwxrwxrwx. 1 root root 22 Jun 20 01:41 K15htcacheclean ->
../init.d/htcacheclean
lrwxrwxrwx. 1 root root 15 Jun 20 01:41 K15httpd -> ../init.d/httpd
lrwxrwxrwx. 1 root root 17 Jun 20 01:41 K50dnsmasq -> ../init.d/dnsmasq
lrwxrwxrwx. 1 root root 20 Jun 20 01:40 K50netconsole ->
```

```
../init.d/netconsole
lrwxrwxrwx. 1 root root 15 Jun 20 01:41 K50snmpd -> ../init.d/snmpd
lrwxrwxrwx. 1 root root 19 Jun 20 01:41 K50snmptrapd ->
../init.d/snmptrapd
lrwxrwxrwx. 1 root root 17 Jun 20 01:47 K73winbind -> ../init.d/winbind
lrwxrwxrwx. 1 root root 14 Jun 20 01:41 K74ntpd -> ../init.d/ntpd
lrwxrwxrwx. 1 root root 17 Jun 20 01:41 K75ntpdate -> ../init.d/ntpdate
lrwxrwxrwx. 1 root root 19 Jun 20 01:44 K75quota_nld ->
../init.d/quota_nld
lrwxrwxrwx. 1 root root 24 Jun 20 01:44 K84wpa_supplicant ->
../init.d/wpa_supplicant
lrwxrwxrwx. 1 root root 21 Jun 20 01:40 K87restorecond ->
../init.d/restorecond
lrwxrwxrwx. 1 root root 15 Jun 20 01:40 K89rdisc -> ../init.d/rdisc
lrwxrwxrwx. 1 root root 14 Jun 20 01:44 K99rngd -> ../init.d/rngd
lrwxrwxrwx. 1 root root 17 Jun 20 01:43 S01sysstat -> ../init.d/sysstat
lrwxrwxrwx. 1 root root 22 Jun 20 01:43 S02lvm2-monitor -> ../init.d/lvm2-
monitor
lrwxrwxrwx. 1 root root 22 Jun 20 01:49 S03vmware-tools ->
../init.d/vmware-tools
lrwxrwxrwx. 1 root root 19 Jun 20 01:41 S08ip6tables ->
../init.d/ip6tables
lrwxrwxrwx. 1 root root 18 Jun 20 01:40 S08iptables -> ../init.d/iptables
lrwxrwxrwx. 1 root root 17 Jun 20 01:40 S10network -> ../init.d/network
lrwxrwxrwx. 1 root root 16 Jun 20 01:44 S11auditd -> ../init.d/auditd
lrwxrwxrwx. 1 root root 21 Jun 20 01:38 S11portreserve ->
../init.d/portreserve
lrwxrwxrwx. 1 root root 17 Jun 20 01:41 S12rsyslog -> ../init.d/rsyslog
lrwxrwxrwx. 1 root root 18 Jun 20 01:44 S13cpuspeed -> ../init.d/cpuspeed
```

 Throughout the chapter, some output is omitted for the sake of brevity.

From the preceding output, there are a number of daemons for runlevel 5. The way by which we identify the daemon would be by the naming convention in use. The files that start with K are used to kill/stop the process and the files that start with S are used to start a process. Also, most of the scripts are symbolic links pointing to the /etc/rc.d/init.d/ directory.

Similarly, we can expose the various start/stop scripts in a later CentOS distribution. For instance, let's choose CentOS 6.5 and dissect one of its directories. On the CentOS 6.5 system, here is one of the stop scripts being displayed:

```
[philip@localhost Desktop]$ cat /etc/rc.d/rc5.d/S13irqbalance
#! /bin/sh
### BEGIN INIT INFO
# Provides: irqbalance
# Default-Start: 3 4 5
# Default-Stop: 0 1 6
# Short-Description: start and stop irqbalance daemon
# Description: The irqbalance daemon will distribute interrupts across
# the cpus on a multiprocessor system with the purpose of
# spreading the load
### END INIT INFO
# chkconfig: 2345 13 87
# This is an interactive program, we need the current locale
# Source function library.
. /etc/init.d/functions
```

As we can see, the scripts are a lot more involved. Moving down, we can see the following code:

```
# Check that we're a privileged user
  [ `id -u` = 0 ] || exit 0
prog="irqbalance"
[ -f /usr/sbin/irqbalance ] || exit 0
# fetch configuration if it exists
  # ONESHOT=yes says to wait for a minute, then look at the interrupt
  # load and balance it once; after balancing exit and do not change
  # it again.
  # The default is to keep rebalancing once every 10 seconds.
  ONESHOT=
  [ -f /etc/sysconfig/irqbalance ] && . /etc/sysconfig/irqbalance
  case "$IRQBALANCE_ONESHOT" in
  y*|Y*|on) ONESHOT=--oneshot ;;
  *) ONESHOT= ;;
  esac
RETVAL=0
start() {
  if [ -n "$ONESHOT" -a -f /var/run/irqbalance.pid ]; then
  exit 0
  fi
  echo -n $"Starting $prog: "
  if [ -n "$IRQBALANCE_BANNED_CPUS" ];
  then
  export IRQBALANCE_BANNED_CPUS=$IRQBALANCE_BANNED_CPUS
  fi
```

```
 daemon irqbalance --pid=/var/run/irqbalance.pid $IRQBALANCE_ARGS $ONESHOT
 RETVAL=$?
 echo
 return $RETVAL
 }
stop() {
 echo -n $"Stopping $prog: "
 killproc irqbalance
 RETVAL=$?
 echo
 [ $RETVAL -eq 0 ] && rm -f /var/lock/subsys/irqbalance
 return $RETVAL
 }
restart() {
 stop
 start
 }
# See how we were called.
 case "$1" in
 start)
 start
 ;;
 stop)
 stop
 ;;
 status)
 status irqbalance
 ;;
 restart|reload|force-reload)
 restart
 ;;
 condrestart)
 [ -f /var/lock/subsys/irqbalance ] && restart || :
 ;;
 *)
 echo $"Usage: $0 {start|stop|status|restart|reload|condrestart|force-
reload}"
 exit 1
 ;;
 esac
exit $?
 [philip@localhost Desktop]$
```

Finally, from the preceding output, we can clearly see that the scripts are programmatic in nature.

Introduction to boot targets

The concept of boot targets is a whole new ball game. Boot targets are used when working with `systemd`. We can see increased performance, because only requests for a particular socket are started as needed. Also, `systemd` emulates init for compatibility, while in the background `systemd` is doing the work. When we use boot targets, we work with units. For a given boot target, a number of daemons reside. Let's see the available boot targets in an Ubuntu distribution:

```
root@ubuntu:/home/philip# systemctl list-units --type target
  UNIT              LOAD    ACTIVE    SUB  DESCRIPTION
  basic.target          loaded active active Basic System
  cryptsetup.target loaded active active Encrypted Volumes
  getty.target          loaded active active Login Prompts
  graphical.target  loaded active active Graphical Interface
  local-fs-pre.target loaded active active Local File Systems (Pre)
  local-fs.target   loaded active active Local File Systems
  multi-user.target loaded active active Multi-User System
  network.target        loaded active active Network
  nss-user-lookup.target loaded active active User and Group Name Lookups
  paths.target          loaded active active Paths
  remote-fs-pre.target loaded active active Remote File Systems (Pre)
  remote-fs.target loaded active active Remote File Systems
  slices.target     loaded active active Slices
  sockets.target    loaded active active Sockets
  sound.target      loaded active active Sound Card
  swap.target       loaded active active Swap
  sysinit.target    loaded active active System Initialization
  time-sync.target loaded active active System Time Synchronized
  timers.target     loaded active active Timers
  LOAD = Reflects whether the unit definition was properly loaded.
  ACTIVE = The high-level unit activation state, i.e. generalization of SUB.
  SUB = The low-level unit activation state, values depend on unit type.
  19 loaded units listed. Pass --all to see loaded but inactive units, too.
  To show all installed unit files use 'systemctl list-unit-files'.
  root@ubuntu:/home/philip#
```

From the preceding output, only the targets that are currently loaded will be displayed. The `graphical.target` is similar to runlevel 5 in `init`. To see all of the boot targets, we would do this:

```
root@ubuntu:/home/philip# systemctl list-units --type target --all
  UNIT               LOAD ACTIVE SUB DESCRIPTION
  basic.target           loaded active active Basic System
  cryptsetup.target  loaded active active Encrypted Volumes
  emergency.target   loaded inactive dead Emergency Mode
```

```
failsafe-graphical.target loaded inactive dead Graphical failsafe fallback
final.target          loaded inactive dead Final Step
getty.target          loaded active active Login Prompts
graphical.target      loaded active active Graphical Interface
halt.target           loaded inactive dead Halt
local-fs-pre.target loaded active active Local File Systems (Pre)
local-fs.target       loaded active active Local File Systems
multi-user.target     loaded active active Multi-User System
network-online.target loaded inactive dead Network is Online
network-pre.target    loaded inactive dead Network (Pre)
network.target          loaded active active Network
nss-user-lookup.target  loaded active active User and Group Name Lookups
paths.target            loaded active active Paths
reboot.target           loaded inactive dead Reboot
remote-fs-pre.target    loaded active active
```

From the preceding output, we can see the boot targets that are active and also those that are inactive.

Now, let's say we want to see the actual daemons associated with a given target. We would run the following command:

```
root@ubuntu:/home/philip# systemctl list-dependencies graphical.target
```

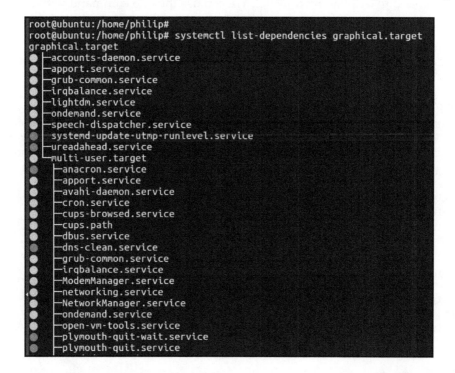

From the preceding output, we can see a number of daemons in `graphical.target`. One such daemon is the `NetworkManager.service`, which is used for networking within our system. The way to read this would be:

- **Green circle**: Indicates that the service is currently running
- **Red circle**: Indicates that the service is not presently running

Working with runlevels

We can use various runlevels for various tasks, as we've seen earlier in this chapter. Let's use the CentOS 6.5 distribution. To see the runlevel at the shell in real time, we can use the `runlevel` command:

```
[philip@localhost Desktop]$ runlevel
N 5
[philip@localhost Desktop]$
```

From the preceding output, the `N` means the previous runlevel. In our case, we have not changed the runlevel. The 5 indicates we are currently in runlevel 5. We can also run another command to display the runlevel. We can use the `who` command with the `-r` option, as can be seen here:

```
[philip@localhost Desktop]$ who -r
  run-level 5 2018-06-20 08:09
  [philip@localhost Desktop]$
```

From the preceding output, we can see a further description, namely `run-level 5` using the `who -r` command.

Now, we can change the runlevel in our CentOS 6.5 distribution by leveraging the `init` or `telinit` commands. Let's see how we would change from runlevel 5 to runlevel 1:

```
[philip@localhost Desktop]$ who -r
  run-level 5 2018-06-20 08:09
  [philip@localhost Desktop]$ init 1
```

We will get an error when we press *Enter*; the reason being, we need root permission to change runlevel 5 to runlevel 1 in the CentOS 6.5 distribution:

```
[philip@localhost Desktop]$ init 1
  init: Need to be root
  [philip@localhost Desktop]$
```

Now, let's authenticate as the root user and retry the `init 1` command:

```
[philip@localhost Desktop]$ su -
Password:
[root@localhost ~]# init 1
```

Now, we will be placed into runlevel 1, which removes the GUI and takes us directly into the shell. This runlevel 1 is typically known as a **single user**, which we would use for recovery:

```
Telling INIT to go to single user mode.
init: rc main process (2501) killed by TERM signal
[root@localhost /]# runlevel
1 S
[root@localhost /]# who -r
         run-level S  2018-06-20 08:15                        last=1
[root@localhost /]#
```

From the preceding output, we have run the `runlevel` and `who -r` commands and verified that we are indeed in runlevel 1.

Now, let's bring back up the system into GUI state, namely runlevel 5:

```
Telling INIT to go to single user mode.
init: rc main process (2501) killed by TERM signal
[root@localhost /]# runlevel
1 S
[root@localhost /]# who -r
         run-level S  2018-06-20 08:15                        last=1
[root@localhost /]# init 5
```

Now, when we run the `runlevel` command in the GUI, we will see the previous runlevel 1 replacing the `N` with an `S` in the `runlevel` command:

```
[philip@localhost Desktop]$ runlevel
S 5
[philip@localhost Desktop]$
```

Similarly, we can run the `who` command with the `-r` option to see more information:

```
[philip@localhost Desktop]$ who -r
run-level 5 2018-06-20 08:20 last=S
[philip@localhost Desktop]$
```

Now, let's say we want to turn on a daemon in some runlevel. We will use `dnsmasq` for demonstration. First, let's verify that the `dnsmasq` service is presently off:

```
[philip@localhost Desktop]$ chkconfig | grep dnsmasq
dnsmasq 0:off 1:off 2:off 3:off 4:off 5:off 6:off
[philip@localhost Desktop]$
```

Great! Let's now turn on the `dnsmasq` daemon only for runlevels 3-5:

```
[philip@localhost Desktop]$ chkconfig --levels 345 dnsmasq on
You do not have enough privileges to perform this operation.
[philip@localhost Desktop]$
```

From the preceding output, we get an error because we need root privilege to turn on/off the daemon in the respective runlevels. Let's retry as the root user:

```
[philip@localhost Desktop]$ su -
Password:
[root@localhost ~]# chkconfig --levels 345 dnsmasq on
[root@localhost ~]#
```

Great! Now let's rerun the `chkconfig` command and only look for the `dnsmasq` daemon:

```
[root@localhost ~]# chkconfig | grep dnsmasq
dnsmasq 0:off 1:off 2:off 3:on 4:on 5:on 6:off
[root@localhost ~]#
```

From the preceding output, we can see that the `dnsmasq` daemon is now set to `on` in runlevels 3-5.

Working with boot targets

We can work with boot targets using the `systemctl` command. We touched on `systemctl` earlier in this chapter. Let's use the Ubuntu distribution. We can check which `target` is currently the default and running in the shell in real time by doing the following:

```
philip@ubuntu:~$ systemctl get-default
graphical.target
philip@ubuntu:~$
```

From the preceding output, we can see that `graphical.target` is the default running target. Now, if we want to change between targets, we can use the `systemctl` command. Let's change to `multi-user.target`:

```
philip@ubuntu:~$ systemctl isolate multi-user.target
```

As soon as we press the *Enter* key, the system will ask us to authenticate:

We can also run `systemctl` to verify the status of `multi-user.target`:

```
philip@trainer-vm:~$
philip@trainer-vm:~$
philip@trainer-vm:~$
philip@trainer-vm:~$
philip@trainer-vm:~$
philip@trainer-vm:~$
philip@trainer-vm:~$
philip@trainer-vm:~$ systemctl status multi-user.target
■ multi-user.target - Multi-User System
   Loaded: loaded (/lib/systemd/system/multi-user.target; static; vendor preset: enabled)
   Active: active since Thu 2018-06-14 11:21:49 -04; 1h 59min ago
     Docs: man:systemd.special(7)

Jun 14 11:21:49 trainer-vm systemd[1]: Reached target Multi-User System.
philip@trainer-vm:~$ _
```

We can return the system to the GUI environment by using the `systemctl` command:

```
philip@ubuntu:~$ systemctl isolate graphical.target
==== AUTHENTICATING FOR org.freedesktop.systemd1.manage-units ===
Authentication is required to start 'graphical.target'.
Authenticating as: philip,,, (philip)
Password: _
```

Also, we can take a look at one of the targets to see its structure, using the `systemctl` command:

```
philip@ubuntu:~$ systemctl show network.target
 Id=network.target
 Names=network.target
 WantedBy=networking.service systemd-networkd.service
NetworkManager.service
 Conflicts=shutdown.target
 Before=network-online.target rc-local.service
 After=NetworkManager.service network-pre.target systemd-networkd.service
network
 Documentation=man:systemd.special(7)
http://www.freedesktop.org/wiki/Software/sy
 Description=Network
```

```
LoadState=loaded
ActiveState=active
SubState=active
FragmentPath=/lib/systemd/system/network.target
UnitFileState=static
UnitFilePreset=enabled
StateChangeTimestamp=Wed 2018-06-20 10:50:52 PDT
StateChangeTimestampMonotonic=18205063
InactiveExitTimestamp=Wed 2018-06-20 10:50:52 PDT
InactiveExitTimestampMonotonic=18205063
ActiveEnterTimestamp=Wed 2018-06-20 10:50:52 PDT
ActiveEnterTimestampMonotonic=18205063
ActiveExitTimestampMonotonic=0
InactiveEnterTimestampMonotonic=0
CanStart=no
```

From the preceding output, one of the key values is `WantedBy`. This tells us who relies on the `network.target`. We can see that `NetworkManager.service` relies on the `network.target`. There are also details regarding `StateChangeTimestamp`, `Documentation`, `LoadState`, and `Description`, to name a few.

Summary

In this chapter, we interacted with runlevels. We saw the various runlevels available, and we switched between runlevels. We saw the default runlevel (runlevel 5), and we made usage of the `runlevel`, `who`, and `init` commands for interaction. We then focused on boot targets. We looked at the default boot targets and saw the various units under each boot target. We then changed between boot targets and saw that authentication was required. We used the `systemctl` commands with various options, and the `runlevel` and `who` commands. We verified we are indeed in another boot target. We derived that the `graphical.target` is similar to runlevel 5 and that `multi-user.target` is similar to runlevel 3. Finally, we took a brief looked at the structure of a boot target.

In the next chapter, we will focus on the design of a hard disk layout. The hard disk layout is critical before any deployment is carried out. Hence, this next chapter carries a lot of weight in that a lot of thought needs to be placed on how we manage our hard disks. The `fdisk` and `parted`, to name a few, are going to be covered. The techniques that you will grasp from the next chapter will aid you in your future deployments as a Linux engineer. This empowerment gained from the next chapter is a key factor in building confidence for your future success in terms of certification.

Questions

1. Which runlevel is a GUI presented in a CentOS distribution?

    A. 1
    B. 5
    C. 2
    D. 3

2. What is the command to print the current runlevel in an Ubuntu distribution?

    A. `run-level`
    B. `systemdctl`
    C. `runlevel`
    D. `who -b`

3. Which alternate command displays the runlevel information?

    A. `who -v`
    B. `who -l`
    C. `who -b`
    D. `who -r`

4. What does the *N* refer to when reading the runlevel output?

    A. The current runlevel
    B. The previous runlevel before it was changed to the current runlevel
    C. The previous current runlevel before it was changed to the previous runlevel
    D. The runlevel that is in use currently

5. What does the *S* refer to when reading the runlevel output?

    A. Single sign-on user
    B. Super user
    C. Single-entry super user
    D. Single user

6. Which command is used to change the runlevel?

    A. `int`
    B. `init`
    C. `runlevel`
    D. `change-run-level`

7. Which other command can be used to change the runlevel?

    A. `runlevel`
    B. `shutdown`
    C. `telinit`
    D. `telnit`

8. Which command is used to view the default boot target?

    A. `systemctl get-default`
    B. `systemctl set-default`
    C. `systemctl-default`
    D. `systemctl-get-default`

9. Which command can be used to list the daemons for a given target?

    A. `systemctl list-dependencies`
    B. `systemctl list-dependencies -type list`
    C. `systemctl list-dependencies -type target`
    D. `systemctl list-dependencies target`

10. Which command switches between targets?

    A. `systemctl isolate target`
    B. `systemctl isolate multi-user.target`
    C. `systemctl isolate-target-multi-user`
    D. `systemctl isolate-multiuser.target`

11. Which command displays the status of a target?

    A. `systemctl status multi-user.target`
    B. `systemctl status-multi-user.target`
    C. `systemctl-status multi-user.target`
    D. `systemctl-status-multiuser.target`

Further reading

- You can get more information about the CentOS distributions, such as installing, configuration best practices, and so on at `https://www.centos.org`.
- The following website gives you a lot of useful tips and best practices from users in the Linux community, particularly for the Debian distributions, such as Ubuntu: `https://askubuntu.com`.
- The following link gives you information in general that relates to various commands that work on both CentOS and Ubuntu. You can post your questions at the following link and other community members will respond: `https://www.linuxquestions.org`.

4
Designing a Hard Disk Layout

In the previous chapter, we focused on runlevels and boot targets. We interacted with a Linux system running `init` and also `systemd`. We saw how to turn on a service, and we saw how to switch between runlevels and boot targets. We looked at the various start and stop scripts, and we also looked at the structure of a script.

This chapter focuses on creating partitions and segmenting a physical hard disk at the CLI. We will be particularly focusing on the usage of the `fdisk` utility and the `parted` utility. Then we will go through the steps to create, remove, and define the partition type as well as formatting the hard disk with the various `mkfs` commands. Finally, we will look at ways of mounting and unmounting a partition.

So, we will cover the following topics in this chapter:

- Using the `fdisk` utility
- Using the `parted` utility
- Steps for formatting a hard disk
- Mounting and unmounting a partition

Using the fdisk utility

In Linux, whenever we're working with hard disks, chances are we will have to **partition a hard disk** at some point in time. *Partitioning* simply means separating the hard disk. This enables us to have varying sizes of partition and gives us the ability to satisfy various software installation requirements. Furthermore, when we partition a hard disk, each partition is treated as an entirely separate hard disk by the operating system. The `fdisk` (fixed disk or format disk) is a command-line based utility that can be used for manipulating a hard disk. With `fdisk`, you can view, create, delete, and change, among other things.

To start with, let's expose the hard disk within our Ubuntu distribution:

```
philip@ubuntu:~$ ls /dev/ | grep sd
sda
sda1
sda2
sda5
philip@ubuntu:~$
```

From the preceding output, the hard disk in the system is represented by /dev/sda. The first partition is /dev/sda1, the second partition is /dev/sda2, and so on. For us to see the partition information, we will run the following command:

```
philip@ubuntu:~$ fdisk -l /dev/sda
fdisk: cannot open /dev/sda: Permission denied
philip@ubuntu:~$
```

From the preceding output, we get Permission denied. This is because we require a root privilege to view and change the partition of a hard disk. Let's retry as the root user:

```
philip@ubuntu:~$ sudo su
[sudo] password for philip:
root@ubuntu:/home/philip#
root@ubuntu:/home/philip# fdisk -l /dev/sda
Disk /dev/sda: 20 GiB, 21474836480 bytes, 41943040 sectors
Units: sectors of 1 * 512 = 512 bytes
Sector size (logical/physical): 512 bytes / 512 bytes
I/O size (minimum/optimal): 512 bytes / 512 bytes
Disklabel type: dos
Disk identifier: 0xf54f42a0

Device     Boot Start      End       Sectors  Size Id  Type
/dev/sda1  *    2048       39845887  39843840 19G  83     Linux
/dev/sda2       39847934   41940991  2093058  1022M 5 Extended
/dev/sda5       39847936   41940991  2093056  1022M 82 Linux swap / Solaris
root@ubuntu:/home/philip#
```

From the preceding output, the way to read this would be as follows:

Disk /dev/sda: 20 GiB, 21,474,836,480 bytes, 41,943,040 sectors. This is the actual physical hard disk:

Device	Boot	Start	End	Sectors	Size	Id	Type	Comment
/dev/sda1	*	2048	39,845,887	39,843,840	19 G	83	Linux	First partition is 19 GB
/dev/sda2		39,847,934	41,940,991	2,093,058	1,022 M	5	Extended	Second partition is 1,022 MB
/dev/sda5		39,847,936	41,940,991	2,093,056	1,022 M	82	Linux swap / Solaris	Fifth partition is 1,022 MB

Now, for us to be able to make any changes, we will use the fdisk command once again. This time we will leave out the -l option:

```
root@ubuntu:/home/philip# fdisk /dev/sda

Welcome to fdisk (util-linux 2.27.1).
Changes will remain in memory only, until you decide to write them.
Be careful before using the write command.

Command (m for help):
```

From the previous code, we are now inside the fdisk utility and we are presented with a nice little message.

 Do not commit any changes before first making sure you understand the dangers surrounding removing partition; the system could become unstable if you remove a partition that stores system files such as /boot/ and /, to name a few.

For us to view the available options, we can press the m key:

```
Command (m for help): m
Help:
  DOS (MBR)
   a   toggle a bootable flag
   b   edit nested BSD disklabel
   c   toggle the dos compatibility flag
Generic
   d   delete a partition
   F   list free unpartitioned space
   l   list known partition types
   n   add a new partition
   p   print the partition table
   t   change a partition type
   v   verify the partition table
   i   print information about a partition

Misc
   m   print this menu
   u   change display/entry units
   x   extra functionality (experts only)
Script
   I   load disk layout from sfdisk script file
   O   dump disk layout to sfdisk script file

Save & Exit
   w   write table to disk and exit
```

```
    q   quit without saving changes
Create a new label
    g   create a new empty GPT partition table
    G   create a new empty SGI (IRIX) partition table
    o   create a new empty DOS partition table
    s   create a new empty Sun partition table

Command (m for help):
```

From the preceding output, we can see a variety of options to choose from. We can even use l to see the known partition types:

```
buntu: /home/philip
Command (m for help): l

  0   Empty            24  NEC DOS          81  Minix / old Lin  bf  Solaris
  1   FAT12            27  Hidden NTFS Win  82  Linux swap / So  c1  DRDOS/sec (FAT-
  2   XENIX root       39  Plan 9           83  Linux            c4  DRDOS/sec (FAT-
  3   XENIX usr        3c  PartitionMagic   84  OS/2 hidden or   c6  DRDOS/sec (FAT-
  4   FAT16 <32M       40  Venix 80286      85  Linux extended   c7  Syrinx
  5   Extended         41  PPC PReP Boot    86  NTFS volume set  da  Non-FS data
  6   FAT16            42  SFS              87  NTFS volume set  db  CP/M / CTOS / .
  7   HPFS/NTFS/exFAT  4d  QNX4.x           88  Linux plaintext  de  Dell Utility
  8   AIX              4e  QNX4.x 2nd part  8e  Linux LVM        df  BootIt
  9   AIX bootable     4f  QNX4.x 3rd part  93  Amoeba           e1  DOS access
  a   OS/2 Boot Manag  50  OnTrack DM       94  Amoeba BBT       e3  DOS R/O
  b   W95 FAT32        51  OnTrack DM6 Aux  9f  BSD/OS           e4  SpeedStor
  c   W95 FAT32 (LBA)  52  CP/M             a0  IBM Thinkpad hi  ea  Rufus alignment
  e   W95 FAT16 (LBA)  53  OnTrack DM6 Aux  a5  FreeBSD          eb  BeOS fs
  f   W95 Ext'd (LBA)  54  OnTrackDM6       a6  OpenBSD          ee  GPT
 10   OPUS             55  EZ-Drive         a7  NeXTSTEP         ef  EFI (FAT-12/16/
 11   Hidden FAT12     56  Golden Bow       a8  Darwin UFS       f0  Linux/PA-RISC b
 12   Compaq diagnost  5c  Priam Edisk      a9  NetBSD           f1  SpeedStor
 14   Hidden FAT16 <3  61  SpeedStor        ab  Darwin boot      f4  SpeedStor
 16   Hidden FAT16     63  GNU HURD or Sys  af  HFS / HFS+       f2  DOS secondary
 17   Hidden HPFS/NTF  64  Novell Netware   b7  BSDI fs          fb  VMware VMFS
 18   AST SmartSleep   65  Novell Netware   b8  BSDI swap        fc  VMware VMKCORE
 1b   Hidden W95 FAT3  70  DiskSecure Mult  bb  Boot Wizard hid  fd  Linux raid auto
 1c   Hidden W95 FAT3  75  PC/IX            bc  Acronis FAT32 L  fe  LANstep
 1e   Hidden W95 FAT1  80  Old Minix        be  Solaris boot     ff  BBT
```

From the preceding screenshot, we can see a range of different partition types available for usage. The common types are 5 Extended, 7 NTFS Windows, 82 Linux swap, 83 (Linux), a5 FreeBSD, ee GPT, and ef EFI, to name a few.

Now, to view the partitions created, we can use p:

```
Command (m for help): p
Disk /dev/sda: 20 GiB, 21474836480 bytes, 41943040 sectors
Geometry: 255 heads, 63 sectors/track, 2610 cylinders
Units: sectors of 1 * 512 = 512 bytes
Sector size (logical/physical): 512 bytes / 512 bytes
I/O size (minimum/optimal): 512 bytes / 512 bytes
Disklabel type: dos
Disk identifier: 0xf54f42a0

Device     Boot    Start      End  Sectors  Size Id Type
/dev/sda1  *        2048 39845887 39843840  19G 83 Linux
/dev/sda2       39847934 41940991  2093058 1022M  5 Extended
/dev/sda5       39847936 41940991  2093056 1022M 82 Linux swap / Solaris

Command (m for help):
```

I've added a second hard disk to this system, so let's verify this:

```
root@ubuntu:/home/philip# ls /dev/ | grep sd
sda
sda1
sda2
sda5
sdb
root@ubuntu:/home/philip#
```

Awesome! We can now see /dev/sdb. We will use fdisk with this new hard disk:

```
root@ubuntu:/home/philip# fdisk /dev/sdb

Welcome to fdisk (util-linux 2.27.1).
Changes will remain in memory only, until you decide to write them.
Be careful before using the write command.

Device does not contain a recognized partition table.
Created a new DOS disklabel with disk identifier 0x0079e169.
Command (m for help):
```

Now let's press p, which will print the current partition(s) on the /dev/sdb:

```
Command (m for help): p
Disk /dev/sdb: 15 GiB, 16106127360 bytes, 31457280 sectors
Units: sectors of 1 * 512 = 512 bytes
Sector size (logical/physical): 512 bytes / 512 bytes
I/O size (minimum/optimal): 512 bytes / 512 bytes
Disklabel type: dos
Disk identifier: 0x0079e169

Command (m for help):
```

As you can see, there is no partition on the /dev/sdb. For us to create a partition, we will use the n key:

```
Command (m for help): n
Partition type
   p   primary (0 primary, 0 extended, 4 free)
   e   extended (container for logical partitions)
Select (default p):
```

This will ask us to declare the type of partition. There are primary and extended partition types available with the fdisk utility. There is also a logical partition type. For us to install an operating system, we will choose p, which stands for *primary partition type*.

> You would not install an operating system on a logical partition type.

As you can see, we use the n to create new partitions. An important point to note is the fact that the partitions that we have created thus far are all Linux-type partitions. If for some reason we want to change the partition type, we can use t to change it. Let's change the /dev/sdb2 to an HPFS/NTFS/exFAT partition. We will use type 7 in the fdisk utility:

```
Command (m for help): t
Partition number (1-3, default 3): 2
Partition type (type L to list all types): 1
0   Empty   24  NEC DOS 81  Minix / old Lin bf  Solaris
1   FAT12   27  Hidden NTFS Win 82  Linux swap / So c1  DRDOS/sec (FAT-
2   XENIX root  39  Plan 9  83  Linux   c4  DRDOS/sec (FAT-
3   XENIX usr   3c  PartitionMagic 84 OS/2 hidden or c6 DRDOS/sec (FAT-
4   FAT16 <32M  40  Venix 80286     85  Linux extended  c7  Syrinx
5   Extended    41  PPC PReP Boot   86  NTFS volume set da  Non-FS data
6   FAT16       42  SFS 87  NTFS volume set db  CP/M / CTOS / .
7   HPFS/NTFS/exFAT
```

Awesome! Now we can see the partition type as type 7:

```
Partition type (type L to list all types): 7
Changed type of partition 'Empty' to 'HPFS/NTFS/exFAT'.
Command (m for help): p
Disk /dev/sdb: 15 GiB, 16106127360 bytes, 31457280 sectors
Units: sectors of 1 * 512 = 512 bytes
Sector size (logical/physical): 512 bytes / 512 bytes
I/O size (minimum/optimal): 512 bytes / 512 bytes
Disklabel type: dos
Disk identifier: 0x2584b986
```

Device	Boot	Start	End	Sectors	Size	Id	Type
/dev/sdb1	2048	10487807	10485760	5G		83	Linux
/dev/sdb2	10487808	18876415	8388608	4G		7	HPFS/NTFS/exFAT
/dev/sdb3	18876416	31457279	12580864	6G		0	Empty

We will also change the /dev/sdb3 partition to type ef:

```
buntu: /home/philip
Command (m for help): l

 0   Empty              24  NEC DOS          81  Minix / old Lin bf  Solaris
 1   FAT12              27  Hidden NTFS Win  82  Linux swap / So c1  DRDOS/sec (FAT-
 2   XENIX root         39  Plan 9           83  Linux           c4  DRDOS/sec (FAT-
 3   XENIX usr          3c  PartitionMagic   84  OS/2 hidden or  c6  DRDOS/sec (FAT-
 4   FAT16 <32M         40  Venix 80286      85  Linux extended  c7  Syrinx
 5   Extended           41  PPC PReP Boot    86  NTFS volume set da  Non-FS data
 6   FAT16              42  SFS              87  NTFS volume set db  CP/M / CTOS / .
 7   HPFS/NTFS/exFAT    4d  QNX4.x           88  Linux plaintext de  Dell Utility
 8   AIX                4e  QNX4.x 2nd part  8e  Linux LVM       df  BootIt
 9   AIX bootable       4f  QNX4.x 3rd part  93  Amoeba          e1  DOS access
 a   OS/2 Boot Manag    50  OnTrack DM       94  Amoeba BBT      e3  DOS R/O
 b   W95 FAT32          51  OnTrack DM6 Aux  9f  BSD/OS          e4  SpeedStor
 c   W95 FAT32 (LBA)    52  CP/M             a0  IBM Thinkpad hi ea  Rufus alignment
 e   W95 FAT16 (LBA)    53  OnTrack DM6 Aux  a5  FreeBSD         eb  BeOS fs
 f   W95 Ext'd (LBA)    54  OnTrackDM6       a6  OpenBSD         ee  GPT
10   OPUS               55  EZ-Drive         a7  NeXTSTEP        ef  EFI (FAT-12/16/
11   Hidden FAT12       56  Golden Bow       a8  Darwin UFS      f0  Linux/PA-RISC b
12   Compaq diagnost    5c  Priam Edisk      a9  NetBSD          f1  SpeedStor
14   Hidden FAT16 <3    61  SpeedStor        ab  Darwin boot     f4  SpeedStor
16   Hidden FAT16       63  GNU HURD or Sys  af  HFS / HFS+      f2  DOS secondary
17   Hidden HPFS/NTF    64  Novell Netware   b7  BSDI fs         fb  VMware VMFS
18   AST SmartSleep     65  Novell Netware   b8  BSDI swap       fc  VMware VMKCORE
1b   Hidden W95 FAT3    70  DiskSecure Mult  bb  Boot Wizard hid fd  Linux raid auto
1c   Hidden W95 FAT3    75  PC/IX            bc  Acronis FAT32 L fe  LANstep
1e   Hidden W95 FAT1    80  Old Minix        be  Solaris boot    ff  BBT
```

Now when we rerun the p command, we can see that our newly created partition type is set to ef:

Device	Boot	Start	End	Sectors	Size	Id	Type
/dev/sdb1	2048	10487807	10485760	5G		83	Linux
/dev/sdb2	10487808	18876415	8388608	4G		7	HPFS/NTFS/exFAT
/dev/sdb3	18876416	31457279	12580864	6G		ef	EFI (FAT-12/16/32)

Now if we decide to install an operating system, we will have to make one of these partitions bootable. We will make the third partition /dev/sdb3 bootable:

```
Command (m for help): a
Partition number (1-3, default 3): 3
The bootable flag on partition 3 is enabled now.
Command (m for help): p
Disk /dev/sdb: 15 GiB, 16106127360 bytes, 31457280 sectors
Units: sectors of 1 * 512 = 512 bytes
```

```
Sector size (logical/physical): 512 bytes / 512 bytes
I/O size (minimum/optimal): 512 bytes / 512 bytes
Disklabel type: dos
Disk identifier: 0x2584b986
Device     Boot    Start       End  Sectors Size Id Type
/dev/sdb1           2048  10487807 10485760   5G 83 Linux
/dev/sdb2       10487808  18876415  8388608   4G  7 HPFS/NTFS/exFAT
/dev/sdb3   *   18876416  31457279 12580864   6G ef EFI (FAT-12/16/32)
```

From the previous output, the /dev/sdb3 is now marked as bootable.

Finally, to change or write our changes, we will press w to save and exit:

```
Command (m for help): w
The partition table has been altered.
Calling ioctl() to re-read partition table.
Syncing disks.
```

The output of these commands can be seen in the following screenshot:

```
Device     Boot    Start       End  Sectors Size Id Type
/dev/sdb1           2048  10487807 10485760   5G 83 Linux
/dev/sdb2       10487808  18876415  8388608   4G  7 HPFS/NTFS/exFAT
/dev/sdb3       18876416  31457279 12580864   6G ef EFI (FAT-12/16/32)

Command (m for help): a
Partition number (1-3, default 3): 3

The bootable flag on partition 3 is enabled now.

Command (m for help): p
Disk /dev/sdb: 15 GiB, 16106127360 bytes, 31457280 sectors
Units: sectors of 1 * 512 = 512 bytes
Sector size (logical/physical): 512 bytes / 512 bytes
I/O size (minimum/optimal): 512 bytes / 512 bytes
Disklabel type: dos
Disk identifier: 0x2584b986

Device     Boot    Start       End  Sectors Size Id Type
/dev/sdb1           2048  10487807 10485760   5G 83 Linux
/dev/sdb2       10487808  18876415  8388608   4G  7 HPFS/NTFS/exFAT
/dev/sdb3   *   18876416  31457279 12580864   6G ef EFI (FAT-12/16/32)

Command (m for help): w
The partition table has been altered.
Calling ioctl() to re-read partition table.
Syncing disks.

root@ubuntu:/home/philip#
```

Using the parted utility

The parted utility is geared towards situations where we have a hard disk or hard disks larger than 2 TB. Additionally, we can a resize a partition; the fdisk utility cannot resize a partition. Almost all of the newer Linux distributions support the parted utility. parted comes from GNU; it's a text-based partitioning utility that works with a variety of disk types such as MBR, GPT, and BSD, to name a few.

 Always backup your data before doing any partitioning.

To start with, we will use the parted command on the /dev/sdb:

```
root@ubuntu:/home/philip# parted /dev/sdb
GNU Parted 3.2
Using /dev/sdb
Welcome to GNU Parted! Type 'help' to view a list of commands.
(parted)
```

From here, we are placed into the parted utility. Similar to the fdisk utility, the parted utility is interactive. Now let's say we want to view the help menu. Here, we can enlist the help at the CLI:

```
(parted) help
 align-check TYPE N check partition N for TYPE(min|opt) alignment
 help [COMMAND] print general help, or help on COMMAND
 mklabel,mktable LABEL-TYPE create a new disklabel (partition table)
 mkpart PART-TYPE [FS-TYPE] START END make a partition
 name NUMBER NAME name partition NUMBER as NAME
 print [devices|free|list,all|NUMBER] display the partition table,
available devices, free space, all found partitions, or a particular
partition
 quit exit program
 rescue START END rescue a lost partition near START and END
 resizepart NUMBER END resize partition NUMBER
 rm NUMBER delete partition NUMBER
 select DEVICE choose the device to edit
 disk_set FLAG STATE change the FLAG on selected device
 disk_toggle [FLAG] toggle the state of FLAG on selected device
 set NUMBER FLAG STATE change the FLAG on partition NUMBER
 toggle [NUMBER [FLAG]] toggle the state of FLAG on partition NUMBER
 unit UNIT set the default unit to UNIT
 version display the version number and copyright information of GNU Parted
(parted)
```

From the preceding output, we have a long list of commands at our disposal.

Remember to do a backup before making any change(s) to your partition.

Now, to view the current partition table for the /dev/sdb, we would type print:

```
(parted) print
Model: VMware, VMware Virtual S (scsi)
Disk /dev/sdb: 16.1GB
Sector size (logical/physical): 512B/512B
Partition Table: msdos
Disk Flags:
Number  Start    End     Size     Type     File system  Flags
 1      1049kB   5370MB  5369MB   primary
 2      5370MB   9665MB  4295MB   primary
 3      9665MB   16.1GB  6441MB   primary boot, esp
(parted)
```

This will print out the partition table for the /dev/sdb. However, we can use the print command with the list option to view all the hard disks available in this system. Let's give it a try:

```
(parted) print list
Model: VMware, VMware Virtual S (scsi)
Disk /dev/sdb: 16.1GB
Sector size (logical/physical): 512B/512B
Partition Table: msdos
Disk Flags:
Number  Start    End     Size     Type     File system  Flags
 1      1049kB   5370MB  5369MB   primary
 2      5370MB   9665MB  4295MB   primary
 3      9665MB   16.1GB  6441MB   primary                boot, esp
  Model: VMware, VMware Virtual S (scsi)
Disk /dev/sda: 21.5GB
Sector size (logical/physical): 512B/512B
Partition Table: msdos
Disk Flags:
Number  Start    End     Size     Type      File system    Flags
 1      1049kB   20.4GB  20.4GB   primary   ext4           boot
 2      20.4GB   21.5GB  1072MB   extended
 5      20.4GB   21.5GB  1072MB   logical   linux-swap(v1)
(parted)
```

Great! As you can see, the /dev/sda is now also listed. Next, let's look at how we would resize a partition. To accomplish this, we're going to leverage another powerful command, the resizepart command, which in itself is appropriately named.

We will choose the second partition for this exercise; we'll say resizepart 2, and we will reduce it to 2 GB:

```
(parted) resizepart
Partition number? 2
End? [5370MB]? 7518
(parted) print
Disk /dev/sdb: 16.1GB
Sector size (logical/physical): 512B/512B
Partition Table: msdos
Disk Flags:
Number Start End Size Type File system Flags
 1 1049kB 5370MB 5369MB primary
 2 5370MB 7518MB 2148MB primary
 3 9665MB 16.1GB 6441MB primary boot, esp
(parted)
```

From the preceding output, you can see that the parted utility is very powerful. We have effectively taken away 2 GB (roughly) from the second partition. Now, if you think about it, we have 2 GB of free space to use at our disposal.

 Hard disk space is critical in a large data center, so bear that in mind when provisioning your servers.

Now, for the purpose of demonstrating how we would use the 2 GB of free space, let's create another partition. The parted utility is powerful, in that it can recognize partitions that were created from another disk utility such as fdisk. In parted, we would use the mkpart command to create a partition:

```
(parted)
(parted) mkpart
Partition type?  primary/extended?
```

As you can see by now, there are similarities between fdisk and parted, and they both ask whether the partition is going to be a primary or extended partition. This is vital whenever we're working with operating system installations. For our purposes, we're going to create yet another primary partition:

```
Partition type?  primary/extended? primary
File system type?   [ext2]?
Start?
```

Now, at this point, we will have to specify the starting size of the partition we are about to create. We will use the size where the second partition ends:

```
File system type? [ext2]?
Start? 7518
End? 9665
(parted)
```

Awesome! Now let's rerun the print command:

```
(parted) print
Model: VMware, VMware Virtual S (scsi)
Disk /dev/sdb: 16.1GB
Sector size (logical/physical): 512B/512B
Partition Table: msdos
Disk Flags:
Number Start     End      Size     Type     File system  Flags
 1       1049kB  5370MB   5369MB   primary
 2       5370MB  7518MB   2148MB   primary
 4       7518MB  9665MB   2146MB   primary  ext2         lba
 3       9665MB  16.1GB   6441MB   primary               boot, esp
(parted)
```

From the preceding output, we can now see our newly created partition at 2 GB (roughly).

Now we can change the boot flag from its present partition 3 /dev/sdb3 to part partition 4 /dev/sdb4. We would use the set command for this:

```
(parted) set
Partition number? 4
Flag to Invert?
```

From here, we have to tell the parted utility that we want to move the boot flag:

```
Flag to Invert? boot
New state?   [on]/off?
```

Now we need to confirm our changes. on is the default, so we press *Enter*:

```
New state?   [on]/off?
(parted) print
Model: VMware, VMware Virtual S (scsi)
Disk /dev/sdb: 16.1GB
Sector size (logical/physical): 512B/512B
Partition Table: msdos
Disk Flags:
Number  Start    End      Size     Type      File system  Flags
 1      1049kB   5370MB   5369MB   primary
 2      5370MB   7518MB   2148MB   primary
 4      7518MB   9665MB   2146MB   primary   ext2         boot, lba
 3      9665MB   16.1GB   6441MB   primary                esp
(parted)
```

Great! Now we can see that the boot flag has been shifted to the fourth partition
/dev/sdb4.

Finally, to save our changes, we can simply type quit:

```
(parted) quit
Information: You may need to update /etc/fstab.
root@ubuntu:/home/philip#
```

> You would add entries as needed in the /etc/fstab to automount your
> partitions to their respective mount points.

Steps to format a hard disk

After we have created our partitions, the next step would be to make the partitions
accessible by way of a filesystem. In Linux, when we format a partition(s), the system wipes
the partition, and this enables the system to store data on the partition.

We have a number of filesystem types available in a Linux system. We use the mkfs
command in combination with the desired filesystem type. To see the available filesystems,
we can do this:

```
root@ubuntu:/home/philip# mkfs
mkfs            mkfs.cramfs    mkfs.ext3     mkfs.ext4dev   mkfs.minix    mkfs.ntfs
mkfs.bfs        mkfs.ext2      mkfs.ext4     mkfs.fat       mkfs.msdos    mkfs.vfat
root@ubuntu:/home/philip# mkfs
```

From the preceding screenshot, in this Ubuntu distribution, the ext4 type is primarily what the distribution is currently using. We can also use the lsblk command with the -f option to verify this:

```
root@ubuntu:/home/philip# lsblk -f
```

The output of the preceding command can be seen in the following screenshot:

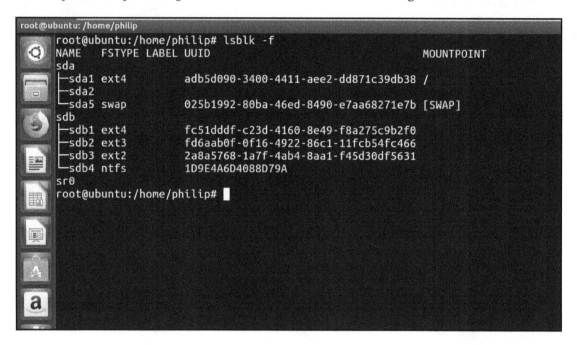

From the preceding screenshot, we can see both hard disks: /dev/sda and /dev/sdb. Additionally, we see a column FSTYPE. This identifies which filesystem is currently in use. We can see that the FSTYPE is blank for the entire /dev/sdb(1-4).

We can also use the blkid command to view the filesystems in use by the system:

```
root@ubuntu:/home/philip# blkid
/dev/sda1: UUID="adb5d090-3400-4411-aee2-dd871c39db38" TYPE="ext4" PARTUUID="f54f42a0-01"
/dev/sda5: UUID="025b1992-80ba-46ed-8490-e7aa68271e7b" TYPE="swap" PARTUUID="f54f42a0-05"
/dev/sdb1: PARTUUID="7e707ac0-01"
/dev/sdb2: PARTUUID="7e707ac0-02"
/dev/sdb3: PARTUUID="7e707ac0-03"
/dev/sdb4: PARTUUID="7e707ac0-04"
root@ubuntu:/home/philip#
```

From the output given, the part that says TYPE= displays the filesystem in use. Please note that the TYPE= is missing for the /dev/sdb(1-4). This simply means that we have not formatted any of the partitions that reside on the /dev/sdb.

Now let's start formatting our partitions. For this, we'll use the ext4 filesystem on the /dev/sdb1:

```
root@ubuntu:/home/philip# mkfs.ext4 /dev/sdb1
mke2fs 1.42.13 (17-May-2015)
Creating filesystem with 1310720 4k blocks and 327680 inodes
Filesystem UUID: fc51dddf-c23d-4160-8e49-f8a275c9b2f0
Superblock backups stored on blocks:
            32768, 98304, 163840, 229376, 294912, 819200, 884736
Allocating group tables: done
Writing inode tables: done
Creating journal (32768 blocks): done
Writing superblocks and filesystem accounting information: done
root@ubuntu:/home/philip#
```

From the preceding output, the mkfs utility, particularly mkfs.ext4, creates the filesystem on the raw partition; then it assigns a UUID to uniquely identify the /dev/sdb1 partition.

You need to have a root privilege before you can format a partition.

Next, let's use the ext3 filesystem for the /dev/sdb2:

```
root@ubuntu:/home/philip# mkfs.ext3 /dev/sdb2
mke2fs 1.42.13 (17-May-2015)
Creating filesystem with 524288 4k blocks and 131328 inodes
Filesystem UUID: fd6aab0f-0f16-4922-86c1-11fcb54fc466
Superblock backups stored on blocks:
            32768, 98304, 163840, 229376, 294912
Allocating group tables: done
Writing inode tables: done
Creating journal (16384 blocks): done
Writing superblocks and filesystem accounting information: done
root@ubuntu:/home/philip#
```

Now we'll use the `ext2` for the `/dev/sdb3` and the `ntfs` for the `/dev/sdb4`:

```
root@ubuntu:/home/philip# mkfs.ext2 /dev/sdb3
mke2fs 1.42.13 (17-May-2015)
Creating filesystem with 1572608 4k blocks and 393216 inodes
Filesystem UUID: b7e075df-541d-468d-ab16-e3ec2e5fb5f8
Superblock backups stored on blocks:
           32768, 98304, 163840, 229376, 294912, 819200, 884736
Allocating group tables: done
Writing inode tables: done
Writing superblocks and filesystem accounting information: done
root@ubuntu:/home/philip# mkfs.ntfs /dev/sdb4
Cluster size has been automatically set to 4096 bytes.
Initializing device with zeroes: 100% - Done.
Creating NTFS volume structures.
mkntfs completed successfully. Have a nice day.
root@ubuntu:/home/philip#
```

You can also use the `mk2fs` to create an `ext2` filesystem.

Great! Now we have just formatted the `/dev/sdb1`, `/dev/sdb2`, `dev/sdb3` and the `/dev/sdb4`. If we now rerun the `lsblk` command with the `-f` option, we will see the filesystem type (`FSTYPE`) populated for the two respective partitions:

```
root@ubuntu:/home/philip# lsblk -f
NAME    FSTYPE LABEL UUID                                MOUNTPOINT
sda
├─sda1 ext4          adb5d090-3400-4411-aee2-dd871c39db38 /
├─sda2
└─sda5 swap          025b1992-80ba-46ed-8490-e7aa68271e7b [SWAP]
sdb
├─sdb1 ext4          fc51dddf-c23d-4160-8e49-f8a275c9b2f0
├─sdb2 ext3          fd6aab0f-0f16-4922-86c1-11fcb54fc466
├─sdb3 ext2          b7e075df-541d-468d-ab16-e3ec2e5fb5f8
└─sdb4 ntfs          1D9E4A6D4088D79A
sr0
root@ubuntu:/home/philip#
```

From the preceding output, we can see that the `FSTYPE` is reflecting the changes that we made.

We can also rerun the `blkid` command to view the UUIDs created for the `/dev/sdb1` and `/dev/sdb2`:

```
root@ubuntu:/home/philip# blkid
/dev/sda1: UUID="adb5d090-3400-4411-aee2-dd871c39db38" TYPE="ext4"
PARTUUID="f54f42a0-01"
/dev/sda5: UUID="025b1992-80ba-46ed-8490-e7aa68271e7b" TYPE="swap"
PARTUUID="f54f42a0-05"
/dev/sdb1: UUID="fc51dddf-c23d-4160-8e49-f8a275c9b2f0" TYPE="ext4"
PARTUUID="7e707ac0-01"
/dev/sdb2: UUID="fd6aab0f-0f16-4922-86c1-11fcb54fc466" SEC_TYPE="ext2"
TYPE="ext3" PARTUUID="7e707ac0-02"
/dev/sdb3: UUID="2a8a5768-1a7f-4ab4-8aa1-f45d30df5631" TYPE="ext2"
PARTUUID="7e707ac0-03"
/dev/sdb4: UUID="1D9E4A6D4088D79A" TYPE="ntfs" PARTUUID="7e707ac0-04"
root@ubuntu:/home/philip#
```

As you can see, the system can now store information on the respective partitions.

Mounting and unmounting a partition

The final step after formatting a partition is to mount the partition. We use the `mount` command to mount a partition and the `unmount` command to unmount a partition. The mount command is also used for viewing the current mount points in our system. However, after a reboot, all partitions are unmounted, unless we created entries in the `/etc/fstab` directory.

You need a root privilege to save any change in the `/etc/fstab`. It's also important to back up any configuration file(s) before making any change(s).

The mount command

We can issue the `mount` command without any arguments to view the current mount points:

```
root@ubuntu:/home/philip# mount
sysfs on /sys type sysfs (rw,nosuid,nodev,noexec,relatime)
proc on /proc type proc (rw,nosuid,nodev,noexec,relatime)
udev on /dev type devtmpfs
(rw,nosuid,relatime,size=478356k,nr_inodes=119589,mode=755)
devpts on /dev/pts type devpts
(rw,nosuid,noexec,relatime,gid=5,mode=620,ptmxmode=000)
tmpfs on /run type tmpfs (rw,nosuid,noexec,relatime,size=99764k,mode=755)
```

```
/dev/sda1 on / type ext4 (rw,relatime,errors=remount-ro,data=ordered)
securityfs on /sys/kernel/security type securityfs
(rw,nosuid,nodev,noexec,relatime)
tmpfs on /dev/shm type tmpfs (rw,nosuid,nodev)
tmpfs on /run/lock type tmpfs (rw,nosuid,nodev,noexec,relatime,size=5120k)
tmpfs on /sys/fs/cgroup type tmpfs (ro,nosuid,nodev,noexec,mode=755)
cgroup on /sys/fs/cgroup/systemd type cgroup
(rw,nosuid,nodev,noexec,relatime,xattr,release_agent=/lib/systemd/systemd-
cgroups-agent,name=systemd)
pstore on /sys/fs/pstore type pstore (rw,nosuid,nodev,noexec,relatime)
cgroup on /sys/fs/cgroup/cpuset type cgroup
(rw,nosuid,nodev,noexec,relatime,cpuset)
cgroup on /sys/fs/cgroup/cpu,cpuacct type cgroup
(rw,nosuid,nodev,noexec,relatime,cpu,cpuacct)
cgroup on /sys/fs/cgroup/net_cls,net_prio type
cgroup(rw,relatime,user_id=0,group_id=0,default_permissions,allow_other)
tmpfs on /run/user/1000 type tmpfs
(rw,nosuid,nodev,relatime,size=99764k,mode=700,uid=1000,gid=1000)
gvfsd-fuse on /run/user/1000/gvfs type fuse.gvfsd-fuse
(rw,nosuid,nodev,relatime,user_id=1000,group_id=1000)
root@ubuntu:/home/philip#
```

Some of the output was omitted for brevity purposes.

From the preceding output, we can see a number of mount points (a mount point is simply associating a partition/drive to a folder/directory). We can filter the mount command to only display the /dev/:

```
root@ubuntu:/home/philip# mount | grep /dev
udev on /dev type devtmpfs
(rw,nosuid,relatime,size=478356k,nr_inodes=119589,mode=755)
devpts on /dev/pts type devpts
(rw,nosuid,noexec,relatime,gid=5,mode=620,ptmxmode=000)
/dev/sda1 on / type ext4 (rw,relatime,errors=remount-ro,data=ordered)
tmpfs on /dev/shm type tmpfs (rw,nosuid,nodev)
cgroup on /sys/fs/cgroup/devices type cgroup
(rw,nosuid,nodev,noexec,relatime,devices)
mqueue on /dev/mqueue type mqueue (rw,relatime)
hugetlbfs on /dev/hugepages type hugetlbfs (rw,relatime)
root@ubuntu:/home/philip#
```

Based on the filter, we can see the /dev/sda1 is currently mounted on the / directory. As you know, the / directory is the root directory. All other directories fall under the / directory.

We can also use the `df` command with the `-h` option to view a more concise output:

```
root@ubuntu:/home/philip# df -h
Filesystem      Size  Used Avail Use% Mounted on
udev            468M     0  468M   0% /dev
tmpfs            98M  6.2M   92M   7% /run
/dev/sda1        19G  5.1G   13G  29% /
tmpfs           488M  212K  487M   1% /dev/shm
tmpfs           5.0M  4.0K  5.0M   1% /run/lock
tmpfs           488M     0  488M   0% /sys/fs/cgroup
tmpfs            98M   44K   98M   1% /run/user/1000
root@ubuntu:/home/philip#
```

Great! Now this is presented in a structured format and is easier to read. Based on the output, only the `/dev/sda1` partition is currently mounted.

We can now go ahead and mount the `/dev/sdb1` on the `/mnt`. The `/mnt` is an empty directory which we use whenever we want to mount a partition.

Only one partition can be mounted at any given time.

We will run the `mount` command as follows:

```
root@ubuntu:/# mount /dev/sdb1 /mnt
root@ubuntu:/#
```

Note that without any options, the `mount` command worked without an error. Now let's rerun the `mount` command and filter for only the `/dev`:

```
root@ubuntu:/# mount | grep /dev
udev on /dev type devtmpfs
(rw,nosuid,relatime,size=478356k,nr_inodes=119589,mode=755)
devpts on /dev/pts type devpts
(rw,nosuid,noexec,relatime,gid=5,mode=620,ptmxmode=000)
/dev/sda1 on / type ext4 (rw,relatime,errors=remount-ro,data=ordered)
tmpfs on /dev/shm type tmpfs (rw,nosuid,nodev)
cgroup on /sys/fs/cgroup/devices type cgroup
(rw,nosuid,nodev,noexec,relatime,devices)
mqueue on /dev/mqueue type mqueue (rw,relatime)
hugetlbfs on /dev/hugepages type hugetlbfs (rw,relatime)
/dev/sdb1 on /mnt type ext4 (rw,relatime,data=ordered)
root@ubuntu:/#
```

Based on the preceding output, we can see that the /dev/sdb1 is currently mounted on the /mnt.

We can also leverage the df command with the h option to see similar results:

```
root@ubuntu:/# df -h
Filesystem     Size  Used Avail Use% Mounted on
udev           468M     0  468M   0% /dev
tmpfs           98M  6.2M   92M   7% /run
/dev/sda1       19G  5.1G   13G  29% /
tmpfs          488M  212K  487M   1% /dev/shm
tmpfs          5.0M  4.0K  5.0M   1% /run/lock
tmpfs          488M     0  488M   0% /sys/fs/cgroup
tmpfs           98M   44K   98M   1% /run/user/1000
/dev/sdb1      4.8G   10M  4.6G   1% /mnt
root@ubuntu:/#
```

From the preceding output, we can see the size of the partition along with the mount point associated with the partition.

Let's now create two directories to be used for the /dev/sdb2 and the /dev/sdb4 partitions:

```
root@ubuntu:/# mkdir /folder1
root@ubuntu:/# mkdir /folder2
root@ubuntu:/# ls
bin  dev    folder2 initrd.img.old  lost+found  opt run srv usr
vmlinuz.old
boot etc  home lib    media     proc sbin  sys  var
cdrom  folder1 initrd.img  lib64     mnt           root  snap tmp  vmlinuz
root@ubuntu:/#
```

Now we'll mount the /dev/sdb2 and the /dev/sdb4 on the /folder1 and /folder2 directories, respectively:

```
root@ubuntu:/# mount /dev/sdb2 /folder1
root@ubuntu:/# mount /dev/sdb4 /folder2
root@ubuntu:/#
root@ubuntu:/# mount | grep /dev
/dev/sda1 on / type ext4 (rw,relatime,errors=remount-ro,data=ordered)
/dev/sdb1 on /mnt type ext4 (rw,relatime,data=ordered)
/dev/sdb2 on /folder1 type ext3 (rw,relatime,data=ordered)
/dev/sdb4 on /folder2 type fuseblk
(rw,relatime,user_id=0,group_id=0,allow_other,blksize=4096)
root@ubuntu:/#
```

Great! Now we can see our mount points being displayed with the `mount` command. Likewise, we can use the `df` command with the `-h` option for a readable format:

```
root@ubuntu:/# df -h
Filesystem      Size  Used Avail Use% Mounted on
udev            468M     0  468M   0% /dev
tmpfs            98M  6.2M   92M   7% /run
/dev/sda1        19G  5.1G   13G  29% /
tmpfs           488M  212K  487M   1% /dev/shm
tmpfs           5.0M  4.0K  5.0M   1% /run/lock
tmpfs           488M     0  488M   0% /sys/fs/cgroup
tmpfs            98M   44K   98M   1% /run/user/1000
/dev/sdb1       4.8G   10M  4.6G   1% /mnt
/dev/sdb2       2.0G  3.1M  1.9G   1% /folder1
/dev/sdb4       2.0G   11M  2.0G   1% /folder2
root@ubuntu:/#
```

As you can see, the steps involved in mounting a partition are fairly straightforward. However, on some distributions, you will have to specify the filesystem type. In a network, mounting a share is common. An example of mounting a share would be as follows:

```
root@ubuntu:/#mount //172.16.175.144/share /netshare -t cifs  -o
user=philip,password=pass123,uid=1000,gid=1000,rw
```

The umount command

After we would have mounted our partitions and made changes, it's always a good idea to clean up and unmount our partitions. We use the `umount` command to unmount a partition.

> Always change/move out of a directory before running the `umount` command.

Let's unmount the `/dev/sdb1`. The format would be as follows:

```
root@ubuntu:/# umount /dev/sdb1
root@ubuntu:/#
root@ubuntu:/# mount | grep /dev
udev on /dev type devtmpfs
(rw,nosuid,relatime,size=478356k,nr_inodes=119589,mode=755)
devpts on /dev/pts type devpts
(rw,nosuid,noexec,relatime,gid=5,mode=620,ptmxmode=000)
/dev/sda1 on / type ext4 (rw,relatime,errors=remount-ro,data=ordered)
```

```
tmpfs on /dev/shm type tmpfs (rw,nosuid,nodev)
cgroup on /sys/fs/cgroup/devices type cgroup
(rw,nosuid,nodev,noexec,relatime,devices)
mqueue on /dev/mqueue type mqueue (rw,relatime)
hugetlbfs on /dev/hugepages type hugetlbfs (rw,relatime)
/dev/sdb2 on /folder1 type ext3 (rw,relatime,data=ordered)
/dev/sdb4 on /folder2 type fuseblk
(rw,relatime,user_id=0,group_id=0,allow_other,blksize=4096)
root@ubuntu:/#
```

Now we can see that the /dev/sdb1 is no longer mounted; we can also confirm this by using the df command:

```
root@ubuntu:/# df -h
Filesystem Size Used Avail Use% Mounted on
udev 468M 0 468M 0% /dev
tmpfs 98M 7.5M 91M 8% /run
/dev/sda1 19G 5.2G 13G 30% /
tmpfs 488M 212K 487M 1% /dev/shm
tmpfs 5.0M 4.0K 5.0M 1% /run/lock
tmpfs 488M 0 488M 0% /sys/fs/cgroup
tmpfs 98M 48K 98M 1% /run/user/1000
/dev/sdb2 2.0G 3.1M 1.9G 1% /folder1
/dev/sdb4 2.0G 11M 2.0G 1% /folder2
root@ubuntu:/#
```

We can also use the lsblk command to confirm the same:

```
root@ubuntu:/# lsblk -f
NAME    FSTYPE LABEL UUID              MOUNTPOINT
sda
├─sda1 ext4         adb5d090-3400-4411-aee2-dd871c39db38 /
├─sda2
└─sda5 swap         025b1992-80ba-46ed-8490-e7aa68271e7b [SWAP]
sdb
├─sdb1 ext4         fc51dddf-c23d-4160-8e49-f8a275c9b2f0
├─sdb2 ext3         fd6aab0f-0f16-4922-86c1-11fcb54fc466 /folder1
├─sdb3 ext2         2a8a5768-1a7f-4ab4-8aa1-f45d30df5631
└─sdb4 ntfs         1D9E4A6D4088D79A                     /folder2
sr0
root@ubuntu:/#
```

Now let's also unmount the /dev/sdb2:

```
root@ubuntu:/# umount /folder1
```

The output of the preceding command can be seen in the following screenshot:

```
root@ubuntu: /home/philip
root@ubuntu:/home/philip# lsblk -f
NAME    FSTYPE LABEL UUID                                    MOUNTPOINT
sda
 ├─sda1 ext4         adb5d090-3400-4411-aee2-dd871c39db38 /
 ├─sda2
 └─sda5 swap         025b1992-80ba-46ed-8490-e7aa68271e7b [SWAP]
sdb
 ├─sdb1 ext4         fc51dddf-c23d-4160-8e49-f8a275c9b2f0
 ├─sdb2 ext3         fd6aab0f-0f16-4922-86c1-11fcb54fc466
 ├─sdb3 ext2         2a8a5768-1a7f-4ab4-8aa1-f45d30df5631
 └─sdb4 ntfs         1D9E4A6D4088D79A                        /folder2
sr0
root@ubuntu:/home/philip#
```

From the preceding screenshot, you will notice that instead of the /dev/sdb2 partition, I used the directory /folder1; this is entirely up to you; they are both accepted. Also, we can see from the lsblk command that there is no mount point listed for /dev/sdb2.

Now, let's say that you want your mount points to persist during a system reboot. Well, rest assured, we can make this happen by creating entries in the /etc/fstab.

First, let's create an entry for the /dev/sdb4 inside the /etc/fstab. We'll use the UUID for the /dev/sdb4 to assist us. Let's run blkid and save the UUID for the /dev/sdb4:

```
root@ubuntu:/# blkid
/dev/sdb4: UUID="1D9E4A6D4088D79A" TYPE="ntfs" PARTUUID="7e707ac0-04"
root@ubuntu:/#
```

Now let's edit the /etc/fstab file:

```
# /etc/fstab: static file system information.
#
# Use 'blkid' to print the universally unique identifier for a
# device; this may be used with UUID= as a more robust way to name devices
# that works even if disks are added and removed. See fstab(5).
```

```
#
# <file system> <mount point>   <type>  <options>        <dump>  <pass>
# / was on /dev/sda1 during installation
UUID=adb5d090-3400-4411-aee2-dd871c39db38 / ext4 errors=remount-ro 0
1
# swap was on /dev/sda5 during installation
UUID=025b1992-80ba-46ed-8490-e7aa68271e7b none swap sw 0    0
/dev/fd0  /media/floppy0  auto   rw,user,noauto,exec,utf8 0   0
UUID=1D9E4A6D4088D79A   /folder2   ntfs    0        0
```

Now the last entry is referencing the `/dev/sdb4`. The format starts with the partition, represented by the UUID, followed by the `mount point, file system`, dump, and pass.

When the system reboots, the `/dev/sdb4` will be mounted on to the `/folder2`. This saves us from repetitive typing.

Summary

In this chapter, we took a look at how to format a hard disk and the various partitioning utilities available. We used the `fdisk` utility to create partitions, and we turned on the `boot` flag. We then took a look at the `parted` utility, and we saw how to create a partition. In addition, we saw how we could resize a partition. This is very useful in data center environments. We then formatted our partitions, which enabled us to start storing data. We looked at using various `mkfs` commands, followed by focusing on how we would mount our partitions. After saving data on our mount points, we unmounted our partitions/mount point. Finally, we saw how we could save ourselves from repetitive typing by creating entries in the `/etc/fstab` file; this mounted our partitions for us upon boot up.

Coming up in the next chapter, we will cover the installation of various Linux distributions. We will particularly focus on Red-Hat distributions—namely CentOS. On the flip side of things, we will cover Debian distributions, specifically Ubuntu and the best techniques used to install Linux distributions, which slightly vary among distributions. Furthermore, we will cover dual boot environments - let's face it, sooner or later, you're bound to come into contact with a Windows OS in your Linux career. You don't need to worry, though, because we slowly go through every step of the installation process in detail. You will definitely become much more sound in your approach to installing a Linux distribution across all platforms after you've completed the next chapter. The skills gained from installing a Linux distribution will help you greatly as a Linux engineer.

Questions

1. Which letter is used to list the partitions of a hard disk without going into the fdisk utility?

    A. fdisk -a /dev/sda
    B. fdisk -c /dev/sda
    C. fdisk -l /dev/sda
    D. fdisk -r /dev/sda

2. Which letter is used to create a partition inside the fdisk utility?

    A. b
    B. c
    C. r
    D. n

3. Which letter is used to toggle a boot flag inside the fdisk utility?

    A. b
    B. a
    C. d
    D. c

4. Which letter is used to print the known partition types inside the fdisk utility?

    A. l
    B. r
    C. n
    D. b

5. Which letter is used to create a partition inside the fdisk utility?

    A. p
    B. n
    C. c
    D. d

6. Which letter is used to write changes inside the `fdisk` utility?

    A. `q`
    B. `c`
    C. `d`
    D. `w`

7. Which command is used to start the `parted` utility?

    A. `part -ad`
    B. `parted`
    C. `part -ed`
    D. `part`

8. Which option is used to display a partition table inside the `parted` utility?

    A. `display`
    B. `parted`
    C. `print`
    D. `console`

9. Which option is used to mount a partition from the CLI?

    A. `mount /dev/sdb1`
    B. `mnt /dev/sdb1`
    C. `mt /dev/sdb1`
    D. `mont /dev/sdb1`

10. Which command displays the UUID of the known partitions on the CLI?

    A. `blkid`
    B. `df -h`
    C. `du -h`
    D. `mount`

Further reading

- You can get more info about the CentOS distributions such as installing, configuration best practices, and so on, by checking out the following: `https://www.centos.org`.
- The following website gives you a lot of useful tips and best practices from users in the Linux community, particularly for Debian distributions such as Ubuntu: `https://askubuntu.com`.
- Finally, this last link gives you general information that relates to various commands that work on both CentOS and Ubuntu. You can post your questions here, and other community members will respond: `https://www.linuxquestions.org`.

Installing a Linux Distribution

5

In the previous chapter, we looked at preparing the hard disk for use. We worked with the `fdisk` and `parted` utilities, looked at the steps to create and remove a partition, saw how we could resize a partition, and then turned our focus to formatting a partition for usage. In addition to this, we looked at the various filesystems available on today's Linux distributions. After that, we took a look at how to mount a partition to be able to start storing data. We then looked at unmounting a partition. Finally, we created entries in the `/etc/fstab` file to have our mount point(s) load upon system boot. In this chapter, our focus is now on the actual installation of a Linux distribution, the process involved with booting into a LiveCD, when installing Linux from scratch. Then we will focus on installing Linux side by side with a Windows OS. Finally, we will look at installing Linux side by side with another Linux distribution.

We will cover the following topics in this chapter:

- Understanding the use of a LiveCD
- Installing a Linux distribution as a fresh installation
- Installing a Linux distribution side by side with a Windows OS
- Installing a Linux distribution side by side with another version of Linux

Understanding the use of the LiveCD

When we boot up our system, we have a number of options to choose when installing a Linux distribution. Instead of us wiping our hard drive(s), we can install Linux using what is known as a LiveCD. Keep in mind that the experience may seem as though we are installing a Linux distribution, but in fact, we are actually temporarily loading up files into RAM, and the LiveCD is acting as though it is installed on an actual hard drive. That is the main concept of a LiveCD.

We will use the Ubuntu distribution for this demo. First, we set our system to boot from CD/DVD. Then we power on our system:

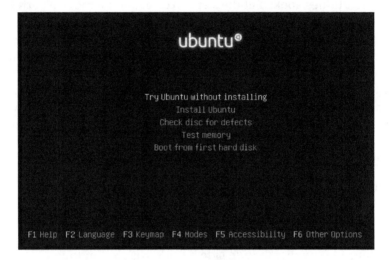

Here, we have a number of options available for us to choose from. The first option will load the Linux distribution into memory. The other options, such as **Install Ubuntu**, would be used for a normal installation. We can also check the disc for defects and so on.

Now, using the cursor, highlight **Try Ubuntu without installing**, then press *Enter*. After this, the system will boot into the Linux distribution:

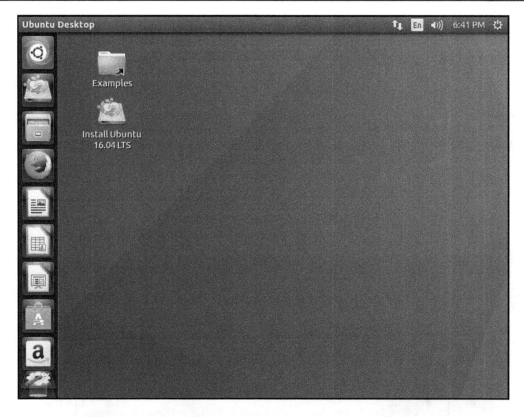

From here, we can carry out a variety of tasks just as we would on an installed operating system. The benefit comes when you are running low on hardware or have very old hardware that cannot support the latest operating systems. Rest assured, there are a number of Linux distributions available that cater to such environments.

 Note that we can remove the CD/DVD from the drive and the system will continue to work without any error(s). Mostly, we will use a LiveCD to perform administrative task(s).

Installing a Linux distribution as a fresh installation

Working within a LiveCD is fine when we just want to do some administrative tasks. For this, we can install a Linux distribution as a full installation; in that, we install Linux on a hard disk. To continue from the LiveCD demo, we will use the **Install Ubuntu...** option on the desktop to perform a fresh installation. This will present the following setup:

1. From here, we then have to select the language with which setup will continue. There is a wide range of languages to choose from. In our case, we will accept the default, **English**, and select **Continue**:

2. Now we have options to download updates during installation and/or install third-party software for graphics and so on. For this section, you will need an active internet connection; the reason being, the system will go out and download the most recent updates which have been released. Also, when we add additional hardware that is not part of the system, they require modules (think drivers) which will not be installed by default. Hence, there is the second option to download third-party software. In our case, because we're in a lab environment, we will leave these options unchecked and select **Continue**:

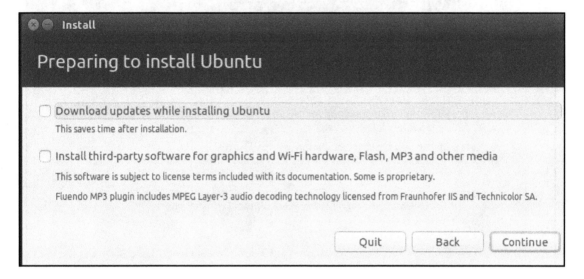

You will need an active internet connection to download updates.

3. Here, we have the option to install the Linux distribution on the entire hard disk. If, for some reason, we want to add one or more partitions to the hard disk, then we will select **Something else**. Also, if we are trying to do a dual boot with Windows or a side-by-side installation with another Linux distribution, we would choose this option:

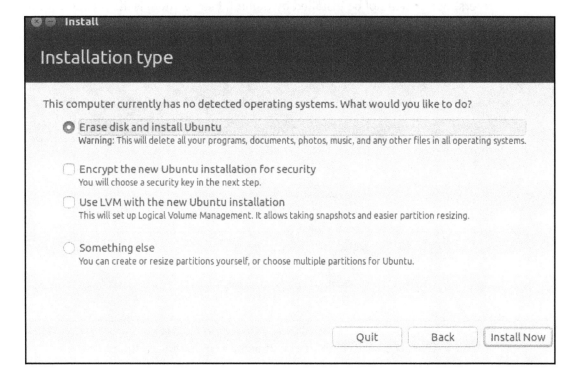

4. For the fresh installation, let's choose the **Something else** option, create our own partitions and specify what we want to mount:

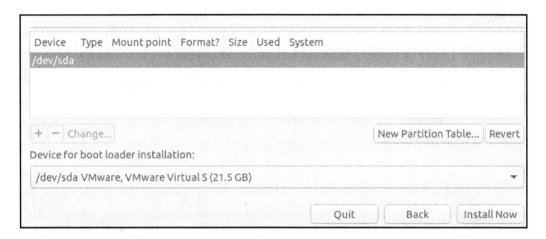

5. Great! We only have a single hard disk in our environment. We will select **New Partition Table**. Let's first create a 200 MB partition and mount /boot; this is where the boot files will be stored:

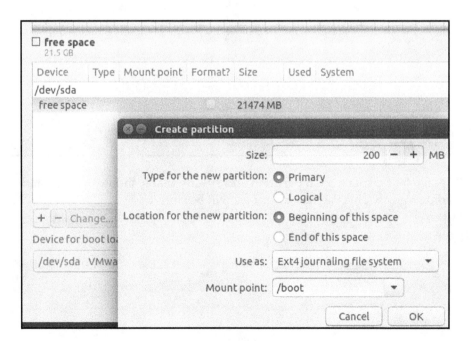

It's always a good idea to create a partition for /boot so as to safeguard the boot files.

6. Next, let's create a 13 GB partition and specify that it should be mounted onto the / directory. In addition, we are also specifying the partition type as a **Primary** partition and we are formatting the partition as an ext3 file system:

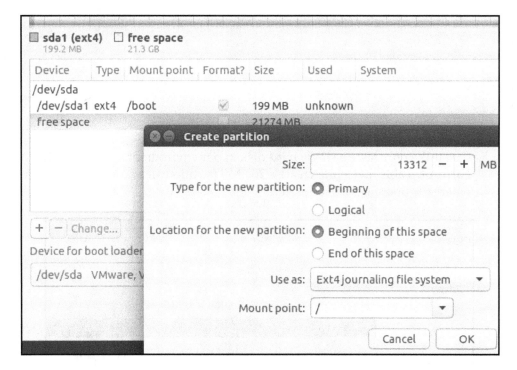

7. Next, let's create a 5 GB partition and specify that it should be mounted onto /home. This is where user files will be stored:

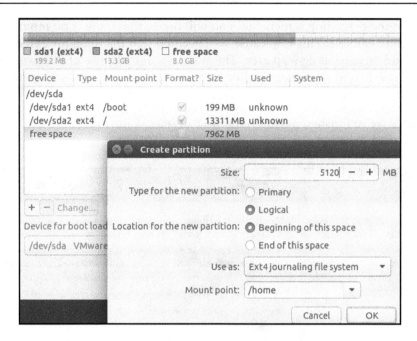

8. Awesome! Lastly, let's make use of the remaining free space and allow the Linux distribution to assign it to swap memory:

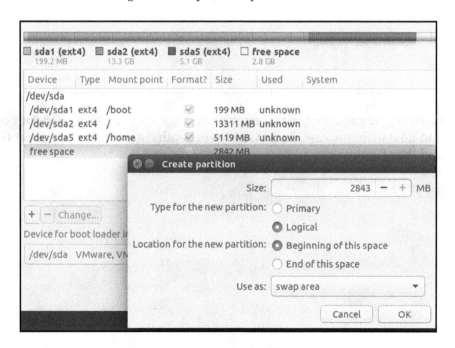

From the preceding screenshot, you will notice that there is no **mount point** option available. This is because we specified that the remaining free space should be used as a **swap area**. The system will make use of the swap as needed (we saw this in an earlier chapter; namely, `Chapter 1`, *Configuring the Hardware Settings*, in the *Viewing CPU, RAM, SWAP info* section).

9. Once we're finished partitioning, we can select **Continue**. This will present a warning message:

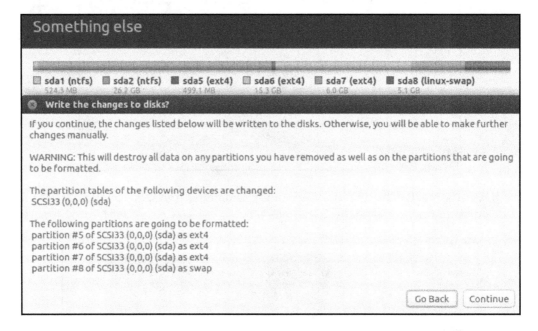

Next, we are presented with the region settings, and you search for your country and fill it in. In my case, I'm in Guyana in South America, and so I select **Guyana** and then **Continue**.

10. After that, the keyboard selection is presented and you select the appropriate settings. This brings us to a crucial part of the setup: the user creation screen. We specify a name for the computer and create a user account with a super-secret password:

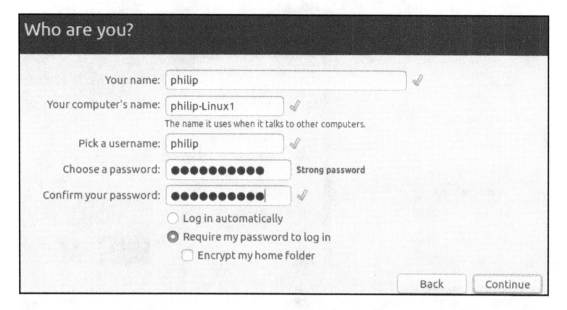

Great! Now we're on our way to a freshly installed Linux distribution.

11. You can always check which files are being downloaded or installed by selecting the drop-down arrow located next to **Installing system**:

Now the installation is going to download the various language packs (internet connectivity required). After that, the setup will continue installing the necessary files onto the hard disk.

Finally, the system will ask us to reboot in order to start up the system using the freshly installed Linux distribution.

 Remove the CD, DVD, or USB drive after installation and before the system boots up.

Installing a Linux distribution side by side with a Windows OS

In most environments, you may come across a system that has an existing installation of another operating system such as Windows. Ideally, you would not remove the Windows installation completely as you may require some software that runs only on a Windows installation, or maybe it's the company policy to have a Windows installation on the system. In this case, you can install a Linux distribution alongside Windows without wiping the Windows partition. This is made possible because Linux has the ability to recognize a Windows partition type, such as NTFS. Linux would not in any way alter the Windows partition.

Let's boot up an existing Windows system and configure the system to start from a Ubuntu ISO image to see how we implement a dual boot installation:

1. From here, the Ubuntu installation recognizes the Windows 10 operating system. Here, we will choose the last option, **Something else**:

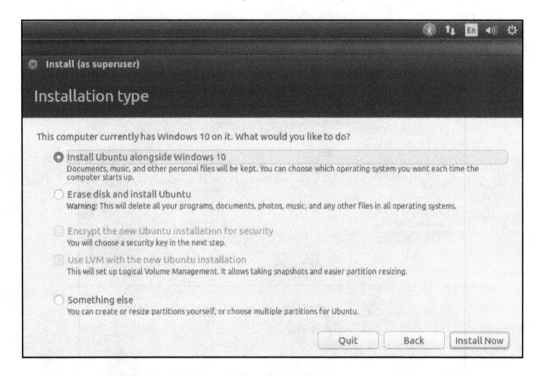

2. Next, we will create the /boot partition:

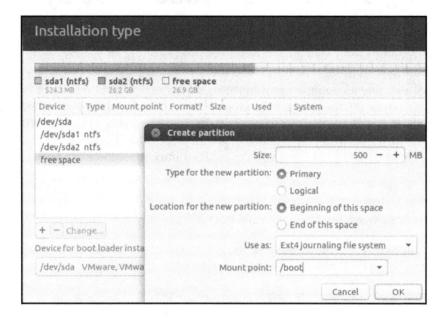

3. After this, we will create the / partition:

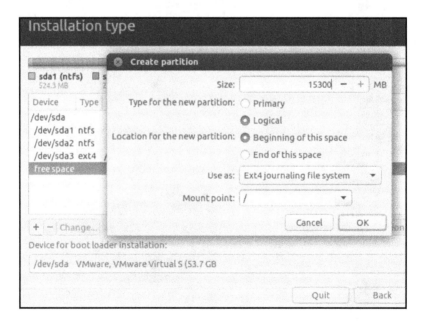

From the preceding screenshot, we can see that we have just successfully created the / partition. You may have noticed the pattern with which we are creating the partitions. It's always a good idea to separate your system files from the user files.

4. Next, we will create the /home partition:

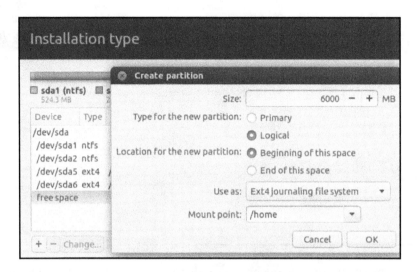

5. Finally, we will create the swap space and use the remaining free space:

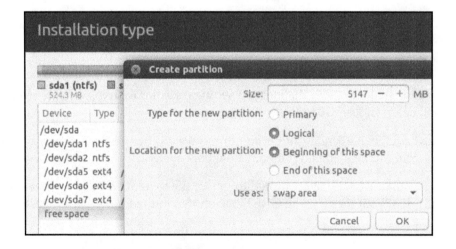

6. The last step is to select **Install Now**:

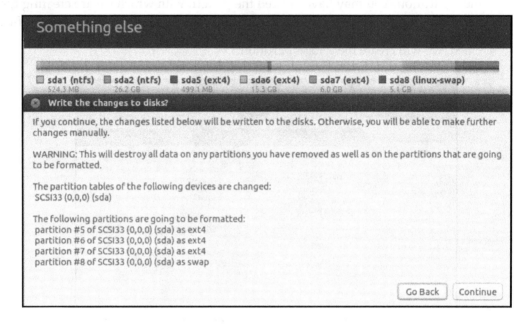

From the preceding screenshot, we will have to confirm that we would like to write the changes to the disk. We are going to select **Continue**.

We can always go back and make changes to the partition table by selecting **Go Back**.

Now we have to fill in the location settings, similar to doing a fresh installation. I will again choose **Guyana**.

Next, we have to create a user account as we did before. The necessary Linux files are going to be installed onto our dual boot system.

7. After that, we will be prompted to reboot the system and will be greeted with our dual boot menu using GRUB2, as shown in the following screenshot:

To direct input to this virtual machine, press Ctrl+G.

```
GNU GRUB  version 2.02 beta2-36ubuntu3

Ubuntu
Advanced options for Ubuntu
Memory test (memtest86+)
Memory test (memtest86+, serial console 115200)
*Windows 10 (loader) (on /dev/sda1)
```

 In some cases, if we have Linux as the first OS and then install Windows, sometimes Windows will remove the Linux boot entry. The best way to remedy this is to run `grub-install`.

Installing Linux side by side with another version of Linux

In some environments, you may be required to adapt to different Linux distributions. Instead of gutting your current Linux distribution, you can install another distribution without losing your current Linux distribution.

Let's use our existing Ubuntu system and install CentOS 7 alongside to demonstrate how we would dual boot:

1. First, we set our system to boot from the CentOS 7 ISO image:

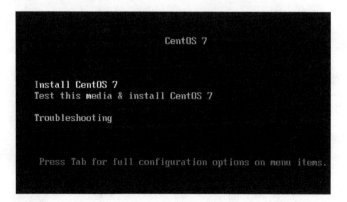

2. From here, we select the first option and press *Enter*. This will launch the setup for CentOS 7:

We then choose our language and select **Continue**.

3. On the **INSTALLATION SUMMARY** page, the key important sections are **SOFTWARE SELECTION** and **SYSTEM**:

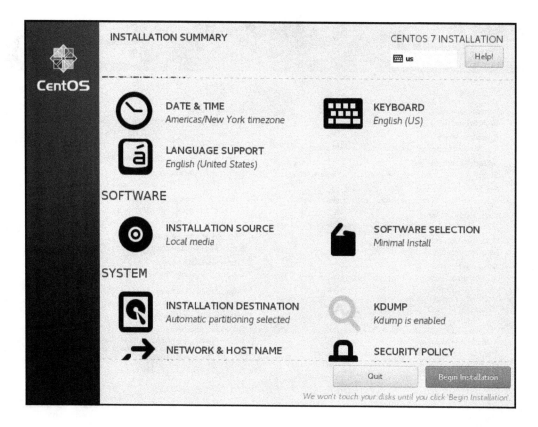

4. By default, CentOS 7 will do a **Minimal Install**. We want to do a full installation so select **SOFTWARE SELECTION**:

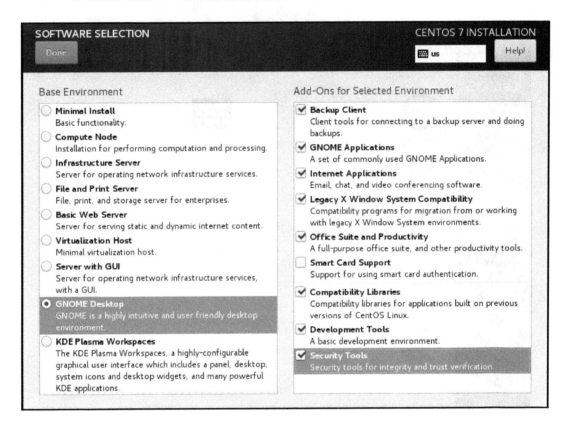

From the preceding screenshot, by default, the **Minimal Install** is selected. I've selected **GNOME Desktop** under **Base Environment**, and I've chosen the checked add-ons. Once I have finished making my selections, I will click **Done**.

You can choose to add some or all the add-ons for a particular base environment.

5. The next section of importance, particularly in a dual boot environment, is under the **SYSTEM** section: **INSTALLATION DESTINATION**.

6. Here is where we are going to partition the hard disk:

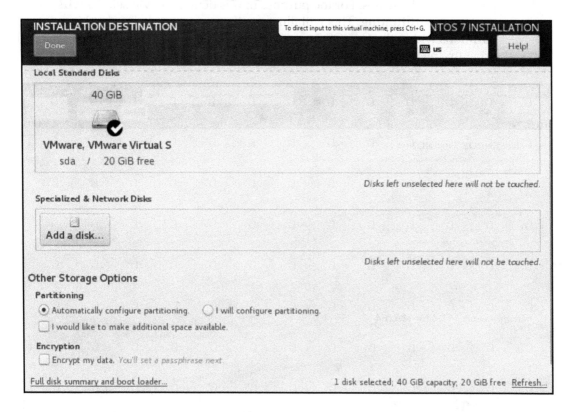

7. By default, the system will choose to partition the hard disk automatically. If we leave this option and allow the system to create the partitioning for us, then the system is going to create partitions based on the recommended size for each partition that it creates. For the purpose of this demo, we will select **I will configure partitioning**. This will illustrate the various steps involved in creating partitions within the CentOS 7 environment. Next, we will select **Done**. This will bring up the following partitioning screen:

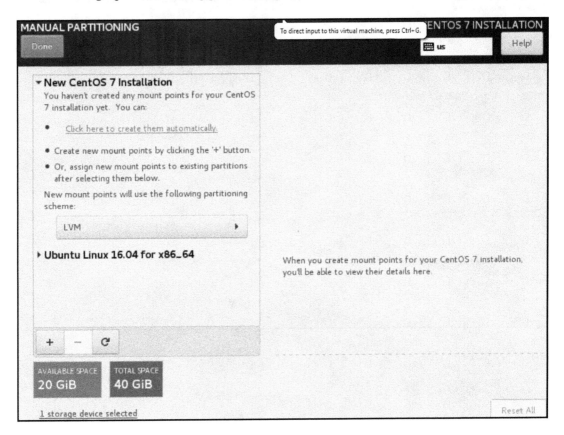

From the preceding screenshot, we can see that the CentOS 7 installation has detected the Ubuntu installation.

For this CentOS 7 installation, we mount `/boot` to the `/boot` mount point for CentOS 7.

> Be careful when removing partitions as this can have some adverse effects on the operational status of your system. In other words, you may accidentally remove some critical configuration files that were stored on a partition, or, even worse, your system may be unable to boot.

8. Next, we create the / partition for CentOS 7:

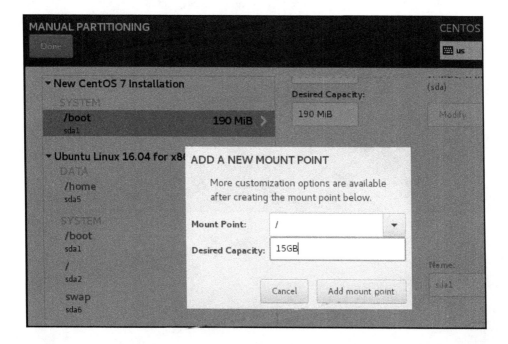

9. Then we create the /home partition:

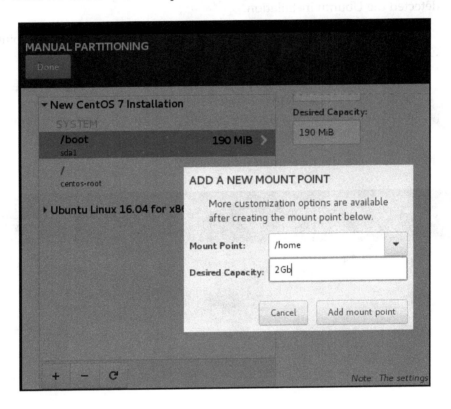

10. Finally, we create our swap space, using up the remaining free space:

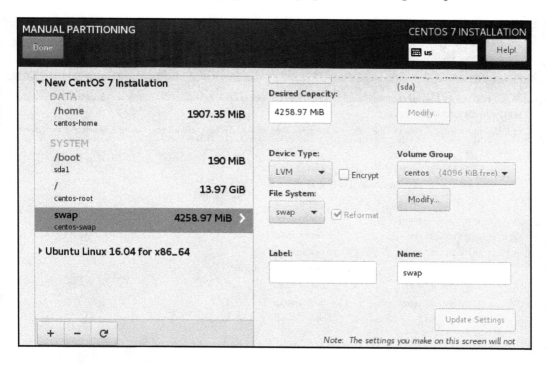

11. Once we're finished, we then select **Done**:

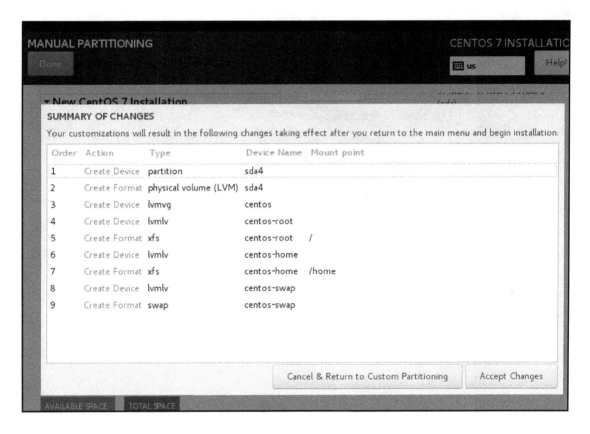

12. Now, we must confirm our changes by selecting **Accept Changes**:

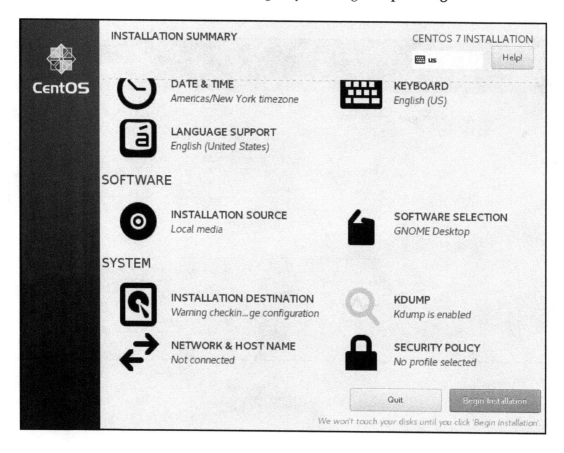

13. When we select **Begin Installation**, the actual installation will begin. We will have to create a user account:

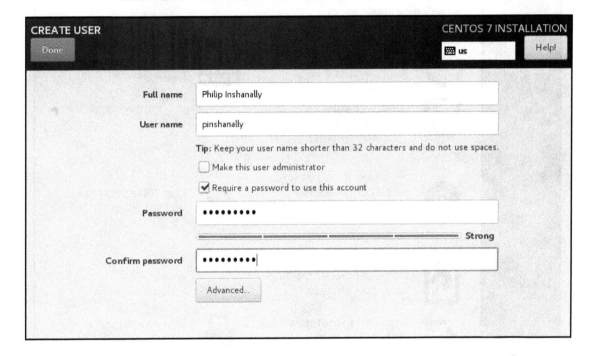

14. Then we need to see a root password:

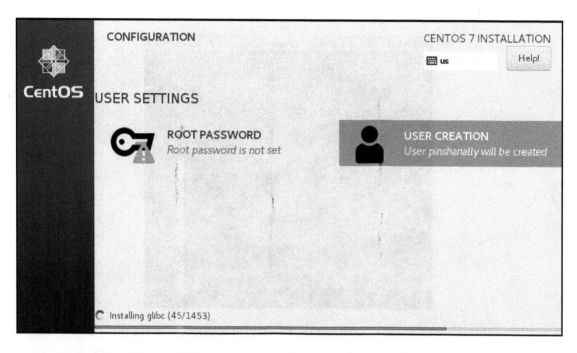

15. We should set a difficult password that no one can guess:

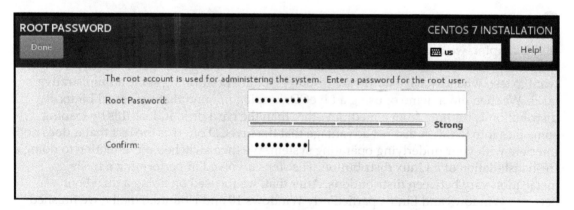

16. Now, we are going to allow the CentOS 7 to perform the installation—give it some time. Finally, we are prompted to reboot, so we will select **Reboot**.

17. Finally, we are then greeted with our dual boot menu, displaying both CentOS 7 and Ubuntu, as shown in the following screenshot:

```
CentOS Linux (3.10.0-693.el7.x86_64)
CentOS Linux (0-rescue-e966a8c83fcf4
Ubuntu 16.04.4 LTS (16.04) (on /dev/
Advanced options for Ubuntu 16.04.4




Use the ↑ and ↓ keys to change the s
Press 'e' to edit the selected item,
```

As you can see, we now have the options to choose which Linux distribution to load.

Summary

In this chapter, we dived deep into the installations of Linux Distributions. We also covered the concept of a LiveCD and discussed the scenarios for using a LiveCD; namely, when we want to test, when we have hardware resources, or are performing some administrative tasks. We then did a demo of using a LiveCD, keeping in mind that the actual Linux distribution is running from a medium other than the hard disk. It does this by loading some files into RAM. A distinct advantage that the LiveCD offers is the fact that it does not interfere with your underlying operating system. We then switched our attention to doing a fresh installation of a Linux distribution. The steps involved in performing a fresh installation vary between distributions. After that, we focused on doing a dual boot between Windows and Linux, particularly Windows 10 and Ubuntu. Finally, we finished off this chapter by doing a dual boot between Linux distributions, particularly CentOS and Ubuntu.

Coming up, we're going to be covering the opposite side of the Red Hat world: the Debian environment. Namely, we're going to be focusing primarily on package management within the context of Ubuntu, covering various techniques used such as `dpkg`, `apt`, and `aptitude`, to name a few. I hope you join me for another exciting chapter, taking you one step closer to achieving your goal of certification.

Questions

1. Where are temporary files stored when using a LiveCD?

    A. Hard disk
    B. LiveCD
    C. RAM
    D. None of the above

2. Which option starts up a Ubuntu LiveCD?

    A. Boot from first hard disk
    B. Test integrity
    C. Install now
    D. Try Ubuntu without installing

3. Which option on the desktop in a Ubuntu LiveCD would you choose to do a fresh installation?

    A. Install Ubuntu…
    B. Try Ubuntu and install
    C. Reboot and start from hard disk
    D. Fresh install

4. When downloading updates while doing a fresh installation, what is required?

    A. Complex coding
    B. An active internet connection
    C. Copying files from the installation media onto the hard disk
    D. No requirements needed

5. What option allows us to create our own partitions under **Installation type**?

    A. Something else
    B. Erase the entire hard disk
    C. Copy the entire hard disk
    D. Encrypt the entire hard disk

6. Which type of partition is required for the system to be able to boot?

    A. Logical
    B. Extended
    C. Primary
    D. Secondary

7. Why should we separate the /boot partition from the other partitions?

    A. To be able to download our videos in /boot
    B. To prevent the system from becoming unbootable by accidentally deleting files in /boot
    C. To prove that we know how to partition
    D. To prove that all of the system files are installed in /boot

8. Which command is chosen to create custom partitions in a CentOS 7 installation?

    A. Automatically configure partitioning
    B. I will configure partitioning
    C. Encrypt my data
    D. Create Logical Volume

9. Which command is used to install GRUB if a Windows installation removed GRUB while trying to do a **Dual** boot?

    A. grub-install
    B. grub
    C. grub-update
    D. grub-configure

10. Which is the default **SOFTWARE SELECTION** for CentOS 7?

> A. GNOME Desktop
> B. KDE Desktop
> C. XFCE Desktop
> D. Minimal Install

Further reading

- You can get more information about the CentOS distributions, such as installing, configuration best practices, and so on, at `https://www.centos.org`.
- This website gives you a lot of useful tips and best practices from users in the Linux community, particularly for the Debian distributions, such as Ubuntu: `https://askubuntu.com`.
- This last link gives you information that relates to various commands that work on both CentOS and Ubuntu. You can post your questions here, and other community members will respond: `https://www.linuxquestions.org`.

6
Using Debian Package Management

In the previous chapter, we focused on the steps to install a Linux distribution. We first worked with the concept of a LiveCD, as opposed to a regular installation. We saw how the system could be booted up without having a hard disk. Then we discussed why we would use a LiveCD. After that, we switched our attention to a demo of performing a fresh installation of Linux distribution. Emphasis was placed on the partitioning, particularly the common mount points. Next, we saw how to do an installation side-by-side with a Windows OS. Following this, we carried out a side-by-side installation between Linux distributions.

In this chapter, we will continue our lesson by focusing on the points surrounding software installation. We will begin by looking at the Debian style of package management. First, we will start with the dpkg command, and look at the various methods of using the dpkg command. After this, we will look at the various options which can be passed with the dpkg command. Next, we will turn our attention toward the apt-get utility. This is another popular command for installing applications within a Debian environment. We will pay close attention to the options that can be passed with the apt-get command. Following this, the focus will be switched to the aptitude utility. Finally, we will close the chapter by looking at the synaptic utility. In a similar way to the previous commands, here we will focus on the syntax for deploying software within a Debian environment. All the utilities discussed in this chapter are commonly used for managing software within a Debian environment.

We will cover the following topics in this chapter:

- The `dpkg` command
- The `apt-get` command
- The `aptitude` command
- The `synaptic` utility

The dpkg command

Firstly, the `dpkg` utility is a low-level system tool to extract, analyze, unpack, install, and remove packages with a `.deb` extension. The scripts read by `dpkg` inside each `.deb` file are important as they give information to the program regarding the packages' installation, removal, and configuration. The `dpkg` utility resides at the base of the package management system in Debian-based distributions. The Debian package, `dpkg`, provides the `dpkg` utility, as well as several other programs necessary for runtime functioning of the packaging system; namely: `dpkg-deb`, `dpkg-split`, `dpkg-query`, `dpkg-statoverride`, `dpkg-divert`, and `dpkg-trigger`. We can take a glance at the `/var/log/dpkg.log` file. There are a lot of verbose details about triggers and packages going through varying stages of unpacking and configuration.

Let's take a look at `/var/log/dpkg.log`:

```
philip@ubuntu:~$ cat /var/log/dpkg.log
2018-07-02 06:43:57 startup archives unpack
2018-07-02 06:44:01 install linux-image-4.4.0-130-generic:amd64 <none>
4.4.0-130.156
2018-07-02 06:44:01 status half-installed linux-image-4.4.0-130-
generic:amd64 4.4.0-130.156
2018-07-02 06:44:09 status unpacked linux-image-4.4.0-130-generic:amd64
4.4.0-130.156
2018-07-02 06:44:09 status unpacked linux-image-4.4.0-130-generic:amd64
4.4.0-130.156
2018-07-02 06:44:09 install linux-image-extra-4.4.0-130-generic:amd64
<none> 4.4.0-130.156
2018-07-02 06:44:09 status half-installed linux-image-extra-4.4.0-130-
generic:amd64 4.4.0-130.156
2018-07-02 06:44:20 status unpacked linux-image-extra-4.4.0-130-
generic:amd64 4.4.0-130.156
2018-07-02 06:44:20 status unpacked linux-image-extra-4.4.0-130-
generic:amd64 4.4.0-130.156
2018-07-02 06:44:21 upgrade linux-generic:amd64 4.4.0.128.134 4.4.0.130.136
2018-07-02 06:44:21 status half-configured linux-generic:amd64
```

```
4.4.0.128.134
2018-07-02 06:44:21 status unpacked linux-generic:amd64 4.4.0.128.134
2018-07-02 06:44:21 status half-installed linux-generic:amd64 4.4.0.128.134
2018-07-02 06:44:21 status half-installed linux-generic:amd64 4.4.0.128.134
2018-07-02 06:44:21 status unpacked linux-generic:amd64 4.4.0.130.136
2018-07-02 06:44:21 status unpacked linux-generic:amd64 4.4.0.130.136
2018-07-02 06:44:21 upgrade linux-image-generic:amd64 4.4.0.128.134
4.4.0.130.136
2018-07-02 06:44:21 status half-configured linux-image-generic:amd64
4.4.0.128.134
2018-07-02 06:44:21 status unpacked linux-image-generic:amd64 4.4.0.128.134
2018-07-02 06:44:21 status half-installed linux-image-generic:amd64
4.4.0.128.134
```

From the preceding output, we have learned about the various packages that the dpkg
utility is managing. If we want to see a list of packages on this system, we can use the l
option:

```
philip@ubuntu:~$ dpkg -l
Desired=Unknown/Install/Remove/Purge/Hold
| Status=Not/Inst/Conf-files/Unpacked/halF-conf/Half-inst/trig-aWait/Trig-
pend
|/ Err?=(none)/Reinst-required (Status,Err: uppercase=bad)
||/ Name                          Version             Architecture
Description
+++-=============================-===================-===================-
==============================================================
ii  a11y-profile-manager-indicato 0.1.10-0ubuntu3      amd64
Accessibility Profile Manager - Unity desktop indicator
ii  account-plugin-facebook       0.12+16.04.20160126 all
GNOME Control Center account plugin for single signon - facebook
ii  account-plugin-flickr         0.12+16.04.20160126 all
GNOME Control Center account plugin for single signon - flickr
ii  account-plugin-google         0.12+16.04.20160126 all
GNOME Control Center account plugin for single signon
ii  accountsservice               0.6.40-2ubuntu11.3  amd64
query and manipulate user account information
ii  activity-log-manager          0.9.7-0ubuntu23.16. amd64
blacklist configuration user interface for Zeitgeist
ii  adduser                       3.113+nmu3ubuntu4   all
add and remove users and groups
ii  adium-theme-ubuntu            0.3.4-0ubuntu1.1    all
Adium message style for Ubuntu
ii  app-install-data              15.10               all
Ubuntu applications (data files)
ii  app-install-data-partner      16.04               all
Application Installer (data files for partner applications/repos
ii  apparmor                      2.10.95-0ubuntu2.9  amd64
```

```
user-space parser utility for AppArmor
ii  appmenu-qt:amd64            0.2.7+14.04.2014030  amd64
application menu for Qt
ii  appmenu-qt5                 0.3.0+16.04.2017021  amd64
application menu for Qt5
ii  apport                      2.20.1-0ubuntu2.18   all
automatically generate crash reports for debugging
ii  apport-gtk                  2.20.1-0ubuntu2.18   all
GTK+ frontend for the apport crash report system
```

In the preceding output, we read this from left to right. We should now focus our attention on the far right of the output. This is the description section; the packages are presented in a human-readable summary for each package that is currently installed onto the system.

We can also narrow down our output by filtering the dpkg command; let's look for the xterm program:

```
philip@ubuntu:~$ dpkg -l xterm
Desired=Unknown/Install/Remove/Purge/Hold
| Status=Not/Inst/Conf-files/Unpacked/halF-conf/Half-inst/trig-aWait/Trig-
pend
|/ Err?=(none)/Reinst-required (Status,Err: uppercase=bad)
||/ Name                       Version            Architecture
Description
+++-==============================-===================-===================-
=====================================================================
ii  xterm                      322-1ubuntu1       amd64                  X
terminal emulator
philip@ubuntu:~$
```

We can verify whether or not a package is installed with --get-selections:

```
philip@ubuntu:~$ dpkg --get-selections
a11y-profile-manager-indicator    install
account-plugin-facebook           install
account-plugin-flickr             install
account-plugin-google             install
accountsservice                   install
acl                               install
acpi-support                      install
acpid                             install
activity-log-manager              install
adduser                           install
adium-theme-ubuntu                install
adwaita-icon-theme                install
aisleriot                         install
alsa-base                         install
alsa-utils                        install
```

```
amd64-microcode                          install
anacron                                  install
apg                                      install
app-install-data                         install
app-install-data-partner                 install
apparmor                                 install
appmenu-qt:amd64                         install
appmenu-qt5                              install
apport                                   install
```

We can view the locations in which a package is installed by using the L option. Let's continue with our example:

```
philip@ubuntu:~$ dpkg -L xterm
/.
/etc
/etc/X11
/etc/X11/app-defaults
/etc/X11/app-defaults/UXTerm-color
/etc/X11/app-defaults/UXTerm
/etc/X11/app-defaults/KOI8RXTerm-color
/etc/X11/app-defaults/KOI8RXTerm
/etc/X11/app-defaults/XTerm-color
/usr/share/man/man1/koi8rxterm.1.gz
/usr/share/man/man1/resize.1.gz
/usr/share/man/man1/xterm.1.gz
/usr/share/man/man1/lxterm.1.gz
philip@ubuntu:~$
```

We can search for a particular package in this system by using the s option:

```
philip@ubuntu:~$ dpkg -s apache
dpkg-query: package 'apache' is not installed and no information is
available
Use dpkg --info (= dpkg-deb --info) to examine archive files,
and dpkg --contents (= dpkg-deb --contents) to list their contents.
philip@ubuntu:~$ dpkg --info apache
dpkg-deb: error: failed to read archive 'apache': No such file or directory
philip@ubuntu:~$
```

In this case, Apache is not installed by default on this system.

I've downloaded a `tftp` client for this demonstration. Let's verify that the `tftp` client isn't installed on this system:

```
philip@ubuntu:~/Downloads$ dpkg -l tftp
dpkg-query: no packages found matching tftp
philip@ubuntu:~/Downloads$
```

Now we'll install a package using the `dpkg` command. Let's try to install the `tftp` client package using the `i` option:

```
philip@ubuntu:~/Downloads$ dpkg -i tftp_0.17-18_i386.deb
dpkg: error: requested operation requires superuser privilege
philip@ubuntu:~/Downloads$
```

From the preceding output, you can see that we would need root privileges to install or remove a package. Let's retry as root:

```
root@ubuntu:/home/philip/Downloads# ls -l | grep tftp
-rw-rw-r-- 1 philip philip  17208 Jul 18 08:15 tftp_0.17-18_i386.deb
root@ubuntu:/home/philip/Downloads#
root@ubuntu:/home/philip/Downloads# dpkg -i tftp_0.17-18_i386.deb
Selecting previously unselected package tftp:i386.
(Reading database ... 241431 files and directories currently installed.)
Preparing to unpack tftp_0.17-18_i386.deb ...
Unpacking tftp:i386 (0.17-18) ...
Setting up tftp:i386 (0.17-18) ...
Processing triggers for man-db (2.7.5-1) ...
root@ubuntu:/home/philip/Downloads#
```

Great! Now, let's retry the `dpkg` command with the `l` option:

```
root@ubuntu:/home/philip/Downloads# dpkg -l tftp
Desired=Unknown/Install/Remove/Purge/Hold
| Status=Not/Inst/Conf-files/Unpacked/halF-conf/Half-inst/trig-aWait/Trig-
pend
|/ Err?=(none)/Reinst-required (Status,Err: uppercase=bad)
||/ Name                        Version             Architecture
Description
+++-===========================-===================-===================-
=============================================================
ii  tftp:i386                   0.17-18             i386
Trivial file transfer protocol client
root@ubuntu:/home/philip/Downloads#
```

Awesome! We can now see that our `tftp` client is listed. We can also run the `dpkg` with the `--get-selections` to verify the following:

```
root@ubuntu:/home/philip/Downloads# dpkg --get-selections | grep tftp
tftp:i386
install
root@ubuntu:/home/philip/Downloads#
```

 When you use `dpkg` to install a package, you may sometimes run into dependency issues. To work around this, you will need to download and install each of the dependencies before you install your package using `dpkg`.

We can also remove a package using the `dpkg` command. Let's remove the `tftp` package which we installed in the previous example. We will use the `-r` option for this:

```
root@ubuntu:/home/philip/Downloads# dpkg -r tftp
(Reading database ... 241438 files and directories currently installed.)
Removing tftp:i386 (0.17-18) ...
Processing triggers for man-db (2.7.5-1) ...
root@ubuntu:/home/philip/Downloads#
```

Now, let's verify that the `tftp` package has indeed been uninstalled:

```
root@ubuntu:/home/philip/Downloads# dpkg -l tftp
dpkg-query: no packages found matching tftp
root@ubuntu:/home/philip/Downloads#
```

Great! However, when we use the `-r` option, it does not remove the configuration file(s). In order to remove the package, along with the configuration files, we should use the `-P` (purge) option. Here is how that works:

```
root@ubuntu:/home/philip/Downloads# dpkg -P tftp
(Reading database ... 241438 files and directories currently installed.)
Removing tftp:i386 (0.17-18) ...
Processing triggers for man-db (2.7.5-1) ...
root@ubuntu:/home/philip/Downloads#
```

We can also extract the content of a package without installing it. We should use the `-x` option for this:

```
root@ubuntu:/home/philip/Downloads# dpkg -x tftp_0.17-18_i386.deb
./tftp_0.17-18_i386
root@ubuntu:/home/philip/Downloads# ls
root@ubuntu:/home/philip/Downloads# ls tftp_0.17-18_i386
usr
root@ubuntu:/home/philip/Downloads# ls tftp_0.17-18_i386/usr/
```

```
bin   share
root@ubuntu:/home/philip/Downloads#
root@ubuntu:/home/philip/Downloads# ls tftp_0.17-18_i386/usr/bin/
tftp
root@ubuntu:/home/philip/Downloads# ls tftp_0.17-18_i386/usr/share/
doc/ man/
root@ubuntu:/home/philip/Downloads# ls tftp_0.17-18_i386/usr/share/
doc   man
root@ubuntu:/home/philip/Downloads#
```

Before we can download any packages and install them using the dpkg utility, we need to know the correct hardware architecture of the system. Fortunately, we can use the dpkg-architecture command:

```
root@ubuntu:/home/philip/Downloads# dpkg-architecture
DEB_BUILD_ARCH=amd64
DEB_BUILD_ARCH_BITS=64
DEB_BUILD_ARCH_CPU=amd64
DEB_BUILD_ARCH_ENDIAN=little
DEB_BUILD_ARCH_OS=linux
DEB_BUILD_GNU_CPU=x86_64
DEB_BUILD_GNU_SYSTEM=linux-gnu
DEB_BUILD_GNU_TYPE=x86_64-linux-gnu
DEB_TARGET_ARCH_CPU=amd64
DEB_TARGET_ARCH_ENDIAN=little
DEB_TARGET_ARCH_OS=linux
DEB_TARGET_GNU_CPU=x86_64
DEB_TARGET_GNU_SYSTEM=linux-gnu
DEB_TARGET_GNU_TYPE=x86_64-linux-gnu
DEB_TARGET_MULTIARCH=x86_64-linux-gnu
root@ubuntu:/home/philip/Downloads#
```

Based on the preceding output, we can see that this system supports either 32-bit or 64-bit packages. We can also garner useful information regarding the purpose of a package. We need to use the dpkg-query command with the -s option here:

```
root@ubuntu:/home/philip/Downloads# dpkg-query -s tftp
Package: tftp
Status: install ok unpacked
Priority: optional
Section: net
Installed-Size: 80
Maintainer: Alberto Gonzalez Iniesta <agi@inittab.org>
Architecture: i386
Source: netkit-tftp
Version: 0.17-18
Config-Version: 0.17-18
```

```
Replaces: netstd
Depends: netbase, libc6 (>= 2.3)
Description: Trivial file transfer protocol client
Tftp is the user interface to the Internet TFTP (Trivial File Transfer
Protocol), which allows users to transfer files to and from a remote
machine.
The remote host may be specified on the command line, in which case tftp
uses
host as the default host for future transfers.
root@ubuntu:/home/philip/Downloads#
```

From the preceding output, we are given a description at the bottom regarding the use of the tftp package.

The apt-get command

The **Advanced Package Tool** (**APT**) is a command-line tool that is used for easy interaction with the dpkg packaging system. APT is the ideal method used for managing software within Debian-based Linux distributions, such as Ubuntu. It manages dependencies effectively, maintains large configuration files, and properly handles upgrades and downgrades to ensure system stability. On its own, dpkg does not handle dependencies properly. apt-get performs installations, package searches, updates, and many other operations for packages available to your system. Keeping packages up to date is extremely important, as using out-of-date packages can lead to security issues on your system. The apt-get utility requires root privileges, similar to the dpkg utility.

First, before we make it perform in any software installation, it's always best practice to update the package database. We should run the apt-get update for this:

```
root@ubuntu:/home/philip/Downloads# apt-get update
Get:1 http://security.ubuntu.com/ubuntu xenial-security InRelease [107 kB]
Hit:2 http://us.archive.ubuntu.com/ubuntu xenial InRelease
Get:3 http://security.debian.org/debian-security wheezy/updates InRelease
[54.0 kB]
Get:4 http://us.archive.ubuntu.com/ubuntu xenial-updates InRelease [109 kB]
Ign:3 http://security.debian.org/debian-security wheezy/updates InRelease
Get:5 http://us.archive.ubuntu.com/ubuntu xenial-backports InRelease [107
kB]
Get:6 http://security.debian.org/debian-security wheezy/updates/main amd64
Packages [589 kB]
Get:21 http://us.archive.ubuntu.com/ubuntu xenial-updates/multiverse amd64
DEP-11 Metadata [5,964 B]
Get:22 http://us.archive.ubuntu.com/ubuntu xenial-backports/main amd64
DEP-11 Metadata [3,328 B]
```

```
Get:23 http://us.archive.ubuntu.com/ubuntu xenial-backports/universe amd64
DEP-11 Metadata [5,096 B]
Fetched 6,189 kB in 6s (1,031 kB/s)
Reading package lists... Done
root@ubuntu:/home/philip/Downloads#
```

Based on the preceding output, the first section will be Hit, Get, Ign. Now, Hit means that there is no change in the package version, and Get means that there is a new version available. Then Ign means that the package is being ignored. There are various reasons why you would see Ign, ranging from a package being too recent to there being an error in retrieving the file. Usually, the errors are harmless.

Now, before we install an application, we can search for it using the apt-cache command. Let's say that we want to install a messenger application. We can do this in the following way:

```
root@ubuntu:/home/philip/Downloads# apt-cache search messenger
adium-theme-ubuntu - Adium message style for Ubuntu
totem-plugins - Plugins for the Totem media player
ayttm - Universal instant messaging client
banshee-extension-telepathy - Telepathy extension for Banshee
droopy - mini web server to let others upload files to your computer
dsniff - Various tools to sniff network traffic for cleartext insecurities
ekg2 - instant messenger and IRC client for UNIX systems
ekg2-api-docs - instant messenger and IRC client for UNIX systems - API
documentation
ekg2-core - instant messenger and IRC client for UNIX systems - main
program
yate-qt4 - YATE-based universal telephony client
yowsup-cli - command line tool that acts as WhatsApp client
empathy-skype - Skype plugin for libpurple messengers (Empathy-specific
files)
pidgin-skype - Skype plugin for libpurple messengers (Pidgin-specific
files)
pidgin-skype-common - Skype plugin for libpurple messengers (common files)
pidgin-skype-dbg - Skype plugin for libpurple messengers (debug symbols)
root@ubuntu:/home/philip/Downloads#
```

Based on the preceding output, we can see that a wide range of messenger packages are available to be installed. If, for some reason, we wanted to see all the available packages, we could use the pkgnames option:

```
root@ubuntu:/home/philip/Downloads# apt-cache pkgnames | less
libdatrie-doc
libfstrcmp0-dbg
librime-data-sampheng
xxdiff-scripts
```

```
globus-xioperf
edenmath.app
libghc-ansi-wl-pprint-doc
libjson0
zathura-cb
root@ubuntu:/home/philip/Downloads#
```

We can see a variety of packages which we can install onto this system. We can also see a brief description of each package by specifying the correct package name:

```
root@ubuntu:/home/philip/Downloads# apt-cache search zathura-cb
zathura-cb - comic book archive support for zathura
root@ubuntu:/home/philip/Downloads# apt-cache search virtaal
virtaal - graphical localisation editor
root@ubuntu:/home/philip/Downloads# apt-cache search python-logbook
python-logbook - logging system for Python that replaces the standard
library's module
python-logbook-doc - logging system for Python that replaces the standard
library's module (doc)
root@ubuntu:/home/philip/Downloads#
```

Based on the preceding output, we can see the descriptions for various packages that we passed with the search option. We can also check the details of a package by using the show option:

```
root@ubuntu:/home/philip/Downloads# apt-cache show python-logbook
Package: python-logbook
Priority: optional
Section: universe/python
Source: logbook
Version: 0.12.3-1
Depends: python:any (<< 2.8), python:any (>= 2.7.5-5~)
Suggests: python-logbook-doc
Filename: pool/universe/l/logbook/python-logbook_0.12.3-1_all.deb
Size: 47896
MD5sum: 865ee97095b97f74e362ce3d93a26a9e
SHA1: 812b08f4e4e4dbcd40264a99fa4cd4dff4f62961
SHA256: 3091d5c491e54007da8b510a6f2e463b63f62364938c4f371406cb4511b6232c
Origin: Ubuntu
root@ubuntu:/home/philip/Downloads#
```

We can even filter this information to only look for dependencies. We should use the showpkg option for this:

```
root@ubuntu:/home/philip/Downloads# apt-cache showpkg python-logbook
Package: python-logbook
Versions:
0.12.3-1
(/var/lib/apt/lists/us.archive.ubuntu.com_ubuntu_dists_xenial_universe_bina
```

```
ry-amd64_Packages)
(/var/lib/apt/lists/us.archive.ubuntu.com_ubuntu_dists_xenial_universe_bina
ry-i386_Packages)
Dependencies:
0.12.3-1 - python:any (3 2.8) python:any (2 2.7.5-5~) python-logbook-doc (0
(null))
Provides:
0.12.3-1 -
Reverse Provides:
root@ubuntu:/home/philip/Downloads#
```

We can also view the statistics for the cache on this system by using the `stats` option:

```
root@ubuntu:/home/philip/Downloads# apt-cache stats
Total package names: 73419 (1,468 k)
Total package structures: 113356 (4,988 k)
  Normal packages: 84328
  Total buckets in PkgHashTable: 50503
  Unused: 11792
  Used: 38711
  Utilization: 76.6509%
  Average entries: 2.92826
  Longest: 15
  Shortest: 1
Total buckets in GrpHashTable: 50503
  Unused: 11792
  Used: 38711
  Utilization: 76.6509%
  Average entries: 1.89659
  Longest: 8
  Shortest: 1
root@ubuntu:/home/philip/Downloads#
```

Now, we can download a package without installing it. For this, we can use the `download` option with `apt-get`:

```
root@ubuntu:/tmp# apt-get download zathura-cb
Get:1 http://us.archive.ubuntu.com/ubuntu xenial/universe amd64 zathura-cb
amd64 0.1.5-1 [8,812 B]
Fetched 8,812 B in 0s (40.0 kB/s)
root@ubuntu:/tmp# ls | grep zathura
zathura-cb_0.1.5-1_amd64.deb
root@ubuntu:/tmp#
```

We can also install a package that has been downloaded. We need to specify the path with the `apt-get` command:

```
root@ubuntu:/tmp# apt-get install ./zathura-cb_0.1.5-1_amd64.deb
Reading package lists... Done
Building dependency tree
Reading state information... Done
You might want to run 'apt-get -f install' to correct these.
The following packages have unmet dependencies:
openssh-server:i386 : Depends: openssh-client:i386 (= 1:6.0p1-4+deb7u7)
   Recommends: ncurses-term:i386
   Recommends: openssh-blacklist:i386 but it is not installable
   Recommends: openssh-blacklist-extra:i386 but it is not installable
openssh-sftp-server:i386 : Breaks: openssh-server (< 1:6.5p1-5)
Breaks: openssh-server:i386 (< 1:6.5p1-5)
E: Unmet dependencies. Try using -f.
root@ubuntu:/tmp#
```

Now, sometimes you may run into the problem seen in the previous example. The easiest way to fix this would be to rerun the `apt-get` command with the `-f` option, leaving out the package name:

```
root@ubuntu:/tmp# apt-get -f install
Reading package lists... Done
Building dependency tree
Reading state information... Done
Correcting dependencies... Done
The following packages were automatically installed and are no longer
required:
Do you want to continue? [Y/n] y
Preconfiguring packages ...
 (Reading database ... 241439 files and directories currently installed.)
Preparing to unpack .../openssh-server_1%3a7.2p2-4ubuntu2.4_i386.deb ...
Unpacking openssh-server:i386 (1:7.2p2-4ubuntu2.4) over (1:6.0p1-4+deb7u7)
...
Processing triggers for ufw (0.35-0ubuntu2) ...
Processing triggers for systemd (229-4ubuntu21.2) ...
Processing triggers for ureadahead (0.100.0-19) ...
Processing triggers for man-db (2.7.5-1) ...
Setting up openssh-server:i386 (1:7.2p2-4ubuntu2.4) ...
Setting up tftp:i386 (0.17-18) ...
root@ubuntu:/tmp#
```

There we go! As we can see, the installation was successful. This is what is so great about the `apt-get` utility: it finds the dependencies that are needed and offers to install them to fix the problem being reported. We can also install multiple applications simultaneously. We simply place each package name on the same line, separated by a space:

```
root@ubuntu:/tmp# apt-get install virtaal vsftpd
Reading package lists... Done
Building dependency tree
Reading state information... Done
The following packages were automatically installed and are no longer
required:
  libllvm3.8 libpango1.0-0 libpangox-1.0-0 libqmi-glib1 linux-
headers-4.4.0-21 linux-headers-4.4.0-21-generic linux-image-4.4.0-21-
generic
  linux-image-extra-4.4.0-21-generic
Use 'sudo apt autoremove' to remove them.
The following additional packages will be installed:
  javascript-common libglade2-0 libjs-jquery libjs-sph
Do you want to continue? [Y/n] y
Get:1 http://us.archive.ubuntu.com/ubuntu xenial/main amd64 libglade2-0
amd64 1:2.6.4-2 [44.6 kB]
Get:2 http://us.archive.ubuntu.com/ubuntu xenial/main amd64 javascript-
common all 11 [6,066 B]
Get:3 http://us.archive.ubuntu.com/ubuntu xenial/main amd64 libjs-jquery
all 1.11.3+dfsg-4 [161 kB]
Get:4 http://us.archive.ubuntu.com/ubuntu xenial/main amd64 libjs-
underscore all 1.7.0~dfsg-1ubuntu1 [46.7 kB]
Get:5 http://us.archive.ubuntu.com/ubuntu xenial-updates/main amd64 libjs-
sphinxdoc all 1.3.6-2ubuntu1.1 [57.6 kB]
Get:6 http://us.archive.ubuntu.com/ubuntu xenial-updates/main amd64 libpq5
amd64 9.5.13-0ubuntu0.16.04 [78.7 kB]
Setting up virtaal (0.7.1-1) ...
Setting up python-iniparse (0.4-2.2) ...
Setting up vsftpd (3.0.3-3ubuntu2) ...
Processing triggers for libc-bin (2.23-0ubuntu10) ...
Processing triggers for systemd (229-4ubuntu21.2) ...
Processing triggers for ureadahead (0.100.0-19) ...
root@ubuntu:/tmp#
```

Great! So, now you can see the power of the `apt-get` utility in action. We can also upgrade all of the packages that are currently installed by using the `upgrade` option:

```
root@ubuntu:/tmp# apt-get upgrade
Reading package lists... Done
Building dependency tree
Reading state information... Done
Calculating upgrade... Done
```

```
The following packages were automatically installed and are no longer
required:
The following packages were automatically installed and are no longer
required:
  libllvm3.8 libpango1.0-0 libpangox-1.0-0 libqmi-glib1 linux-
headers-4.4.0-21 linux-headers-4.4.0-21-generic linux-image-4.4.0-21-
generic
  linux-image-extra-4.4.0-21-generic
Use 'sudo apt autoremove' to remove them.
The following packages have been kept back:
  libegl1-mesa libgbm1 libgl1-mesa-dri libwayland-egl1-mesa libxatracker2
The following packages will be upgraded:
  apt apt-transport-https apt-utils base-files cups cups-bsd cups-client
cups-common cups-core-drivers cups-daemon cups-ppdc
63 upgraded, 0 newly installed, 0 to remove and 5 not upgraded.
Need to get 67.1 MB/160 MB of archives.
After this operation, 1,333 kB disk space will be freed.
Do you want to continue? [Y/n] y
root@ubuntu:/tmp#
```

Some output was omitted for brevity.

We can also remove some packages that were previously used, to ensure a particular package was installed correctly. In our case, if we rerun the upgrade option, we should see this:

```
root@ubuntu:/tmp# apt-get upgrade
Reading package lists... Done
Building dependency tree
Reading state information... Done
Calculating upgrade... Done
The following packages were automatically installed and are no longer
required:
libllvm3.8 libpango1.0-0 libpangox-1.0-0 libqmi-glib1 linux-
headers-4.4.0-21 linux-headers-4.4.0-21-generic linux-image-4.4.0-21-
generic
linux-image-extra-4.4.0-21-generic
Use 'sudo apt autoremove' to remove them.
The following packages have been kept back:
libegl1-mesa libgbm1 libgl1-mesa-dri libwayland-egl1-mesa libxatracker2
0 upgraded, 0 newly installed, 0 to remove and 5 not upgraded.
root@ubuntu:/tmp#
```

We should use the `autoremove` option, as suggested, to free up some disk space:

```
root@ubuntu:/tmp# apt-get autoremove
Reading package lists... Done
Building dependency tree
Reading state information... Done
The following packages will be REMOVED:
libllvm3.8 libpango1.0-0 libpangox-1.0-0 libqmi-glib1 linux-
headers-4.4.0-21 linux-headers-4.4.0-21-generic linux-image-4.4.0-21-
generic
linux-image-extra-4.4.0-21-generic
0 upgraded, 0 newly installed, 8 to remove and 5 not upgraded.
After this operation, 339 MB disk space will be freed.
Do you want to continue? [Y/n] y
(Reading database ... 244059 files and directories currently installed.)
Removing libllvm3.8:amd64 (1:3.8-2ubuntu4) ...
Removing libpango1.0-0:amd64 (1.38.1-1) ...
Removing libpangox-1.0-0:amd64 (0.0.2-5) ...
done
Processing triggers for libc-bin (2.23-0ubuntu10) ...
root@ubuntu:/tmp#
```

We can also free up disk space by using the `clean` option:

```
root@ubuntu:/tmp# apt-get clean
root@ubuntu:/tmp#
```

As we can see, the command ran very quickly.

It's always best practice to clean up disk space regularly.

We can also remove an application by using the `remove` option. This would remove the application but not the configuration:

```
root@ubuntu:/tmp# apt-get remove virtaal
Reading package lists... Done
Building dependency tree
Reading state information... Done
The following packages were automatically installed and are no longer
required:
javascript-common libglade2-0 libjs-jquery libjs-sphinxdoc libjs-underscore
libpq5 libtidy-0.99-0 python-babel python-babel-localedata
python-bs4 python-cairo python-chardet python-dateutil python-diff-match-
patch python-egenix-mxdatetime python-egenix-mxtools
python-enchant python-gi python-glade2 python-gobject python-gobject-2
```

```
python-gtk2 python-html5lib python-iniparse python-levenshtein
python-lxml python-pkg-resources python-psycopg2 python-pycurl python-
simplejson python-six python-tz python-utidylib python-vobject
python-xapian translate-toolkit
Use 'sudo apt autoremove' to remove them.
The following packages will be REMOVED:
virtaal
0 upgraded, 0 newly installed, 1 to remove and 5 not upgraded.
After this operation, 3,496 kB disk space will be freed.
Do you want to continue? [Y/n] y
root@ubuntu:/tmp#
```

We would then run the `autoremove` option to clean up unnecessary packages.

The autoremove option

Often, when we uninstall a package, there are some unnecessary packages which were initially installed in order for the specific package to function. These unneeded packages take up hard disk space; we could reclaim this space by using the `autoremove` option:

```
root@ubuntu:/tmp# apt-get autoremove virtaal
Reading package lists... Done
Building dependency tree
Reading state information... Done
Package 'virtaal' is not installed, so not removed
The following packages will be REMOVED:
javascript-common libglade2-0 libjs-jquery libjs-sphinxdoc libjs-underscore
libpq5 libtidy-0.99-0 python-babel python-babel-localedata
python-bs4 python-cairo python-chardet python-dateutil python-diff-match-
patch python-egenix-mxdatetime python-egenix-mxtools
python-enchant python-gi python-glade2 python-gobject python-gobject-2
python-gtk2 python-html5lib python-iniparse python-levenshtein
python-lxml python-pkg-resources python-psycopg2 python-pycurl python-
simplejson python-six python-tz python-utidylib python-vobject
python-xapian translate-toolkit
0 upgraded, 0 newly installed, 36 to remove and 5 not upgraded.
After this operation, 34.6 MB disk space will be freed.
Do you want to continue? [Y/n] y
Processing triggers for libc-bin (2.23-0ubuntu10) ...
Processing triggers for man-db (2.7.5-1) ...
Processing triggers for doc-base (0.10.7) ...
Processing 4 removed doc-base files...
root@ubuntu:/tmp#
```

Awesome! We can remove the package and its configuration by using the `purge` option.

The purge option

The purge option, when used, not only removes a package, but also removes a package configuration file. This is ideal because most of the time when we uninstall a package using uninstall, it leaves unwanted configuration files in our system. Here is how we use the purge option:

```
root@ubuntu:/tmp# apt-get purge virtaal
Reading package lists... Done
Building dependency tree
Reading state information... Done
The following packages will be REMOVED:
  virtaal*
0 upgraded, 0 newly installed, 1 to remove and 5 not upgraded.
After this operation, 0 B of additional disk space will be used.
Do you want to continue? [Y/n] y
Removing virtaal (0.7.1-1) ...
Purging configuration files for virtaal (0.7.1-1) ...
root@ubuntu:/tmp#
```

Great!

It is always a good idea to regularly run the apt-get command with the clean option.

Whenever we install a package using the apt utility, it uses repositories to download the packages into the cache. By default, when we install a Debian distribution, the installation comes with official repositories. These are stored in the /etc/apt/sources.list file. Let's take a look at that file:

```
root@ubuntu:/tmp# cat /etc/apt/sources.list
#deb cdrom:[Ubuntu 16.04 LTS _Xenial Xerus_ - Release amd64 (20160420.1)]/
xenial main restricted
  # See http://help.ubuntu.com/community/UpgradeNotes for how to upgrade to
# newer versions of the distribution.
deb http://us.archive.ubuntu.com/ubuntu/ xenial main restricted
# deb-src http://us.archive.ubuntu.com/ubuntu/ xenial main restricted
  ## Major bug fix updates produced after the final release of the
## distribution.
deb http://us.archive.ubuntu.com/ubuntu/ xenial-updates main restricted
# deb-src http://us.archive.ubuntu.com/ubuntu/ xenial-updates main
restricted
## N.B. software from this repository is ENTIRELY UNSUPPORTED by the Ubuntu
## team, and may not be under a free licence. Please satisfy yourself as to
```

```
## your rights to use the software. Also, please note that software in
## universe WILL NOT receive any review or updates from the Ubuntu security
## team.
deb http://us.archive.ubuntu.com/ubuntu/ xenial universe
# deb-src http://us.archive.ubuntu.com/ubuntu/ xenial universe
# deb-src http://security.ubuntu.com/ubuntu xenial-security universe
deb http://security.ubuntu.com/ubuntu xenial-security multiverse
# deb-src http://security.ubuntu.com/ubuntu xenial-security multiverse
root@ubuntu:/tmp#
```

The entries that start with `deb` refer to where to search for packages. The entries that start with `deb-src` refer to source packages.

The aptitude command

Aptitude is a frontend to APT, which is the Debian package manager. It's best suited in shell environments where a GUI is not present. The `aptitude` command allows users to view the list of packages, and perform package management tasks such as installing, removing or upgrading packages. There is an interactive mode; also, it could be used as a command-line tool, similar to `apt-get`.

We can see this in action by simply entering the `aptitude` command without passing any option(s):

```
 Actions  Undo  Package  Resolver  Search  Options  Views  Help
C-T: Menu  ?: Help  q: Quit  u: Update  g: Preview/Download/Install/Remove Pkgs
aptitude 0.7.4
--- Upgradable Packages (5)
--- New Packages (187)
--- Installed Packages (1768)
--- Not Installed Packages (85321)
--- Virtual Packages (11107)
--- Tasks (53360)




A newer version of these packages is available.

This group contains 5 packages.
```

In the screen shown in the preceding screenshot, we can interact by using our keyboard or mouse to navigate. At the top, there is a menu. We can select **Actions** from the menu and here we will see the available options:

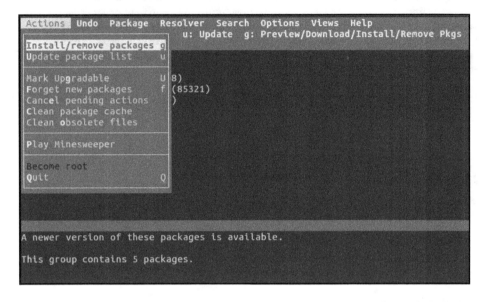

We can also go directly to **Package** from the menu and see options similar to doing package management from the command line:

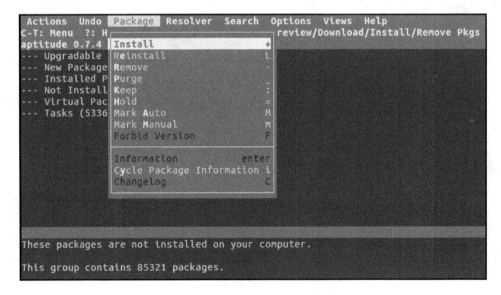

As we can see, `aptitude` is very intuitive when we use this method for package management.

We can also manage packages using the command line. This would require us to pass options with the `aptitude` command, if we prefer typing commands over a menu type of environment. The `aptitude` command supports most of the options that we would pass with the `apt-get` command. Let's start with the `search` option:

The search option

When we execute the `search` option, the `aptitude` command does a search for possible matches based on the criteria specified after the `search` option:

```
root@ubuntu:/home/philip# aptitude search vlc
p    browser-plugin-vlc                    - multimedia plugin
for web browsers based on VLC
p    browser-plugin-vlc:i386               - multimedia plugin
for web browsers based on VLC
p    libvlc-dev                            - development files
for libvlc
p    libvlc-dev:i386                       - development files
for libvlc
p    libvlc5                               - multimedia player
and streamer library
p    vlc                                   - multimedia player
and streamer
p    vlc:i386                              - multimedia player
and streamer
root@ubuntu:/home/philip#
```

Based on the preceding output, we can see similar patterns of the `aptitude` command to that of APT. We can also install and update the package list by passing the `update` option:

```
root@ubuntu:/home/philip# aptitude update
Hit http://us.archive.ubuntu.com/ubuntu xenial InRelease
Get: 1 http://security.ubuntu.com/ubuntu xenial-security InRelease [107 kB]
Get: 2 http://us.archive.ubuntu.com/ubuntu xenial-updates InRelease [109
kB]
Get: 3 http://us.archive.ubuntu.com/ubuntu xenial-backports InRelease [107
kB]
Get: 4 http://us.archive.ubuntu.com/ubuntu xenial-updates/main amd64
Packages [809 kB]
Get: 5 http://security.ubuntu.com/ubuntu xenial-security/main amd64
Packages [524 kB]
Get: 6 http://us.archive.ubuntu.com/ubuntu xenial-updates/main i386
```

```
Packages [738 kB]
Get: 7 http://security.ubuntu.com/ubuntu xenial-security/main i386 Packages
[461 kB]
root@ubuntu:/home/philip#
```

After we have updated the package list, we can upgrade the packages by passing the `safe-upgrade` option:

```
root@ubuntu:/home/philip# aptitude safe-upgrade
Resolving dependencies...
The following NEW packages will be installed:
  libllvm6.0{a}
The following packages will be REMOVED:
  libllvm5.0{u}
The following packages will be upgraded:
  libegl1-mesa libgbm1 libgl1-mesa-dri libwayland-egl1-mesa libxatracker2
5 packages upgraded, 1 newly installed, 1 to remove and 0 not upgraded.
Need to get 21.6 MB of archives. After unpacking 14.1 MB will be used.
Do you want to continue? [Y/n/?] y
Installing new version of config file /etc/drirc ...
Setting up libegl1-mesa:amd64 (18.0.5-0ubuntu0~16.04.1) ...
Setting up libwayland-egl1-mesa:amd64 (18.0.5-0ubuntu0~16.04.1) ...
Processing triggers for libc-bin (2.23-0ubuntu10) ...
Current status: 0 (-5) upgradable.
root@ubuntu:/home/philip#
```

We can also install a package by passing the `install` option:

```
root@ubuntu:/home/philip# aptitude install vlc
The following NEW packages will be installed:
i965-va-driver{a} liba52-0.7.4{a} libaacs0{a} libass5{a} libavcodec-
ffmpeg56{a} libavformat-ffmpeg56{a}
libavutil-ffmpeg54{a} libbasicusageenvironment1{a} libbdplus0{a}
libbluray1{a} libcddb2{a} libchromaprint0{a}
libcrystalhd3{a} libdc1394-22{a} libdca0{a} libdirectfb-1.2-9{a}
libdvbpsi10{a} libdvdnav4{a} libdvdread4{a}
vlc-plugin-notify{a} vlc-plugin-samba{a}
0 packages upgraded, 73 newly installed, 0 to remove and 0 not upgraded.
Need to get 23.7 MB of archives. After unpacking 119 MB will be used.
Do you want to continue? [Y/n/?] y
Setting up va-driver-all:amd64 (1.7.0-1ubuntu0.1) ...
Processing triggers for libc-bin (2.23-0ubuntu10) ...
Processing triggers for vlc-nox (2.2.2-5ubuntu0.16.04.4) ...
root@ubuntu:/home/philip#
```

Awesome! We can also remove a package. To do this, we would simply pass the `remove` option:

```
root@ubuntu:/home/philip# aptitude remove vlc
The following packages will be removed:
  i965-va-driver{u} liba52-0.7.4{u} libaacs0{u} libass5{u} libavcodec-
ffmpeg56{u} libavformat-ffmpeg56{u}
    libzvbi-common{u} libzvbi0{u} mesa-va-drivers{u} va-driver-all{u} vlc
vlc-data{u} vlc-nox{u} vlc-plugin-notify{u} vlc-plugin-samba{u}
Do you want to continue? [Y/n/?] y
Processing triggers for desktop-file-utils (0.22-1ubuntu5.2) ...
Processing triggers for libc-bin (2.23-0ubuntu10) ...
Processing triggers for hicolor-icon-theme (0.15-0ubuntu1) ...
root@ubuntu:/home/philip#
```

Great! As we can see, the `aptitude` command is very useful for any Linux administrator.

The synaptic utility

This is a graphical form of package management; it is based on the APT. This powerful GUI utility enables us to install, update, or remove packages within an easy-to-use environment. Using the `synaptic` utility enables us to manage packages without requiring us to work at the Command Prompt. Let's take a look at the `synaptic` utility within the Ubuntu 18 system. The `synaptic` utility is not installed within Ubuntu 18 by default. We can see information about the `synaptic` utility before we install it by using the `apt-cache` command:

```
root@ubuntu:/home/philip# apt-cache showpkg synaptic
 Package: synaptic
 Versions:
 0.83
(/var/lib/apt/lists/us.archive.ubuntu.com_ubuntu_dists_xenial_universe_bina
ry-amd64_Packages)
 Description Language:
 File:
/var/lib/apt/lists/us.archive.ubuntu.com_ubuntu_dists_xenial_universe_binar
y-amd64_Packages
 MD5: d4fb8e90c9684f1113e56123c017d85f
 Reverse Depends:
 aptoncd,synaptic 0.57.7
 apt,synaptic
 mate-menu,synaptic
 lubuntu-desktop,synaptic
 cinnamon-desktop-environment,synaptic
 update-notifier,synaptic 0.75.12
```

```
apt,synaptic
update-manager,synaptic
Dependencies:
 0.83 - libapt-inst2.0 (2 0.8.16~exp12) libapt-pkg5.0 (2 1.1~exp9) libc6 (2
2.14) libept1.5.0 (0 (null)) libgcc1 (2 1:3.0) libgdk-pixbuf2.0-0 (2
2.22.0) libglib2.0-0 (2 2.14.0) libgtk-3-0 (2 3.3.16) libpango-1.0-0 (2
1.14.0) libstdc++6 (2 5.2) libvte-2.91-
root@ubuntu:/home/philip#
```

Based on the preceding screenshot, we can see that there are a number of dependencies that the `synaptic` utility depends on. Let's install the `synaptic` utility by using the `apt-get` command:

```
root@ubuntu:/home/philip# apt-get install synaptic
 Reading package lists... Done
 Building dependency tree
 Reading state information... Done
 The following NEW packages will be installed:
 docbook-xml libept1.5.0 librarian0 rarian-compat sgml-data synaptic
 0 upgraded, 6 newly installed, 0 to remove and 81 not upgraded.
 Need to get 1,785 kB of archives.
 After this operation, 11.6 MB of additional disk space will be used.
 Do you want to continue? [Y/n] y
Setting up docbook-xml (4.5-7.3) ...
 Processing triggers for sgml-base (1.26+nmu4ubuntu1) ...
 root@ubuntu:/home/philip#
```

We have just installed the `synaptic` utility. We could launch the `synaptic` utility to explore its features from the **Search your computer** button at the top left-hand corner of the Ubuntu 18 system, based on the following screenshot:

As soon as we select the `synaptic` package manager, it will prompt us for authentication, as can be seen in the following screenshot:

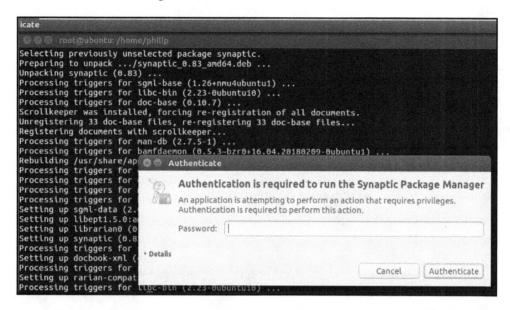

Once this is authenticated, we will then be presented with the `synaptic` utility. We can use the **Search** button to find specific packages. The following screenshot depicts the **Search** function dialog box:

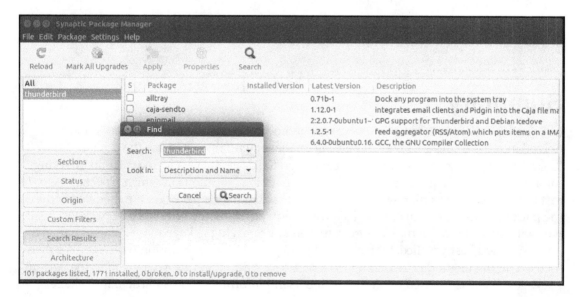

Awesome job! As can be seen in the preceding screenshot, we can perform searches by simply entering the desired package name. When compared to the command-line counterpart, it's much easier to use a GUI. To perform a search, we would simply select the **Search** button. Also, we can update the package database from within the synaptic utility by simply selecting the **Reload** button:

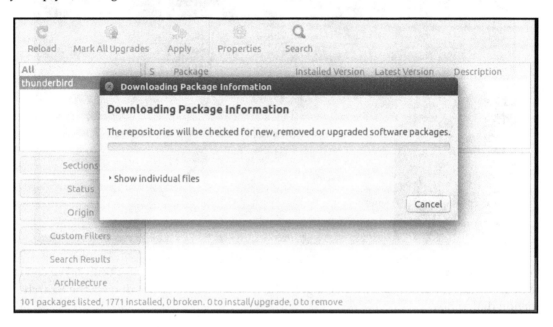

Great! As you can see, the synaptic utility is very intuitive in nature. It can be navigated in a similar way to other GUI programs.

Summary

In this chapter, we focused on the various methods for package management. First, we delved into the traditional way of package management; that is, to use the dpkg utility. We looked at ways to view the current packages on the system. We also touched on querying for a particular package. Then we looked at the various locations in which a package would install files. Adding to that, we did an actual installation of a package. We then verified that the package was indeed installed. This was followed up by the removal of a package. Next, we switched our attention to a more common approach to package management; namely, APT. We used best practice, which is to always pass the update option with apt. We then focused on the method of searching for a package. Adding to this, we looked at the current packages. We also focused on getting some useful information on a particular package.

This was followed up by the installation of a package. At this point, we saw that we can install multiple packages on a single `apt-get` command. This was followed by a demo on updating the packages. In addition to this, we looked at how to remove a package using the `apt-get` command. Finally, we worked with `aptitude`. On its own, the `aptitude` command presents a user-interactive, menu-driven environment. We also looked at passing options with the `aptitude` command. Initially, we updated the package list. This was followed by an upgrade of the packages. Adding to this, we saw the technique for searching for packages. Then a package installation was performed using the command line. Following this, we did a demo on removing a package at the command line. Finally, we ended with an alternative to the command line: the `synaptic` utility. The `synaptic` utility, which is based on APT, is a GUI for package management.

In the next chapter, we take a deep dive into the world of Red Hat package management; particularly Fedora. There, we will cover the various techniques we would use to manage packages, such as `rpm`, `yum`, `dnf`, and `yumex`. I hope you come and join in, because I'm confident you will become better equipped to managing packages in the Red Hat world after going through the next chapter. This will ultimately take you one step closer to certification.

Questions

1. Which option with the `dpkg` command is used to display the packages that `dpkg` is managing on a system?

     A. `dpkg -a`
     B. `dpkg -l`
     C. `dpkg -i`
     D. `dpkg -d`

2. Which option with `dpkg-query` is used to show a human-readable description of a package?

     A. `dpkg-query -a`
     B. `dpkg-query-c`
     C. `dpkg-query -s`
     D. `dpkg-query-r`

3. Which log file is used to display dpkg package-related messages?

    A. cat /var/log/dpkg.log
    B. cat /var/dpkg/dpkg.log
    C. cat /var/dpkg-query/dpkg.log
    D. cat /var/log/dpkg.dpkg

4. Which option is used to display packages that are installed with the dpkg command?

    A. dpkg --get-selections
    B. dpkg -set-selections
    C. dpkg -get-selection
    D. dpkg-query -get-selection

5. Which option is used to add a package using the dpkg command?

    A. dpkg -e
    B. dpkg -r
    C. dpkg -Add
    D. dpkg -i

6. Which option is used to remove a package along with its configuration files using the dpkg command?

    A. dpkg -p
    B. dpkg-e
    C. dpkg -P
    D. dpkg-a

7. Which option is used to update apt cache?

    A. apt-get -c
    B. apt-get update
    C. apt-get upgrade
    D. apt-get -u

8. Which command is used to search the cache for a package?

    A. `apt-get search`
    B. `apt-cache search`
    C. `apt-get -update`
    D. `apt-get clean`

9. Which option is used to remove a package and its configuration using the `apt` command?

    A. `apt-get remove`
    B. `apt-get purge`
    C. `apt-get --remove`
    D. `apt-get --update`

10. Which option is used to update the package list using the `aptitude` command?

    A. `aptitude purge`
    B. `aptitude clean`
    C. `aptitude update`
    D. `aptitude --clean`

Further reading

- This first website gives you useful information about the Debian distributions: `https://wiki.debian.org`.
- This website gives you tips and best practices for the Debian distributions: `https://www.debian.org`.
- This next website gives you a lot of useful tips and best practices from users in the Linux community, particularly for the Debian distributions such as Ubuntu: `https://askubuntu.com`.
- This last website gives you a lot of useful resources on various problems faced by other Linux users for various tasks: `https://unix.stackexchange.com`.

7
Using YUM Package Management

In the previous chapter, package management was our focal point. Here, we learned about the Debian package manager. There are a number of ways to install packages inside a Debian environment. Our attention was focused on the common methods of managing packages within a Debian environment.

In this chapter, we continue our journey. This time we focus on the Red Hat approach to package management. We will begin with the very popular **Yellowdog Updater, Modified**, also known as **YUM**. Next, we turn our attention toward the dnf utility. The dnf utility acts similarly to YUM. This is followed by the rpm utility for managing packages. Finally, the yumex utility will be covered.

We will be covering the following topics in this chapter:

- yum
- dnf
- rpm
- yumex

YUM

Yellowdog Updater, Modified, is commonly known as **YUM**. YUM is an open source command-line method for package management for systems using a Red Hat distribution. As Linux administrators, YUM enables us to perform automatic updates and package and dependency management on RPM-based distributions. YUM is similar in nature to its Debian counterpart, APT. The YUM utility makes use of various software repositories.

A software repo, as it is commonly called, stores a variety of packages. One of the main reasons for using YUM is that it detects whether any dependency files are needed for a particular package. It then prompts the user of the needed files and offers to install them as part of the package installation, which the user should have initiated from the get-go.

An interesting point to note is the fact that YUM works with RPM packages.

To begin with, we can view the available packages in the YUM database by using the `list` option:

```
[philip@localhost ~]$ yum list | less
Repodata is over 2 weeks old. Install yum-cron? Or run: yum makecache fast
Loading mirror speeds from cached hostfile
  * base: centos.mirror.iweb.ca
  * extras: centos.mirror.iweb.ca
  * updates: centos.mirror.iweb.ca
Installed Packages
GConf2.x86_64                         3.2.6-8.el7                    @anaconda
GeoIP.x86_64                          1.5.0-11.el7                   @anaconda
ModemManager.x86_64                   1.6.0-2.el7                    @anaconda
ModemManager-glib.x86_64              1.6.0-2.el7                    @anaconda
NetworkManager.x86_64                 1:1.8.0-9.el7                  @anaconda
NetworkManager-adsl.x86_64            1:1.8.0-9.el7                  @anaconda
NetworkManager-glib.x86_64            1:1.8.0-9.el7                  @anaconda
NetworkManager-libnm.x86_64           1:1.8.0-9.el7                  @anaconda
NetworkManager-libreswan.x86_64  1.2.4-2.el7                        @anaconda
NetworkManager-libreswan-gnome.x86_64 1.2.4-2.el7                        @anaconda
NetworkManager-ppp.x86_64             1:1.8.0-9.el7                  @anaconda
NetworkManager-team.x86_64            1:1.8.0-9.el7                  @anaconda
NetworkManager-tui.x86_64             1:1.8.0-9.el7                  @anaconda
NetworkManager-wifi.x86_64            1:1.8.0-9.el7                  @anaconda
PackageKit.x86_64                     1.1.5-1.el7.centos             @anaconda
```

From the preceding output, the repo data is precisely two-weeks old. This can be solved by running `makecache fast` with YUM:

```
[philip@localhost ~]$ yum makecache fast
Loaded plugins: fastestmirror, langpacks
Existing lock /var/tmp/yum-philip-FdEYSO/x86_64/7/yum.pid: another copy is
running as pid 2322.
Another app is currently holding the yum lock; waiting for it to exit...
   The other application is: yum
   Memory :  24 M RSS (415 MB VSZ)
   Started: Tue Jul 31 05:49:03 2018 - 00:11 ago
```

```
   State   : Traced/Stopped, pid: 2322
Another app is currently holding the yum lock; waiting for it to exit...
   The other application is: yum
   Memory :   24 M RSS (415 MB VSZ)
   Started: Tue Jul 31 05:49:03 2018 - 00:13 ago
   State   : Traced/Stopped, pid: 2322
Another app is currently holding the yum lock; waiting for it to exit...
   The other application is: yum
   Memory :   24 M RSS (415 MB VSZ)
   Started: Tue Jul 31 05:49:03 2018 - 00:15 ago
   State   : Traced/Stopped, pid: 2322
^C
Exiting on user cancel.
[philip@localhost ~]$
```

If you are faced with this message whilst attempting to update the cache, then we can remove the lock file, which will remedy this:

```
[philip@localhost ~]$ rm /var/tmp/yum-philip-FdEYSO/x86_64/7/yum.pid
[philip@localhost ~]$ yum makecache fast
Loaded plugins: fastestmirror, langpacks
http://ftp.jaist.ac.jp/pub/Linux/CentOS/7/os/x86_64/repodata/repomd.xml:
[Errno 14] curl#6 - "Could not resolve host: ftp.jaist.ac.jp; Name or
service not known"
Trying other mirror.
base
| 3.6 kB   00:00:00
extras
| 3.4 kB   00:00:00
http://centos.mirror.iweb.ca/7/updates/x86_64/repodata/repomd.xml: [Errno
14] curl#6 - "Could not resolve host: centos.mirror.iweb.ca; Name or
service not known"
Trying other mirror.
updates
| 3.4 kB   00:00:00
(1/2): extras/7/x86_64/primary_db
| 172 kB   00:00:10
(2/2): updates/7/x86_64/primary_db
| 4.3 MB   00:00:13
Loading mirror speeds from cached hostfile
 * base: centos.mirror.iweb.ca
 * extras: centos.mirror.iweb.ca
 * updates: centos.mirror.iweb.ca
Metadata Cache Created
[philip@localhost ~]$
```

Awesome job! We can see that the cache has been updated. We can further narrow down the packages being displayed by YUM. To do this, we use the `installed` option:

```
[philip@localhost ~]$ yum list installed | less
Loaded plugins: fastestmirror, langpacks
Installed Packages
GConf2.x86_64                3.2.6-8.el7                    @anaconda
GeoIP.x86_64                 1.5.0-11.el7                   @anaconda
ModemManager.x86_64          1.6.0-2.el7                    @anaconda
ModemManager-glib.x86_64 1.6.0-2.el7                       @anaconda
NetworkManager.x86_64       1:1.8.0-9.el7                   @anaconda
NetworkManager-adsl.x86_641:1.8.0-9.el7                     @anaconda
NetworkManager-glib.x86_64 1:1.8.0-9.el7                    @anaconda
NetworkManager-libnm.x86_641:1.8.0-9.el7                    @anaconda
NetworkManager-libreswan.x86_64 1.2.4-2.el7                     @anaconda
NetworkManager-libreswan-gnome.x86_64 1.2.4-2.el7                @anaconda
NetworkManager-ppp.x86_64   1:1.8.0-9.el7                   @anaconda
NetworkManager-team.x86_64 1:1.8.0-9.el7                    @anaconda
NetworkManager-tui.x86_64   1:1.8.0-9.el7                   @anaconda
NetworkManager-wifi.x86_64 1:1.8.0-9.el7                    @anaconda
PackageKit.x86_64           1.1.5-1.el7.centos             @anaconda
PackageKit-command-not-found.x86_64 1.1.5-1.el7.centos         @anaconda
PackageKit-glib.x86_64      1.1.5-1.el7.centos             @anaconda
PackageKit-gstreamer-plugin.x86_64  1.1.5-1.el7.centos         @anaconda
```

From the output, the packages are displayed by package name, package version, and installer. We can also view packages in a group format. For this, we use the `grouplist` option:

```
[philip@localhost ~]$ yum grouplist
Loaded plugins: fastestmirror, langpacks
There is no installed groups file.
Maybe run: yum groups mark convert (see man yum)
Loading mirror speeds from cached hostfile
 * base: centos.mirror.iweb.ca
 * extras: centos.mirror.iweb.ca
 * updates: centos.mirror.iweb.ca
Available Environment Groups:
     Minimal Install
     Compute Node
     Infrastructure Server
     File and Print Server
     Basic Web Server
     Virtualization Host
     Server with GUI
     GNOME Desktop
      KDE Plasma Workspaces
     Development and Creative Workstation
```

```
Available Groups:
    Compatibility Libraries
    Console Internet Tools
    Development Tools
    Graphical Administration Tools
    Legacy UNIX Compatibility
    Scientific Support
    Security Tools
    Smart Card Support
    System Administration Tools
    System Management
Done
[philip@localhost ~]$
```

Great! To view information about a particular package, we can use the `info` option:

```
[philip@localhost ~]$ yum info firefox
Installed Packages
Name        : firefox
Arch        : x86_64
Version     : 52.2.0
Release     : 2.el7.centos
Size        : 149 M
Repo        : installed
From repo   : anaconda
Summary     : Mozilla Firefox Web browser
URL         : http://www.mozilla.org/projects/firefox/
License     : MPLv1.1 or GPLv2+ or LGPLv2+
Description : Mozilla Firefox is an open-source web browser, designed for
standards
            : compliance, performance and portability.
Available Packages
Name        : firefox
Arch        : i686
Version     : 60.1.0
Name        : firefox
Arch        : x86_64
Version     : 60.1.0
Description : Mozilla Firefox is an open-source web browser, designed for
standards
            : compliance, performance and portability.
[philip@localhost ~]$
```

From the preceding output, there is a lot of useful information pertaining to the package.

We can identify a package for a file by using the `provides` option:

```
[philip@localhost ~]$ yum provides /etc/my.cnf
Loaded plugins: fastestmirror, langpacks
1:mariadb-libs-5.5.56-2.el7.i686 : The shared libraries required for
MariaDB/MySQL clients
Repo        : base
Matched from:
Filename    : /etc/my.cnf
1:mariadb-libs-5.5.56-2.el7.x86_64 : The shared libraries required for
MariaDB/MySQL clients
Repo        : base
Matched from:
Filename    : /etc/my.cnf
1:mariadb-libs-5.5.56-2.el7.x86_64 : The shared libraries required for
MariaDB/MySQL clients
Repo        : @anaconda
Matched from:
Filename    : /etc/my.cnf
[philip@localhost ~]$
```

Based on the output, it is clear that /etc/my.cnf belongs to mariadb-libs-5.5.56-2.el7.x86_64. We can also search for a package by using the search option:

```
[philip@localhost ~]$ yum search gedit
Loaded plugins: fastestmirror, langpacks
 * updates: centos.mirror.iweb.ca
=================================================================== N/S
matched: gedit
=================================================================
gedit-devel.i686 : Support for developing plugins for the gedit text editor
gedit-devel.x86_64 : Support for developing plugins for the gedit text
editor
gedit-plugins-data.x86_64 : Common data required by plugins
Name and summary matches only, use "search all" for everything.
[philip@localhost ~]$
```

Now to update our system, we first use the `clean all` option:

You need root privilege before doing package maintenance.

```
[root@localhost philip]# yum clean all
Loaded plugins: fastestmirror, langpacks
```

```
Repodata is over 2 weeks old. Install yum-cron? Or run: yum makecache fast
Cleaning repos: base extras updates
Cleaning up everything
Cleaning up list of fastest mirrors
[root@localhost philip]#
```

Next, we use the `check-update` option:

```
[root@localhost philip]# yum check-update
Loaded plugins: fastestmirror, langpacks
http://ftp.hosteurope.de/mirror/centos.org/7/os/x86_64/repodata/repomd.xml:
[Errno 14] curl#6 - "Could not resolve host: ftp.hosteurope.de; Name or
service not known"
Trying other mirror.
base
| 3.6 kB   00:00:00
extras
| 3.4 kB   00:00:00
updates
| 3.4 kB   00:00:00
(1/4): base/7/x86_64/group_gz
| 166 kB   00:00:09
(2/4): extras/7/x86_64/primary_db
| 172 kB   00:00:08
(3/4): updates/7/x86_64/primary_db
| 4.3 MB   00:00:14
(4/4): base/7/x86_64/primary_db
| 5.9 MB   00:00:16
Determining fastest mirrors
 * base: mirror.us.leaseweb.net
 * extras: mirror.us.leaseweb.net
 * updates: mirror.us.leaseweb.net
ModemManager.x86_64
1.6.10-1.el7                    base      accountsservice.x86_64
0.6.45-7.el7                    base      accountsservice-libs.x86_64
0.6.45-7.el7                    base      acl.x86_64
2.2.51-14.el7                   base      attr.x86_64
2.4.46-13.el7                   base      avahi-gobject.x86_64
0.6.31-19.el7                   base      avahi-libs.x86_64
0.6.31-19.el7                   base      yum.noarch
3.4.3-158.el7.centos            base      yum-plugin-fastestmirror.noarch
1.1.31-45.el7                   base      yum-utils.noarch
1.1.31-45.el7                   base      Obsoleting Packages grub2.x86_64
1:2.02-0.65.el7.centos.2        base      grub2-tools.x86_64
1:2.02-0.64.el7.centos          @anaconda grub2-tools-minimal.x86_64
1:2.02-0.65.el7.centos.2        base
[root@localhost philip]#
```

Some output has been omitted for brevity. We can also install a package by using the `install` option:

```
[root@localhost philip]# yum install talk.x86_64
Loaded plugins: fastestmirror, langpacks
* updates: mirror.us.leaseweb.net
Resolving Dependencies
--> Running transaction check
Dependencies Resolved
================================================================
Package        Arch      Version      Repository   Size
================================================================
Installing:
talk           x86_64    0.17-46.el7     base      24 k
Transaction Summary
================================================================
Install  1 Package
Total download size: 24 k
Installed size: 31 k
Is this ok [y/d/N]: y
Downloading packages:
talk-0.17-46.el7.x86_64.rpm
|  24 kB  00:00:04
Running transaction check
Running transaction test
Transaction test succeeded
Running transaction
Installing : talk-0.17-46.el7.x86_64
1/1
Verifying  : talk-0.17-46.el7.x86_64
1/1
Installed:
 talk.x86_64 0:0.17-46.el7
Complete!
[root@localhost philip]#
```

Awesome! We can also remove a package in the reverse order. To do this, we use the `remove` option:

```
[root@localhost philip]# yum remove talk.x86_64
Loaded plugins: fastestmirror, langpacks
Resolving Dependencies
--> Running transaction check
---> Package talk.x86_64 0:0.17-46.el7 will be erased
--> Finished Dependency Resolution
Dependencies Resolved
================================================================
Package         Arch      Version    Repository    Size
```

```
========================================================================
Removing:
talk          x86_64  0.17-46.el7     @base       31 k
Transaction Summary
========================================================================
Remove  1 Package
Installed size: 31 k
Is this ok [y/N]: y
Downloading packages:
Transaction test succeeded
Running transaction
Erasing    : talk-0.17-46.el7.x86_64
1/1
Verifying  : talk-0.17-46.el7.x86_64
1/1
Removed:
talk.x86_64 0:0.17-46.el7
Complete!
[root@localhost philip]#
```

If, for some reason, we want to update all packages on the system, we use the update option:

```
[root@localhost philip]# yum update
Loaded plugins: fastestmirror, langpacks
Loading mirror speeds from cached hostfile
 * base: mirror.us.leaseweb.net
 * extras: mirror.us.leaseweb.net
 * updates: mirror.us.leaseweb.net
Resolving Dependencies
---> Package python-gobject.x86_64 0:3.22.0-1.el7_4.1 will be an update
---> Package python-gobject-base.x86_64 0:3.22.0-1.el7 will be updated
---> Package python-libs.x86_64 0:2.7.5-58.el7 will be updated
---> Package python-libs.x86_64 0:2.7.5-69.el7_5 will be an update
---> Package python-netaddr.noarch 0:0.7.5-7.el7 will be updated
libwayland-server x86_64 1.14.0-2.el7 base 38 k
unbound-libs x86_64 1.6.6-1.el7 base 405 k
volume_key-libs x86_64 0.3.9-8.el7 base 140 k
Transaction Summary
========================================================================
========================================================================
Install 6 Packages (+20 Dependent packages)
Upgrade 586 Packages
Total download size: 691 M
Is this ok [y/d/N]: y
```

Finally, we can view the YUM repo by passing the `repolist` option:

```
[root@localhost philip]# yum repolist
Loaded plugins: fastestmirror, langpacks
Loading mirror speeds from cached hostfile
 * base: mirror.us.leaseweb.net
repo id              repo name            status
base/7/x86_64       CentOS-7 - Base      9,911
extras/7/x86_64     CentOS-7 - Extras    363
updates/7/x86_64    CentOS-7 - Updates   1,004
repolist: 11,278
[root@localhost philip]#
```

DNF

Dandified YUM or DNF is the name of the package management utility. DNF is the next-generation version of YUM. It's used in RPM-based distributions. DNF was introduced in Fedora 18, and has been the default package manager for Fedora since version 22. In fact, when we run YUM commands in later releases of Fedora, we are actually running `dnf` in the background. The `dnf` utility offers, among other things, performance, memory usages, and dependency resolution.

To get started, we can check the version of `dnf` on our Fedora 28 system by using the `--version` option:

```
[root@localhost philip]# dnf --version
2.7.5
Installed: dnf-0:2.7.5-12.fc28.noarch at Wed 25 Apr 2018 06:35:34 AM GMT
Built    : Fedora Project at Wed 18 Apr 2018 02:29:51 PM GMT
Installed: rpm-0:4.14.1-7.fc28.x86_64 at Wed 25 Apr 2018 06:34:14 AM GMT
Built    : Fedora Project at Mon 19 Feb 2018 09:29:01 AM GMT
[root@localhost philip]#
```

Based on the preceding output, we have version 2.7.5 of the `dnf` utility installed. We can even view the repositories on our system by passing the `repolist` option:

```
[root@localhost philip]# dnf repolist
Last metadata expiration check: 0:01:09 ago on Tue 31 Jul 2018 03:10:57 PM
EDT.
repo id      repo name                     status
*fedora      Fedora 28 - x86_64            57,327
*updates     Fedora 28 - x86_64 - Updates  16,337
[root@localhost philip]#
```

In addition to this, we can even expose the YUM command in Fedora 28 to prove that it is an alias to the dnf utility. We can do a listing of /usr/bin and search for YUM as follows:

```
[root@localhost philip]# ll /usr/bin | grep yum
lrwxrwxrwx. 1 root root              5 Apr 18 10:29 yum -> dnf-3
[root@localhost philip]#
```

Based on the preceding output, YUM is an alias inside the Fedora 28 system. We can also check to see whether repositories are enabled or not. For this, we use the repolist all option:

```
[root@localhost philip]# dnf repolist all
```

Once we run the preceding command, we get the following output:

Now, to view all the available packages on our system, we use the `list` option:

```
[root@localhost philip]# dnf list
Last metadata expiration check: 0:06:37 ago on Tue 31 Jul 2018 03:10:57 PM
EDT.
Installed Packages
GConf2.x86_64                3.2.6-20.fc28              @anaconda
GeoIP.x86_64                 1.6.12-3.fc28             @anaconda
GeoIP-GeoLite-data.noarch 2018.04-1.fc28              @anaconda
ImageMagick.x86_64          1:6.9.9.38-1.fc28         @anaconda
ImageMagick-libs.x86_64     1:6.9.9.38-1.fc28         @anaconda
LibRaw.x86_64               0.18.8-1.fc28             @anaconda
ModemManager.x86_64         1.6.12-3.fc28             @anaconda
ModemManager-glib.x86_64    1.6.12-3.fc28             @anaconda
NetworkManager.x86_64       1:1.10.6-1.fc28           @anaconda
NetworkManager-adsl.x86_64 1:1.10.6-1.fc28            @anaconda
NetworkManager-bluetooth.x86_64 1:1.10.6-1.fc28              @anaconda
NetworkManager-config-connectivity-fedora.noarch  1:1.10.6-1.fc28
@anaconda
NetworkManager-libnm.x86_64 1:1.10.6-1.fc28 @anaconda
NetworkManager-openconnect.x86_64 1.2.4-9.fc28                @anaconda
NetworkManager-openconnect-gnome.x86_64  1.2.4-9.fc28
@anaconda
zziplib-utils.x86_64
0.13.68-1.fc28 fedora
zzuf.x86_64 0.15-5.fc28  fedora
[root@localhost philip]#
```

We can perform searches similar to YUM. For this, we use the `search` option:

```
[root@localhost philip]# dnf search firefox
Last metadata expiration check: 0:11:22 ago on Tue 31 Jul 2018 03:10:57 PM
EDT.
============================================ Summary & Name Matched:
firefox ==============================================
firefox.x86_64 : Mozilla Firefox Web browser
============================================== Summary Matched: firefox
==============================================
icecat.x86_64 : GNU version of Firefox browser
mozilla-ublock-origin.noarch : An efficient blocker for Firefox
mozilla-https-everywhere.noarch : HTTPS enforcement extension for Mozilla
Firefox
mozilla-requestpolicy.noarch : Firefox and Seamonkey extension that gives
you control over cross-site requests
python-mozrunner.noarch : Reliable start/stop/configuration of Mozilla
Applications (Firefox, Thunderbird)
[root@localhost philip]#
```

Awesome! Furthermore, to view which package provides a particular utility, we use the `provides` option:

```
[root@localhost philip]# dnf provides /bin/ksh
Last metadata expiration check: 0:14:22 ago on Tue 31 Jul 2018 03:10:57 PM
EDT.
ksh-20120801-247.fc28.x86_64 : The Original ATT Korn Shell
Repo        : updates
Matched from:
Provide     : /bin/ksh
ksh-20120801-245.fc28.x86_64 : The Original ATT Korn Shell
Repo        : fedora
Matched from:
Provide     : /bin/ksh
[root@localhost philip]#
```

In addition to this, we can view information for a specific package using the `info` option:

```
root@localhost philip]# dnf info libreoffice
Available Packages
Name        : libreoffice
Epoch       : 1
Version     : 6.0.6.1
Summary     : Free Software Productivity Suite
URL         : http://www.libreoffice.org/
License     : (MPLv1.1 or LGPLv3+) and LGPLv3 and LGPLv2+ and BSD and
(MPLv1.1 or GPLv2 or LGPLv2 or Netscape) and Public
            : Domain and ASL 2.0 and MPLv2.0 and CC0
Description : LibreOffice is an Open Source, community-developed, office
productivity suite.
            : It includes the key desktop applications, such as a word
processor,
            : spreadsheet, presentation manager, formula editor and
drawing program, with a
            : user interface and feature set similar to other office
suites.  Sophisticated
            : and flexible, LibreOffice also works transparently with a
variety of file
            : formats, including Microsoft Office File Formats.
[root@localhost philip]#
```

Based on the preceding screenshot, we can see a lot of useful information for a given package. We can also check for system updates by using the `check-update` option:

```
[root@localhost philip]# dnf check-update
Last metadata expiration check: 0:18:17 ago on Tue 31 Jul 2018 03:10:57 PM
EDT.
GeoIP-GeoLite-data.noarch
```

```
2018.06-1.fc28                          updates
LibRaw.x86_64
0.18.13-1.fc28                          updates
rkManager-openvpn.x86_64                1:1.8.4-1.fc28
updates
NetworkManager-openvpn-gnome.x86_64
1:1.8.4-1.fc28                          updates
grub2-tools-extra.x86_64
1:2.02-38.fc28                          updates
grub2-tools.x86_64                      1:2.02-34.fc28
@anaconda
grub2-tools-minimal.x86_64
1:2.02-38.fc28                          updates
grub2-tools.x86_64                      1:2.02-34.fc28
@anaconda
kernel-headers.x86_64
4.17.9-200.fc28                         updates
kernel-headers.x86_64                   4.16.3-301.fc28
@anaconda
[root@localhost philip]#
```

To install a package, we use the `install` option:

```
[root@localhost philip]# dnf install BitchX.x86_64
Last metadata expiration check: 0:20:30 ago on Tue 31 Jul 2018 03:10:57 PM
EDT.
Dependencies resolved.
================================================================================
==================================================
Package                    Arch                     Version
Repository                 Size
================================================================================
==================================================
Installing:
BitchX                     x86_64                   1.2.1-15.fc28
fedora                     1.6 M
Transaction Summary
================================================================================
==================================================
Install  1 Package
Total download size: 1.6 M
Installed size: 3.3 M
Is this ok [y/N]: y
Installed:
  BitchX.x86_64 1.2.1-15.fc28
Complete!
[root@localhost philip]#
```

Great job! As you will be able to see by now, the options are similar to their older YUM counterparts. Similarly, to remove a package, we use the `remove` option:

```
[root@localhost philip]# dnf remove BitchX.x86_64
Dependencies resolved.
================================================================================
===============================================
Package Arch Version Repository Size
================================================================================
===============================================
Removing:
BitchX x86_64 1.2.1-15.fc28 @fedora 3.3 M
Transaction Summary
================================================================================
===============================================
Remove 1 Package
Freed space: 3.3 M
Is this ok [y/N]: y
Running transaction check
Preparing : 1/1
Erasing : BitchX-1.2.1-15.fc28.x86_64 1/1
Verifying : BitchX-1.2.1-15.fc28.x86_64 1/1
Removed:
BitchX.x8
6_64 1.2.1-15.fc28
Complete!
[root@localhost philip]#
```

We can also remove packages that were only needed to satisfy dependencies. To do so, we use the `autoremove` option:

```
[root@localhost philip]# dnf autoremove
Last metadata expiration check: 0:25:12 ago on Tue 31 Jul 2018 03:10:57 PM
EDT.
Dependencies resolved.
Nothing to do.
Complete!
[root@localhost philip]#
```

If we would like to see the various `dnf` commands that were executed, we can use the `history` option:

```
[root@localhost philip]# dnf history
ID     | Command line           | Date and time   | Action(s)        |
Altered
--------------------------------------------------------------------------------
----
```

```
3 | remove BitchX.x86_64        | 2018-07-31 15:33 | Erase    |    1
2 | install BitchX.x86_64       | 2018-07-31 15:31 | Install  |    1
1 |                             | 2018-04-25 02:33 | Install  | 1596 EE
[root@localhost philip]#
```

This is very useful when we're trying to track what has changed in our system. Before we perform any updates to our system, it's always a good idea to do some housekeeping. We can use the `clean all` option for this:

```
[root@localhost philip]# dnf clean all
18 files removed
[root@localhost philip]#
```

Finally, to update all packages on the system, we use the `update` option:

```
[root@localhost philip]# dnf update
Last metadata expiration check: 0:11:49 ago on Tue 31 Jul 2018 03:48:23 PM
EDT.
Dependencies resolved.
================================================================================
================================================
Package                                       Arch          Version
Repository      Size
================================================================================
================================================
Upgrading:
GeoIP-GeoLite-data    noarch 2018.06-1.fc28                      updates
551 k
LibRaw          x86_64        0.18.13-1.fc28                      updates
libkcapi        x86_64        1.1.1-6.fc28
updates         44 k
libkcapi-hmaccalc         x86_64        1.1.1-6.fc28
updates         26 k
libnice         x86_64        0.1.14-7.20180504git34d6044.fc28
updates         173 k
libvirt-daemon-config-network    x86_64        4.1.0-3.fc28
updates         10 k
rpm-sign-libs   x86_64        4.14.1-9.fc28                       updates
73 k
xmlsec1-nss     x86_64        1.2.25-4.fc28                       updates
79 k
Transaction Summary
================================================================================
================================================
Install    11 Packages
Upgrade   736 Packages
Total download size: 1.0 G
Is this ok [y/N]: y
```

We can also pass the `upgrade` option, which is newer:

```
[root@localhost philip]# dnf upgrade
Last metadata expiration check: 0:11:49 ago on Tue 31 Jul 2018 03:48:23 PM
EDT.
Dependencies resolved.
================================================================================
================================================================
Package                                         Arch          Version
Repository      Size
================================================================================
================================================================
Upgrading:
GeoIP-GeoLite-data                              noarch        2018.06-1.fc28
updates        551 k
LibRaw                                          x86_64        0.18.13-1.fc28
updates
libkcapi                                        x86_64        1.1.1-6.fc28
updates         44 k
libkcapi-hmaccalc                               x86_64        1.1.1-6.fc28
updates         26 k
libnice                                         x86_64
0.1.14-7.20180504git34d6044.fc28         updates        173 k
libvirt-daemon-config-network                   x86_64        4.1.0-3.fc28
updates         10 k
rpm-sign-libs                                   x86_64        4.14.1-9.fc28
updates         73 k
xmlsec1-nss                                     x86_64        1.2.25-4.fc28
updates         79 k
Transaction Summary
================================================================================
================================================================
Install   11 Packages
Upgrade   736 Packages
Total download size: 1.0 G
Is this ok [y/N]: y
```

As we can see, the process is identical.

RPM

Red Hat Package Manager, also known as **RPM**, is a program for installing, uninstalling, and managing software packages in RPM-based Linux distributions. There are various utilities that make use of the rpm utility in the backend, such as yum and dnf, to name two. This is similar in nature to its counterpart, the dpkg utility. Whenever there are dependency requirements, you usually have to go out and manually find the necessary files in order to install them. The packages that rpm manages all end with an rpm extension.

To begin with, we can check for an rpm signature against a package, and we will use the --checksig option:

```
[root@localhost Downloads]# rpm --checksig gnome-
calculator-3.22.3-1.el7.x86_64.rpm
gnome-calculator-3.22.3-1.el7.x86_64.rpm: rsa sha1 (md5) pgp md5 OK
[root@localhost Downloads]#
```

Based on the preceding output, the signatures have passed the checks using the rpm utility. We can also check for dependencies for a particular package. We use the qpR options for this:

```
[root@localhost Downloads]# rpm -qpR gnome-
calculator-3.22.3-1.el7.x86_64.rpm
/bin/sh
/bin/sh
libatk-1.0.so.0()(64bit)
libc.so.6()(64bit)
libc.so.6(GLIBC_2.14)(64bit)
libc.so.6(GLIBC_2.2.5)(64bit)
libc.so.6(GLIBC_2.3.4)(64bit)
libgmp.so.10()(64bit)
rtld(GNU_HASH)
rpmlib(PayloadIsXz) <= 5.2-1
[root@localhost Downloads]#
```

Note that q means to query, p means to list the capabilities the package provides, and R means to list the capabilities on which the package depends.

In order to view all packages which were recently installed, we can use qa in combination with --last:

```
[root@localhost Downloads]# rpm -qa --last
gpg-pubkey-f4a80eb5-53a7ff4b                    Tue 31 Jul 2018 08:30:07 AM
PDT
words-3.0-22.el7.noarch                         Wed 20 Jun 2018 09:29:01 AM
PDT
```

```
iwl6000-firmware-9.221.4.1-56.el7.noarch       Wed 20 Jun 2018 09:29:01 AM
PDT
iwl6050-firmware-41.28.5.1-56.el7.noarch       Wed 20 Jun 2018 09:29:00 AM
PDT
iwl6000g2b-firmware-17.168.5.2-56.el7.noarch   Wed 20 Jun 2018 09:29:00 AM
PDT
iwl4965-firmware-228.61.2.24-56.el7.noarch     Wed 20 Jun 2018 09:29:00 AM
PDT
iwl3945-firmware-15.32.2.9-56.el7.noarch       Wed 20 Jun 2018 09:29:00 AM
PDT
iwl100-firmware-39.31.5.1-56.el7.noarch        Wed 20 Jun 2018 09:29:00 AM
PDT
iwl7265-firmware-22.0.7.0-56.el7.noarch        Wed 20 Jun 2018 09:28:59 AM
PDT
fontpackages-filesystem-1.44-8.el7.noarch      Wed 20 Jun 2018 09:15:44 AM
PDT
centos-release-7-4.1708.el7.centos.x86_64      Wed 20 Jun 2018 09:15:44 AM
PDT
[root@localhost Downloads]#
```

We can also search for a specific package by passing the package name:

```
[root@localhost Downloads]# rpm -qa ntp
ntp-4.2.6p5-25.el7.centos.2.x86_64
[root@localhost Downloads]#
```

In this case, we search for the `ntp` package. We can get more information about a particular package. We can pass the `qi` options:

```
[root@localhost Downloads]# rpm -qi ntp
Name : ntp
Version : 4.2.6p5
Vendor : CentOS
URL : http://www.ntp.org
Summary : The NTP daemon and utilities
Description :
The Network Time Protocol (NTP) is used to synchronize a computer's
time with another reference time source. This package includes ntpd
(a daemon which continuously adjusts system time) and utilities used
to query and configure the ntpd daemon.
 [root@localhost Downloads]#
```

Interestingly, before we install a package, we can actually get information on the said package and then make a decision as to whether to abort or continue installation:

```
[root@localhost Downloads]# rpm -qa gnome-calculator
gnome-calculator-3.22.3-1.el7.x86_64
[root@localhost Downloads]# rpm -e gnome-calculator
[root@localhost Downloads]# rpm -qa gnome-calculator
[root@localhost Downloads]#
```

We queried for the GNOME calculator because it came preinstalled in this CentOS 7 system. We then removed the package and queried once again. Now we'll pass qip on the rpm package, which we downloaded as follows:

```
[root@localhost Downloads]# rpm -qip gnome-
calculator-3.22.3-1.el7.x86_64.rpm
Name        : gnome-calculator
Version     : 3.22.3
Release     : 1.el7
Architecture: x86_64
Install Date: (not installed)
Group       : Unspecified
Size        : 5053847
Summary     : A desktop calculator
Description :
gnome-calculator is a powerful graphical calculator with financial,
logical and scientific modes. It uses a multiple precision package
to do its arithmetic to give a high degree of accuracy.
[root@localhost Downloads]#
```

And voila! As we can see, the rpm utility is very powerful. To install a package, we use the -i or --install options:

```
[root@localhost Downloads]# rpm --install gnome-
calculator-3.22.3-1.el7.x86_64.rpm
  [root@localhost Downloads]# rpm -qa  gnome-calculator
gnome-calculator-3.22.3-1.el7.x86_64
[root@localhost Downloads]#
```

From the preceding output, we can see that our package was successfully installed using the rpm utility.

We can view all of the files for a particular package:

```
[root@localhost Downloads]# rpm -ql gnome-calculator
/usr/bin/gcalccmd
/usr/bin/gnome-calculator
/usr/lib64/gnome-calculator
/usr/share/applications/gnome-calculator.desktop
/usr/share/man/man1/gnome-calculator.1.gz
[root@localhost Downloads]#
```

Likewise, we can remove a package by passing the -e option. We can also view the process of removing a package by adding the -v option:

```
[root@localhost Downloads]# rpm -ev gnome-calculator
Preparing packages...
gnome-calculator-3.22.3-1.el7.x86_64
[root@localhost Downloads]#
```

Awesome! Finally, we can determine which package a particular configuration file belongs to using the -qf option:

```
[root@localhost Downloads]#  rpm -qf /etc/rsyslog.conf
rsyslog-8.24.0-12.el7.x86_64
[root@localhost Downloads]#
```

yumex

YUM extender, or **yumex** for short, is a frontend to the yum and dnf utilities. By default, yumex does not come preinstalled with Fedora 28. This can easily be addressed by installing the yumex utility at the shell:

```
[root@localhost philip]# dnf install yumex-dnf
Last metadata expiration check: 0:01:38 ago on Thu 02 Aug 2018 10:30:42 AM
EDT.
Dependencies resolved.
================================================================================
================================================
 Package                              Arch         Version
 Repository      Size
================================================================================
================================================
Installing:
dnfdragora                           noarch
 1.0.1-10.git20180108.b0e8a66.fc28      fedora         364 k
Installing dependencies:
```

```
checkpolicy                                 x86_64           2.8-1.fc28
updates            336 k
dnfdaemon                                   noarch           0.3.18-6.fc28
fedora              64 k
python3-dnfdaemon                           noarch           0.3.18-6.fc28
fedora              23 k
python3-libsemanage                         x86_64           2.7-12.fc28
fedora             125 k
Transaction Summary
================================================================================
================================================
Install  23 Packages
Total download size: 5.6 M
Installed size: 17 M
Is this ok [y/N]: y
```

As you can see, installing yumex on Fedora 28 is fairly simple. For CentOS 7, we first install the **Extra Packages for Enterprise Linux** (EPEL):

```
[root@localhost philip]# yum install epel-release
Loaded plugins: fastestmirror, langpacks
Loading mirror speeds from cached hostfile
 * base: mirror.as24220.net
 * extras: mirror.as24220.net
 * updates: mirror.as24220.net
Resolving Dependencies
--> Running transaction check
---> Package epel-release.noarch 0:7-11 will be installed
--> Finished Dependency Resolution
Dependencies Resolved
================================================================================
=====
Package                 Arch            Version          Repository
Size
================================================================================
=====
Installing:
epel-release            noarch          7-11             extras
15 k
Transaction Summary
================================================================================
=====
Install  1 Package
Total download size: 15 k
Installed size: 24 k
Is this ok [y/d/N]: y
Downloading packages:
epel-release-7-11.noarch.rpm                                    |  15 kB   00:03
```

```
Installing : epel-release-7-11.noarch
1/1
Verifying  : epel-release-7-11.noarch
1/1
Installed:
epel-release.noarch 0:7-11
Complete!
[root@localhost philip]#
```

Next, we install the actual yumex utility:

```
[root@localhost philip]# yum install yumex
Loaded plugins: fastestmirror, langpacks
epel/x86_64/metalink | 4.0 kB 00:00
epel | 3.2 kB 00:00
(1/3): epel/x86_64/group_gz | 88 kB 00:01
(2/3): epel/x86_64/updateinfo | 927 kB 00:02
(3/3): epel/x86_64/primary | 3.6 MB 00:00:16
Loading mirror speeds from cached hostfile
 * base: mirror.as24220.net
.net
epel 12639/12639
Resolving Dependencies
--> Running transaction check
---> Package yumex.noarch 0:3.0.17-1.el7 will be installed
--> Processing Dependency: pexpect for package: yumex-3.0.17-1.el7.noarch
---> Package python2-pyxdg.noarch 0:0.25-6.el7 will be installed
--> Finished Dependency Resolution
Dependencies Resolved
============
Package Arch Version Repository Size
===========
Installing:
yumex noarch 3.0.17-1.el7 epel 444 k
Installing for dependencies:
pexpect noarch 2.3-11.el7 base 142 k
python2-pyxdg noarch 0.25-6.el7 epel 89 k
Transaction Summary
=======================================================================
=======================================================================
Install 1 Package (+2 Dependent packages)
Total download size: 675 k
Installed size: 2.7 M
Is this ok [y/d/N]: y
Downloading packages:
warning: /var/cache/yum/x86_64/7/epel/packages/python2-
pyxdg-0.25-6.el7.noarch.rpm: Header V3 RSA/SHA256 Signature, key ID
352c64e5: NOKEY-:--:-- ETA
```

```
---------------------------------------------------------------
---------------------------------------------------------------
Total 167 kB/s | 675 kB 00:00:04
Retrieving key from file:///etc/pki/rpm-gpg/RPM-GPG-KEY-EPEL-7
Importing GPG key 0x352C64E5:
Userid : "Fedora EPEL (7) <epel@fedoraproject.org>"
Fingerprint: 91e9 7d7c 4a5e 96f1 7f3e 888f 6a2f aea2 352c 64e5
 Package : epel-release-7-11.noarch (@extras)
 From : /etc/pki/rpm-gpg/RPM-GPG-KEY-EPEL-7
Is this ok [y/N]: y
Transaction test succeeded
Running transaction
  Installing : yumex-3.0.17-1.el7.noarch 3/3
warning: /etc/yumex.conf created as /etc/yumex.conf.rpmnew
  Verifying : yumex-3.0.17-1.el7.noarch 1/3
  Verifying : pexpect-2.3-11.el7.noarch 3/3
Installed:
  yumex.noarch 0:3.0.17-1.el7
Dependency Installed:
pexpect.noarch 0:2.3-11.el7 python2-pyxdg.noarch 0:0.25-6.el7
Complete!
[root@localhost philip]#
```

The steps illustrated for installing yumex on CentOS 7 are fairly similar to those for Fedora 28. Finally, we can launch the yumex utility either at the shell or via the GUI. We'll demonstrate the shell method:

```
[root@localhost philip]# yumex &
[1] 2884
[root@localhost philip]# Don't run yumex as root it is unsafe (Use --root
to force)
```

From the preceding output, there is a clear indication that we should not run the yumex utility as a root. Instead, we'll run the yumex utility as a non-root user:

```
root@localhost philip]# exit
exit
[philip@localhost ~]$ yumex &
[1] 2937
[philip@localhost ~]$ 07:48:33 : INFO - Using config file :
/home/philip/.config/yumex/yumex.conf
07:48:33 : INFO - Using config file : /home/philip/.config/yumex/yumex.conf
(<class 'dbus.exceptions.DBusException'>, DBusException('Rejected send
message, 2 matched rules; type="method_call", sender=":1.115" (uid=1000
pid=2937 comm="/usr/bin/python -tt /usr/bin/yumex ") interface="(unset)"
member="GetDevices" error name="(unset)" requested_reply="0"
destination=":1.8" (uid=0 pid=633 comm="/usr/sbin/NetworkManager --no-
daemon ")',), <traceback object at 0x2ac5ef0>)
```

```
(<class 'dbus.exceptions.DBusException'>, DBusException('Rejected send
message, 2 matched rules; type="method_call", sender=":1.115" (uid=1000
pid=2937 comm="/usr/bin/python -tt /usr/bin/yumex ") interface="(unset)"
member="GetDevices" error name="(unset)" requested_reply="0"
destination=":1.8" (uid=0 pid=633 comm="/usr/sbin/NetworkManager --no-
daemon ")',), <traceback object at 0x2ac6ef0>)
```

Once we run the preceding commands, we get the following screen:

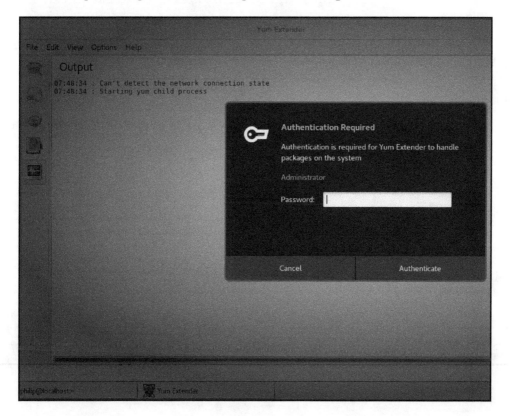

Ironically, we're being prompted for the root password—yes, it may seem confusing for some, but not us. This is because we started the `yumex` utility as a non-root user. For the `yumex` utility to run, we need root privileges. This is because it manages packages. A non-root user is unable to manage packages by default. So, we'll authenticate and then we will be greeted with the `nifty yumex` utility:

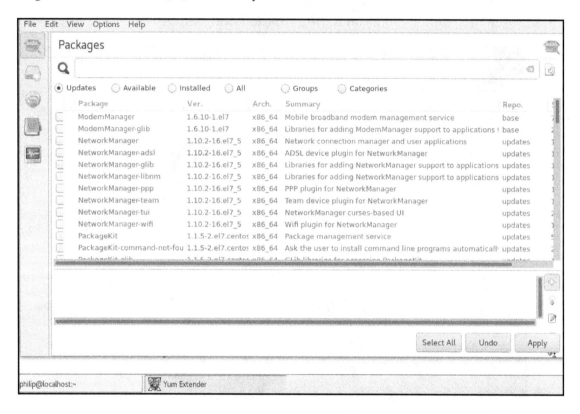

We notice right off the bat that we have a nice user-friendly GUI with which we can work. There is a menu bar at the top and a search field for finding a particular package. We simply type the name of a package, for instance:

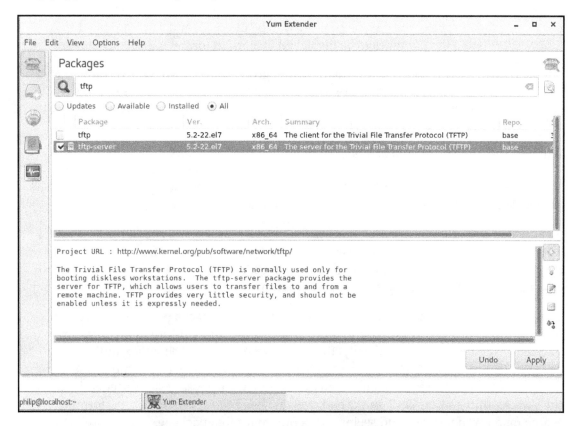

Awesome! We get a nice description for a given package, we can select the checkbox and then click **Apply**, and the package will be installed.

Summary

In this chapter, we really dived deep into package management within the Red Hat world; particularly, the yum, dnf, rpm, and yumex utilities. We first covered yum and viewed the packages available; next, the yum cache needed to be updated, and so we updated it. After that, we formatted the packages to be displayed in a group format.

Following this, we exposed the information for a given package. We then did some reverse engineering by selecting a file and discovering which package it came from. This was followed by demonstrating the steps to searching for a package. After this, we removed unneeded files before performing an update to the system.

Furthermore, we did a demo on installing a package, followed up on the flip side by illustrating the steps to remove a package. Finally, we performed a system update using YUM. We then covered the dnf utility and saw the similarities between dnf and yum. The Fedora 28 demo showed that yum is merely an alias to dnf.

Next, we looked at the method of viewing the repo list using dnf, and at the method for searching for a given package. Similar to yum, using a configuration file, we located the corresponding package for the configuration file. Ultimately a demo was done on how to add a package using yum. The reverse side of removing a package was also demonstrated.

Working with rpm, we saw how to check the signature of a package. Also, we exposed information for a given package, and there was an illustration for installing and removing a package using the rpm utility. Finally, the focus was on yumex. The yumex utility is a frontend to yum and dnf. It is not preinstalled by default. There was a demo on installing yumex in a Fedora 28 environment; likewise, we saw the necessary steps needed to install the yumex utility in CentOS 7. In the end, we navigated the yumex utility, performing a search for a given package and seeing a description for that package.

In the next chapter, we will work with various utilities in the shell. After reading this, you will be better prepared to navigate the filesystem, create files, directories, and so on. We will look at file permissions, viewing hidden files and directories, and performing searches inside the shell. The skill sets covered in the next chapter are essential for any Linux engineer to work efficiently in a command-line environment. You will be more confident with file management after completing the next chapter. This will enable you to conquer another milestone in your quest for certification.

Questions

1. Which option with the `yum` command is used to display the packages on the system?

   A. yum --display
   B. yum --list
   C. yum list
   D. yum --verbose

2. Which command is used to update `cache`?

   A. yum makecache fast
   B. yum cache --update
   C. yum –update --cache
   D. yum –make --list

3. Which command can be passed to identify a package from a configuration file?

   A. yum --get-information
   B. yum --display-information
   C. yum --provides
   D. yum provides

4. Which option is used to display packages that are installed with the `dpkg` command?

   A. dpkg --get-selections
   B. dpkg –set-selections
   C. dpkg –get-selection
   D. dpkg-query –get-selection

5. Which command is used to remove any `temp` files that are no longer needed?

   A. yum remove cache
   B. yum clean all
   C. yum clean temp
   D. yum remove temp

6. Which command is used to update the system?

   A. `yum update`
   B. `yum auto-update`
   C. `yum clean update`
   D. `yum purge update`

7. Which command is used to display both enabled and disabled repositories?

   A. `dnf --repo-list`
   B. `dnf repolist all`
   C. `dnf list repo`
   D. `dnf --repo-list --all`

8. Which command is used to check for updates?

   A. `dnf check-update`
   B. `dnf --update-check`
   C. `dnf --list-update`
   D. `dnf --get-list -updates`

9. Which command is used to expose information for a package before it is installed?

   A. `rpm -qa`
   B. `rpm -qic`
   C. `rpm -qip`
   D. `rpm -qe`

10. Which command is used to remove a package?

    A. `rpm --remove`
    B. `rpm --erase`
    C. `rpm --delete`
    D. `aptitude --purge`

Further reading

- You can get more info about the CentOS distributions such as installing, configuration best practices, and so on at `https://centos`.
- For more information about Fedora, to download a copy and get some hands-on experience, see `https://getfedora.org`.

Performing File Management

8

In the previous chapter, we dealt with package management within the Red Hat world. Particularly, we covered the `yum`, `dnf`, `rpm`, and `yumex` utilities.

In this chapter, our focus will shift toward file management. We will look at ways to work in the shell. We will work on creating, modifying, and removing files. Additionally, we will work with directories, illustrating how to create, move, and remove a directory. Next, we will touch upon performing searches for files and directories. Finally, we will cover pipes and redirects.

We will cover the following topics in this chapter:

- Viewing and moving files and directories in the CLI
- Creating, copying, moving, renaming, and removing files
- Creating and removing directories
- Finding files and directories
- Pipes and redirects

Viewing and moving files and directories in the CLI

First, you will need to be familiar with working in the CLI. Throughout the previous chapters, we interacted with the shell. Now we want to become efficient in the CLI. When we first open a Terminal, we are placed into the user's home directory, as follows:

```
[philip@localhost ~]$
```

In the preceding output, we're being placed into the home directory of the user `philip`. This can be confirmed by issuing the print working directory (`pwd`) command, as follows:

```
[philip@localhost ~]$ pwd
/home/philip
[philip@localhost ~]$
```

In the preceding output, we've confirmed that we are indeed in the `/home/philip` directory. However, it gets even more interesting. There are various directories inside of `/home/philip`. We can confirm this by using the list's (`ls`) command, as follows:

```
[philip@localhost ~]$ ls
Desktop   Documents   Downloads   Music   Pictures   Public   Templates   Videos
[philip@localhost ~]$
```

The directories (folders) listed in the preceding output are created for each user in the system. Now, the way in which the directories are displayed doesn't really tell us a lot. To dig deeper, we can issue the `ls` command once again; this time, we will pass the `-l` option. The `-l` option exposes things such as the file type, user permissions, group permissions, user ownership, group ownership, size, and date last modified, as follows:

```
[philip@localhost ~]$ ls -l
total 32
drwxr-xr-x. 2 philip philip 4096 Jul 31 14:59 Desktop
drwxr-xr-x. 2 philip philip 4096 Jul 31 14:59 Documents
drwxr-xr-x. 2 philip philip 4096 Jul 31 14:59 Downloads
drwxr-xr-x. 2 philip philip 4096 Jul 31 14:59 Music
drwxr-xr-x. 2 philip philip 4096 Jul 31 14:59 Pictures
drwxr-xr-x. 2 philip philip 4096 Jul 31 14:59 Public
drwxr-xr-x. 2 philip philip 4096 Jul 31 14:59 Templates
drwxr-xr-x. 2 philip philip 4096 Jul 31 14:59 Videos
[philip@localhost ~]$
```

We can get some useful information from the preceding output. For instance, there are permissions for each directory; we can also see the ownership and size. Adding to this, in Linux, we have what are known as hidden files/folders. They are not displayed by default when we perform a listing; to get them, we have to add on the `-a` option:

```
[philip@localhost ~]$ ls -al
drwx------. 15 philip philip 4096 Aug  2 10:28 .
drwxr-xr-x.  3 root   root   4096 Jul 31 14:58 ..
-rw-r--r--.  1 philip philip   18 Mar 15 09:56 .bash_logout
-rw-r--r--.  1 philip philip  193 Mar 15 09:56 .bash_profile
-rw-r--r--.  1 philip philip  231 Mar 15 09:56 .bashrc
drwx------. 14 philip philip 4096 Jul 31 14:59 .cache
drwx------. 14 philip philip 4096 Jul 31 14:59 .config
```

```
drwxr-xr-x.  2 philip philip 4096 Jul 31 14:59 Desktop
drwxr-xr-x.  2 philip philip 4096 Jul 31 14:59 Documents
drwxr-xr-x.  2 philip philip 4096 Jul 31 14:59 Downloads
-rw-------.  1 philip philip   16 Jul 31 14:58 .esd_auth
-rw-------.  1 philip philip  620 Aug  2 10:28 .ICEauthority
drwx------.  3 philip philip 4096 Jul 31 14:59 .local
drwxr-xr-x.  4 philip philip 4096 Apr 25 02:33 .mozilla
drwxr-xr-x.  2 philip philip 4096 Jul 31 14:59 Music
drwxr-xr-x.  2 philip philip 4096 Jul 31 14:59 Pictures
drwxrw----.  3 philip philip 4096 Jul 31 14:59 .pki
[philip@localhost ~]$
```

Awesome! This way, we can tell whether a file or directory is hidden; these files/directories begin with a period in front of the name of the file or folder. In order to move between directories, we use the cd command. Change directory or cd allows us to navigate the Linux filesystem. So, let's move on to /home/philip/Documents. Here, we use the following command:

```
[philip@localhost ~]$ cd /home/philip/Documents
[philip@localhost Documents]$
```

There is another way to move between directories. The first method that we used is known as the absolute path; this means that we specified the complete path to the directory. The next method for moving between the directories is specifying the relative path, as follows:

```
[philip@localhost ~]$ cd Documents/
[philip@localhost Documents]$
```

> You have to be in the parent directory of the child directory for the relative method to work.

Once we're in the child directory, we can perform the ls command, as follows:

```
[philip@localhost Documents]$ ls
[philip@localhost Documents]$
```

Currently, there is no content in this directory. In order to move back up to the parent directory, we can use the cd command, as follows:

```
[philip@localhost Documents]$ cd /home/philip
[philip@localhost ~]$ pwd
/home/philip
[philip@localhost ~]$
```

In the preceding output, we specified the path. This method will always work. We can also use the `cd` command in another manner, as follows:

```
[philip@localhost Documents]$ cd ..
[philip@localhost ~]$
```

In the preceding method, we used a double period. The double period indicates the parent directory. If we had specified a single period, the following would have been the outcome:

```
[philip@localhost Documents]$ cd .
[philip@localhost Documents]$
```

The single period references the current directory itself. The following method can be used in a directory, regardless of where you are:

```
[philip@localhost Documents]$ cd ~
[philip@localhost ~]$
```

The tilde (~) character will always bring us back to the `home` directory of the user. To illustrate this, we will go to the `/etc` directory as follows:

```
[philip@localhost ~]$ cd /etc
[philip@localhost etc]$ pwd
/etc
[philip@localhost etc]$
```

Now we will issue the `cd` command once again, passing the tilde (~):

```
[philip@localhost etc]$ cd ~
[philip@localhost ~]$ pwd
/home/philip
[philip@localhost ~]$
```

Awesome job! You can now see the power of the tilde (~) character. At the very top of the filesystem hierarchy lies the root. We usually refer to the root as /; this is not to be confused with the `/root` directory. The latter is the home directory of the root user. From the /, every other directory is created. We can get to the / as follows:

```
[philip@localhost ~]$ cd /
[philip@localhost /]$ pwd
/
[philip@localhost /]$
```

In the preceding output, we are placed at the root of the filesystem. We can view this directory in a similar way to the other directories, as follows:

```
[philip@localhost /]$ ls
bin   dev   home   lib64        media   opt    root   sbin   sys   usr
boot  etc   lib    lost+found   mnt     proc   run    srv    tmp   var
[philip@localhost /]$
```

You'll notice that we have some familiar directories here, such as /home and /dev. Interestingly, we can see the /root directory listed. We can change to that directory and perform a listing, as follows:

```
[philip@localhost /]$ cd /root
bash: cd: /root: Permission denied
[philip@localhost /]$
```

We got the preceding error due to the fact that we do not have permission to view the /root directory. Let's authenticate as the root user and retry, as follows:

```
[root@localhost /]# cd /root
[root@localhost ~]#
```

Voila! We are placed into the /root directory. This time, when we do a listing, we will notice right off the bat that this is not the / directory:

```
[root@localhost ~]# ls
anaconda-ks.cfg
[root@localhost ~]#
```

Based on the preceding output, navigating the directory structure is fairly intuitive.

Creating, copying, moving, renaming, and removing files

This section sounds like a mouthful. Not to worry; it covers the techniques for creating and removing files. It also covers the methods for copying and renaming files.

There are various files that we use on a daily basis. We can do an `ls` on the
`/home/philip/Documents/NewTest` directory, as follows:

```
philip@localhost Documents]$ cd NewTest/
[philip@localhost NewTest]$ ll -a
total 8
drwxrwxr-x. 2 philip philip 4096 Aug  6 12:04 .
drwxr-xr-x. 3 philip philip 4096 Aug  6 13:45 ..
[philip@localhost NewTest]$
```

Currently, there aren't any files inside of this directory. In Linux, we can create a file from
the shell; we can use the `touch` command to accomplish this:

```
[philip@localhost NewTest]$ touch OurFile
[philip@localhost NewTest]$ ll
total 0
-rw-rw-r--. 1 philip philip 0 Aug  6 13:52 OurFile
[philip@localhost NewTest]$
```

The file was created using some default permissions. Notably, the `-rw-rw-r--` object
stands for the user (`-rw`), the group (`-rw`), and the other (`-r--`). The first dash (`-`) is
referencing the file type. In this case, it's a regular file. The (`rw-`) means that the user/owner
has read and write permissions. The second set of `rw-` means that the group also has read
and execute permissions. Lastly, the `r--` means that the other (everyone else) has read
permissions. Also, the part which states `philip philip` refers to the owner of the file and
the group that the file belongs to. We can change the permissions for this file by using the
`chmod` command. Let's suppose that we want to give the others (everyone else) read and
write permissions. We can do so as follows:

```
[philip@localhost NewTest]$ chmod o+w OurFile
[philip@localhost NewTest]$ ll
total 0
-rw-rw-rw-. 1 philip philip 0 Aug  6 13:52 OurFile
[philip@localhost NewTest]$
```

Great! We can now see that the other permission says `rw-`. There is another way to change
the permissions, rather than using `o+w`. Instead, we can use the numerical value. I will
change the other back to `r--` by using the numerical format, as follows:

```
[philip@localhost NewTest]$ chmod 664 OurFile
[philip@localhost NewTest]$ ll
total 0
-rw-rw-r--. 1 philip philip 0 Aug  6 13:52 OurFile
[philip@localhost NewTest]$
```

We can read the preceding code as follows: in the 664, 6 is equal to read and write, 6 is equal to read and write, and 4 is equal to read. The first digit is a placeholder for the user. The second digit is a placeholder for the group, and the last digit is a placeholder for the other. To further illustrate this, we can take off the read and leave the write for the group permissions, as follows:

```
[philip@localhost NewTest]$ chmod 624 OurFile
[philip@localhost NewTest]$ ll
total 0
-rw--w-r--. 1 philip philip 0 Aug  6 13:52 OurFile
[philip@localhost NewTest]$
```

Similarly, we can add on permissions by increasing the value. Let's pick the others; we will give the others the read and execute permissions, as follows:

```
[philip@localhost NewTest]$ chmod 625 OurFile
[philip@localhost NewTest]$ ll
total 0
-rw--w-r-x. 1 philip philip 0 Aug  6 13:52 OurFile
[philip@localhost NewTest]$
```

Wonderful! We can even give all of the permissions (read, write, and execute) for the user, the group, or the others in a single command. Let's start with the user, as follows:

```
[philip@localhost NewTest]$ ll
total 0
-rwx-w-r-x. 1 philip philip 0 Aug  6 13:52 OurFile
[philip@localhost NewTest]$
```

Now, we can see that the user has read, write, and execute permissions. I got the value of 7 by adding read as equal to 4, write as equal to 2, and execute as equal to 1. We will now give the group all of the permissions, as follows:

```
[philip@localhost NewTest]$ chmod 775 OurFile
[philip@localhost NewTest]$ ll
total 0
-rwxrwxr-x. 1 philip philip 0 Aug  6 13:52 OurFile
[philip@localhost NewTest]$
```

Awesome job! We can also remove all of the permissions for the user, group, or others in a single command. Let's remove the permissions (read, write, and execute) for the others, as follows:

```
[philip@localhost NewTest]$ chmod 770 OurFile
[philip@localhost NewTest]$ ll
total 0
-rwxrwx---. 1 philip philip 0 Aug  6 13:52 OurFile
[philip@localhost NewTest]$
```

Placing a zero (0) negates all of the permissions for the particular section (user, group, or others). You can see the power of permissions. Similarly, we can use letters, as seen previously. The u means user, g means group, and o means others. We can remove the execute permission from the group as follows:

```
[philip@localhost NewTest]$ chmod g-x OurFile
[philip@localhost NewTest]$ ll
total 0
-rwxrw----. 1 philip philip 0 Aug  6 13:52 OurFile
[philip@localhost NewTest]$
```

We can use either a plus (+) symbol (to add a permission) or a minus (-) symbol (to remove a permission). We can also copy a file from one location to another, or inside the same location. A different name will have to be given if the destination for the file is inside the same location as the source.

The cp command is used for copying. We will make a copy of the file and place it in /home/philip/Documents/, as follows:

```
[philip@localhost NewTest]$ cp OurFile /home/philip/Documents/NewFile
[philip@localhost NewTest]$ ll /home/philip/Documents/
-rwxrw----. 1 philip philip 0 Aug  6 14:34 NewFile
drwxrwxr-x. 2 philip philip 4096 Aug  6 13:52 NewTest
[philip@localhost NewTest]$
```

Excellent!

 Directories have a d in front of their permissions.

We can also move a file; the mv command is used for moving files. Let's move /home/philip/Documents/NewFile and place it inside /home/philip/Documents/NewTest:

```
[philip@localhost NewTest]$ mv /home/philip/Documents/NewFile .
[philip@localhost NewTest]$ ll
-rwxrw----. 1 philip philip 0 Aug  6 14:34 NewFile
-rwxrw----. 1 philip philip 0 Aug  6 13:52 OurFile
[philip@localhost NewTest]$
```

The method that we used was to specify a period (.) for the location. This indicates the current working directory; so, instead of typing out the full destination path, we can use the period (.).

We can also rename a file by using the mv command. Let's rename the NewFile:

```
[philip@localhost NewTest]$ mv NewFile RenameFile
[philip@localhost NewTest]$ ll
total 0
-rwxrw----. 1 philip philip 0 Aug  6 13:52 OurFile
-rwxrw----. 1 philip philip 0 Aug  6 14:34 RenameFile
[philip@localhost NewTest]$
```

Voila! We can also rename a file and place it in another directory, as follows:

```
[philip@localhost NewTest]$ mv RenameFile /home/philip/Documents/
[philip@localhost NewTest]$ ll
-rwxrw----. 1 philip philip 0 Aug  6 13:52 OurFile
[philip@localhost NewTest]$
```

The file is no longer inside the present directory, but is now inside the /home/philip/Documents directory:

```
[philip@localhost NewTest]$ ll /home/philip/Documents/
total 4
drwxrwxr-x. 2 philip philip 4096 Aug  6 14:57 NewTest
-rwxrw----. 1 philip philip    0 Aug  6 14:34 RenameFile
[philip@localhost NewTest]$
```

Great! We can also remove a file by using the rm command. Let's remove the /home/philip/Documents/NewTest/OurFile, as follows:

```
[philip@localhost NewTest]$ ll
total 0
-rwxrw----. 1 philip philip 0 Aug  6 13:52 OurFile
[philip@localhost NewTest]$ rm OurFile
```

```
[philip@localhost NewTest]$ ll
total 0
[philip@localhost NewTest]$
```

Creating and removing directories

We can create directories by using another popular command. The `mkdir` command can be used to create a directory. Let's do a listing, using the `ls` command, as follows:

```
[philip@localhost ~]$ ls
Desktop Documents Downloads Music Pictures Public Templates Videos
[philip@localhost ~]$
```

Now, let's create our own directory inside of `/home/philip`:

```
[philip@localhost ~]$ mkdir NewTest
[philip@localhost ~]$ ll
total 36
drwxr-xr-x. 2 philip philip 4096 Jul 31 14:59 Desktop
drwxr-xr-x. 2 philip philip 4096 Jul 31 14:59 Documents
drwxr-xr-x. 2 philip philip 4096 Jul 31 14:59 Downloads
drwxr-xr-x. 2 philip philip 4096 Jul 31 14:59 Music
drwxr-xr-x. 2 philip philip 4096 Jul 31 14:59 Pictures
drwxr-xr-x. 2 philip philip 4096 Jul 31 14:59 Public
drwxr-xr-x. 2 philip philip 4096 Jul 31 14:59 Templates
drwxrwxr-x. 2 philip philip 4096 Aug  6 12:04 NewTest
drwxr-xr-x. 2 philip philip 4096 Jul 31 14:59 Videos
[philip@localhost ~]$
```

In the preceding code, our new directory is listed at the bottom. You'll also notice that we used the `ll` command; this is just an alias for the `ls -l` command. This can be verified quickly by using the `which` command, as follows:

```
philip@localhost ~]$ which ll
alias ll='ls -l --color=auto'
 /usr/bin/ls
[philip@localhost ~]$
```

Great job! We can move into our newly created directory by using the `cd` command:

```
[philip@localhost ~]$ cd NewTest/
[philip@localhost NewTest]$ ls
[philip@localhost NewTest]$ pwd
/home/philip/NewTest
[philip@localhost NewTest]$
```

Next, suppose that we have created a directory and have made a typo. Not to worry; we can leverage the mv command, which has the ability to rename a directory. Let's attempt to rename the /home/Test directory:

```
[philip@localhost NewTest]$ pwd
/home/philip/Documents/NewTest
[philip@localhost NewTest]$ mv /home/philip/Documents/NewTest/
/home/philip/
[philip@localhost NewTest]$ pwd
/home/philip/Documents/NewTest
[philip@localhost NewTest]$
```

We are encountering this error due to the fact that we are inside the directory. Let's try the command with the -v option:

```
[philip@localhost NewTest]$ mv -v /home/philip/Documents/NewTest/
/home/philip/
mv: cannot stat '/home/philip/Documents/NewTest/'
[philip@localhost NewTest]$
```

To get around this, we need to navigate out of the directory, and then retry the mv command, as follows:

```
[philip@localhost ~]$ mv /home/philip/Documents/NewTest/ .
[philip@localhost ~]$ ll
total 36
drwxr-xr-x. 2 philip philip 4096 Jul 31 14:59 Desktop
drwxr-xr-x. 2 philip philip 4096 Aug  6 15:12 Documents
drwxr-xr-x. 2 philip philip 4096 Jul 31 14:59 Downloads
drwxr-xr-x. 2 philip philip 4096 Jul 31 14:59 Music
drwxrwxr-x. 2 philip philip 4096 Aug  6 15:00 NewTest
drwxr-xr-x. 2 philip philip 4096 Jul 31 14:59 Pictures
drwxr-xr-x. 2 philip philip 4096 Jul 31 14:59 Public
drwxr-xr-x. 2 philip philip 4096 Jul 31 14:59 Templates
drwxr-xr-x. 2 philip philip 4096 Jul 31 14:59 Videos
[philip@localhost ~]$
```

Awesome! Now, the NewTest file no longer exists inside of /home/philip/Documents/; this can be shown by executing the following:

```
[philip@localhost ~]$ ll Documents/
total 0
-rwxrw----. 1 philip philip 0 Aug  6 14:34 RenameFile
[philip@localhost ~]$
```

We can also rename a directory by using the mv command. The trick is to specify a directory name when we call the mv command, as follows:

```
[philip@localhost ~]$ mv NewTest/ ReName
[philip@localhost ~]$ ll
total 36
drwxr-xr-x. 2 philip philip 4096 Jul 31 14:59 Desktop
drwxr-xr-x. 2 philip philip 4096 Aug  6 15:12 Documents
drwxr-xr-x. 2 philip philip 4096 Jul 31 14:59 Downloads
drwxr-xr-x. 2 philip philip 4096 Jul 31 14:59 Music
drwxr-xr-x. 2 philip philip 4096 Jul 31 14:59 Pictures
drwxr-xr-x. 2 philip philip 4096 Jul 31 14:59 Public
drwxrwxr-x. 2 philip philip 4096 Aug  6 15:00 ReName
drwxr-xr-x. 2 philip philip 4096 Jul 31 14:59 Templates
drwxr-xr-x. 2 philip philip 4096 Jul 31 14:59 Videos
[philip@localhost ~]$
```

Renaming a directory is that simple. We can also change the permissions on a directory. Let's remove the read, write, and execute permissions from the group, as follows:

```
[philip@localhost ~]$ chmod -R 705 ReName/
[philip@localhost ~]$ ll
drwxr-xr-x. 2 philip philip 4096 Jul 31 14:59 Desktop
drwxr-xr-x. 2 philip philip 4096 Aug  6 15:12 Documents
drwxr-xr-x. 2 philip philip 4096 Jul 31 14:59 Downloads
drwxr-xr-x. 2 philip philip 4096 Jul 31 14:59 Music
drwxr-xr-x. 2 philip philip 4096 Jul 31 14:59 Pictures
drwxr-xr-x. 2 philip philip 4096 Jul 31 14:59 Public
drwx---r-x. 2 philip philip 4096 Aug  6 15:00 ReName
drwxr-xr-x. 2 philip philip 4096 Jul 31 14:59 Templates
drwxr-xr-x. 2 philip philip 4096 Jul 31 14:59 Videos
[philip@localhost ~]$
```

Awesome! The -R option tells the chmod command to apply the permissions to everything that resides inside of the /home/philip/ReName directory. When we are finished with a directory, we can remove it. The rmdir command is used to remove directories. Let's remove the /home/philip/ReName directory, as follows:

```
[philip@localhost ~]$ rmdir ReName/
[philip@localhost ~]$ ll
drwxr-xr-x. 2 philip philip 4096 Jul 31 14:59 Desktop
drwxr-xr-x. 2 philip philip 4096 Aug  6 15:12 Documents
drwxr-xr-x. 2 philip philip 4096 Jul 31 14:59 Downloads
drwxr-xr-x. 2 philip philip 4096 Jul 31 14:59 Music
drwxr-xr-x. 2 philip philip 4096 Jul 31 14:59 Pictures
```

```
drwxr-xr-x. 2 philip philip 4096 Jul 31 14:59 Public
drwxr-xr-x. 2 philip philip 4096 Jul 31 14:59 Templates
drwxr-xr-x. 2 philip philip 4096 Jul 31 14:59 Videos
[philip@localhost ~]$
```

Based on the preceding code, no errors were encountered. This might not be the case in your environment. Most often, you will either have files or other directories that reside in the directory that you are attempting to remove. Let's quickly create a directory and place three files inside it. Then we will attempt to remove the directory:

```
[philip@localhost ~]$ mkdir TempDir
[philip@localhost ~]$ ll
drwxr-xr-x. 2 philip philip 4096 Jul 31 14:59 Desktop
drwxrwxr-x. 2 philip philip 4096 Aug  6 15:46 TempDir
drwxr-xr-x. 2 philip philip 4096 Jul 31 14:59 Templates
drwxr-xr-x. 2 philip philip 4096 Jul 31 14:59 Videos
[philip@localhost ~]$ touch TempDir/File1
[philip@localhost ~]$ touch TempDir/File2
[philip@localhost ~]$ touch TempDir/File3
[philip@localhost ~]$ ll TempDir/
total 0
-rw-rw-r--. 1 philip philip 0 Aug  6 15:47 File1
-rw-rw-r--. 1 philip philip 0 Aug  6 15:47 File2
-rw-rw-r--. 1 philip philip 0 Aug  6 15:47 File3
[philip@localhost ~]$
```

Now we will retry the rm command and look at the differences:

```
[philip@localhost ~]$ rmdir TempDir/
rmdir: failed to remove 'TempDir/': Directory not empty
[philip@localhost ~]$
```

Lo and behold, we encountered an error. This is common when a directory is not empty. We can work around it quite easily, however. This time, we will use the rm command with −r, which means to delete everything that follows. We can also add the −v option, which will show the details of any potential permissions issues:

```
[philip@localhost ~]$ ll TempDir/
total 0
-rw-rw-r--. 1 philip philip 0 Aug  6 15:53 File1
-rw-rw-r--. 1 philip philip 0 Aug  6 15:53 File2
-rw-rw-r--. 1 philip philip 0 Aug  6 15:53 File3
[philip@localhost ~]$ rm −rv TempDir/
removed 'TempDir/File3'
removed 'TempDir/File1'
removed 'TempDir/File2'
removed directory 'TempDir/'
```

```
[philip@localhost ~]$ ll TempDir/
ls: cannot access 'TempDir/': No such file or directory
[philip@localhost ~]$
```

Great!

> You can use −f to delete an entire directory without being prompted for confirmation.

Finding files and directories

Often, we are searching for files and directories from the GUI. We can also perform searches in the shell. First, we can use the find command; let's look for files that have a .conf extension. The search function would be as follows:

```
[philip@localhost ~]$ find /etc -iname "*.cfg"
find: '/etc/grub.d': Permission denied
find: '/etc/cups/ssl': Permission denied
/etc/libblockdev/conf.d/00-default.cfg
find: '/etc/audit': Permission denied
find: '/etc/dhcp': Permission denied
find: '/etc/sssd': Permission denied
/etc/grub2.cfg
find: '/etc/audisp': Permission denied
find: '/etc/polkit-1/rules.d': Permission denied
find: '/etc/polkit-1/localauthority': Permission denied
find: '/etc/openvpn/server': Permission denied
find: '/etc/openvpn/client': Permission denied
 [philip@localhost ~]$
```

Now, if you encounter these errors, it's an indication that you need some advanced permissions. Let's try the search once again, as the root user:

```
[philip@localhost ~]$ su
Password:
[root@localhost philip]# find /etc -iname "*.cfg"'
/etc/libblockdev/conf.d/00-default.cfg
/etc/grub2-efi.cfg
/etc/vdpau_wrapper.cfg
/etc/grub2.cfg
[root@localhost philip]#
```

Awesome! We can even broaden the area where we want to perform a search. Let's search the entire filesystem, as follows:

```
[root@localhost philip]# find / -iname "*.cfg"
/home/philip/.config/yelp/yelp.cfg
/run/media/philip/Fedora-WS-Live-28-1-1/EFI/BOOT/grub.cfg
/run/media/philip/Fedora-WS-Live-28-1-1/isolinux/isolinux.cfg
find: '/run/user/1000/gvfs': Permission denied
/usr/lib64/libreoffice/share/config/soffice.cfg
/usr/lib64/libreoffice/help/en-US/schart.cfg
/usr/lib64/libreoffice/help/en-US/smath.cfg
/usr/lib64/libreoffice/help/en-US/sbasic.cfg
grub2.cfg
/boot/grub2/grub.cfg
[root@localhost philip]
```

 Some output has been omitted for brevity.

We can also search based on a part of a name. Let's look for any file that begins with gru:

```
[root@localhost philip]# find /boot -iname "gru*"
/boot/efi/EFI/fedora/grubia32.efi
/boot/efi/EFI/fedora/grubenv
/boot/efi/EFI/fedora/grubx64.efi
/boot/grub2
/boot/grub2/grub.cfg
/boot/grub2/grubenv
[root@localhost philip]#
```

In the preceding output, we searched inside of the /boot directory. Empty files are often just sitting inside of a directory without being used. We can search for empty files by using the find command. The -type option is passed to specify what we're searching for:

```
[root@localhost philip]# find /home/philip/Documents  -empty
/home/philip/Documents/RenameFile
[root@localhost philip]#
```

Awesome job! But, wait; we can do some housekeeping by passing the −delete option to remove any files that the find command has returned from our search. We can do so as follows:

> Be careful when using the −delete option as it will remove the files, and even the directories, in some cases. Always back up your data before running find with the −delete option.

```
[root@localhost philip]# find /home/philip/Documents  -empty -delete
[root@localhost philip]# ll /home/philip/Documents
ls: cannot access '/home/philip/Documents': No such file or directory
```

In the preceding output, you will notice that /home/philip/Documents/RenameFile, in addition to /home/philip/Documents, has been removed. Be very cautious whenever you pass the −delete option. Although in our case, we are using a lab environment, be sure to keep this in mind in your real systems. Perform a backup before attempting to pass the −delete option.

We can also search for a file or directory based on permissions. Yes! We would pass the −readable, −writable, and −executable options with the find command. This would look as follows:

```
[root@localhost philip]# find /etc/yum.repos.d/ -readable
/etc/yum.repos.d/
/etc/yum.repos.d/fedora-updates.repo
/etc/yum.repos.d/fedora.repo
/etc/yum.repos.d/fedora-cisco-openh264.repo
/etc/yum.repos.d/fedora-updates-testing.repo
  [root@localhost philip]# ll /etc/yum.repos.d/
total 16
-rw-r--r--. 1 root root  707 Apr 23 13:03 fedora-cisco-openh264.repo
-rw-r--r--. 1 root root 1331 Apr 23 13:03 fedora.repo
-rw-r--r--. 1 root root 1392 Apr 23 13:03 fedora-updates.repo
-rw-r--r--. 1 root root 1450 Apr 23 13:03 fedora-updates-testing.repo
[root@localhost philip]#
```

Awesome job! You can see that the result of the find command matches the listing for files with the read permission. Likewise, we can search for the files and directories with execute permissions, as follows:

```
[root@localhost philip]# ll /etc/init.d/
total 52
-rw-r--r--. 1 root root 18561 Jan  2  2018 functions
-rwxr-xr-x. 1 root root  7288 Apr 25 02:39 livesys
-rwxr-xr-x. 1 root root  1054 Apr 25 02:39 livesys-late
```

```
-rwxr-xr-x. 1 root root  4334 Jan  2  2018 netconsole
-rwxr-xr-x. 1 root root  7613 Jan  2  2018 network
-rw-r--r--. 1 root root  1161 Apr 18 17:59 README
[root@localhost philip]# find /etc/init.d/ -perm -o+x
/etc/init.d/
/etc/init.d/livesys
/etc/init.d/livesys-late
/etc/init.d/netconsole
/etc/init.d/network
[root@localhost philip]#
```

In the preceding output, only the files with execute permissions for the others are displayed.

Adding to this, we can search for files and directories with write permissions, as follows:

```
[root@localhost philip]# find /etc/init.d/ -perm -o+w
[root@localhost philip]#
```

Great job! The results came back empty because none of the files or directories have write permissions for the others. Similarly, we can search using numbers. We could look for execute permissions, as follows:

```
[root@localhost philip]# find /etc/init.d/ -perm -005
/etc/init.d/
/etc/init.d/livesys
/etc/init.d/livesys-late
/etc/init.d/netconsole
/etc/init.d/network
[root@localhost philip]#
```

In the preceding output, only directories with execute permissions are displayed. We can search for files and directories with write permissions, as follows:

```
[root@localhost philip]# find /etc/init.d/ -perm -002
[root@localhost philip]#
```

Interestingly enough, the results came back as expected, because the others do not have write permissions. Likewise, we can search for write permissions for groups, as follows:

```
[root@localhost philip]# ll /etc/init.d/
total 52
-rw-r--r--. 1 root root 18561 Jan  2  2018 functions
-rwxr-xr-x. 1 root root  7288 Apr 25 02:39 livesys
-rwxr-xr-x. 1 root root  1054 Apr 25 02:39 livesys-late
-rwxr-xr-x. 1 root root  4334 Jan  2  2018 netconsole
```

```
-rwxr-xr-x. 1 root root  7613 Jan  2  2018 network
-rw-r--r--. 1 root root  1161 Apr 18 17:59 README
[root@localhost philip]# find /etc/init.d/ -perm -020
[root@localhost philip]#
```

Awesome! The results are empty, because the groups do not have write permissions. Lastly, we can search for write permissions for the user; this will yield the following:

```
[root@localhost philip]# find /etc/init.d/ -perm -200
/etc/init.d/
/etc/init.d/functions
/etc/init.d/livesys
/etc/init.d/README
/etc/init.d/livesys-late
/etc/init.d/netconsole
/etc/init.d/network
[root@localhost philip]#
```

Great job! The syntax is -perm, followed by the user (the first digit), the group (the second digit), and the others (the last digit).

Another popular method for searching files and directories is to use the locate command. The locate utility is faster in terms of results compared to the find utility; this is due to the fact that the locate command uses a database to perform lookups. The database is called mlocate. We can perform a simple search of a file we have created, as follows:

```
[philip@localhost ~]$ locate TestFile
[philip@localhost ~]$
```

In the preceding output, the locate command is unaware of the specified file. Not to worry; we simply have to update the database, as follows:

```
[philip@localhost ~]$ updatedb
updatedb: cannot open a temporary file for `/var/lib/mlocate/mlocate.db'
[philip@localhost ~]$
```

If you run into this error, it means that you need to run the command as the root user, as follows:

```
[philip@localhost ~]$ su
Password:
[root@localhost philip]# updatedb
[root@localhost philip]#
Now, let's retry the locate command for the given file:
[root@localhost philip]# locate TestFile
/home/philip/Documents/TestFile1
[root@localhost philip]#
```

That's more like it! We can also search by extensions. To do so, we can use a wildcard, as follows:

```
[root@localhost philip]# locate *.key
/etc/brlapi.key
/etc/trusted-key.key
/usr/lib64/libreoffice/help/en-US/sbasic.key
/usr/lib64/libreoffice/help/en-US/scalc.key
/usr/lib64/libreoffice/help/en-US/schart.key
/usr/lib64/libreoffice/help/en-US/sdatabase.key
/usr/lib64/libreoffice/help/en-US/sdraw.key
/usr/lib64/libreoffice/help/en-US/simpress.key
/usr/lib64/libreoffice/help/en-US/smath.key
/usr/lib64/libreoffice/help/en-US/swriter.key
/usr/share/doc/openssh/PROTOCOL.key
/usr/share/doc/python3-pycurl/tests/certs/server.key
[root@localhost philip]#
```

In the preceding output, only the results with lowercase names are displayed; we can fix this by passing -i, which tells the locate command to ignore the case:

```
[root@localhost philip]# locate -i *.key
/etc/brlapi.key
/etc/trusted-key.key
/usr/lib64/libreoffice/help/en-US/sbasic.key
/usr/lib64/libreoffice/help/en-US/scalc.key
/usr/lib64/libreoffice/help/en-US/schart.key/usr/lib64/libreoffice/help/en-
US/sdatabase.key
/usr/lib64/libreoffice/help/en-US/sdraw.key
/usr/lib64/libreoffice/help/en-US/simpress.key
/usr/lib64/libreoffice/help/en-US/smath.key
/usr/lib64/libreoffice/help/en-US/swriter.key
/usr/share/doc/openssh/PROTOCOL.key
/usr/share/doc/python3-pycurl/tests/certs/server.key
[root@localhost philip]#
```

In this case, the results are the same, due to the fact that the files are in lowercase. We can also control how the output is displayed; we can pass the --null option, as follows:

```
[root@localhost philip]# locate --null *types
/etc/ethertypes/etc/mime.types/etc/firewalld/icmptypes/etc/selinux/targeted
/contexts/customizable_types/etc/selinux/targeted/contexts/securetty_types/
usr/include/bits/types/usr/lib/firewalld/icmptypes/usr/lib64/libreoffice/pr
ogram/types/usr/lib64/libreoffice/share/filter/vml-shape-
types/usr/lib64/perl5/bits/types/usr/lib64/python2.7/ctypes/usr/lib64/pytho
n2.7/ctypes/macholib/REAshare/icons/hicolor/512x512/mimetypes/usr/share/ico
ns/hicolor/64x64/mimetypes/usr/share/icons/hicolor/72x72/mimetypes/usr/shar
e/icons/hicolor/96x96/mimetypes/usr/share/icons/hicolor/scalable/mimetypes/
```

```
usr/share/icons/locolor/16x16/mimetypes/usr/share/icons/locolor/32x32/mimet
ypes/usr/share/mime/types
[root@localhost philip]#
```

In the preceding output, we can see the desired results. Finally, we can view information about the database; to do so, we can use the -S option:

```
[root@localhost philip]# locate -S
Database /var/lib/mlocate/mlocate.db:
        12,517 directories
        162,475 files
        8,292,135 bytes in file names
        3,883,960 bytes used to store database
[root@localhost philip]#
```

Great job! In addition to the size, we can also see the location of the database.

Pipes and redirects

Often, when we are viewing output from various commands, it is a bit fuzzy. Fear no more; we have what is known as pipes and redirects. Basically, when working with pipes (|), we take the output of a command and pass it as the input of another command. Redirects (>, <, >>, 2>, and 2>&1) are similar to taking output from a command, but this time, we send it to a location, such as a file or another location, to name a few.

To begin, let's use the ls command. The code is as follows:

```
[root@localhost philip]# ls /etc
abrt              default      gdbinit.d           kernel
networks          rc4.d        subuid-
adjtime           depmod.d     gdm                 krb5.conf
nfs.conf          rc5.d        sudoers
aliases           dhcp         geoclue             krb5.conf.d
nfsmount.conf     rc6.d        sudoers.d
alsa              DIR_COLORS   glvnd               ld.so.cache     nsswitch.conf
rc.d          sysconfig
alternatives      DIR_COLORS.256color             gnupg           ld.so.conf
nsswitch.conf.bak rdma     sysctl.conf
[root@localhost philip]#
```

We can view the output one page at a time by bringing in yet another powerful command—the `less` command:

```
[root@localhost philip]# ls /etc | less
cron.daily
cron.deny
cron.hourly
cron.monthly
crontab
cron.weekly
crypto-policies
crypttab
csh.cshrc
csh.login
cups
cupshelpers
:
[root@localhost philip]#
```

In order to exit the `less` command, we can use the `q` on the keyboard. The benefit of using the `less` command is the fact that we can move back and forward, as opposed to the `more` command, which can only move forward. We can also use the pipe (`|`) character to pass values that another command is expecting. We can use the `wc` command to illustrate this, as follows:

```
[root@localhost philip]# ls /etc | wc -w
263
[root@localhost philip]#
```

In the preceding output, we took the output from the `ls` command and passed it as the input to the `wc` command. The `wc` command is used for the word count; the `-w` option is used to display the total amount of words.

Next, we can use redirects in a number of ways. In Linux, we have three types of streams, as follows:

- STDIN = input <
- STDOUT = output >
- STDERR = standard error 2>

Also, we can mix and match the streams, as you will see later in this section. Let's start with STDIN; we can use the `wc` command and call the input from a file, as follows:

```
[root@localhost philip]# wc -w < /boot/grub2/grub.cfg
435
[root@localhost philip]#
```

Awesome! The word count of `/boot/grub2/grub.cfg` is passed to the `wc` command. Moving on to STDOUT, we can get the output of a command and store it in a file. Let's use the `ls` command, as follows:

```
[root@localhost philip]# ls /etc/init.d/ > /home/philip/Documents/ls.txt
[root@localhost philip]#
```

In the preceding output, we did a listing of `/etc/init.d/` and saved the output to `/home/philip/Documents/ls.txt`. This can be verified as follows:

```
[root@localhost philip]# cat /home/philip/Documents/ls.txt
functions
livesys
livesys-late
netconsole
network
README
[root@localhost philip]#
```

Now, suppose that we use the `ls` command for another directory; this will overwrite the existing content of `/home/philip/Documents/ls.txt`:

```
[root@localhost philip]# ls /boot/grub2/ > /home/philip/Documents/ls.txt
[root@localhost philip]# cat /home/philip/Documents/ls.txt
device.map
fonts
grub.cfg
grubenv
i386-pc
localethemes
[root@localhost philip]#
```

As you can see, the proof is in the pudding. A way around this would be to tell the STDOUT that we want to append the output, instead of overwriting it:

```
[root@localhost philip]# ls /var/ >> /home/philip/Documents/ls.txt
[root@localhost philip]# cat /home/philip/Documents/ls.txt
device.map
fonts
grub.cfg
```

```
grubenv
i386-pc
locale
themes
account
adm
cache
crash
db
empty
ftp
games
gopher
kerberos
lib
spool
tmp
www
yp
[root@localhost philip]#
```

There we go! So, we use >> to append data to an existing file. Next, we can combine the results of the STDIN of a command and send it to the STDOUT. That would look as follows:

```
[root@localhost philip]# wc -w < /var/log/boot.log  >
/home/philip/Documents/STDIN_STDOUT.txt
[root@localhost philip]# cat /home/philip/Documents/STDIN_STDOUT.txt
2021
[root@localhost philip]#
```

Great job! We can also redirect STDERR to a file. Let's use the `file` command, as follows:

```
[root@localhost philip]# ls -l /tmp TestFileWithError 2>
/home/philip/Documents/STDERR.txt
/tmp:
drwx------. 3 root root 60 Aug 2 10:23 systemd-private-
a7a23120abff44c8bca6807f1711c1c2-bolt.service-7uNmVr
drwx------. 3 root root 60 Aug 2 10:22 systemd-private-
a7a23120abff44c8bca6807f1711c1c2-chronyd.service-LPD8zu
drwx------. 3 root root 60 Aug 2 10:23 systemd-private-
a7a23120abff44c8bca6807f1711c1c2-colord.service-13Vcs8
drwx------. 3 root root 60 Aug 2 10:28 systemd-private-
a7a23120abff44c8bca6807f1711c1c2-fwupd.service-XOnyvf
drwx------. 3 root root 60 Aug 2 10:22 systemd-private-
a7a23120abff44c8bca6807f1711c1c2-rtkit-daemon.service-ZD5mO7
drwx------. 2 philip philip 40 Aug 2 10:31 tracker-extract-files.1000
drwx------. 2 root root 40 Aug 2 10:22 vmware-root
```

```
[root@localhost philip]#
```

In the preceding output, it appears as though the command worked. Well, the truth of the matter is that the listing for /tmp worked, but the error for the TestFileWithError file was not displayed. Instead, the error was sent to /home/philip/Documents/STDERR.txt. This can be verified as follows:

```
[root@localhost philip]# cat /home/philip/Documents/STDERR.txt
ls: cannot access 'TestFileWithError': No such file or directory
[root@localhost philip]#
```

Awesome job! We can also combine the STDOUT with the STDERR in a single file. This is accomplished by telling the shell that we would like to store the STDERR, along with the STDOUT, inside the file 2>&1. This can be done as follows:

```
[root@localhost philip]# ls -l  /tmp TestFileWithError >
/home/philip/Documents/STDERR.txt 2>&1
[root@localhost philip]# cat /home/philip/Documents/STDERR.txt
ls: cannot access 'TestFileWithError': No such file or directory
/tmp:
total 0
drwx------. 3 root   root   60 Aug  2 10:23 systemd-private-
a7a23120abff44c8bca6807f1711c1c2-bolt.service-7uNmVr
drwx------. 3 root   root   60 Aug  2 10:22 systemd-private-
a7a23120abff44c8bca6807f1711c1c2-chronyd.service-LPD8zu
drwx------. 3 root   root   60 Aug  2 10:23 systemd-private-
a7a23120abff44c8bca6807f1711c1c2-colord.service-13Vcs8
drwx------. 3 root   root   60 Aug  2 10:28 systemd-private-
a7a23120abff44c8bca6807f1711c1c2-fwupd.service-XOnyvf
drwx------. 3 root   root   60 Aug  2 10:22 systemd-private-
a7a23120abff44c8bca6807f1711c1c2-rtkit-daemon.service-ZD5mO7
drwx------. 2 philip philip 40 Aug  7 14:45 tracker-extract-files.1000
drwx------. 2 root   root   40 Aug  2 10:22 vmware-root
[root@localhost philip]#
```

In the preceding output, we can see the error at the beginning of the file, followed by the listing of the /tmp. Finally, it's possible to display the output of a command and simultaneously redirect the output to a file; this is made possible by yet another powerful command—the tee command. The following shows the tee command in action:

```
[root@localhost philip]# cat  /etc/hosts.allow | tee
/home/philip/Documents/The_Tee_command.txt
#
# hosts.allow     This file contains access rules which are used to
#       allow or deny connections to network services that
#       either use the tcp_wrappers library or that have been
#       started through a tcp_wrappers-enabled xinetd.
```

```
#
#          See 'man 5 hosts_options' and 'man 5 hosts_access'
#          for information on rule syntax.
#          See 'man tcpd' for information on tcp_wrappers
[root@localhost philip]#
[root@localhost philip]# cat /home/philip/Documents/The_Tee_command.txt
#
# hosts.allow    This file contains access rules which are used to
#          allow or deny connections to network services that
#          either use the tcp_wrappers library or that have been
#          started through a tcp_wrappers-enabled xinetd.
#
#          See 'man 5 hosts_options' and 'man 5 hosts_access'
#          for information on rule syntax.
#          See 'man tcpd' for information on tcp_wrappers
[root@localhost philip]#
```

In the preceding output, you can see the power of the tee command.

Summary

This chapter was very detailed. I must say that I had a lot of fun working on it. We covered the filesystem structure. You learned how to navigate the filesystem using the cd command. Then we looked at how to identify the working directory. After that, we covered the method for viewing the contents of a directory. Adding to that, we exposed hidden files and directories within directories that weren't displayed by default.

Next, we covered how to create a file in the shell. Furthermore, we looked at the various permissions for a file and how to change these permissions. Following this, we moved on to directories inside a Linux environment. The various methods to create, move, rename, and remove a directory were explored. The next topic involved techniques to search for files and directories. First, we worked with the find command extensively. Next, the locate command was explored. Finally, we worked with pipes and redirects, within the context of the shell environment. We saw how we can leverage the output of a command and pass it as the input for another command. We then explored how to redirect to and from a file, including STDOUT and STDERR. Finally, we took a look at another powerful command: the tee command.

In the next chapter, we will look at processes in the context of the shell environment. In particular, we will look at a technique to manage processes. Some popular commands will be covered, such as `top`, `service`, and `systemctl`, used for identifying and managing processes. The next chapter will be concise, in the sense that we will focus on the methods that it is essential for every Linux engineer to be aware of when working inside a shell environment. The skill set that you will gain will foster even more confidence as you progress in your path to certification.

Questions

1. Which of the following directories is the `root` directory?

   A. `/root/`
   B. `/root`
   C. `/home/root`
   D. `/`

2. Which of the following commands is used to change to another directory?

   A. `pwd`
   B. `change`
   C. `cd`
   D. `change dir`

3. Which of the following commands will print the current working directory?

   A. `print dir`
   B. `pwd`
   C. `display`
   D. `cd`

4. Which of the following commands is used to print the content of a directory?

   A. `ls`
   B. `which`
   C. `whereis`
   D. `cat`

5. Which of the following options can be used to display file and directory permissions, using the `ls` command?

        A. `-r`
        B. `-b`
        C. `-a`
        D. `-l`

6. Which of the following options can be used to display hidden files and directories, with the `ls` command?

        A. `-l`
        B. `-b`
        C. `-a`
        D. `-u`

7. Which of the following commands is used to remove a directory, even when it's not empty?

        A. `rmdir`
        B. `rm`
        C. `remove`
        D. `mv`

8. Which of the following options are used to find and remove empty files and directories, with the `find` command?

        A. `empty -remove`
        B. `-empty -clean`
        C. `-empty -delete`
        D. `-empty -cycle`

9. Which of the following commands is used to update the database that the `locate` command uses?

        A. `updatelocate`
        B. `updatedatabase`
        C. `locateupdate`
        D. `updatedb`

10. Which of the following commands displays the output of a command and simultaneously saves the results to a file?

    A. `less`
    B. `more`
    C. `wc`
    D. `tee`

Further reading

- You can get more information about various distributions and file manipulation at: `https://unix.stackexchange.com`
- For general information that relates to various commands that work on both CentOS and Ubuntu, and for the ability to post your questions for other community members to respond to, refer to `https://www.linuxquestions.org`

Creating, Monitoring, Killing, and Restarting Processes

9

In the previous chapter, we looked in detail at file management. Then, we covered how to create a file at the shell. Furthermore, we saw the various permissions for a file, and we learned how to change them. Following this, we moved onto directories inside a Linux environment. Finally, we worked with pipes and redirects, within the context of the shell environment. Also, we took a look at another powerful command—the `tee` command.

In this chapter, we are going to explore various techniques that can be used for managing various processes. First, we will investigate processes in real time using a very popular command—the `ps` command. This `ps` command was briefly covered in Chapter 2, *Booting the System*, in the *The boot process – explained* section. In this chapter, we place more emphasis on the `ps` command, exploring more options that can be passed, thereby exposing vital information. After this, we venture into methods of managing daemons; first, we start off with the very popular `top` command. This method of handling processes is widely used throughout the Linux community. This is mainly because the `top` command gives real-time statistics for various daemons. In addition to this, we can also control daemon behavior. Following this, we move onto another common method for managing processes: the `service` command. Finally, we cover the latest method for daemon management; namely, the `systemctl` command. This was covered in Chapter 2, *Booting the System*, in the *The boot process: Explained* section. In this chapter, we go into more depth on common practices used for daemon management, using the `systemctl` command.

We will cover the following topics in this chapter:

- The `ps` command
- Viewing and managing processes using the `top` command
- Managing processes with the `service` command
- Managing processes with the `systemctl` command

The ps command

The ps command, which stands for **Process Status**, is one of the most popular commands used in today's environment. It displays the current processes running within a system; when we work within a Linux environment, we often overlook the underlying processes that make it all possible. All the information that the ps command displays comes from a very popular directory; namely, the /proc filesystem. The /proc filesystem is not actually a real filesystem, per se; it is in fact a virtual filesystem. It's loaded upon boot time, and you will find the /proc filesystem in almost every Linux distribution available today. Let's dive into the ps command.

To begin with, we can display any process that has started in the current shell:

```
[philip@localhost ~]$ ps
  PID          TTY          TIME        CMD
  2220         pts/0        00:00:00    bash
  95677        pts/0        00:00:00    ps
[philip@localhost ~]$
```

Based on the preceding output, we have not started any other process in the current shell, except for the ps command itself and the Bash shell. We can also list all of the processes currently present within a system, using the ps command; we would pass the -A parameter:

```
[philip@localhost ~]$ ps -A
  PID    TTY      TIME       CMD
    1    ?        00:00:31   systemd
    2    ?        00:00:00   kthreadd
    3    ?        00:00:02   ksoftirqd/0
    5    ?        00:00:00   kworker/0:0H
    7    ?        00:00:00   migration/0
    8    ?        00:00:00   rcu_bh
    9    ?        00:00:12   rcu_sched
   10    ?        00:00:11   watchdog/0
   12    ?        00:00:00   kdevtmpfs
   13    ?        00:00:00   netns
   14    ?        00:00:00   khungtaskd
   15    ?        00:00:00   writeback
95730    ?        00:00:00   kworker/0:3
95747    ?        00:00:00   sleep
95748    pts/0    00:00:00   ps
[philip@localhost ~]$
```

When we run the `ps` command with either `-A` or `-e` parameter, it will only print out the process IDs and the name of each process. But wait, we can expand this output even further. We can pass `-a` along with `-u`. This will print out processes for the current user who opened the Terminal:

```
[philip@localhost ~]$ ps -au
```

To see all processes owned by the current user in the system, we pass the `-x` option:

```
[philip@localhost ~]$ ps -x
PID   TTY   STAT   TIME  COMMAND
1487   ?     Sl     0:00  /usr/bin/gnome-keyring-daemon --daemonize --login
1491   ?     Ssl    0:01  /usr/libexec/gnome-session-binary --session gnome-
classic
1498   ?     S      0:00  dbus-launch --sh-syntax --exit-with-session
1499   ?     Ssl    0:00  /bin/dbus-daemon --fork --print-pid 4 --print-address
6 --session
1567   ?     Sl     0:00  /usr/libexec/gvfsd
1572   ?     Sl     0:00  /usr/libexec/gvfsd-fuse /run/user/1000/gvfs -f -o
big_writes
1664   ?     Ss     0:00  /usr/bin/ssh-agent /bin/sh -c exec -l /bin/bash -c
"env
GNOME_SHELL_SESSION_MODE=classic gnome-session --session gnome-cla
1683   ?     Sl     0:00  /usr/libexec/at-spi-bus-launcher
1688   ?     Sl     0:00  /bin/dbus-daemon --config-file=/usr/share/defaults/at-
spi2/accessibility.conf --nofork --print-address 3
```

We can also specify a user as part of the argument with −u:

```
[philip@localhost ~]$ ps -au root
  PID  TTY    TIME      CMD
    1  ?      00:00:31  systemd
    2  ?      00:00:00  kthreadd
    3  ?      00:00:02  ksoftirqd/0
    5  ?      00:00:00  kworker/0:0H
```

We can also see all the users in addition to the path to the executable for each daemon; we pass −aux or aux−; this is the **Berkeley Software Distribution (BSD)** syntax. The BSD is another flavor of Unix. Following is an example of the Linux syntax:

```
[philip@localhost ~]$ ps -aux
USER     PID  %CPU %MEM VSZ       RSS    TTY  STAT  START    TIME
COMMAND
root       1   0.0  0.4 193700   4216   ?    Ss    Aug08   0:31
/usr/lib/systemd/systemd --switched-root --system --deserialize 21
root       2   0.0  0.0 0         0     ?    S     Aug08   0:00
[kthreadd]
root       3   0.0  0.0 0         0     ?    S     Aug08   0:02 [ksoftirqd/0]
root       5   0.0  0.0 0         0     ?    S     Aug08   0:00
[kworker/0:0H]
dbus     570   0.0  0.2 36524    2236   ?    Ssl   Aug08   0:14 /bin/dbus-
daemon --system --address=systemd: --nofork --nopidfile --systemd-activati
chrony   571   0.0  0.0 115640   672    ?    S     Aug08   0:00
/usr/sbin/chronyd
avahi    585   0.0  0.0 30072    28     ?    S     Aug08   0:00 avahi-daemon:
chroot helper
philip  2209   0.0  0.0 313472   644    ?    Sl    Aug08   0:00
/usr/libexec/gvfsd-metadata
philip  2213   0.0  1.0 720692   10608  ?    Sl    Aug08   0:05
/usr/libexec/gnome-terminal-server
```

Awesome! Based on the preceding output, we can see various user accounts. Some of the accounts are actual system accounts, such as the dbus account. We can also specify a user account ID:

```
[philip@localhost ~]$ ps -ux 1000
USER     PID   %CPU  %MEM  VSZ      RSS    TTY  STAT START    TIME
COMMAND
philip  1487   0.0   0.0   462496   996    ?    Sl   Aug08   0:00
/usr/bin/gnome-keyring-daemon --daemonize --login
philip  1491   0.0   0.1   761348   1512   ?    Ssl  Aug08   0:01
/usr/libexec/gnome-session-binary --session gnome-classic
philip  1498   0.0   0.0   13976    0      ?    S    Aug08   0:00
dbus-launch --sh-syntax --exit-with-session
philip  1499   0.0   0.1   36284    1276  ?     Ssl  Aug08   0:00 /bin/dbus-
```

```
daemon --fork --print-pid 4 --print-address 6 --session
philip   1567   0.0   0.0     386352   0   ?   S1   Aug08   0:00
/usr/libexec/gvfsd
philip   1572   0.0   0.0     415548   52  ?   S1   Aug08   0:00
/usr/libexec/gvfsd-fuse /run/user/1000/gvfs -f -o big_writes
```

In addition to this, it is also possible to display processes that are owned by a particular group. Yes! It's possible by passing either the group name or ID. If we're passing the group name, then we use -g:

```
[philip@localhost ~]$ ps -fg postfix
UID         PID    PPID  C  STIME  TTY      TIME      CMD
postfix    1110   1108  0  Aug08  ?    00:00:00  qmgr -l -t unix -u
postfix   95714   1108  0  06:12  ?    00:00:00  pickup -l -t unix -u
[philip@localhost ~]$
```

To pass the group ID, we pass the -G option:

```
[philip@localhost ~]$ ps -fg 89
UID         PID    PPID  C  STIME  TTY          TIME   CMD
[philip@localhost ~]$
[philip@localhost ~]$ ps -fG 89
UID         PID    PPID  C  STIME  TTY   TIME      CMD
postfix    1110   1108  0  Aug08  ?   00:00:00  qmgr -l -t unix -u
postfix   95714   1108  0  06:12  ?   00:00:00  pickup -l -t unix -u
[philip@localhost ~]$
```

Great job! We can also search for a process by specifying the **process ID (PID)**. We pass -f that will print a long listing along with the -p option, which expects a numerical value:

```
[philip@localhost ~]$ ps -fp 1982
UID        PID   PPID  C  STIME  TTY  TIME        CMD
philip    1982   1     0  Aug08  ?    00:00:00  /usr/libexec/tracker-store
[philip@localhost ~]$
```

Interestingly enough, we can even specify multiple processes on the same line; we separate the processes by a comma:

```
[philip@localhost ~]$ ps -fp 1982,2001,2219
UID        PID   PPID  C  STIME  TTY  TIME        CMD
philip    1982   1     0  Aug08  ?    00:00:00  /usr/libexec/tracker-store
philip    2001   1730  0  Aug08  ?    00:00:00  /usr/libexec/ibus-engine-
simple
philip    2219   2213  0  Aug08  ?    00:00:00  gnome-pty-helper
[philip@localhost ~]$
```

Great job! It is also possible to find a command by specifying the process ID by passing the −o option:

```
[philip@localhost ~]$ ps −fp 955 −o comm=sshd
[philip@localhost ~]$
```

Based on the preceding output, only the actual executable for the respective PID is displayed.

It is also possible to get memory and CPU information using the `ps` command; we pass the −e option along with the −o option. We then need to pass the column names that interest us. Here is how we accomplish this:

```
[philip@localhost ~]$ ps −eo pid,ppid,cmd,%mem,%cpu −−sort=−%mem | head
−14
PID     PPID    CMD                             %MEM    %CPU
1710    1491    /usr/bin/gnome-shell            17.9    0.0
1926    1491    /usr/bin/gnome-software −−g      7.1    0.0
1042    989     /usr/bin/X :0 −background n      2.5    0.0
95581   633     /sbin/dhclient −d −q −sf /u      1.3    0.0
2213    1       /usr/libexec/gnome-terminal      1.1    0.0
605     1       /usr/lib/polkit-1/polkitd −      1.1    0.0
1872    1491    /usr/libexec/gnome-settings      0.8    0.0
633     1       /usr/sbin/NetworkManager −−      0.8    0.0
1890    1491    nautilus-desktop −−force         0.7    0.0
2050    1915    /usr/libexec/evolution-cale      0.6    0.0
1291    1       /usr/libexec/packagekitd         0.6    0.0
632     1       /usr/bin/python −Es /usr/sb      0.4    0.0
1990    1915    /usr/libexec/evolution-cale      0.4    0.0
[philip@localhost ~]$
```

Awesome! Based on the preceding output, we've specified `pid`, `ppid`, `cmd`, `%mem`, `%cpu`. In addition to this, the `−−sort` option was added. This looks for the processes that have used up most of the system RAM and displays those first starting from highest to lowest. In addition, we've added the `head` command; this will only display the top portion of the content.

We specified that we would only like to see the first 14 lines. But wait, the output from the `ps` command isn't refreshed in real time; we can use yet another popular command to see the output refresh in real time instead of us having to rerun the command. We use the `watch` command to accomplish this task:

```
[philip@localhost ~]$ watch -n 1 'ps -eo pid,ppid,cmd,%mem,%cpu --sort=-
%cpu | head'
```

The output of running the preceding command is as follows:

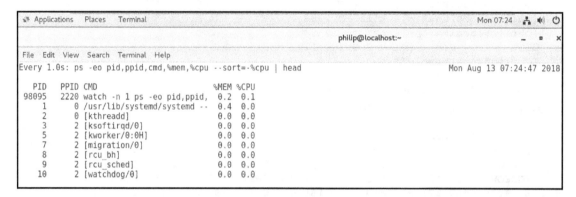

Based on the preceding screenshot, we have sorted the output to view the processes that are taking up most of the CPU within the system. We can view the output of the `ps` command in a hierarchical view; we would add the `-f` and `--forest` options:

```
[philip@localhost ~]$ ps -af --forest
UID          PID    PPID  C  STIME   TTY      TIME        CMD
philip       99053  2220  0  07:29   pts/0    00:00:00    ps -af --forest
[philip@localhost ~]$ ps -axf --forest
PID TTY        STAT    TIME  COMMAND
  2 ?          S       0:00  [kthreadd]
  3 ?          S       0:02   \_ [ksoftirqd/0]
517?           S<sl    0:00  /sbin/auditd
519 ?          S<sl    0:01   \_ /sbin/audispd
521 ?          S<      0:00    \_ /usr/sbin/sedispatch
543 ?          SNsl    0:04      /usr/libexec/rtkit-daemon
1664 ?         Ss      0:00     \_ /usr/bin/ssh-agent /bin/sh -c exec -l
/bin/bash -c "env GNOME_SHELL_SESSION_MODE=classic gnome-session --sessi
1710 ?         Sl      5:01      \_ /usr/bin/gnome-shell
1730 ?         Sl      0:00      |  \_ ibus-daemon --xim --panel disable
1743 ?         Sl      0:00      |     \_ /usr/libexec/ibus-dconf
2001 ?         Sl      0:00      |        \_ /usr/libexec/ibus-engine-simple
1872 ?         Sl      0:18      \_ /usr/libexec/gnome-settings-daemon
```

The kill command

The `kill` command is used for terminating processes. We can leverage the `ps` command, which we just covered, to identify a process, then call the `kill` command to end the process. Here is how we stop a process using the `kill` command:

```
[philip@localhost ~]$ ps -p 1788
PID   TTY        TIME       CMD
1788   ?         00:00:00 goa-daemon
[philip@localhost ~]$
[philip@localhost ~]$ kill -9 1788
[philip@localhost ~]$ ps -fp 1788
UID         PID   PPID C STIME TTY        TIME CMD
[philip@localhost ~]$
```

Awesome job! We used the 9 number, which means to send a `SIGKILL`. To see the various signals we can pass, we can use the `-l` option with the `kill` command:

```
[philip@localhost ~]$ kill -l
 1) SIGHUP       2) SIGINT      3) SIGQUIT     4) SIGILL      5) SIGTRAP
 6) SIGABRT      7) SIGBUS      8) SIGFPE      9) SIGKILL    10) SIGUSR111)
SIGSEGV        12) SIGUSR2     13) SIGPIPE    14) SIGALRM   15) SIGTERM
16) SIGSTKFLT  17) SIGCHLD     18) SIGCONT    19) SIGSTOP   20) SIGTSTP
21) SIGTTIN    22) SIGTTOU     23) SIGURG     24) SIGXCPU   25) SIGXFSZ
26) SIGVTALRM  27) SIGPROF     28) SIGWINCH   29) SIGIO     30) SIGPWR
31) SIGSYS     34) SIGRTMIN    35) SIGRTMIN+1 36) SIGRTMIN+2
37) SIGRTMIN+3 38) SIGRTMIN+4  39) SIGRTMIN+5 40) SIGRTMIN+6
41) SIGRTMIN+7 42) SIGRTMIN+8  43) SIGRTMIN+9 44) SIGRTMIN+10
45) SIGRTMIN+11 46) SIGRTMIN+12 47) SIGRTMIN+13 48) SIGRTMIN+14
49) SIGRTMIN+15 50) SIGRTMAX-14 51) SIGRTMAX-13 52) SIGRTMAX-12
53) SIGRTMAX-11 54) SIGRTMAX-10 55) SIGRTMAX-9 56) SIGRTMAX-8
57) SIGRTMAX-7  58) SIGRTMAX-6 59) SIGRTMAX-5 60) SIGRTMAX-4
61) SIGRTMAX-3  62) SIGRTMAX-2 63) SIGRTMAX-1 64) SIGRTMAX
[philip@localhost ~]$
```

To stop a process using the signal name, we pass the `-s` option:

```
[philip@localhost ~]$ ps -fp 1990
UID      PID   PPID C STIME  TTY    TIME       CMD
philip 1990  1915  0 Aug08   ?      00:00:00 /usr/libexec/evolution-
calendar-factory-subprocess --factory contacts --bus-name
org.gnome.evolution
[philip@localhost ~]$ kill -s SIGKILL 1915
[philip@localhost ~]$ ps -fp 1915
UID         PID   PPID C STIME TTY        TIME CMD
[philip@localhost ~]$
```

Caution should be taken whenever stopping a process with the SIGTERM while calling the kill command.

The pstree command

There is also another flavor of the ps command that can be used to view processes within a system—the pstree command. This will present all processes in a hierarchical layout. This is what it looks like:

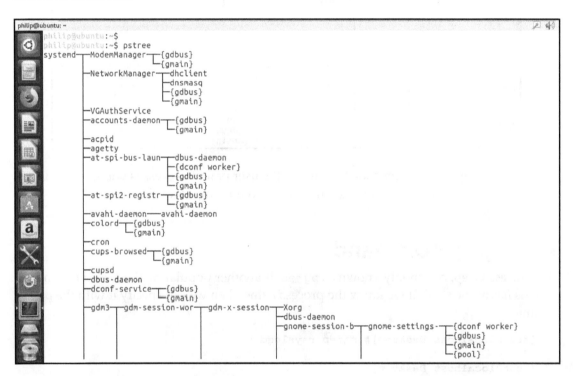

Based on the preceding screenshot, some processes are parent processes: they have child processes. We can also highlight a specific process by passing the -h option:

```
[root@localhost Desktop]# pstree -h 1735
rsyslogd────3*[{rsyslogd}]
[root@localhost Desktop]#The Process Grep commonly known as pgrep is
another popular method
```

We can also display only the processes specific to a user; we pass `username`:

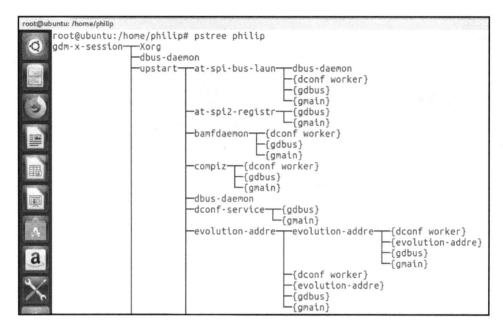

Based on the preceding screenshot, we can see the user parent process is `gdm-x-session`; this then has child processes, starting with `Xorg` and moving down the tree.

The pgrep command

The **Process Grep**, commonly known as `pgrep`, is another popular method used for finding process IDs at the shell. If we know the process name, then we can specify it with the `pgrep` command:

```
[root@localhost Desktop]# pgrep rsyslogd
545
[root@localhost Desktop]#
```

Based on the preceding command, we can see the PID for `rsyslogd`. We can also find processes for a particular user. To do this, we pass the `-u` option:

```
[root@localhost Desktop]# pgrep -u root rsyslogd
545
[root@localhost Desktop]#
```

Awesome job!

The pkill command

The `pkill` command is another method used for terminating processes. It enables us to use the process name when terminating a given process. In its simplest form, it is as follows:

```
[philip@localhost ~]$ pgrep rsyslogd
545
[philip@localhost ~]$ pkill rsyslogd
pkill: killing pid 545 failed: Operation not permitted
[philip@localhost ~]$ su
Password:
[root@localhost philip]# pkill rsyslogd
[root@localhost philip]# pgrep rsyslogd
[root@localhost philip]#
```

Awesome job! Based on the preceding code output, we can see the effectiveness of the `pkill` command.

Viewing and managing processes using the top command

The `top` command, which means *table of processes*, is similar in nature to Windows Task Manager. You will find a wide variety of Linux distributions that support the `top` command. The `top` command is essentially used to derive the system's CPU and memory utilization. The output is structured by creating a list of running processes selected by user-specified criteria; the output is in real time. The PID for each process is listed in the first column. Let's fire it up:

```
[philip@localhost ~]$ top
top - 12:50:44 up 5 days, 11:44,  2 users,  load average: 0.01, 0.02, 0.05
Tasks: 165 total,  1 running, 164 sleeping,  0 stopped,  0 zombie
%Cpu(s): 12.1 us,  1.4 sy,  0.0 ni, 86.1 id,  0.0 wa,  0.0 hi,  0.4 si,
0.0 st
KiB Mem :   999696 total,    95804 free,    633636 used,    270256 buff/cache
KiB Swap:  2097148 total,  1852900 free,    244248 used.   137728 avail Mem
PID    USER     PR   NI VIRT    RES   SHR S %CPU %MEM   TIME+   COMMAND
1710 philip    20    0  1943720 175920  15680 S  9.3 17.6 5:32.99 gnome-
shell
1042 root      20    0  306324  26188   1864 S  5.6 2.6 1:13.99 X
2213 philip    20    0  721204  11976   5992 S  2.7 1.2 0:15.04 gnome-
terminal-
1934 philip    20    0  389192   6308   1952 S  0.3  0.6   5:25.10 vmtoolsd
103282 philip 20    0  157716   2260   1540 R  0.3  0.2   0:00.28 top
```

```
1  root        20   0  193700   4248   2484 S  0.0  0.4   0:33.67 systemd
2  root        20   0       0      0      0 S  0.0  0.0   0:00.21 kthreadd
```

To the far right, there is a COMMAND column; this shows the executable. We can filter which user we would like to be displayed and their corresponding processes; we pass the -u option with top:

```
[philip@localhost ~]$ top -u philip
top - 12:55:24 up 5 days, 11:49,  2 users,  load average: 0.25, 0.08, 0.06
Tasks: 164 total,   2 running, 162 sleeping,   0 stopped,   0 zombie
%Cpu(s): 55.4 us,  6.8 sy,  0.0 ni, 36.5 id,  1.4 wa,  0.0 hi,  0.0 si,
0.0 st
KiB Mem :   999696 total,    73184 free,   641804 used,    284708 buff/cache
KiB Swap:  2097148 total,  1856364 free,   240784 used.   128952 avail Mem
PID   USER   PR NI VIRT      RES     SHR    S %CPU %MEM  TIME+    COMMAND
1710  philip 20 0 1943720  177568  16612  S 42.7 17.8 5:39.32 gnome-shell
2213  philip 20 0 721204   12256    6228  S  2.6  1.2 0:15.61 gnome-terminal-
1934  philip 20 0 389192    6308    1952  S  0.3  0.6 5:25.37 vmtoolsd
103360 philip 20 0 157716    2260    1544  R  0.3  0.2 0:00.06 top
1487  philip 20 0 462496    1504    1004  S  0.0  0.2 0:00.08 gnome-keyring-d
1491  philip 20 0 761348    2140    1220  S  0.0  0.2 0:01.77 gnome-session-b
1498  philip 20 0 13976        0       0  S  0.0  0.0 0:00.00 dbus-launch
1499  philip 20 0 36284      160     600  S  0.0  0.2 0:00.72 dbus-daemon
1567  philip 20 0 386352      864     592  S 0.0  0.1 0:00.02 gvfsd
```

Based on the preceding output, only the user philip is displayed with the processes. We can view the absolute path for all processes by pressing *C* inside the top command. Here is a screenshot of what you get when *C* is pressed:

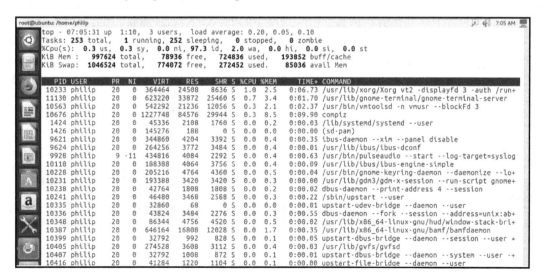

Awesome job! Now we can see the location for each process. We can also change how often the output is refreshed; the default is every three seconds. We press the *D* key from within the `top` command:

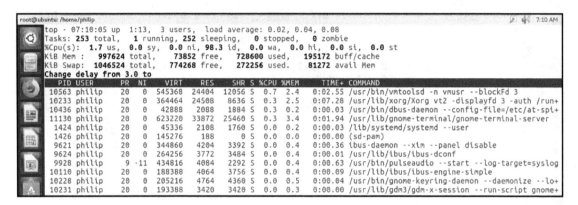

Based on the preceding screenshot, when the *D* key is pressed, a new line appears: `Change delay from 3.0 to`. This prompts us to specify a number. I'll type 2 here so the updates will refresh every two seconds. Now, when I press *D* once again, we will notice the difference in the prompt:

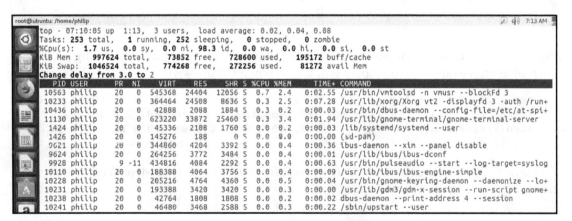

Great job! To see help with `top`, we can press *H*:

```
root@ubuntu: /home/philip
Help for Interactive Commands - procps-ng version 3.3.10
Window 1:Def: Cumulative mode Off.  System: Delay 2.0 secs; Secure mode Off.

  Z,B,E,e   Global: 'Z' colors; 'B' bold; 'E'/'e' summary/task memory scale
  l,t,m     Toggle Summary: 'l' load avg; 't' task/cpu stats; 'm' memory info
  0,1,2,3,I Toggle: '0' zeros; '1/2/3' cpus or numa node views; 'I' Irix mode
  f,F,X     Fields: 'f'/'F' add/remove/order/sort; 'X' increase fixed-width

  L,&,<,> . Locate: 'L'/'&' find/again; Move sort column: '<'/'>' left/right
  R,H,V,J . Toggle: 'R' Sort; 'H' Threads; 'V' Forest view; 'J' Num justify
  c,i,S,j . Toggle: 'c' Cmd name/line; 'i' Idle; 'S' Time; 'j' Str justify
  x,y       . Toggle highlights: 'x' sort field; 'y' running tasks
  z,b       . Toggle: 'z' color/mono; 'b' bold/reverse (only if 'x' or 'y')
  u,U,o,O . Filter by: 'u'/'U' effective/any user; 'o'/'O' other criteria
  n,#,^O  . Set: 'n'/'#' max tasks displayed; Show: Ctrl+'O' other filter(s)
  C,...   . Toggle scroll coordinates msg for: up,down,left,right,home,end

  k,r       Manipulate tasks: 'k' kill; 'r' renice
  d or s    Set update interval
  W,Y       Write configuration file 'W'; Inspect other output 'Y'
  q         Quit
            ( commands shown with '.' require a visible task display window )
Press 'h' or '?' for help with Windows,
Type 'q' or <Esc> to continue █
```

We can change how the memory is displayed inside in the `top` utility; depending on the current memory output, the display will toggle when we press *M*:

```
top - 13:09:50 up 5 days, 12:03,  2 users, load average: 0.00, 0.04, 0.05
Tasks: 164 total,   1 running, 163 sleeping,   0 stopped,   0 zombie
%Cpu(s):  4.1 us,  0.7 sy,  0.0 ni, 95.2 id,  0.0 wa,  0.0 hi,  0.0 si,
0.0 st
```

Based on the preceding screenshot, the section for the memory is hidden. When we press the *M* key once again, this will change:

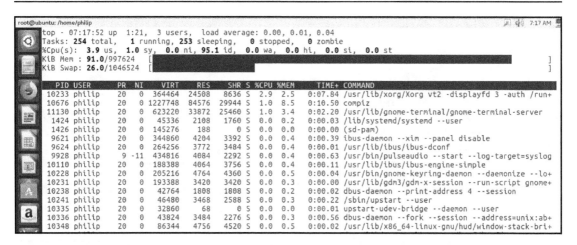

Awesome! If we press the *M* key once again, we will see a sort of graphical design:

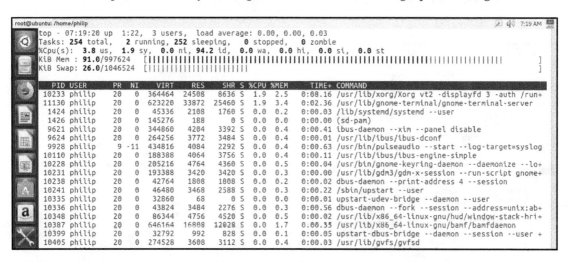

Great job! Now we have the nice bars indicating the memory usage for both RAM and swap. Similarly, we can change the display of the output by CPU; to do so, we press *T*:

```
top - 13:19:23 up 5 days, 12:13,  2 users,  load average: 0.30, 0.11, 0.07
Tasks: 163 total,   3 running, 160 sleeping,   0 stopped,   0 zombie
2 sleeping,   0 stopped,   0 zombie
%Cpu(s):    9.6/1.4     11[|||||||||||||
]
KiB Mem :   999696 total,    73524 free,    641328 used,    284844 buff/cache
KiB Swap:  2097148 total,  1856532 free,    240616 used.   129444 avail Mem
```

Awesome! When we press *T*, it will then turn the bars into a shaded output:

```
 Applications   Places   Terminal

                                                        philip@localhost:~

File  Edit  View  Search  Terminal  Help
top - 13:21:09 up 5 days, 12:14,  2 users,  load average: 0.19, 0.13, 0.08
Tasks: 164 total,   4 running, 160 sleeping,   0 stopped,   0 zombie
%Cpu(s):   2.5/1.0    4[               ]                                      ]
KiB Mem :   999696 total,     73252 free,    641584 used,    284860 buff/cache
KiB Swap:  2097148 total,   1856536 free,    240612 used.    129180 avail Mem

  PID USER      PR  NI    VIRT    RES    SHR S %CPU %MEM     TIME+ COMMAND
 1710 philip    20   0 1943720 178288  16624 S  1.0 17.8   6:17.98 gnome-shell
 1926 philip    20   0 1048800  70932   3204 S  0.5  7.1   0:23.02 gnome-software
 1934 philip    20   0  389192   6308   1952 S  0.5  0.6   5:26.99 vmtoolsd
103541 philip   20   0  157716   2260   1544 R  0.5  0.2   0:02.29 top
```

In addition to this, the processes can also be displayed in a hierarchical output; we press *Shift + V*:

```
 Applications   Places   Terminal

                                                philip@localhost:/home/philip

File  Edit  View  Search  Terminal  Help
top - 07:23:33 up 8 days,  8:54,  2 users,  load average: 0.37, 0.23, 0.12
Tasks: 165 total,   3 running, 162 sleeping,   0 stopped,   0 zombie
%Cpu(s):   1.0/0.7    2[||]                                                  ]
KiB Mem :   999696 total,    293592 free,    471420 used,    234684 buff/cache
KiB Swap:  2097148 total,   1602464 free,    494684 used.    328164 avail Mem

  PID USER      PR  NI    VIRT    RES    SHR S %CPU %MEM     TIME+ COMMAND
    1 root      20   0  193700   2416    616 S  0.0  0.2   0:50.59 systemd
  352 root      20   0   35016   3716   3508 S  0.0  0.4   0:23.21 `- systemd-journal
  373 root      20   0  121356      0      0 S  0.0  0.0   0:00.00 `- lvmetad
  390 root      20   0   48172    460    316 S  0.0  0.0   0:00.76 `- systemd-udevd
  517 root      16  -4   55452    148     52 S  0.0  0.0   0:01.37 `- auditd
  519 root      12  -8   84500    192     52 S  0.0  0.0   0:01.81    `- audispd
  521 root      16  -4   24052    156     88 S  0.0  0.0   0:00.49       `- sedispatch
  543 rtkit     21   1  164656    108     80 S  0.0  0.0   0:09.51 `- rtkit-daemon
  547 root      39  19   16840     28      0 S  0.0  0.0   0:00.21 `- alsactl
  550 root      20   0   99612      0      0 S  0.0  0.0   0:00.01 `- VGAuthService
  551 root      20   0  305080   1528   1172 S  0.0  0.2  11:28.93 `- vmtoolsd
  552 libstor+  20   0    8532     32      0 S  0.0  0.0   0:01.90 `- lsmd
  553 root      20   0   24260    836    648 S  0.0  0.1   0:13.13 `- systemd-logind
  555 root      20   0  219408      8      4 S  0.0  0.0   0:00.00 `- abrtd
  557 avahi     20   0   30200    376    136 S  0.0  0.0   0:01.53 `- avahi-daemon
  585 avahi     20   0   30072      4      0 S  0.0  0.0   0:00.00    `- avahi-daemon
  558 root      20   0  425952    592    172 S  0.0  0.1   0:00.85 `- ModemManager
  559 root      20   0  216908    168    128 S  0.0  0.0   0:01.75 `- abrt-watch-log
```

To turn off the forest view, we simply toggle *Shift + V* once again:

```
 Applications   Places   Terminal

                                           philip@localhost:/home/philip

 File  Edit  View  Search  Terminal  Help
top - 07:25:27 up 8 days,  8:56,  2 users,  load average: 0.26, 0.22, 0.13
Tasks: 166 total,   4 running, 162 sleeping,   0 stopped,   0 zombie
%Cpu(s):   1.3/0.0      1[|                                                    ]
KiB Mem :   999696 total,   272572 free,   474076 used,   253048 buff/cache
KiB Swap:  2097148 total,  1602464 free,   494684 used.   325516 avail Mem

  PID USER      PR  NI    VIRT    RES    SHR S %CPU %MEM     TIME+ COMMAND
 1710 philip    20   0 1977684 200548  10488 S  0.9 20.1   9:32.82 gnome-shell
 1042 root      20   0  305840  25196   1124 R  0.4  2.5   4:17.68 X
25621 root      20   0  157716   1968   1248 R  0.4  0.2   0:00.57 top
    1 root      20   0  193700   2416    616 S  0.0  0.2   0:50.59 systemd
    2 root      20   0       0      0      0 S  0.0  0.0   0:00.39 kthreadd
    3 root      20   0       0      0      0 S  0.0  0.0   0:08.15 ksoftirqd/0
    5 root       0 -20       0      0      0 S  0.0  0.0   0:00.00 kworker/0:0H
    7 root      rt   0       0      0      0 S  0.0  0.0   0:00.00 migration/0
    8 root      20   0       0      0      0 S  0.0  0.0   0:00.00 rcu_bh
    9 root      20   0       0      0      0 S  0.0  0.0   0:20.27 rcu_sched
   10 root      rt   0       0      0      0 S  0.0  0.0   0:13.42 watchdog/0
   12 root      20   0       0      0      0 S  0.0  0.0   0:00.00 kdevtmpfs
   13 root       0 -20       0      0      0 S  0.0  0.0   0:00.00 netns
   14 root      20   0       0      0      0 S  0.0  0.0   0:00.35 khungtaskd
   15 root       0 -20       0      0      0 S  0.0  0.0   0:00.00 writeback
   16 root       0 -20       0      0      0 S  0.0  0.0   0:00.00 kintegrityd
   17 root       0 -20       0      0      0 S  0.0  0.0   0:00.00 bioset
   18 root       0 -20       0      0      0 S  0.0  0.0   0:00.00 kblockd
   19 root       0 -20       0      0      0 S  0.0  0.0   0:00.00 md
   25 root      20   0       0      0      0 S  0.0  0.0   0:53.60 kswapd0
   26 root      25   5       0      0      0 S  0.0  0.0   0:00.00 ksmd
   27 root      39  19       0      0      0 S  0.0  0.0   0:03.16 khugepaged
   28 root       0 -20       0      0      0 S  0.0  0.0   0:00.00 crypto
```

We can also stop a process using the `top` command; we press *K*, which is for killing processes inside the `top` command:

```
  Applications   Places    Terminal

                                              philip@localhost:/home/philip

 File  Edit  View  Search  Terminal  Help
top - 07:27:24 up 8 days,  8:58,  2 users,  load average: 0.06, 0.17, 0.13
Tasks: 165 total,   1 running, 164 sleeping,   0 stopped,   0 zombie
%Cpu(s):   2.3/0.3    3[||                                                     ]
KiB Mem :   999696 total,    264528 free,    474208 used,    260960 buff/cache
KiB Swap:  2097148 total,   1602472 free,    494676 used.   325384 avail Mem
PID to signal/kill [default pid = 1710]
  PID USER      PR  NI    VIRT    RES    SHR S %CPU %MEM     TIME+ COMMAND
 1710 philip    20   0 1977684 200664  10596 S  1.3 20.1   9:34.24 gnome-shell
 1934 philip    20   0  392400   9720   1568 S  0.7  1.0   9:53.14 vmtoolsd
25621 root      20   0  157716   1968   1248 R  0.7  0.2   0:00.75 top
 1042 root      20   0  305840  25196   1124 S  0.3  2.5   4:18.14 X
 1809 philip    20   0  518716    296     28 S  0.3  0.0   0:20.70 goa-identity-se
    1 root      20   0  193700   2416    616 S  0.0  0.2   0:50.59 systemd
    2 root      20   0       0      0      0 S  0.0  0.0   0:00.39 kthreadd
    3 root      20   0       0      0      0 S  0.0  0.0   0:08.15 ksoftirqd/0
    5 root       0 -20       0      0      0 S  0.0  0.0   0:00.00 kworker/0:0H
    7 root      rt   0       0      0      0 S  0.0  0.0   0:00.00 migration/0
    8 root      20   0       0      0      0 S  0.0  0.0   0:00.00 rcu_bh
    9 root      20   0       0      0      0 S  0.0  0.0   0:20.28 rcu_sched
   10 root      rt   0       0      0      0 S  0.0  0.0   0:13.42 watchdog/0
   12 root      20   0       0      0      0 S  0.0  0.0   0:00.00 kdevtmpfs
   13 root       0 -20       0      0      0 S  0.0  0.0   0:00.00 netns
   14 root      20   0       0      0      0 S  0.0  0.0   0:00.35 khungtaskd
   15 root       0 -20       0      0      0 S  0.0  0.0   0:00.00 writeback
```

Based on the preceding command, a new line appears: `PID to signal/kill [default pid = 1710]`, and we need to specify a process ID:

```
KiB Swap:2097148 total, 1856800 free, 240348 used. 129084 avail Mem
Send pid 1718 signal [15/sigterm]
PID  USER    PR NI VIRT     RES    SHR   S %CPU %MEM TIME+    COMMAND
1710 philip 20 0 1944552 176788 16840 S  1.5 17.7  6:36.40 gnome-shell
2213 philip 20 0 721724  16020   8740 S  0.5 1.6   0:22.60 gnome-terminal-
```

Now we need to specify the signal to send to the process; the default is `15/sigterm`. We'll accept the default; this will terminate the process without us having to exit the `top` utility.

Managing process(es) with the service command

The `service` command initially was used to run SysV init scripts on early Linux distributions prior to `systemd`. Depending on the what you're trying to accomplish, the method you use to start, stop, or restart a service will depend upon whether your distribution uses `systemd` or `init`. Most Linux engineers prefer to use the `service` command as opposed to the newer methods of handling processes in system environments. Thus in most newer distributions the `service` command is supported. The syntax for the `service` command is:

```
service <process> <status>
```

To view all services on a system running SysV scripts, we'll use the CentOS 6.5 system:

```
[philip@localhost Desktop]$ service --status-all
abrt-ccpp hook is installed
abrtd (pid  2254) is running...
abrt-dump-oops is stopped
acpid (pid  1964) is running...
atd (pid  2273) is running...
auditd (pid  1710) is running...
Usage: /etc/init.d/bluetooth {start|stop}
cpuspeed is stopped
crond (pid  2262) is running...
cupsd (pid  1874) is running...
dnsmasq (pid  2087) is running...
firstboot is not scheduled to run
hald (pid  1975) is running...
htcacheclean is stopped
httpd is stopped
winbindd is stopped
wpa_supplicant (pid  1875) is running...
[philip@localhost Desktop]$
```

The scripts that the `service` command reads start with `rc`. We can quickly view all related scripts:

```
[philip@localhost Desktop]$ ls -l /etc | grep rc.
lrwxrwxrwx. 1 root root    11 Jun 20 01:37 init.d -> rc.d/init.d
lrwxrwxrwx. 1 root root     7 Jun 20 01:40 rc -> rc.d/rc
lrwxrwxrwx. 1 root root    10 Jun 20 01:40 rc0.d -> rc.d/rc0.d
lrwxrwxrwx. 1 root root    10 Jun 20 01:40 rc1.d -> rc.d/rc1.d
lrwxrwxrwx. 1 root root    10 Jun 20 01:40 rc2.d -> rc.d/rc2.d
lrwxrwxrwx. 1 root root    10 Jun 20 01:40 rc3.d -> rc.d/rc3.d
```

```
lrwxrwxrwx. 1 root root      10 Jun 20 01:40 rc4.d -> rc.d/rc4.d
lrwxrwxrwx. 1 root root      10 Jun 20 01:40 rc5.d -> rc.d/rc5.d
lrwxrwxrwx. 1 root root      10 Jun 20 01:40 rc6.d -> rc.d/rc6.d
drwxr-xr-x. 10 root root   4096 Jun 20 05:50 rc.d
lrwxrwxrwx. 1 root root      13 Jun 20 01:40 rc.local -> rc.d/rc.local
lrwxrwxrwx. 1 root root      15 Jun 20 01:40 rc.sysinit -> rc.d/rc.sysinit
[philip@localhost Desktop]$
```

To control the status of a process, we can do this:

```
[philip@localhost Desktop]$ service crond status
crond (pid  4457) is running...
[philip@localhost Desktop]$
```

From the preceding command, this particular process is currently running. We can change this; let's say we want to stop the crond process. We simply replace status with stop:

```
[philip@localhost Desktop]$ service crond stop
User has insufficient privilege.
[philip@localhost Desktop]$
```

Based on the preceding output, we run into a roadblock; this can easily be remedied by becoming the root user:

```
[root@localhost Desktop]# service crond stop
Stopping crond:                                          [  OK  ]
[root@localhost Desktop]#
```

Awesome job! Now we can rerun the service command; this time using the status option:

```
[root@localhost Desktop]# service crond status
crond is stopped
[root@localhost Desktop]#
```

And there we have it. The service has been stopped. To start backing up this process, we simply replace stop with start:

```
[root@localhost Desktop]# service crond start
Starting crond:                                          [  OK  ]
[root@localhost Desktop]#
```

Now let's try to start the process once again:

```
[root@localhost Desktop]# service crond status
crond (pid  6606) is running...
[root@localhost Desktop]#
```

Great job! If, for some reason, we have changes to the process and need to restart the process, then we can do it in a number of ways. We can stop the process and then start it again:

```
[root@localhost Desktop]# service crond stop
Stopping crond:                                         [  OK  ]
[root@localhost Desktop]# service crond start
Starting crond:                                         [  OK  ]
[root@localhost Desktop]#
```

Also, we can use the `restart` option:

```
[root@localhost Desktop]# service crond restart
Stopping crond:                                         [  OK  ]
Starting crond:                                         [  OK  ]
[root@localhost Desktop]#
```

Lastly, we can use the `reload` option; this last option will reread the configuration files for any changes that have been made:

```
[root@localhost Desktop]# service crond reload
Reloading crond:                                        [  OK  ]
[root@localhost Desktop]# service crond status
crond (pid  6703) is running...
[root@localhost Desktop]#
```

Awesome job!

Managing process(es) with the systemctl command

On most new distributions that use system, we would manage processes using the `systemctl` command. The Linux developers have also left support for the `service` command; if we try to terminate a process using the `service` command, then we will see that it is actually going to redirect our request to the `systemctl` command. Let's try this:

```
[root@localhost philip]# service crond status
Redirecting to /bin/systemctl status crond.service
crond.service - Command Scheduler
Loaded: loaded (/usr/lib/systemd/system/crond.service; enabled; vendor
preset: enabled)
Active: active (running) since Thu 2018-08-02 07:13:38 PDT; 1 weeks 5 days
ago
 Main PID: 991 (crond)
```

```
CGroup: /system.slice/crond.service
        └─991 /usr/sbin/crond -n
Aug 02 07:13:38 localhost.localdomain systemd[1]: Started Command
Scheduler.
Aug 02 07:13:38 localhost.localdomain systemd[1]: Starting Command
Scheduler...
Aug 02 07:13:38 localhost.localdomain crond[991]: (CRON) INFO (RANDOM_DELAY
will be scaled with factor 15% if used.)
Aug 02 07:13:43 localhost.localdomain crond[991]: (CRON) INFO (running with
inotify support)
[root@localhost philip]#
```

Awesome! Based on the output, we can see that the `service` command is in fact being redirected:

```
[root@localhost philip]# service crond status
Redirecting to /bin/systemctl status crond.service
crond.service - Command Scheduler
```

Now let's try using the newer approach for managing processes; we'll use the `systemctl` command. The format is as follows:

```
systemctl <action><process>
```

We can use this at the shell:

```
[root@localhost philip]# systemctl status atd
atd.service - Job spooling tools
Loaded: loaded (/usr/lib/systemd/system/atd.service; enabled; vendor
preset: enabled)
Active: active (running) since Thu 2018-08-02 07:13:38 PDT; 1 weeks 5 days
ago
Main PID: 993 (atd)
CGroup: /system.slice/atd.service
        └─993 /usr/sbin/atd -f
Aug 02 07:13:38 localhost.localdomain systemd[1]: Started Job spooling
tools.
Aug 02 07:13:38 localhost.localdomain systemd[1]: Starting Job spooling
tools...
[root@localhost philip]#
```

To start a process using `systemctl`, we pass the `start` option:

```
[root@localhost philip]# systemctl start rsyslog.service
[root@localhost philip]#
```

We can check on the status for a process by passing the `status` option:

```
[root@localhost philip]# systemctl status rsyslog.service
rsyslog.service - System Logging Service
Loaded: loaded (/usr/lib/systemd/system/rsyslog.service; enabled; vendor
preset: enabled)
   Active: active (running) since Tue 2018-08-14 08:29:22 PDT; 5s ago
   Docs:
man:rsyslogd(8)
   http://www.rsyslog.com/doc/
Main PID: 117499 (rsyslogd)
   CGroup: /system.slice/rsyslog.service
           └─117499 /usr/sbin/rsyslogd -n
Aug 14 08:29:22 localhost.localdomain systemd[1]: Starting System Logging
Service...
Aug 14 08:29:22 localhost.localdomain rsyslogd[117499]:   [origin
software="rsyslogd" swVersion="8.24.0" x-pid="117499" x-
info="http://www.rs...] start
Aug 14 08:29:22 localhost.localdomain systemd[1]: Started System Logging
Service.
Hint: Some lines were ellipsized, use -l to show in full.
[root@localhost philip]#
```

You will notice that the output from the `systemctl` command is much more intuitive than the older `service` command in early Linux distributions. We can also stop a process using the `systemctl` command; we pass the `stop` option:

```
[root@localhost philip]# systemctl stop rsyslog.service
[root@localhost philip]# systemctl status rsyslog.service
rsyslog.service - System Logging Service
Loaded: loaded (/usr/lib/systemd/system/rsyslog.service; enabled; vendor
preset: enabled)
Active: inactive (dead) since Tue 2018-08-14 08:38:38 PDT; 8s ago
Docs: man:rsyslogd(8)
http://www.rsyslog.com/doc/
Process: 117499 ExecStart=/usr/sbin/rsyslogd -n $SYSLOGD_OPTIONS
(code=exited, status=0/SUCCESS)
Main PID: 117499 (code=exited, status=0/SUCCESS)
Aug 14 08:29:22 localhost.localdomain systemd[1]: Starting System Logging
Service...
Aug 14 08:29:22 localhost.localdomain rsyslogd[117499]:   [origin
software="rsyslogd" swVersion="8.24.0" x-pid="117499" x-
info="http://www.rs...] start
Aug 14 08:29:22 localhost.localdomain systemd[1]: Started System Logging
Service.
Aug 14 08:38:38 localhost.localdomain rsyslogd[117499]:   [origin
software="rsyslogd" swVersion="8.24.0" x-pid="117499" x-
info="http://www.rs...nal 15.
```

```
Aug 14 08:38:38 localhost.localdomain systemd[1]: Stopping System Logging
Service...
Aug 14 08:38:38 localhost.localdomain systemd[1]: Stopped System Logging
Service.
Hint: Some lines were ellipsized, use -l to show in full.
[root@localhost philip]#
```

Also, we can restart or reload a process:

```
[root@localhost philip]# systemctl restart rsyslog.service
[root@localhost philip]# systemctl status rsyslog.service
rsyslog.service -
System Logging Service
Loaded: loaded (/usr/lib/systemd/system/rsyslog.service; enabled; vendor
preset: enabled)
    Active: active (running) since Tue 2018-08-14 08:39:37 PDT; 2s ago
      Docs: man:rsyslogd(8)
            http://www.rsyslog.com/doc/
Main PID: 117730 (rsyslogd)
CGroup: /system.slice/rsyslog.service
        └─117730 /usr/sbin/rsyslogd -n
Aug 14 08:39:37 localhost.localdomain systemd[1]: Starting System Logging
Service...
Aug 14 08:39:37 localhost.localdomain rsyslogd[117730]:  [origin
software="rsyslogd" swVersion="8.24.0" x-pid="117730" x-
info="http://www.rs...] start
Aug 14 08:39:37 localhost.localdomain systemd[1]: Started System Logging
Service.
Hint: Some lines were ellipsized, use -l to show in full.
[root@localhost philip]#
```

Based on the preceding output, when we passed the `restart` option, it simply started the process. The processes that `systemctl` handles are considered as units when using the `systemctl` command. We can view the units by passing `list-units` files:

```
[root@localhost philip]# systemctl list-units --all --state=active
UNIT    LOAD    ACTIVE SUB        DESCRIPTION
proc-sys-fs-binfmt_misc.automount                          loaded
active waiting   Arbitrary Executable File Formats File System Automount
Point
dev-cdrom.device                                           loaded
active plugged    VMware_Virtual_IDE_CDROM_Drive
dev-disk-by\x2did-
ata\x2dVMware_Virtual_IDE_CDROM_Drive_10000000000000000001.device loaded
active plugged    VMware_Virtual_IDE_CDROM_Drive
dev-disk-by\x2dpath-pci\x2d0000:00:07.1\x2data\x2d2.0.device    loaded
active plugged    VMware_Virtual_IDE_CDROM_Drive
dev-disk-by\x2dpath-pci\x2d0000:00:10.0\x2dscsi\x2d0:0:0:0.device loaded
```

```
active plugged    VMware_Virtual_S
dev-disk-by\x2dpath-pci\x2d0000:00:10.0\x2dscsi\x2d0:0:0:0\x2dpart1.device
loaded active plugged    VMware_Virtual_S 1
dev-disk-by\x2dpath-pci\x2d0000:00:10.0\x2dscsi\x2d0:0:0:0\x2dpart2.device
loaded active plugged    VMware_Virtual_S 2
dev-disk-by\x2dpath-pci\x2d0000:00:10.0\x2dscsi\x2d0:0:0:0\x2dpart3.device
loaded active plugged    VMware_Virtual_S 3
dev-disk-by\x2duuid-16e2de7b\x2db679\x2d4a12\x2d888e\x2d55081af4dad8.device
loaded active plugged    VMware_Virtual_S 3
sys-devices-virtual-net-virbr0\x2dnic.device                     loaded
active plugged    /sys/devices/virtual/net/virbr0-nic
[root@localhost philip]#
```

The various processes are stored in /usr/lib/systemd/system:

```
[root@localhost philip]# ls /usr/lib/systemd/system
abrt-ccpp.service        iscsiuio.socket          shutdown.target
abrtd.service            kdump.service            shutdown.target.wants
abrt-oops.service        kexec.target             sigpwr.target
abrt-pstoreoops.service  kexec.target.wants       sleep.target
abrt-vmcore.service      kmod-static-nodes.service -.slice
abrt-xorg.service        kpatch.service           slices.target
accounts-daemon.service  ksm.service              smartcard.target
alsa-restore.service     ksmtuned.service         smartd.service
alsa-state.service       libstoragemgmt.service   sockets.target
alsa-store.service       libvirtd.service         sockets.target.wants
[root@localhost philip]#
```

As you can see, there are a wide variety of processes that are managed using the systemctl command.

Summary

In this chapter, we dealt with various aspects relating to handling processes from within the shell. We started off with the ps command. The methods to expose processes currently running in the shell were shown. Next, we saw how to print all processes running on the system. This was followed up by exposing the commands used by each process. We then focused on filtering the output for a particular user, also by the user ID. After that, we touched on filtering for a process, also filtering by the process ID. In addition to this, we tackled filtering by groups. This was followed by changing the display into a forest layout.

Furthermore, we saw how to pull memory and CPU information; we called on the `watch` command to update the results in real time. Finally, we saw how to terminate a process using the `ps` command in combination with the `kill` command. Next, we touched on the `pstree` command; this presents the processes in a hierarchical format. We even manipulated its output to narrow in on a specific process; in addition, we also checked for a specific user's processes.

Following this, we touched on the `pgrep` command, also known as process grep. This is another method for finding a process ID; either a process name can be supplied, or we can specify the user whose processes we would like to be displayed. Following this, we touched on the `pkill` command; as the names suggests, it is used to terminate a process. We saw this in the demo. After that, we worked with the `top` command, using various techniques for manipulating the output of the results, and explored how to terminate a process while inside the `top` command.

Next, we worked with the `service` command; we talked about where we usually find it, and looked at its support in newer Linux distributions. Various demos were done using the `service` command. Finally, we worked with the `systemctl` command; this is by far the best method for managing processes in newer Linux distributions that use systems, as opposed to older Linux distributions that use SysV init scripts.

In the next chapter, we go deeper into managing processes. There are times when we want to give preference to one process over another. This is the focus of the next chapter. This will not only enable you to manage your processes on your system, but it will also give you an edge over others, thus taking you one step closer to certification. I hope to see you there.

Questions

1. Which command prints processes that have been started in a new Terminal?

    A. `pkill`
    B. `chmod`
    C. `ps`
    D. `chage`

2. Which option with the `ps` command prints all processes running in a system?

        A. `-B`
        B. `-b`
        C. `-e`
        D. `-x`

3. Which option with the `ps` command can be used to print the output in a hierarchical layout?

        A. `-forest`
        B. `--forest`
        C. `--tree`
        D. `-tree`

4. Which option with the `ps` command is used to specify a user process?

        A. `-x`
        B. `-a`
        C. `-u`
        D. `-d`

5. Which option with the `kill` command is used to display the various SIG terms?

        A. `-`
        B. `-l`
        C. `-i`
        D. `-d`

6. Which number is equivalent to `SIGKILL` when using the `kill` command?

        A. 8
        B. 10
        C. 7
        D. 9

7. Which option with the `top` command can specify the user?

        A. `-u`
        B. `-p`
        C. `-v`
        D. `-a`

8. Which letter is used to set how often the results are refreshed inside the `top` utility?

    A. `-a`
    B. `b`
    C. `d`
    D. `e`

9. Which option can be used to reread a process configuration with the `service` command?

    A. `reboot`
    B. `stop`
    C. `status`
    D. `reload`

10. In which directory are the units `/processes` located in a system that is managed by the `systemctl` command?

    A. `/var/lib/systemd`
    B. `/usr/lib/systemd/system`
    C. `/usr/systemd/system`
    D. `/usr/system/systemd`

Further reading

- For more info about processes, see `https://www.tutorialspoint.com`.
- This website gives you a lot of useful tips for processes: `https://www.linux.com`.
- This last link gives you information in general that relates to various commands. You can post your questions there, and other community members will respond: `https://www.linuxquestions.org`.

10
Modifying Process Execution

In the previous chapter, we discussed various methods to expose processes currently running in the shell. Furthermore, we saw how to pull memory and CPU information, and we saw how to terminate a process using the ps command in combination with the kill command. Next, we touched on the pstree command. Following this, we touched on the pgrep command; also known as Process Grep. We then looked at the pkill command; as its name suggests, this is used to terminate a process. After this, we worked with the top command and then we worked with the service command. Finally, we worked with the systemctl command.

This chapter is small in comparison to the previous ones, but its contents are of great importance when it comes to managing our resources. First, managing processes is further discussed, this time focusing on the importance of a process within the context of the process scheduler (sometimes you may hear the term kernel scheduler; they mean the same thing). Often, we are faced with challenges with regard to resource limitations. This will be addressed in a number of ways. With that in mind, we will explore the various guidelines that should be followed when attempting to change a process's priority within the confines of a Linux distribution. The first section focuses on the nice command. This is followed by the renice command. Finally, the focus will be on foreground processes versus background processes.

We will cover the following topics in this chapter:

- The nice command
- The renice command
- Foreground processes versus background processes

The nice command

In its simplest terms, the `nice` command is used for manipulating process niceness with regard to CPU resource availability. When we say *niceness* in this context, this is referring to the attention or priority given to a particular process for the CPU resources. We can increase or decrease priority for a given process. This becomes relevant whenever the CPU is being bogged down by a number of processes, each fighting for its own attention. By changing the niceness for a particular process, we are affecting the process scheduling.

We can view the current `nice` value for processes using the `ps` command. Here, we would pass the `al` option:

```
root@ubuntu:/home/philip# ps -al
F S UID PID  PPID C PRI  NI ADDR SZ WCHAN TTY   TIME CMD
4 S 0   2423 2271 0 80   0 - 13698 poll_s pts/17   00:00:00 sudo
4 S 0   2437 2423 0 80   0 - 13594 wait   pts/17   00:00:00 su
4 S 0   2438 2437 0 80   0 - 5304 wait    pts/17   00:00:00 bash
0 R 0   3063 2438 0 80   0 - 7229 -       pts/17   00:00:00 ps
root@ubuntu:/home/philip#
```

Some output has been omitted for brevity. Based on the preceding output, the `NI` column represents the current niceness for processes. You'll notice that most processes' niceness value is set to `0`. We can also filter the output of the `ps` command by using the `grep` command:

```
root@ubuntu:/home/philip# ps -eo pid,ppid,ni,comm | grep update
   2402    1841    0 update-notifier
   2421    1611   10 update-manager
root@ubuntu:/home/philip#
```

Awesome job! Based on this, we can see that there are some processes whose niceness value is not `0`, by default. Interestingly enough, we can also leverage another command to view the current niceness of processes; we can use the `top` command:

```
root@ubuntu:/home/philip# top
PID USER   PR  NI    VIRT   RES   SHR S %CPU %MEM    TIME+    COMMAND
3020 root  20   0   41800  3880  3176 R  6.7  0.4   0:00.01 top
1 root      20   0  185164  4532  3100 S  0.0  0.5   0:01.92 systemd
2 root      20   0       0     0     0 S  0.0  0.0   0:00.00  kthreadd
3 root      20   0       0     0     0 S  0.0  0.0   0:00.16  ksoftirqd/0
9 root      rt   0       0     0     0 S  0.0  0.0   0:00.00  migration/0
10 root     rt   0       0     0     0 S  0.0  0.0   0:00.00  watchdog/0
15 root      0 -20       0     0     0 S  0.0  0.0   0:00.00  writeback
16 root     25   5       0     0     0 S  0.0  0.0   0:00.00  ksmd
17 root     39  19       0     0     0 S  0.0  0.0   0:00.00  khugepaged
```

The fourth column, `NI`, represents the niceness for each process. Another key column is the third column, `PR`; this represents the actual priority that the Linux kernel sees. The `PRI` column is not user configurable. Also, the `rt` under the `PRI` column indicates that those processes' priorities are handled in real-time scheduling.

We cannot change values under the `PRI` column.

We can view the syntax of the `nice` command by passing the `--help` option:

```
root@ubuntu:/home/philip# nice --help
Usage: nice [OPTION] [COMMAND [ARG]...]
Run COMMAND with an adjusted niceness, which affects process scheduling.
With no COMMAND, print the current niceness.  Niceness values range from
-20 (most favorable to the process) to 19 (least favorable to the process).
Mandatory arguments to long options are mandatory for short options too.
  -n, --adjustment=N   add integer N to the niceness (default 10)
      --help     display this help and exit
      --version  output version information and exit
```

Your shell may have its own version of `nice`, which usually supersedes the version described here. Please refer to your shell's documentation for details about the options it supports.
GNU coreutils online help can be found at the following link: `http://www.gnu.org/software/coreutils`.
Full documentation can be found at `http://www.gnu.org/software/coreutils/nice`,
or it is available locally via `info coreutils 'nice invocation'`
`root@ubuntu:/home/philip#`

Based on the preceding syntax, the range that we can set is between -19 (`most priority`) to 20 (`least priority`). Let's run the `nice` command without any options:

```
root@ubuntu:/home/philip# nice
0
root@ubuntu:/home/philip#
```

Great! The value 0 represents the priority with which the shell was started. Keep in mind that a normal user cannot change the niceness of another user's process; only the root user can change the niceness for any user. By default, if we run the `nice` command without specifying a niceness value, then the niceness will be set to 10. Let's verify this:

```
root@ubuntu:/home/philip# ps -alx | grep cron
```

```
1   0   3419   1611   30  10   29008   2540 hrtime SNs  ?    0:00 cron
0   0   3435 2438 20 0 14224 952 pipe_w S+ pts/17 0:00 grep --color=auto cron
root@ubuntu:/home/philip# nice cron
cron: can't lock /var/run/crond.pid, otherpid may be 3419: Resource
temporarily unavailable
root@ubuntu:/home/philip#
```

Based on the preceding output, the NI value was not changed. This is due to the fact that
the process had already been started. The `nice` command can't change the niceness of
currently running processes. We can work around this by stopping the process:

```
root@ubuntu:/home/philip# systemctl stop cron
root@ubuntu:/home/philip#
```

Now, let's try to the start the `cron` process using the `nice` command:

```
root@ubuntu:/home/philip# ps -alx | grep cron
0     0   3463   2438   20   0   14224    900 pipe_w S+   pts/17      0:00 grep
--color=auto cron
root@ubuntu:/home/philip# nice cron
root@ubuntu:/home/philip# ps -alx | grep cron
1 0 3467 1611 30 10 29008  2732 hrtime SNs  ? 0:00 cron
0 0 3469 2438 20 0 14224 940 pipe_w S+ pts/17 0:00 grep --color=auto cron
root@ubuntu:/home/philip#
```

Awesome job! We can clearly see that the NI value has been changed to 10, even though we
did not specify a niceness value. If we want to specify a value, then we pass it by placing a
– in front of the number. Let's use the `cron` process once again:

```
root@ubuntu:/home/philip# systemctl stop cron
root@ubuntu:/home/philip# systemctl status cron
cron.service - Regular background program processing daemon
   Loaded: loaded (/lib/systemd/system/cron.service; enabled; vendor preset:
enabled)
  Active: failed (Result: exit-code) since Thu 2018-08-16 11:30:00 PDT; 8min
ago
  Docs: man:cron(8)
  Process: 3430 ExecStart=/usr/sbin/cron -f $EXTRA_OPTS (code=exited,
status=1/FAILURE)
  Main PID: 3430 (code=exited, status=1/FAILURE)
root@ubuntu:/home/philip# pgrep cron
3467
root@ubuntu:/home/philip#
```

Sometimes, you may run into an error similar to this while stopping a process. You can use the `systemctl` command or the `service` command, but the process will still be running. We can easily fix this by using what we've learned in the previous chapter; we can call the `kill` command:

```
root@ubuntu:/home/philip# kill -9 3467
root@ubuntu:/home/philip# pgrep cron
root@ubuntu:/home/philip#
```

Great job! Now let's try to start up the `cron` process with a niceness value:

```
root@ubuntu:/home/philip# nice -15 cron
root@ubuntu:/home/philip# pgrep cron
3636
root@ubuntu:/home/philip# ps -alx | grep cron
1 0 3636 1611   35 15 29008 2616 hrtime SNs  ?  0:00 cron
0 0 3658 2438   20 0 14224 920 pipe_w S+ pts/17 0:00 grep --color=auto cron
root@ubuntu:/home/philip#
```

Awesome job! But there is a problem if we run the `systemctl` command to check the status:

```
root@ubuntu:/home/philip# systemctl status cron
cron.service - Regular background program processing daemon
   Loaded: loaded (/lib/systemd/system/cron.service; enabled; vendor
preset: enabled)
   Active: failed (Result: exit-code) since Thu 2018-08-16 11:30:00 PDT;
21min ago
     Docs: man:cron(8)
  Process: 3430 ExecStart=/usr/sbin/cron -f $EXTRA_OPTS (code=exited,
status=1/FAILURE)
 Main PID: 3430 (code=exited, status=1/FAILURE)
Aug 16 11:30:00 ubuntu systemd[1]: cron.service: Unit entered failed state.
Aug 16 11:30:00 ubuntu systemd[1]: cron.service: Failed with result 'exit-
code'.
root@ubuntu:/home/philip#
```

The reason why we get this error is because when we are working with a Linux distribution that uses `systemd`, we need to edit the service file in `/lib/systemd/system/`. In our case, it would be `/lib/systemd/system/cron.service`. This is the `/lib/systemd/system/cron.service` configuration file:

```
root@ubuntu:/home/philip# cat /lib/systemd/system/cron.service
[Unit]
Description=Regular background program processing daemon
Documentation=man:cron(8)
[Service]
```

```
EnvironmentFile=-/etc/default/cron
ExecStart=/usr/sbin/cron -f $EXTRA_OPTS
IgnoreSIGPIPE=false
KillMode=process
[Install]
WantedBy=multi-user.target
root@ubuntu:/home/philip#
```

The [Service] section is where we would put Nice=value. Here is how we would store the niceness for the cron process and remove the aching error that the systemctl is generating:

```
root@ubuntu:/home/philip# cat /lib/systemd/system/cron.service
[Unit]
Description=Regular background program processing daemon
Documentation=man:cron(8)
[Service]
Nice=15
EnvironmentFile=-/etc/default/cron
ExecStart=/usr/sbin/cron -f $EXTRA_OPTS
IgnoreSIGPIPE=false
KillMode=process
[Install]
WantedBy=multi-user.target
root@ubuntu:/home/philip#
```

Now, once we've made changes to a systemd service, we will need to run this:

```
root@ubuntu:/home/philip# systemctl daemon-reload
root@ubuntu:/home/philip#
```

Awesome job! Also, you want to place Nice= before ExecStart, because, if you place it after, then it will have no effect on the process. We will now stop the existing cron process and use the systemctl to start cron; the errors will go away and systemctl will be happy:

```
root@ubuntu:/home/philip# systemctl stop cron
root@ubuntu:/home/philip# ps -alx | grep cro
0    0 3904 2438 20  0  14224  1016 pipe_w S+ pts/17  0:00 grep --
color=auto cro
root@ubuntu:/home/philip# systemctl start cron
root@ubuntu:/home/philip# ps -alx | grep cro
4    0 3907    1 35 15  29008  2988 hrtime SNs ?   0:00 /usr/sbin/cron -f
0    0 3911 2438 20  0  14224  1024 pipe_w S+  pts/17    0:00 grep --
color=auto cro
root@ubuntu:/home/philip#
```

Great job! We can now see that the `cron` process `NI` is set to `15`. This is only for system services such as `cron` and so on. Another method is to pass the `--adjustment=` option; we would specify a niceness value following the `=` sign:

```
root@ubuntu:/home/philip# systemctl stop cron
root@ubuntu:/home/philip# nice --adjustment=13 cron
root@ubuntu:/home/philip# ps -alx | grep cro
1  0 3941   1611  33  13  29008  2576 hrtime SNs  ?   0:00 cron
0  0 3943   2438  20   0  14224  1008 pipe_w S+  pts/17 0:00 grep --
color=auto cro
root@ubuntu:/home/philip#
```

Of course, `systemctl` will complain:

```
root@ubuntu:/home/philip# systemctl status cron
cron.service - Regular background program processing daemon
   Loaded: loaded (/lib/systemd/system/cron.service; enabled; vendor
preset: enabled)
   Active: inactive (dead) since Thu 2018-08-16 12:13:32 PDT; 1min 3s ago
     Docs: man:cron(8)
  Process: 3907 ExecStart=/usr/sbin/cron -f $EXTRA_OPTS (code=killed,
signal=TERM)
 Main PID: 3907 (code=killed, signal=TERM)
root@ubuntu:/home/philip#
```

But we can easily remedy this using the technique we have just learned; by specifying the declaration inside `/lib/systemd/system/cron.service`:

```
root@ubuntu:/home/philip# cat /lib/systemd/system/cron.service
[Unit]
Description=Regular background program processing daemon
Documentation=man:cron(8)
[Service]
Nice=13
EnvironmentFile=-/etc/default/cron
ExecStart=/usr/sbin/cron -f $EXTRA_OPTS
IgnoreSIGPIPE=false
KillMode=process
[Install]
WantedBy=multi-user.target
root@ubuntu:/home/philip#
root@ubuntu:/home/philip# systemctl daemon-reload
root@ubuntu:/home/philip# systemctl start cron
root@ubuntu:/home/philip# ps -alx | grep cro
4  0 4084   1  33  13  29008  2956 hrtime SNs ? 0:00 /usr/sbin/cron -f
0  0 4088   2438  20   0  14224  1076 pipe_w S+  pts/17  0:00 grep --
color=auto cro
root@ubuntu:/home/philip#
```

Awesome job!

> Be very cautious when modifying system processes as seen in these demos.

The renice command

When we work with the `nice` command, it's clear that it can't change the scheduling priority of running processes. As we've just seen, we would need to stop and then start the process in this case. This is where the `renice` command shines. We can leverage the `renice` command to change the niceness while the process is running. To see the syntax, we would pass the `--help` option:

```
root@ubuntu:/home/philip# renice --help
Usage:
 renice [-n] <priority> [-p|--pid] <pid>...
 renice [-n] <priority> -g|--pgrp <pgid>...
 renice [-n] <priority> -u|--user <user>...
Alter the priority of running processes.
Options:
 -n, --priority <num>   specify the nice increment value
 -p, --pid <id>         interpret argument as process ID (default)
 -g, --pgrp <id>        interpret argument as process group ID
 -u, --user <name>|<id> interpret argument as username or user ID
 -h, --help      display this help and exit
 -V, --version   output version information and exit
For more details see renice(1).
root@ubuntu:/home/philip#
```

First off, let's use the `ps` command to see the niceness of a process and then change its niceness:

```
root@ubuntu:/home/philip# ps -alx | grep ssh
4     0    3375     1   20   0    9996   4900 poll_s Ss    ?              0:00
/usr/sbin/sshd -D
0     0    4196  2438   20   0   14224    936 pipe_w S+    pts/17         0:00 grep
--color=auto ssh
root@ubuntu:/home/philip#
root@ubuntu:/home/philip# renice -2 3375
3375 (process ID) old priority 0, new priority -2
root@ubuntu:/home/philip# ps -alx | grep ssh
4  0  3375  1  18  -2   9996  4900 poll_s S<s  ? 0:00 /usr/sbin/sshd -D
```

```
0  0  4209  2438  20  0  14224  1080 pipe_w S+ pts/17 0:00 grep --
color=auto ssh
root@ubuntu:/home/philip#
```

Based on the preceding output, the `renice` command expects a PID of a process. In addition to this, when we specify a – followed by a number, it interprets it as a negative – sign and assigns a negative value. Also, the `systemctl` command is not going to complain because it's not required to stop and start the process to apply the changes when using the `renice` command:

```
root@ubuntu:/home/philip# systemctl status sshd
ssh.service - OpenBSD Secure Shell server
Loaded: loaded (/lib/systemd/system/ssh.service; enabled; vendor preset:
enabled)
Active: active (running) since Thu 2018-08-16 11:25:39 PDT; 1h 20min ago
 Main PID: 3375 (sshd)
CGroup: /system.slice/ssh.service
 └─3375 /usr/sbin/sshd -D
root@ubuntu:/home/philip#
```

Great job! We can also change the niceness for a specific user; here, we would pass the `-u` option. Let's change the niceness for all the processes owned by a user:

```
root@ubuntu:/home/philip# ps -alu philip
F S UID  PID PPID C  PRI  NI ADDR SZ WCHAN   TTY  TIME CMD
4 S 1000 1507 1  0   80   0 - 11319 ep_pol   ?  00:00:00 systemd
5 S 1000 1508 1507 0 80 0 - 36293 sigtim   ?   00:00:00 (sd-pam)
1 S 1000 1599 1  0   80   0 - 51303 poll_s ? 00:00:00 gnome-keyring-d
4 S 1000 1611 1349 0  80 0 - 11621 poll_s ?  00:00:00 upstart
1 S 1000 1696 1611 0   80  0 - 10932 ep_pol ? 00:00:00 dbus-daemon
0 S 1000  1708  1611 0 80 0 - 21586 poll_s ? 00:00:00 window-stack-br
1 S 1000  1721 1611  0  80 0 - 8215 poll_s ? 00:00:00 upstart-udev-br
1 S 1000  1735  1611 0 80 0 - 8198 poll_s ? 00:00:00 upstart-dbus-br
1 S 1000 1737 1611  0 80  0 -  8198 poll_s ? 00:00:00 upstart-dbus-br
1 S 1000 1743 1611  0 80 0 - 10321 poll_s ? 00:00:00 upstart-file-br
root@ubuntu:/home/philip# renice 3 -u philip
root@ubuntu:/home/philip # ps -alu philip
F S UID PID   PPID  C PRI  NI ADDR SZ WCHAN TTY TIME CMD
4 S 1000 1507  1    0  83 3 - 11319 ep_pol ? 00:00:00 systemd
5 S 1000 1508  1507 0 83  3 - 36293 sigtim ? 00:00:00 (sd-pam)
1 S 1000 1599  1    0  83  3 - 51303 poll_s ? 00:00:00 gnome-keyring-d
4 S 1000 1611  1349 0  83 3 - 11621 poll_s ? 00:00:00 upstart
1 S 1000 1696  1611 0  83  3 - 10932 ep_pol ? 00:00:00 dbus-daemon
0 S 1000 1708  1611 0 83  3 - 21586 poll_s ? 00:00:00 window-stack-br
1 S 1000 1721  1611 0 83  3 - 8215 poll_s ? 00:00:00 upstart-udev-br
1 S 1000 1735  1611 0 83  3 - 8198 poll_s ? 00:00:00 upstart-dbus-br
1 S 1000 1737  1611 0 83  3 - 8198 poll_s ? 00:00:00 upstart-dbus-br
```

```
 1 S  1000 1743  1611 0  83 3 - 10321 poll_s ? 00:00:00 upstart-file-br
```

Great job! The niceness has been changed for each process that is owned by the user we specified.

Foreground processes versus background processes

When working in the shell, we are in fact working in what is known as the foreground; we aren't able to carry out any other tasks unless we stop the current process. There are times when you are going to want to send some processes to the background for processing; this will allow you to continue to work in the shell, while, at the same time, the process in the background is also running. To verify whether there are any processes running in the background, we can use the `jobs` command. Let's try this out:

```
root@ubuntu:/home/philip# jobs
root@ubuntu:/home/philip#
```

From the preceding output, we can see that there are no jobs currently running in the background. To see how a process could affect you when working in the shell, let's look at the `yes` utility; this can be found in most Linux distributions. The `yes` utility will run until we suspend or stop it. When we execute the `yes` utility, it will prevent us from executing any commands:

```
root@ubuntu:/home/philip# yes
y
y
y
```

To stop this utility, we would use a combination of *Ctrl* + *C*:

```
y
^C
root@ubuntu:/home/philip#
```

This will inadvertently stop the `yes` utility. The syntax for the `yes` utility is as follows:

- `yes <STRING>`: If we leave off the string, it will spit out `y` as shown in the preceding code
- `yes <OPTIONS>`: The available options are `--version` and `--help`

If we rerun the `yes` utility, and, instead of stopping it, we decide we would like to suspend it, we would use a combination of *Ctrl + Z*. This will, in effect, place the `yes` utility in the background:

```
root@ubuntu:/home/philip# yes
y
y
y
^Z
[1]+  Stopped                 yes
root@ubuntu:/home/philip#
```

This time, when we run the `jobs` command, we will see that there is a job listed:

```
root@ubuntu:/home/philip# jobs
[1]+  Stopped                 yes
root@ubuntu:/home/philip#
```

This has suspended the `yes` utility and placed it in the background, allowing us to continue to work at the Command Prompt. Another example to illustrate the concept of a foreground process halting the shell, thus preventing us from executing any other commands, would be where we started a utility, such as `vim` or any GUI program.

Let's pick a GUI to demonstrate. This will drive home the point. We will start the `gedit` utility from the shell:

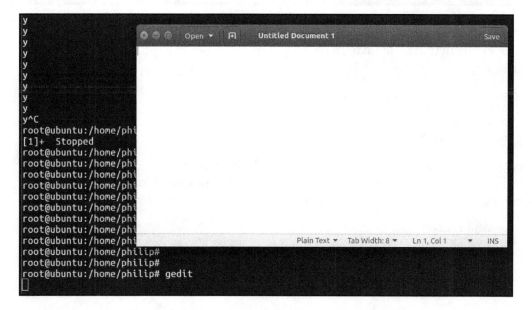

Based on the preceding output, the shell is preventing us from typing any other commands until we either suspend or close the `gedit` utility. Let's suspend the `gedit` utility:

```
y
y
y
y
y
y
y^C
root@ubuntu:/home/phi
[1]+  Stopped
root@ubuntu:/home/phi
root@ubuntu:/home/phi
root@ubuntu:/home/philip#
root@ubuntu:/home/philip#
root@ubuntu:/home/philip#
root@ubuntu:/home/philip#
root@ubuntu:/home/philip#
root@ubuntu:/home/philip#
root@ubuntu:/home/philip#
root@ubuntu:/home/philip#
root@ubuntu:/home/philip# gedit
^Z
[2]+  Stopped                 gedit
root@ubuntu:/home/philip#
```

From the preceding output, you'll notice that the `gedit` utility is frozen, meaning we're unable to do anything from within the `gedit` utility. Now let's run the `jobs` command once again:

```
root@ubuntu:/home/philip# jobs
[1]-  Stopped                 yes
[2]+  Stopped                 gedit
root@ubuntu:/home/philip#
```

Great job! There are now two jobs listed. If we decide that we would like to resume working with one of these jobs, we can use yet another powerful command: the `fg` command. The syntax for the `fg` command is as follows:

```
fg %<job id>
```

To see this in action, let's resume the `gedit` utility from its stopped state:

```
y
y
y^C
root@ubuntu:/home/phil
[1]+  Stopped
root@ubuntu:/home/phi
root@ubuntu:/home/phi
root@ubuntu:/home/phi
root@ubuntu:/home/phi
root@ubuntu:/home/phi
root@ubuntu:/home/phi
root@ubuntu:/home/phi
root@ubuntu:/home/philip#
root@ubuntu:/home/philip#
root@ubuntu:/home/philip#
root@ubuntu:/home/philip# gedit
^Z
[2]+  Stopped                 gedit
root@ubuntu:/home/philip# jobs
[1]-  Stopped                 yes
[2]+  Stopped                 gedit
root@ubuntu:/home/philip# fg %2
gedit
```

Awesome job! Now we're able to work within the `gedit` utility that was started from the Command Prompt. However, there is a problem. When we do *Ctrl + Z*, the program is stopped. In a real environment, we would want the process that we are sending to the background to continue to run. This would speed up our productivity, enabling us to carry out simultaneous jobs. Rest assured that this is, in fact, possible by way of yet another technique, which we can use whenever we're executing a command in the shell. `&` is for starting a process and sending it to the background. Let's close both the `gedit` and `yes` utilities:

```
root@ubuntu:/home/philip# fg
y
y
^C
root@ubuntu:/home/philip# jobs
root@ubuntu:/home/philip#
```

Now we'll use & to start the `gedit` utility and send it straight to the background:

Great job! Now we can work in either the `gedit` utility, or we can continue to work at the Command Prompt. Also, when we run the `jobs` command, we will see that the `gedit` utility's status is `running`:

```
root@ubuntu:/home/philip# jobs
[1]+  Running                 gedit &
root@ubuntu:/home/philip#
```

Awesome! There is another way to resume the jobs that are stopped in the background and instruct them to run in the background. This is made possible by leveraging yet another powerful command: the `bg` command. Here is how we would resume the `gedit` program, if we had stopped it, and instruct it to resume but run in the background:

Great job! The `bg` command did two things. First, it resumed the `gedit` utility. It then placed `&` at the end of the command. As we saw earlier, `&` instructs a process to run in the background. If there are multiple jobs, we would specify either the job ID or the job name:

```
root@ubuntu:/home/philip# gnome-calculator
** (gnome-calculator:9649): WARNING **: currency.vala:407: Currency ZAR is
not provided by IMF or ECB
^Z
[2]+  Stopped                 gnome-calculator
root@ubuntu:/home/philip# jobs
[1]-  Running                 gedit &
[2]+  Stopped                 gnome-calculator
root@ubuntu:/home/philip#
root@ubuntu:/home/philip# bg 2
[2]+ gnome-calculator &
root@ubuntu:/home/philip# jobs
[1]-  Running                 gedit &
[2]+  Running                 gnome-calculator &
root@ubuntu:/home/philip#
```

By running the preceding command, you will see the following output:

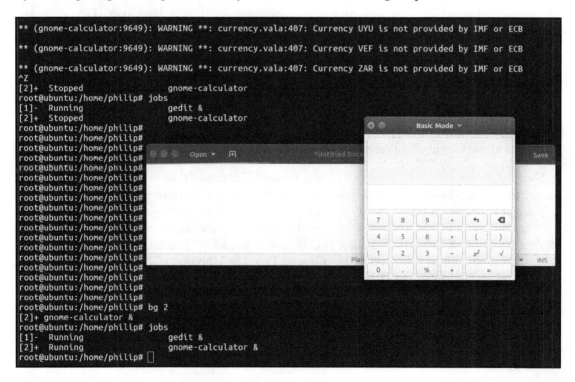

Awesome! We can see that both of the utilities are open and can be used simultaneously alongside the Command Prompt.

Summary

In this chapter, we have covered a variety of methods for handling processes. First, we focused on scheduling processes using the `nice` command. Whenever the workload on your CPU is rising, various processes are contending for the CPU's resources. The niceness for each process was exposed using various commands, such as `ps` and `top`. Next, we did some demos on how we would go about setting the niceness for the processes. This took us to systems that run `systemd`; we saw the problem of changing the niceness of a process on a `systemd` system. This led to us modifying the configuration file for a process so that `systemd` could recognize the niceness when we started the process. After this, we moved on to the `renice` command, particularly dealing with processes that are currently running and the method to change the niceness of running processes. This was illustrated by changing the niceness, not only for a given process, but, also, we were able to change the niceness for all processes owned by a user. `systemd` recognized the changes of the running process without us having to modify any particular configuration. However, if the process is stopped and started or restarted, then the niceness that we set would be removed. To work around this and have the niceness persisting would mean editing the configuration file for a given process. Finally, we worked with processes in the context of foreground versus background. The concept of foreground processes prevents us from working at the Command Prompt until the foreground process is suspended or closed. This greatly reduces productivity when we are tasked to carry out a number of operations. The fix is to have the processes running in the background, thereby allowing you to effectively carry out functions at the Command Prompt.

In the next chapter, we will shift our attention toward the world of display managers. Often, most users are comfortable working within a GUI environment. Therefore, the focus will cover the common display managers that are prevalent in today's Linux distributions. This is also the case for those which are on the current Linux+ exam objectives. First, we will touch on the **X Display Manager** (**XDM**). Next, the KDE Display Manager will be discussed. This will be followed by the **Gnome Display Manager** (**GDM**). Finally, the chapter will cover the **Light Display Manager** (**LDM**). This next chapter is vital for your exam preparation, as are all of the previous chapters. This will allow you to be able to work with the various display managers common in today's Linux environments.

Questions

1. Which option with the `ps` command prints the niceness for each process?

   A. n
   B. l
   C. a
   D. x

2. Which column represents the niceness for each process using the `ps` command?

   A. NI
   B. ni
   C. N1
   D. nice

3. Which column represents the niceness for each process using the `top` command?

   A. ni
   B. PNI
   C. pnic
   D. NI

4. Which value is not a valid one to set when using the `nice` command?

   A. -20
   B. -19
   C. 20
   D. 19

5. Which niceness value has the highest priority?

   A. -21
   B. -32
   C. -19
   D. -20

6. In which directory are the configuration files for processes using `systemd` stored?

    A. `/usr/lib/systemd/system`
    B. `/lib/systemd/system`
    C. `/lib/systemd/system/service`
    D. `/lib/systemd/service`

7. Which command needs to be run after editing a service file using `systemd`?

    A. `systemctl daemon-reload`
    B. `systemctl --daemon-reload`
    C. `systemctl daemon --reload`
    D. `systemctl daemonreload`

8. When using the `renice` command, what is expected after specifying the niceness value?

    A. `Process name`
    B. `PID`
    C. `Process name + PID`
    D. None of the above

9. Which command resumes a process from the background and prevents you from executing any other commands until the current process has ended?

    A. `fg`
    B. `bg`
    C. `jobs`
    D. `job`

10. Which command resumes a process from the background, but places it in the background, allowing you to execute other commands at the Command Prompt?

    A. `fg`
    B. `jobs`
    C. `bg`
    D. `CTRL+C`

Further reading

- You can get more info about managing processes by checking out `https://www.tecmint.com`.
- This website gives you a lot of useful tips and best practices for handling processes: `https://www.digitalocean.com`.
- This last link gives you information in general that relates to various commands that work on both CentOS and Ubuntu. You can post your questions here and other community members will be able to respond: `https://www.linuxquestions.org`.

11
Display Managers

In the previous chapter, we covered a variety of methods for handling processes. First, we focused on scheduling processes using the `nice` command. Whenever the workload on your CPU is rising, various processes are contending for the CPU's resources; the niceness for each process was exposed using various commands, such as `ps` and `top`. After this, we moved on to the `renice` command, particularly dealing with processes that are currently running, and the method to change the niceness of running processes. Finally, we worked with processes in the context of foreground versus background.

In this chapter, display managers are covered. Often, most users are comfortable working within a GUI environment. We will look at the display managers that are prevalent in today's Linux distribution. Display managers are sometimes confused with desktops; a display manager manages the GUI login prompt, which is presented to the user upon boot up. Desktops are collections of X Windows, which the users use to carry out various tasks. Some examples of desktops are XFCE KDE, GNOME, and Unity, to name a few. Moreover, the display managers that are on the current Linux+ exam objectives are covered. First, we will touch on the **X Display Manager (XDM)**. Next, the **KDE Display Manager (KDM)** will be discussed. This is followed by the **GNOME Display Manager (GDM)**. Finally, the chapter will cover the **Light Display Manager (Lightdm)**.

We will cover the following topics in this chapter:

- Working with the XDM
- Working with the KDM
- Working with the GDM
- Working with the Lightdm

Working with the XDM

The XDM manages a collection of X servers. This could either be locally on the system or remotely on another X server on a network. The XDM utility is somewhat similar in nature to the older SysVinit, so you may be wondering about the concept of an X server. An X server is a program in the X Window system; it runs locally on the machine. It usually manages access to the graphics cards, displays, and interaction with the keyboard and mouse on the local machine. So what is an X Window system? Well, an X Window system , commonly called X, is an entire suite that is made up of a cross-platform, free client-server infrastructure for managing **graphical user interfaces** (**GUIs**) on a single or a range of computers, as is the case in networking environments. In the context of X, the way that the client/server works is a bit odd; an X server runs on each local machine. The X server then accesses X clients; X clients are GUI applications. Another interesting point to note is the fact that X clients can be running either locally or they can indeed be running remotely across a network. The X server acts as a middle man in the sense that the actual X clients interact with the X server; the X server then interacts with the actual display devices. An X server uses the **X Display Manager Control Protocol** (**XDMCP**). XDM was meant to be a graphical replacement for the command-line login prompt. After the user provides their login credentials, XDM initiates their X session.

The first step for using XDM would be to install it. We will use the CentOS 6.5 system for this and search for xdm:

```
[root@localhost Desktop]# yum search xdm
Loaded plugins: fastestmirror, refresh-packagekit, security
========================================= N/S Matched: xdm
==========================================
libXdmcp-devel.i686 : Development files for libXdmcp
libXdmcp-devel.x86_64 : Development files for libXdmcp
xorg-x11-xdm.x86_64 : X.Org X11 xdm - X Display Manager
libXdmcp.i686 : X Display Manager Control Protocol library
libXdmcp.x86_64 : X Display Manager Control Protocol library
xorg-x11-server-Xdmx.x86_64 : Distributed Multihead X Server and utilities
  Name and summary matches only, use "search all" for everything.
[root@localhost Desktop]#
```

Awesome! By default, the CentOS 6.5 is using GDM; we will install the XDM for illustration:

```
[root@localhost Desktop]# yum install xorg-x11-xdm.x86_64
Loaded plugins: fastestmirror, refresh-packagekit, security
Loading mirror speeds from cached hostfile
  * updates: centos.mirror.iweb.ca
Setting up Install Process
Resolving Dependencies
```

```
--> Processing Dependency: libXaw.so.7()(64bit) for package: 1:xorg-x11-
xdm-1.1.6-14.1.el6.x86_64
Installed:
  xorg-x11-xdm.x86_64 1:1.1.6-14.1.el6
Dependency Installed:
  libXaw.x86_64 0:1.0.11-2.el6                      libXpm.x86_64
0:3.5.10-2.el6
Complete!
[root@localhost Desktop]#
```

Some output has been omitted for brevity. Next, we will look at the configuration directory; this is inside /etc/X11:

```
[root@localhost Desktop]# ls /etc/X11
applnk  fontpath.d  prefdm  xdm  xinit  Xmodmap  xorg.conf.d  Xresources
[root@localhost Desktop]#
[root@localhost xdm]# ll
total 40
-rwxr-xr-x. 1 root root  510 Aug 19  2010 GiveConsole
-rwxr-xr-x. 1 root root  244 Aug 19  2010 TakeConsole
-rw-r--r--. 1 root root 3597 Aug 19  2010 Xaccess
-rw-r--r--. 1 root root 1394 Aug 19  2010 xdm-config
-rwxr-xr-x. 1 root root  183 Aug 19  2010 Xreset
-rw-r--r--. 1 root root 2381 Aug 19  2010 Xresources
-rw-r--r--. 1 root root  484 Aug 19  2010 Xservers
lrwxrwxrwx. 1 root root   17 Aug 24 07:55 Xsession -> ../xinit/Xsession
-rwxr-xr-x. 1 root root  938 Aug 19  2010 Xsetup_0
-rwxr-xr-x. 1 root root  181 Aug 19  2010 Xstartup
-rwxr-xr-x. 1 root root  303 Aug 19  2010 Xwilling
[root@localhost xdm]#
```

These are the necessary files that make XDM shine. By default, the CentOS 6.5 will not use XDM; this can easily be fixed by editing /etc/X11/prefdm:

```
[root@localhost xdm]# cat /etc/X11/prefdm
#!/bin/sh
PATH=/sbin:/usr/sbin:/bin:/usr/bin
# We need to source this so that the login screens get translated
[ -f /etc/sysconfig/i18n ] && . /etc/sysconfig/i18n
# Run preferred X Display Manager
quit_arg=
preferred=
exit 1
[root@localhost xdm]#
```

Some output has been omitted for brevity. We should specify the display manager in the `preferred=` line. Another approach that we could take would be to edit `/etc/sysconfig/desktop`:

```
[root@localhost xdm]# ls /etc/sysconfig | grep desktop
[root@localhost xdm]#
```

Based on the preceding output, we would need to create the `/etc/sysconfig/` desktop file. Let's try this:

```
[root@localhost xdm]# which xdm
/usr/bin/xdm
[root@localhost xdm]# vim /etc/sysconfig/desktop
[root@localhost philip]# cat /etc/sysconfig/desktop
preferred=/usr/bin/xdm
[root@localhost philip]#
```

Based on the preceding example, we have created a file and stored the location of XDM, which was derived from using the `which` command. The `which` command can be used to find the location of an executable.

Now, let's reboot the system for those changes to take effect:

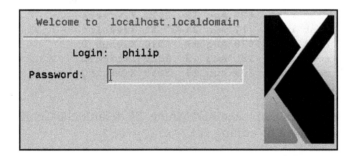

Great job! Now we are presented with the XDM login. The configuration files for XDM are stored inside the `/etc/X11/xdm`:

```
[root@localhost philip]# ll /etc/X11/xdm
total 40
-rwxr-xr-x. 1 root root 510 Aug 19 2010 GiveConsole
-rwxr-xr-x. 1 root root 244 Aug 19 2010 TakeConsole
-rw-r--r--. 1 root root 3597 Aug 19 2010 Xaccess
-rw-r--r--. 1 root root 1394 Aug 19 2010 xdm-config
-rwxr-xr-x. 1 root root 183 Aug 19 2010 Xreset
-rw-r--r--. 1 root root 2381 Aug 19 2010 Xresources
-rw-r--r--. 1 root root 484 Aug 19 2010 Xservers
lrwxrwxrwx. 1 root root 17 Aug 24 07:55 Xsession -> ../xinit/Xsession
```

```
-rwxr-xr-x. 1 root root 938 Aug 19 2010 Xsetup_0
-rwxr-xr-x. 1 root root 181 Aug 19 2010 Xstartup
-rwxr-xr-x. 1 root root 303 Aug 19 2010 Xwilling
[root@localhost philip]#
```

We can now focus on `/etc/X11/xdm/Xaccess`:

```
# To control which addresses xdm listens for requests on:
#   LISTEN      address [list of multicast groups ... ]
# The first form tells xdm which displays to respond to itself.
#   LISTEN      * ff02:0:0:0:0:0:0:12b
# This example shows listening for multicast on all scopes up
# to site-local
#   LISTEN      * ff01:0:0:0:0:0:0:12b ff02:0:0:0:0:0:0:12b
ff03:0:0:0:0:0:0:12b ff04:0:0:0:0:0:0:12b ff05:0:0:0:0:0:0:12b
[root@localhost philip]#
```

Some output has been omitted for brevity. The preceding file controls which addresses XDM will listen to for an incoming request. Another important file, when working remotely with XDM, is `/etc/X11/xdm/xdm-config`:

```
[root@localhost philip]# cat /etc/X11/xdm/xdm-config
! The following three resources set up display :0 as the console.
DisplayManager._0.setup:          /etc/X11/xdm/Xsetup_0
DisplayManager._0.startup:        /etc/X11/xdm/GiveConsole
DisplayManager._0.reset:          /etc/X11/xdm/TakeConsole
DisplayManager*loginmoveInterval:     10
! SECURITY: do not listen for XDMCP or Chooser requests
! Comment out this line if you want to manage X terminals with xdm
DisplayManager.requestPort:    0
[root@localhost philip]#
```

Some output has been omitted for brevity. The last line, `DisplayManager.requestPort: 0`, would need to be commented out for us to manage remote sessions using XDM.

Working with the KDM

The KDM is one of the more popular display managers available in today's Linux distributions. KDM is based on source code from the X Display Manager; it was developed by KDE. It was, for many years, the display manager for the KDE framework, but that has recently changed. To see KDM, we will use our Fedora 28 system by using the `dnf` command. Fedora 28 uses the GDM.

We will install the KDE desktop for this demo using the `groupinstall` option; this will install all of the necessary packages for the KDE desktop:

```
[root@localhost philip]# dnf groupinstall KDE
Install  412 Packages
Upgrade    3 Packages
Total download size: 425 M
Is this ok [y/N]: y
  xorg-x11-apps.x86_64 7.7-20.fc28
  xorg-x11-fonts-misc.noarch 7.5-19.fc28
  xorg-x11-xbitmaps.noarch 1.1.1-13.fc28
Upgraded:
  firewalld.noarch 0.5.3-2.fc28        firewalld-filesystem.noarch
0.5.3-2.fc28
  python3-firewall.noarch 0.5.3-2.fc28
Complete!
[root@localhost philip]#
```

Next, we will install the `kdm` utility and additional components using the `dnf` command:

```
[root@localhost philip]# dnf install kdm kde-settings-kdm
Last metadata expiration check: 0:12:52 ago on Mon 27 Aug 2018 11:16:03 AM
EDT.
Dependencies resolved.
=====================================================================
Package          Arch       Version          Repository  Size
=====================================================================
Installing:
 kdm             x86_64   1:4.11.22-22.fc28    fedora     740 k
 kdm-settings    noarch   1:4.11.22-22.fc28    fedora     186 k
=====================================================================
Install  5 Packages
Total download size: 1.2 M
Installed size: 2.3 M
Is this ok [y/N]: y
Installed:
  kdm.x86_64 1:4.11.22-22.fc28
  kdm-settings.noarch 1:4.11.22-22.fc28
  kgreeter-plugins.x86_64 1:4.11.22-22.fc28
  libkworkspace.x86_64 1:4.11.22-22.fc28
  qimageblitz.x86_64 0.0.6-15.fc28
Complete!
[root@localhost philip]#
```

Awesome! Some output has been omitted for brevity. The kdm utility has been installed.
Finally, we will install the system switcher; this will allow us to switch from GDM to KDM:

```
[root@localhost philip]# dnf install system-switch-displaymanager.noarch
Last metadata expiration check: 0:16:52 ago on Mon 27 Aug 2018 11:16:03 AM
EDT.
Dependencies resolved.
=====================================================================
Package                       Arch    Version       Repository  Size
Installing:
system-switch-displaymanager noarch 1.5.1-3.fc28 fedora 17 k
Transaction Summary
Installed:
 system-switch-displaymanager.noarch 1.5.1-3.fc28
Complete!
[root@localhost philip]#
```

Great job! Now we can call on the system-switch utility to perform the switch from
GDM3 to KDM:

```
[root@localhost philip]# system-switch-displaymanager KDM
Created symlink /etc/systemd/system/display-manager.service →
/usr/lib/systemd/system/kdm.service.
Your default graphical display manager has successfully been switched.
[root@localhost philip]#
```

Awesome! Now, let's reboot our Fedora 28 system for the changes to take effect:

Based on the previous output, we can now see that the Fedora 28 system is using the `kdm` utility as the display manager instead of the `gdm`. We can also see the various desktops listed under the **Session Type**. The **Plasma** is the KDE style of the desktop that we installed. Let's log in to the **Plasma** desktop and confirm that we are indeed using the `kdm` utility:

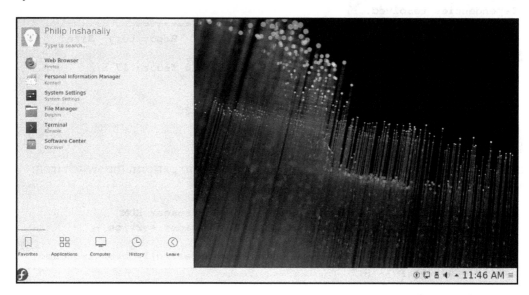

Awesome! So we've successfully changed our desktop to the KDE style **Plasma** and now we can look at the `/etc/systemd/system/display-manager.service` to verify which display manager is in use:

```
[root@localhost philip]# ls -l /etc/systemd/system/display-manager.service
lrwxrwxrwx. 1 root root 35 Aug 27 11:34 /etc/systemd/system/display-
manager.service -> /usr/lib/systemd/system/kdm.service
[root@localhost philip]#
```

Great job! We can clearly see that we have, in fact, changed our display manager to KDM. We can also check the status of KDM with the `systemctl` command:

```
[root@localhost philip]# systemctl status kdm.service
kdm.service - The KDE login manager
   Loaded: loaded (/usr/lib/systemd/system/kdm.service; enabled; vendor
preset: disabled)
   Active: active (running) since Mon 2018-08-27 11:36:40 EDT; 14min ago
 Main PID: 821 (kdm)
    Tasks: 3 (limit: 2331)
   Memory: 121.6M
   CGroup: /system.slice/kdm.service
```

```
        ┌─821 /usr/bin/kdm vt1
        └─894 /usr/libexec/Xorg -br -novtswitch -quiet :0 vt1 -
background none -nolisten tcp -auth /var/run/kdm/A:0-fPUysb
Aug 27 11:36:40 localhost.localdomain systemd[1]: Started The KDE login
manager.
Aug 27 11:36:40 localhost.localdomain kdm[821]: plymouth is running
[root@localhost philip]#
```

Based on the preceding output, we can see that the kdm.service is indeed active and running. To further verify, we can also check the status of GDM:

```
[root@localhost philip]# systemctl status gdm.service
gdm.service - GNOME Display Manager
   Loaded: loaded (/usr/lib/systemd/system/gdm.service; disabled; vendor
preset: disabled)
   Active: inactive (dead)
[root@localhost philip]#
```

Awesome job! Based on the preceding output, we can see that the gdm utility is currently inactive. The various configuration files for KDM can be found in /etc/kde/kdm:

```
[root@localhost philip]# ls -l /etc/kde/kdm
-rw-r--r--. 1 root root 22985 Jun 12  2016 kdmrc
-rw-r--r--. 1 root root  3607 Apr 26  2010 Xaccess
-rw-r--r--. 1 root root  2381 Apr 26  2010 Xresources
-rwxr-xr-x. 1 root root   207 Jul  8  2008 Xsession
-rwxr-xr-x. 1 root root   938 Apr 26  2010 Xsetup
-rwxr-xr-x. 1 root root   303 Apr 26  2010 Xwilling
[root@localhost philip]#
```

Based on the previous example, we can see that the files have similar names to the XDM files that were covered earlier in this chapter.

Working with the GDM

GDM is another popular display manager available in today's Linux environments. Particularly in Red Hat distributions such as CentOS and Fedora, you will find GDM. This provides a GUI login prompt where the user is given an opportunity to provide their login credentials. Furthermore, if we have multiple desktops installed, we can also select which desktop to load once logged in. As we saw earlier, we can determine which display manager we would prefer to work with. Let's choose our Ubuntu system for this demo. First, let's check whether GDM (GDM3 in Ubuntu) is installed on our Ubuntu 16 system:

```
root@ubuntu:/etc# ls /etc/ | grep gdm3
root@ubuntu:/etc# ls /etc/X11/
```

```
app-defaults  default-display-manager  openbox  xdm    xkb
Xreset    Xresources  Xsession.d     xsm
cursors    fonts      rgb.txt  xinit  xorg.conf.failsafe  Xreset.d
Xsession    Xsession.options
root@ubuntu:/etc#
```

Based on the preceding output, GDM3 is not currently installed. Let's also add a desktop so we can see where the option to choose a desktop is located. We will install the GNOME desktop in our Ubuntu system. We will use the `apt-get` command, particularly the `ubuntu-gnome-desktop` package:

```
root@ubuntu:/etc# apt-get install ubuntu-gnome-desktop
Reading package lists... Done
Building dependency tree
Reading state information... Done
The following additional packages will be installed:
python-boto python-cffi-backend python-chardet python-cloudfiles python-
cryptography python-enum34 python-idna python-ipaddress
  python-libxml2 python-lockfile python-ndg-httpsclient python-openssl
python-pkg-resources python-pyasn1 python-requests python-six
  python-urllib3 rhythmbox-plugin-magnatune seahorse-daemon ssh-askpass-
gnome telepathy-gabble telepathy-haze telepathy-idle
  telepathy-logger telepathy-salut tracker tracker-extract tracker-miner-fs
ubuntu-gnome-default-settings ubuntu-gnome-wallpapers
  ubuntu-gnome-wallpapers-xenial unoconv wodim xserver-xorg-legacy xsltproc
yelp-tools zsync
Suggested packages:
  argyll-doc gir1.2-colordgtk-1.0 db5.3-util vcdimager libdvdcss2 dvdauthor
readom python-paramiko python-oauthlib ncftp lftp
After this operation, 447 MB of additional disk space will be used.
Do you want to continue? [Y/n] y
Processing triggers for initramfs-tools (0.122ubuntu8.11) ...
update-initramfs: Generating /boot/initrd.img-4.4.0-134-generic
root@ubuntu:/etc#
```

Some output has been omitted for brevity. Next, let's install the `gdm` utility. Note that its name is `gdm3` in Ubuntu whereas in Fedora its name is `gdm`. Both are the same, this is just a different naming convention.

Think `gdm3` when working with the Debian distributions, and `gdm` when working with Red Hat distributions.

When we installed the `ubuntu-gnome-desktop`, it in fact installed the `gdm3` for us, saving us some time. We can verify this by looking at the `/etc`:

```
root@ubuntu:/etc# ls -l /etc | grep gdm
drwxr-xr-x  8 root root    4096 Aug 27 11:43 gdm3
root@ubuntu:/etc#
```

Awesome! Based on the previous code, we can see that `gdm3` is in fact installed. Currently, this would not change the display manager because we have not specified that we would like to use `gdm3`. To solve this, we would simply run the `dpkg-reconfigure` command and pass `gdm3`:

```
root@ubuntu:/etc# dpkg-reconfigure gdm3
```

Once we run the preceding command, we get the following screen:

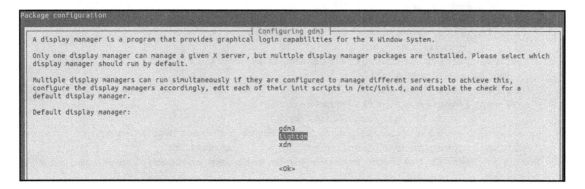

Based on the preceding output, **Lightdm** is set as the default display manager. We could use the keyboard and scroll up or down and select which display manager to set as the default. We will choose **gdm3**:

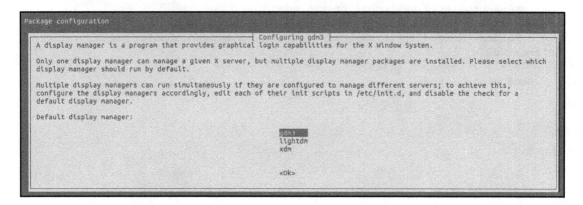

Next, we will run the following command:

```
root@ubuntu:/etc# dpkg-reconfigure gdm3
root@ubuntu:/etc#
```

Great job! Now we can check /etc/X11/ to verify which display manager is currently set:

```
root@ubuntu:/etc# cat /etc/X11/default-display-manager
/usr/sbin/gdm3
root@ubuntu:/etc#
```

Based on the previous code, we can see that the gdm3 has been set. Another technique that we can employ is the systemctl command:

```
root@ubuntu:/etc# systemctl status lightdm
lightdm.service - Light Display Manager
   Loaded: loaded (/lib/systemd/system/lightdm.service; static; vendor
preset: enabled)
   Drop-In: /lib/systemd/system/display-manager.service.d
            └─xdiagnose.conf
   Active: active (running) since Fri 2018-08-24 12:46:32 PDT; 2 days ago
     Docs: man:lightdm(1)
 Main PID: 1011 (lightdm)
   CGroup: /system.slice/lightdm.service
           ├─1011 /usr/sbin/lightdm
           └─1038 /usr/lib/xorg/Xorg -core :0 -seat seat0 -auth
/var/run/lightdm/root/:0 -nolisten tcp vt7 -novtswitch
Warning: Journal has been rotated since unit was started. Log output is
incomplete or unavailable.
root@ubuntu:/etc#
```

Based on the preceding code, we can see that the current Lightdm is still active. So now, let's check for the gdm3:

```
root@ubuntu:/etc# systemctl status gdm3
gdm.service - GNOME Display Manager
   Loaded: loaded (/lib/systemd/system/gdm.service; static; vendor preset:
enabled)
   Active: inactive (dead)
root@ubuntu:/etc#
```

Based on that output, we may think that we have a problem, but the fact of the matter is that only when we reboot the system will the changes be applied:

Awesome! Based on the previous screenshot, we can see that the system has started up GDM3. In addition, we have the option to choose a desktop to load. Let's choose **GNOME**. Now, let's rerun the `systemctl` command to verify that we are indeed running GDM3:

```
root@ubuntu:/home/philip# systemctl status lightdm
lightdm.service - Light Display Manager
   Loaded: loaded (/lib/systemd/system/lightdm.service; static; vendor
preset: e
   Active: inactive (dead)
     Docs: man:lightdm(1)
root@ubuntu:/home/philip#
```

Looks good! Now let's check on GDM3:

```
root@ubuntu:/home/philip# systemctl status gdm
gdm.service - GNOME Display Manager
   Loaded: loaded (/lib/systemd/system/gdm.service; static; vendor preset:
enabl
   Drop-In: /lib/systemd/system/display-manager.service.d
            └─xdiagnose.conf
   Active: active (running) since Mon 2018-08-27 12:33:26 PDT; 3min 22s ago
  Process: 990 ExecStartPre=/usr/share/gdm/generate-config (code=exited,
status=
```

```
  Process: 983 ExecStartPre=/bin/sh -c [ "$(cat /etc/X11/default-display-
manager
 Main PID: 1006 (gdm3)
   CGroup: /system.slice/gdm.service
           └─1006 /usr/sbin/gdm3
root@ubuntu:/home/philip#
```

Awesome job! Based on what we have seen in the preceding output, beyond a shadow of a doubt, we are running GDM3.

Working with the Lightdm

Light Display Manager, known as **Lightdm** or `lightdm` (on the command line), has been making waves in the Linux world. Lightdm had replaced KDM and was the preferred display manager up to Ubuntu 16. This was replaced by GDM in later versions of Ubuntu. It provides a GUI to manage user logins. Lightdm is cross-platform, meaning that it supports various desktops. Let's install Lightdm in our Fedora 28 system. Previously we had KDM. Let's use the `dnf` command:

```
[root@localhost philip]# dnf install lightdm lightdm-gtk
ast metadata expiration check: 4:55:54 ago on Mon 27 Aug 2018 11:16:03 AM
EDT.
Dependencies resolved.
================================================================
Package          Arch       Version        Repository    Size
================================================================
Installing:
lightdm          x86_64     1.26.0-1.fc28     updates     222 k
lightdm-gtk      x86_64     2.0.5-1.fc28      fedora      139 k
Installing dependencies:
lightdm-gobject  x86_64     1.26.0-1.fc28     updates      72 k
Transaction Summary
================================================================
Install  3 Packages
Total download size: 433 k
Installed size: 1.2 M
Is this ok [y/N]: y
Installed:
  lightdm.x86_64 1.26.0-1.fc28    lightdm-gtk.x86_64 2.0.5-1.fc28
lightdm-gobject.x86_64 1.26.0-1.fc28
Complete!
[root@localhost philip]#
```

Great! Now we will use the `system-switch-displaymanger` command to switch to `lightdm`:

```
[root@localhost philip]# system-switch-displaymanager lightdm
Created symlink /etc/systemd/system/display-manager.service →
/usr/lib/systemd/system/lightdm.service.
Your default graphical display manager has successfully been switched.
[root@localhost philip]#
```

To verify, we can use the `ls` command to view the service in `systemd`:

```
[root@localhost philip]# ls -l /etc/systemd/system/display-manager.service
lrwxrwxrwx. 1 root root 39 Aug 27 16:17 /etc/systemd/system/display-
manager.service -> /usr/lib/systemd/system/lightdm.service
[root@localhost philip]#
```

Awesome job! Also, we can check the status of the display manager using the `systemctl` command:

```
[root@localhost philip]# systemctl status kdm
kdm.service - The KDE login manager
   Loaded: loaded (/usr/lib/systemd/system/kdm.service; disabled; vendor
preset: disabled)
     Active: active (running) since Mon 2018-08-27 11:36:40 EDT; 4h 42min ago
  Main PID: 821 (kdm)
     Tasks: 3 (limit: 2331)
     Memory: 101.0M
[root@localhost philip]#
```

Based on the previous code, we can see that KDM is still active. Let's check for `lightdm`:

```
[root@localhost philip]# systemctl status lightdm
lightdm.service - Light Display Manager
  Loaded: loaded (/usr/lib/systemd/system/lightdm.service; enabled; vendor
preset: disabled)
   Active: inactive (dead)
     Docs: man:lightdm(1)
[root@localhost philip]#
```

For the changes to take effect, let's reboot the system:

Awesome job! Based on the preceding code, we are now running Lightdm in our Fedora 28 system. Also, we can choose which desktop to load at the top right-hand corner of the screen. Once logged in, we can then verify. For this, we will use our `systemctl` command:

```
[root@localhost philip]# systemctl status kdm
kdm.service - The KDE login manager
 Loaded: loaded (/usr/lib/systemd/system/kdm.service; disabled; vendor
preset: disabled)
 Active: inactive (dead)
[root@localhost philip]#
```

That's what we expect to see. Likewise, when we check for `lightdm`, we see the following:

```
[root@localhost philip]# systemctl status lightdm
lightdm.service - Light Display Manager
   Loaded: loaded (/usr/lib/systemd/system/lightdm.service; enabled; vendor
preset: disabled)
   Active: active (running) since Mon 2018-08-27 16:23:18 EDT; 4min 0s ago
     Docs: man:lightdm(1)
 Main PID: 840 (lightdm)
    Tasks: 8 (limit: 2331)
   Memory: 84.3M
[root@localhost philip]#
```

Great job! Based on that, we can confirm that we are running Lightdm within our Fedora 28 system.

Summary

In this chapter, our focus was on display managers, particularly XDM, KDM, GDM, and Lightdm. Also, the differences between a display manager and a desktop were identified. We began by working with XDM in a CentOS system. We focused on the directory where XDM is stored. In addition to this, we narrowed in on access control for XDM. Next, we switched our attention to KDM; KDM was dominant in Ubuntu distributions until it was later replaced. The methods of installing and configuring the system to use KDM were outlined. Following this, GDM was next on our agenda. We saw how GDM is being used practically in most Linux distributions. The difference in the name was highlighted when working in Ubuntu as opposed to a Fedora distribution. The steps to installing GDM were illustrated. Moreover, we also covered installing some desktops within the mix; this proven to be quite simple. Then, the process to choose a desktop was also demonstrated. Lastly, Lightdm was covered. Lightdm is also popular in that it has replaced KDM in Ubuntu and was eventually replaced by GDM. The techniques to get Lightdm up and running were highlighted using a Fedora 28 distribution. The process of installing and switching between display managers were the focal points to take away from this chapter.

In the next chapter, the focus will be on users and group accounts. Up until this point, we have been working with various aspects within a Linux environment. Firstly, the process of managing user accounts (things such as user creation and deletion, directory modifications, setting a password, permissions, and ownership) will be the focus. Following this, the scope will be grouped. We will dive into the techniques used for managing groups, the process of creating and removing groups, assigning users to groups, and permissions, to name a few. I encourage you to join me once again in the upcoming chapter to become better equipped in managing users and groups.

Questions

1. What does XDM stand for?

>   A. X Display Manager
>   B. XD Manager
>   C. X Desktop Manager
>   D. none of the above

2. Which directory are the XDM configuration files stored in?

      A. `/etc/XDM/xdm`
      B. `/etc/X11/xdm`
      C. `/etc/X1/xdm`
      D. `/etc/XM/xdm`

3. Which configuration file controls resources for XDM?

      A. `Xaccess`
      B. `Xresources`
      C. `Xsession`
      D. `Xdisplay`

4. Which configuration file specifies the display manager to be used in CentOS 6.5?

      A. `/etc/desktop`
      B. `/etc/X11/xdm`
      C. `/etc/sysconfig/desktop`
      D. `/etc/desktop`

5. Which option with the `dnf` command can be used to install the KDE desktop as a complete package?

      A. `--install`
      B. `groupinstall`
      C. `--group`
      D. `--install-group`

6. Which package is used for changing the display managers in Fedora 28?

      A. `displaymanager-switcher`
      B. `system-displaymanager`
      C. `system-switch-displaymanager`
      D. `switch-displaymanager`

7. Which option in the KDM login prompt allows the user to specify which desktop to load?

      A. Session Type
      B. Desktop Type
      C. Login Desktop Type
      D. Session Desktop

8. Which command is used to change between display managers in Ubuntu 16?

    A. `chage`
    B. `apt-cache`
    C. `system-switcher`
    D. `dpkg-reconfigure`

9. Which configuration file in Ubuntu 16 displays the default display manager?

    A. `/etc/desktop`
    B. `/etc/preferdm`
    C. `/etc/X11/default-display-manager`
    D. `/default-display-manager`

10. Which command identifies the current display manager in Fedora 28 as a service?

    A. `ls -l /etc/systemd/system/display.manager.service`
    B. `ls -l /etc/systemd/system/display-manager.service`
    C. `ls -l /etc/systemd/system/dm.service`
    D. `ls -l /etc/systemd/system/display.service`

Further reading

- This site gives useful information about GDM: `https://wiki.gnome.org`
- This site gives useful information about KDM: `https://forum.kde.org`
- This site gives useful information about various display managers: `https://superuser.com`

12
Managing User and Group Accounts

In the previous chapter, display managers were covered. We touched on XDM, KDM, GDM, and Lightdm. Differences between a display manager and a desktop were identified. We began by working with XDM in a CentOS system. Next, we switched our attention to KDM. Following this, GDM was next on our agenda. Additionally, we also covered installing some desktops within the mix. Lastly, Lightdm was covered. The techniques to get Lightdm up and running were highlighted using a Fedora 28 distribution. The processes for installing various display managers and switching between display managers were the key focal points of the previous chapter.

In this chapter, the topic will be user and group accounts. Thus far, we've covered a number of key areas within a Linux environment. Our focus begins with the process of managing user accounts; things such as user creation and deletion, directory modifications, setting a password, permissions, and ownership will be the focus. Following this, the scope will be grouped; we will dive into the techniques used for managing groups. The process of creating and removing groups, assigning users to groups, permissions, and so on will be covered. I encourage you to join me once again in the upcoming chapter to be better equipped for managing users and groups.

We will cover the following topics in this chapter:

- Directory used when creating a new user
- Managing user accounts
- Managing groups

Directory used when creating a new user

Every time we create a new user using the `useradd` command in a system, a number of events occur. To begin with, there is a structure that is in place in terms of the directories that will be generated for a new user. The structure is stored in the skeleton directory; this is located in the `/etc/skel` directory. The `/etc/skel` directory contains files and folders which are copied in the new user's home directory. We can take a look at the skeleton directory using our Ubuntu system:

```
root@ubuntu:/home/philip# ls -a /etc/skel/
.  ..  .bash_logout  .bashrc  examples.desktop  .profile
root@ubuntu:/home/philip#
```

Each new user pulls its structure from here. The dot (.) indicates a hidden file. This includes files such as `/etc/skel/.logout`, `/etc/.skel/.bashrc`, and `/etc/skel/.profile`.

The .bash_logout

Note that `.bash_history` is where commands executed during logout are stored. This simply clears the screen to ensure privacy upon logout. This can be seen in the following command:

```
root@ubuntu:/home/philip# cat /home/philip/.bash_logout
# ~/.bash_logout: executed by bash(1) when login shell exits.
# when leaving the console clear the screen to increase privacy
if [ "$SHLVL" = 1 ]; then
    [ -x /usr/bin/clear_console ] && /usr/bin/clear_console -q
fi
root@ubuntu:/home/philip#
```

The .bashrc

The `/etc/skel/.bashrc` is usually used for storing alias for various commands. This can be seen by looking at `/etc/skel/.bashrc`:

```
root@ubuntu:/home/philip# cat /etc/skel/.bashrc
# colored GCC warnings and errors
#export
GCC_COLORS='error=01;31:warning=01;35:note=01;36:caret=01;32:locus=01:quote
=01'
# some more ls aliases
```

```
alias ll='ls -alF'
alias la='ls -A'
alias l='ls -CF'
root@ubuntu:/home/philip#
```

Some output has been omitted for brevity. Based on the preceding output, some aliases have been defined for us; one such example is `alias ll='ls -af'`.

The .profile

Let's consider `/etc/skel/.profile` as it does a number of tasks; one of which is to check for the existence of `$Home/.bashrc`. This is evident by looking at `/etc/skel/.profile`:

```
root@ubuntu:/home/philip# cat /etc/skel/.profile
#umask 022
# if running bash
if [ -n "$BASH_VERSION" ]; then
    # include .bashrc if it exists
    if [ -f "$HOME/.bashrc" ]; then
                . "$HOME/.bashrc"
    fi
fi
# set PATH so it includes user's private bin directories
PATH="$HOME/bin:$HOME/.local/bin:$PATH"
root@ubuntu:/home/philip#
```

Some output has been omitted for brevity. Based on the preceding output, we can see the `#if running bash` section. Another way to see that these directories are indeed copied over is by looking at an existing user. We will use the `ls` command in combination with the `egrep` command:

```
root@ubuntu:/home/philip# ls -a ~ | egrep '.bash|.profile'
.bash_history
.bashrc
.profile
root@ubuntu:/home/philip#
```

Awesome job! Based on the preceding output, we can see `.bash_history`, `.bashrc` and `.profile`.

The .bash_history

Every command executed at Command Prompt is stored in `.bash_history`. Furthermore, `.bash_history` is only created after we start running commands at Command Prompt. Here is a brief look at `/home/philip/.bash_history`:

```
root@ubuntu:/home/philip# cat /home/philip/.bash_history
ls /etc/grub.d/
cat /var/log/Xorg.0.log | less
startx
sudo su
Xorg -configure
rm /tmp/.X0-lock
sudo su
su
sudo su
root@ubuntu:/home/philip#
```

Some output has been omitted for brevity.

Also, we can check another user for the existence for the various `.bash` files:

```
root@ubuntu:/home/philip# ls -a /home/philip | egrep '.bash|.profile'
.bash_history
.bash_logout
.bashrc
.profile
root@ubuntu:/home/philip#
```

Great job! We can see `.bash_history`, `.bash_logout`, `.bashrc`, and `.profile`.

Another way to identify that the `/etc/skel` directory is being used when creating a new user with the `useradd` command is to call the `useradd` command and pass the `-D` option:

```
root@ubuntu:/home/philip# useradd -D
GROUP=100
HOME=/home
INACTIVE=-1
EXPIRE=
SHELL=/bin/sh
SKEL=/etc/skel
CREATE_MAIL_SPOOL=no
root@ubuntu:/home/philip#
```

Based on the preceding output, we are given a wealth of information. Particularly, SKEL=/etc/skel indicates which directory to use when creating a new user.

Managing user accounts

So far, we've used two user accounts throughout the previous chapters; a standard user and the root user. In Linux, we can create a user account via a GUI utility or via the command line. In the shell, we use the useradd command in order to create a new user account. In newer distributions, there is also the adduser command. In some distributions, such as CentOS, adduser is a symbolic link. This can be seen here:

```
[root@localhost philip]# ll /usr/sbin/adduser
lrwxrwxrwx. 1 root root 7 Jun 20 09:19 /usr/sbin/adduser -> useradd
[root@localhost philip]#
```

On Ubuntu, the adduser command is separate from the useradd command:

```
root@ubuntu:/home/philip# ll /usr/sbin/adduser
-rwxr-xr-x 1 root root 37276 Jul  2  2015 /usr/sbin/adduser*
root@ubuntu:/home/philip#
```

The basic syntax when using the useradd command is useradd <option> username. By default, a standard user cannot create a user account. This can be seen here:

```
philip@ubuntu:~$ useradd tom
useradd: Permission denied.
useradd: cannot lock /etc/passwd; try again later.
philip@ubuntu:~$
```

Based on the preceding output, we are greeted with a Permission denied message.

By default, standard users cannot create user accounts.

To create a new user, we will continue as a root user. We will cover managing permissions with the sudoers file in Chapter 17, *Perform Security Administration Tasks*. Here it is using the root user:

```
root@ubuntu:/home/philip# useradd tom
root@ubuntu:/home/philip#
```

Based on the preceding output, we aren't given any indication to verify whether the new user was created. Rest assured, we can confirm by looking at the /home directory:

```
root@ubuntu:/home/philip# cat /etc/passwd
rtkit:x:118:126:RealtimeKit,,,:/proc:/bin/false
saned:x:119:127::/var/lib/saned:/bin/false
usbmux:x:120:46:usbmux daemon,,,:/var/lib/usbmux:/bin/false
philip:x:1000:1000:philip,,,:/home/philip:/bin/bash
gdm:x:121:129:Gnome Display Manager:/var/lib/gdm3:/bin/false
geoclue:x:122:130::/var/lib/geoclue:/bin/false
tom:x:1001:1001::/home/tom:
root@ubuntu:/home/philip#
```

Some output has been omitted for brevity. The last entry displays the new user information. The way we read this is as follows:

```
tom=user
x=password placeholder
1001=UID
1001=GID
/home/tome=home directory for Tom
```

However, if we compare the entry for another user, we get this:

```
philip:x:1000:1000:philip,,,:/home/philip:/bin/bash
```

Based on the preceding output, the last :/bin/bash part defines the shell for the user. The user that we created has no shell assigned. Also, we need to see a password for the user. In order to set a password, we will use the passwd command:

```
root@ubuntu:/home/philip# passwd tom
Enter new UNIX password:
Retype new UNIX password:
passwd: password updated successfully
root@ubuntu:/home/philip#
```

Awesome job! Now, let's log out and try to log in using the `tom` account:

Great job! We can see the new user appearing but when we try to log in, the system will keep bouncing us out because we have defined a shell for the user. Let's fix this by removing the user and adding the user once again. We will use the `userdel` command to remove the user:

```
root@ubuntu:/home/philip# userdel -r tom
userdel: tom mail spool (/var/mail/tom) not found
userdel: tom home directory (/home/tom) not found
root@ubuntu:/home/philip#
root@ubuntu:/home/philip# cat /etc/passwd
philip:x:1000:1000:philip,,,:/home/philip:/bin/bash
gdm:x:121:129:Gnome Display Manager:/var/lib/gdm3:/bin/false
geoclue:x:122:130::/var/lib/geoclue:/bin/false
root@ubuntu:/home/philip#
```

Great! Now, let's create the user and pass the `-s` option. This will define the shell for the user to be used with the `useradd` command:

```
root@ubuntu:/home/philip# useradd -s /bin/bash tom
root@ubuntu:/home/philip# cat /etc/passwd:
philip:x:1000:1000:philip,,,:/home/philip:/bin/bash
gdm:x:121:129:Gnome Display Manager:/var/lib/gdm3:/bin/false
geoclue:x:122:130::/var/lib/geoclue:/bin/false
tom:x:1001:1001::/home/tom:/bin/bash
root@ubuntu:/home/philip#
```

Awesome job! Now we can see in the last entry the user `tom` has been assigned a `/bin/bash` shell. Another interesting part of `/etc/passwd` is the x in each of the accounts listed.

We said it represents the password, but we have not set x as the password, so what's the deal with x? Well, x is simply saying that the password is encrypted; it is actually stored in a separate location. The /etc/shadow directory stores the password. We can take a look at the /etc/shadow directory for reference:

```
root@ubuntu:/home/philip# passwd tom
Enter new UNIX password:
Retype new UNIX password:
passwd: password updated successfully
root@ubuntu:/home/philip#
root@ubuntu:/home/philip# cat /etc/shadow
messagebus:*:16911:0:99999:7:::
uuidd:*:16911:0:99999:7:::
lightdm:*:16911:0:99999:7:::
whoopsie:*:16911:0:99999:7:::
avahi-autoipd:*:16911:0:99999:7:::
avahi:*:16911:0:99999:7:::
dnsmasq:*:16911:0:99999:7:::
colord:*:16911:0:99999:7:::
gdm:*:17770:0:99999:7:::
geoclue:*:17770:0:99999:7:::
tom:!:17778:0:99999:7:::
root@ubuntu:/home/philip#
```

Some output has been omitted for brevity. Based on the preceding output, we can see the actual encrypted password for each account.

The chage command

Another interesting aspect regarding user accounts involves the aging time for a password; the expiration for a password. We can view the expiration for a given user by using the chage command. Let's create a password for the user tom and then check the password aging settings for the new user:

 You must have root privileges to change the password aging parameters.

```
root@ubuntu:/home/philip# passwd tom
Enter new UNIX password:
Retype new UNIX password:
passwd: password updated successfully
root@ubuntu:/home/philip#
```

Run the preceding commands and you will see the following output:

Excellent! Based on the preceding output, we used the -l option to display the expiration settings; we can see some valuable information, notably, Last password change, Password expires, and Account expires. We can change these values by passing various options. For instance, let's change Account expires. We use the -E option:

```
root@ubuntu:/home/philip# chage -E 2018-09-04 tom
root@ubuntu:/home/philip# chage -l tom
Last password change
: Sep 04, 2018
Password expires
: never
Password inactive
: never
Account expires
: Sep 04, 2018
Minimum number of days between password change
: 0
Maximum number of days between password change
: 99999
Number of days of warning before password expires
: 7
root@ubuntu:/home/philip#
```

Awesome job! Based on the preceding output, we've set the account to expire to the current time of this demo. Now, to see the effects of this change, we will open another Terminal and try to log in as the user `tom`:

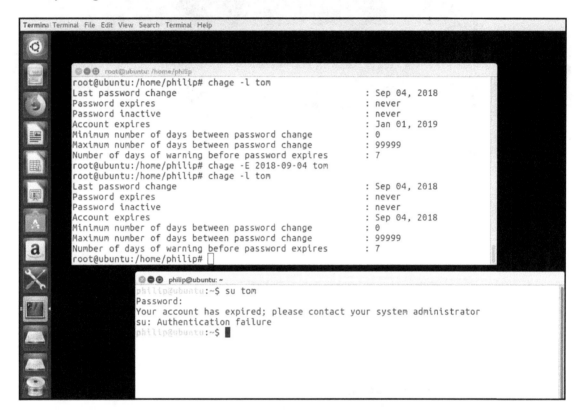

Great job! Based on the preceding output, we see the message that was returned while attempting to log in as the user `tom`. To remove this expiration for the user `tom`, we would use `-1` as the value:

```
root@ubuntu:/home/philip# chage -E -1 tom
root@ubuntu:/home/philip# chage -l tom
Last password change
: Sep 04, 2018
Password expires
: never
Password inactive
: never
Account  expires
: never
Minimum number of days between password change
```

```
 : 0
Maximum number of days between password change
 : 99999
Number of days of warning before password expires
 : 7
root@ubuntu:/home/philip#
```

Now, we will be able to log in as the user `tom`:

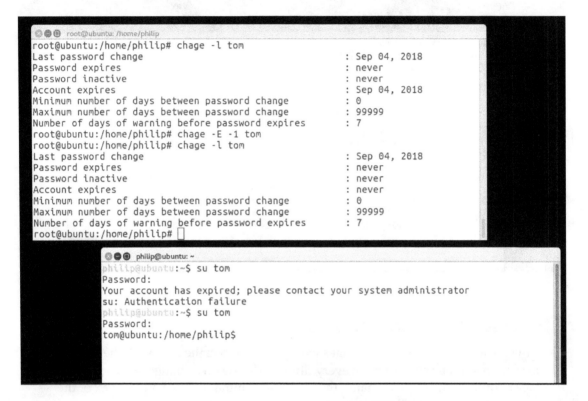

```
root@ubuntu:/home/philip# chage -l tom
Last password change                                      : Sep 04, 2018
Password expires                                          : never
Password inactive                                         : never
Account expires                                           : Sep 04, 2018
Minimum number of days between password change            : 0
Maximum number of days between password change            : 99999
Number of days of warning before password expires         : 7
root@ubuntu:/home/philip# chage -E -1 tom
root@ubuntu:/home/philip# chage -l tom
Last password change                                      : Sep 04, 2018
Password expires                                          : never
Password inactive                                         : never
Account expires                                           : never
Minimum number of days between password change            : 0
Maximum number of days between password change            : 99999
Number of days of warning before password expires         : 7
root@ubuntu:/home/philip#
```

```
philip@ubuntu:~$ su tom
Password:
Your account has expired; please contact your system administrator
su: Authentication failure
philip@ubuntu:~$ su tom
Password:
tom@ubuntu:/home/philip$
```

Excellent! Based on the preceding output, we can see the effectiveness of using the `chage` command. To see the available options that can be passed with the `chage` command, we can do this:

```
root@ubuntu:/home/philip# chage
```

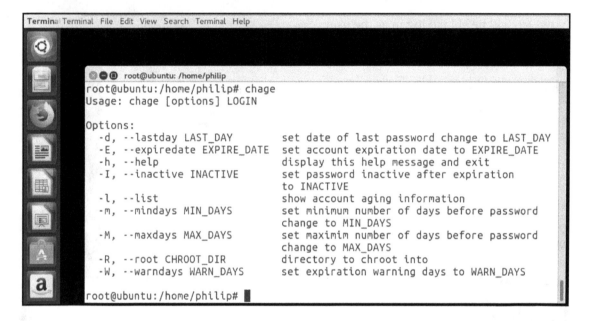

The usermod command

Earlier we saw that to make any changes we have to remove the user with the `useradd` command. This can be cumbersome every time we decide on a change; instead, we can leverage another powerful command: the `usermod` command. The basic syntax of the `usermod` command is as follows:

```
usermod <option> username
```

Using our test user `tom`, we can change a number of parameters with the `usermod` command. For example, we can lock the account for the user `tom`, this will prevent the user `tom` from being able to log into the system. To lock an account, we would use the `-L` option:

```
root@ubuntu:/home/philip# cat /etc/passwd
philip:x:1000:1000:philip,,,:/home/philip:/bin/bash
gdm:x:121:129:Gnome Display Manager:/var/lib/gdm3:/bin/false
geoclue:x:122:130::/var/lib/geoclue:/bin/false
```

```
tom:x:1001:1001::/home/tom:
root@ubuntu:/home/philip# usermod -L tom
root@ubuntu:/home/philip#
```

Awesome job! Based on the preceding output, the user tom is unable to log in. An interesting point to note is the entry for the user tom inside /etc/shadow shows ! in front of the password in the second field, which represents the password:

```
root@ubuntu:/home/philip# cat /etc/shadow | grep tom
tom:!$6$uJ52BA2n$SWGisIpNTTOSygIX6swWdkS/gLPGZacEzCz2Ht6qfUHIr7ZIxkJyUjEyqN
9ncb1yIFIXYnePz4HVzrwqJA1DZ0:17778:0:99999:7:::
root@ubuntu:
 root@ubuntu:/home/philip# cat /etc/shadow | grep philip
 philip:$1$8gQrKziP$v6Uv6
root@ubuntu:/home/philip#
```

Based on the preceding, there is no ! in front of the password for the user philip. Another way to verify whether an account has been locked is to use the passwd command. We pass the --status option:

```
root@ubuntu:/home/philip# passwd --status tom
tom L 09/04/2018 0 99999 7 -1
root@ubuntu:/home/philip#
```

Awesome job! Note L indicates that the user account is currently locked. We can unlock the user account by using the usermod command and passing the -U option:

```
root@ubuntu:/home/philip# usermod -U tom
root@ubuntu:/home/philip# passwd --status tom
tom P 09/04/2018 0 99999 7 -1
root@ubuntu:/home/philip#
```

Great job! Based on the preceding output, the P indicates that the user tom has a usable password; this implies that the account is unlocked:

Excellent! Now, when we look at etc/shadow once again, we will no longer see the ! in front of the hashed password:

```
root@ubuntu:/home/philip# cat /etc/shadow | grep tom
tom:$6$uJ52BA2n$SWGisIpNTTOSygIX6swWdkS/gLPGZacEzCz2Ht6qfUHIr7ZIxkJyUjEyqN9
ncb1yIFIXYnePz4HVzrwqJA1DZ0:17778:0:99999:7:::
root@ubuntu:/home/philip#
```

Awesome! We can also define a shell for a user if we added a user without specifying a shell; we pass the `-s` option with the `usermod` command:

```
root@ubuntu:/home/philip# cat /etc/passwd
gdm:x:121:129:Gnome Display Manager:/var/lib/gdm3:/bin/false
geoclue:x:122:130::/var/lib/geoclue:/bin/false
tom:x:1001:1001::/home/tom:
root@ubuntu:/home/philip# usermod -s /bin/bash tom
root@ubuntu:/home/philip# cat /etc/passwd
gdm:x:121:129:Gnome Display Manager:/var/lib/gdm3:/bin/false
geoclue:x:122:130::/var/lib/geoclue:/bin/false
tom:x:1001:1001::/home/tom:/bin/bash
root@ubuntu:/home/philip#
```

Awesome job! Another method for locking an account is to use the `passwd` command; we pass the `-l` option. Let's lock the user `tom`:

```
root@ubuntu:/home/philip# passwd -l tom
passwd: password expiry information changed.
root@ubuntu:/home/philip# passwd --status tom
tom L 09/04/2018 0 99999 7 -1
root@ubuntu:/home/philip#
```

Once again, when we try to log in as the user `tom`, we will see this:

Great job! Also, we can unlock an account using the `passwd` command; we would pass the `-u` option:

```
root@ubuntu:/home/philip# passwd -u tom
passwd: password expiry information changed.
```

```
root@ubuntu:/home/philip# passwd --status tom
tom P 09/04/2018 0 99999 7 -1
root@ubuntu:/home/philip#
```

Awesome! Note that the root user can still log in using the `tom` user, yes! We can illustrate this by locking the user `tom` once again:

```
root@ubuntu:/home/philip# passwd -l tom
passwd: password expiry information changed.
root@ubuntu:/home/philip# passwd --status tom
tom L 09/04/2018 0 99999 7 -1
root@ubuntu:/home/philip# cat /etc/shadow | grep tom
tom:!$6$uJ52BA2n$SWGisIpNTTOSygIX6swWdkS/gLPGZacEzCz2Ht6qfUHIr7ZIxkJyUjEyqN
9ncb1yIFIXYnePz4HVzrwqJA1DZ0:17778:0:99999:7:::
root@ubuntu:/home/philip#
```

Based on the preceding output, from all indication, it seems that the user `tom` account has been disabled but check this out:

Awesome! Here's what happened, when someone tries to log in as the user `tom`, they will be prevented unless they first become the root user because the lock **does not** prevent the root from accessing the locked account.

The root user can access any account.

When we manage user accounts; some of their base information comes from a special configuration file: the /etc/login.def file. We can take a look at /etc/login.def:

```
root@ubuntu:/home/philip# cat /etc/login.defs
# /etc/login.defs - Configuration control definitions for the login
package.
# Three items must be defined:  MAIL_DIR, ENV_SUPATH, and ENV_PATH.
# If unspecified, some arbitrary (and possibly incorrect) value will
SU_NAME                              su
PASS_MAX_DAYS            99999
PASS_MIN_DAYS               0
PASS_WARN_AGE            7
root@ubuntu:/home/philip#
```

Some output has been omitted for brevity. Based on the preceding output, we can see settings for the su and chage commands.

The w command

The w command displays the currently logged-in users in the system. We can take a look at the w command:

```
root@ubuntu:/home/philip# w
 08:00:03 up 22:14,   4 users,   load average: 0.04, 0.01, 0.00
USER      TTY      FROM              LOGIN@   IDLE   JCPU   PCPU WHAT
philip    tty2       :1              Mon13    7days  1:35   0.29s
/sbin/upstart --user
root@ubuntu:/home/philip#
```

Based on the preceding output, we have the fields starting from the user moving from left to right. Some interesting fields are the FROM field as it shows where the user logged in from (if it is over a network, it will show an IP address) and the LOGIN@ field as it shows which date the user logged in. We can see the available options by passing the --help option:

```
root@ubuntu:/home/philip# w --help
Usage:
 w [options]
Options:
 -h, --no-header      do not print header
```

```
 -u, --no-current     ignore current process username
 -s, --short          short format
 -f, --from           show remote hostname field
 -o, --old-style      old style output
 -i, --ip-addr        display IP address instead of hostname (if possible)
  --help      display this help and exit
 -V, --version  output version information and exit
For more details see w(1).
root@ubuntu:/home/philip#
```

The who command

The who command is another popular command used for displaying currently logged-in users. We simply do who without any options:

```
root@ubuntu:/home/philip# who
philip    tty2           2018-09-03 13:29 (:1)
root@ubuntu:/home/philip#
```

Awesome job! But wait, we can actually identify the date and time when the system booted up, yes! We pass the -a option:

```
root@ubuntu:/home/philip# who -a
        system boot  2018-08-27 12:33
LOGIN      tty1           2018-09-03 13:29                  13792 id=tty1
           run-level 5  2018-08-27 12:33          tty2           2018-08-30
06:34            1434 id=      term=0 exit=0
           tty2           2018-08-30 06:35                   9661 id=      term=0
exit=0
           tty2           2018-09-03 13:17                  10231 id=      term=0
exit=0
philip   + tty2           2018-09-03 13:29  old        13815 (:1)
root@ubuntu:/home/philip#
Excellent! The first entry "system boot", displays the date and time the
system booted up. We can see the available options by passing the "--help"
option:
root@ubuntu:/home/philip# who --help
Usage: who [OPTION]... [ FILE | ARG1 ARG2 ]
Print information about users who are currently logged in.
 -a, --all        same as -b -d --login -p -r -t -T -u  -b, --boot
time of last system boot
 -d, --dead       print dead processes
 -H, --heading    print line of column headings
     --ips        print ips instead of hostnames. with --lookup,
                  canonicalizes based on stored IP, if available,
rather than stored hostname
 -l, --login      print system login processes
```

```
          --lookup      attempt to canonicalize hostnames via DNS   -m
only hostname and user associated with stdin
  -p, --process     print active processes spawned by init
  -q, --count        all login names and number of users logged on   -r, --
runlevel     print current runlevel
  -s, --short        print only name, line, and time (default)   -t, --time
print last system clock change
  -T, -w, --mesg     add user's message status as +, - or ?
  -u, --users        list users logged in
      --message      same as -T
   --writable     same as -T
   --help      display this help and exit
   --version   output version information and exit
root@ubuntu:/home/philip#
```

The last command

Another popular command for displaying the users who have recently logged in is the last command. We simply say last:

```
root@ubuntu:/home/philip# last
tom     pts/18   172.16.175.129   Tue Sep  4 08:31    still logged in
wtmp begins Tue Sep  4 08:31:36 2018
root@ubuntu:/home/philip#
```

Based on the preceding output, the user tom has logged in over the network. We can see the available options by passing the --help option:

```
root@ubuntu:/home/philip# last --help
Usage:
 last [options] [<username>...] [<tty>...]
Show a listing of last logged in users.
Options:
 -<number>           how many lines to show
 -a, --hostlast      display hostnames in the last column
 -d, --dns           translate the IP number back into a hostname
 -f, --file <file>   use a specific file instead of /var/log/wtmp
 -F, --fulltimes     print full login and logout times and dates
 -i, --ip            display IP numbers in numbers-and-dots notation
 -n, --limit <number> how many lines to show
 -R, --nohostname    don't display the hostname field
 -s, --since <time>  display the lines since the specified time
 -t, --until <time>  display the lines until the specified time
 -p, --present <time> display who were present at the specified time
 -w, --fullnames     display full user and domain names
 -x, --system        display system shutdown entries and run level changes
     --time-format <format>  show timestamps in the specified <format>:
```

```
                                        notime|short|full|iso
  -h, --help      display this help and exit
  -V, --version   output version information and exit
root@ubuntu:/home/philip#
```

Awesome job!

The whoami command

We can quickly view information about the current user by using the whoami command. The whoami command displays the owner of the current login session:

```
root@ubuntu:/home/philip# whoami
root
root@ubuntu:/home/philip#
```

Great job! We can view the available options of the whoami command by passing the --help option:

```
root@ubuntu:/home/philip# whoami --help
Usage: whoami [OPTION]...
Print the user name associated with the current effective user ID.
Same as id -un.
      --help      display this help and exit
      --version   output version information and exit
GNU coreutils online help: <http://www.gnu.org/software/coreutils/>
Full documentation at: <http://www.gnu.org/software/coreutils/whoami>
or available locally via: info '(coreutils) whoami invocation'
root@ubuntu:/home/philip#
```

Managing groups

So far, we've been creating user accounts within our system; what about group accounts? Well, here's the thing, when we create an account using the useradd command, we are also indirectly creating a group account using the same name as the user. To prove this, let's take a look at the /etc/login.def file:

```
root@ubuntu:/home/philip# cat /etc/login.defs | grep GRO
#              TTYGROUP            Login tty will be assigned this group
ownership.
# which owns the terminals, define TTYGROUP to the group number and
# TTYPERM to 0620.  Otherwise leave TTYGROUP commented out and assign
TTYGROUP            tty
# If USERGROUPS_ENAB is set to "yes", that will modify this UMASK default
```

```
value
USERGROUPS_ENAB yes
#CONSOLE_GROUPS                              floppy:audio:cdrom
root@ubuntu:/home/philip#
```

Based on the preceding output, the USERGROUPS_ENAB yes variable enables the creation of a group using the same name specified for the username. We can also take a look at the available groups by looking at /etc/group:

```
root@ubuntu:/home/philip# cat /etc/group
pulse-access:x:125:
rtkit:x:126:
saned:x:127:
philip:x:1000:
sambashare:x:128:philip
gdm:x:129:
geoclue:x:130:
tom:x:1001:
root@ubuntu:/home/philip#
```

Some output has been omitted for brevity. Based on the preceding output, a group, tom was created when we created a username tom. However, we can also create a group using another powerful command, the groupadd command:

```
root@ubuntu:/home/philip# groupadd Hacki
root@ubuntu:/home/philip# cat /etc/group
philip:x:1000:
sambashare:x:128:philip
gdm:x:129:
geoclue:x:130:
tom:x:1001:
Hacki:x:1002:
root@ubuntu:/home/philip#
```

Awesome! Now we see our newly created Hacki group being displayed. Likewise, we can remove a group using the groupdel command:

```
root@ubuntu:/home/philip# groupdel Hacki
root@ubuntu:/home/philip# cat /etc/group
philip:x:1000:
sambashare:x:128:philip
gdm:x:129:
geoclue:x:130:
tom:x:1001:
root@ubuntu:/home/philip#
```

Great! Now, let's create recreate a `Hacki` group:

```
root@ubuntu:/home/philip# groupadd Hacki
root@ubuntu:/home/philip# cat /etc/group
tom:x:1001:
Hacki:x:1002:
root@ubuntu:/home/philip#
```

It is possible to add a user to another group using the `usermod` command. Let's use the `tom` user:

```
root@ubuntu:/home/philip# usermod -G Hacki,tom tom
root@ubuntu:/home/philip# cat /etc/group
tom:x:1001:tom
Hacki:x:1002:tom
root@ubuntu:/home/philip#
```

Now, we can see that the user `tom` is part of the `tom` and `Hacki` groups. Another way to group for a user is to use the `id` command:

```
root@ubuntu:/home/philip# id tom
uid=1001(tom) gid=1001(tom) groups=1001(tom),1002(Hacki)
root@ubuntu:/home/philip#
```

Great job! Additionally, we can make a group as the primary group for a user by passing -g with the `usermod` command:

```
root@ubuntu:/home/philip# usermod -g Hacki tom
root@ubuntu:/home/philip# id tom
uid=1001(tom) gid=1002(Hacki) groups=1002(Hacki) ,1001(tom)
root@ubuntu:/home/philip# cat /etc/group | grep tom
tom:x:1001:
Hacki:x:1002:tom
root@ubuntu:/home/philip#
```

Excellent! Based on the preceding output, the only group that the user `tom` belongs to is the `Hacki` group. It is also possible to add a password to a group; we use the `gpasswd` command. Note that `/etc/gshadow` stores each group password. We can take a look at it:

```
root@ubuntu:/home/philip# cat /etc/gshadow
philip:!::
sambashare:!::philip
gdm:!::
geoclue:!::
tom:!::tom
Hacki:!::
root@ubuntu:/home/philip#
```

Some output has been omitted for brevity. The ! exclamation means that no password has been set for the respective groups. Let's set a password for the `Hacki` group:

```
root@ubuntu:/home/philip# gpasswd Hacki
Changing the password for group Hacki
New Password:
Re-enter new password:
root@ubuntu:/home/philip# cat /etc/gshadow
geoclue:!::
tom:!::tom
Hacki:$6$eOvgO//4tAi/0C$v/FxkZyQLE0BLJ9jfrQ3sElm3kyNbhThl8DFXokZmAWzK1AKQFz
tSLOBpNsvOESOsWIz6DXKt4Erg.J7ElZut1::tom
root@ubuntu:/home/philip#
```

Awesome! Now we can see that the hashed version of the password has replaced the ! exclamation.

There is also another command that can be used to create or change a group's password: the `groupmod` command. Let's use the `groupmod` command to assign a password to the `tom` group:

```
root@ubuntu:/home/philip# groupmod -p password tom
root@ubuntu:/home/philip# cat /etc/gshadow
gdm:!::
geoclue:!::
tom:password::tom
Hacki:$6$eOvgO//4tAi/0C$v/FxkZyQLE0BLJ9jfrQ3sElm3kyNbhThl8DFXokZmAWzK1AKQFz
tSLOBpNsvOESOsWIz6DXKt4Erg.J7ElZut1::tom
root@ubuntu:/home/philip#
```

Great job! Based on the preceding output, as opposed to the `gpasswd` command, when we use the `groupmod` command, it expects an encrypted password. We specified a plain password; hence, we see the password being exposed.

Summary

In this chapter, we covered a wide array of techniques for managing user and group accounts. First, we investigated the various directories from which the new users' home directories are populated. Next, we dealt with user account creation. We saw how we add or remove a user account. In addition, we saw how to set a password for a user account. Also, we looked at the various configuration files where the users' passwords are kept, particularly, focusing on the `/etc/passwd` and the `/etc/shadow` files. Following this, we dealt with modifying properties for a user account.

We touched on locking and unlocking a user account. Also, we worked with password expiration settings using the `chage` command. Finally, our focus was on the groups. We covered the steps for creating a group and adding and removing groups. Moreover, we saw how we would assign a group to a user; likewise, we saw how to assign a primary group. Finishing, we looked at methods for setting a password for a group.

In the next chapter, our focus will be automating tasks. We will cover the utilities commonly used for executing tasks. Additionally, we will cover permissions for carrying out tasks within a Linux system. I hope you join me in the next chapter as it contains vital information regarding the automation of tasks.

Questions

1. Which configuration file usually stores alias inside the `/etc/skel` directory?

   A. `/etc/skel/bash`
   B. `/etc/skel/bash_rc`
   C. `/etc/skel/.bash_rc`
   D. `/etc/skel/.bashrc`

2. Which configuration file clears the screen whenever the user signs out of the system?

   A. `/etc.skel/.bash_logout`
   B. `/etc/skel/bash_logout`
   C. `/etc/skel/.logout`
   D. `/etc/skel/.bashlogout`

3. Which configuration file stores the commands executed?

   A. `/etc/skel/.bash_history`
   B. `~/.bash_history`
   C. `/etc/skel/bash_history`
   D. `~/.history`

4. Which option prints the defaults for a new user with the `useradd` command?

   A. `-d`
   B. `-b`
   C. `-D`
   D. `--defaults`

5. Which option allows to specify a shell when using `useradd` ?

        A. `-c`
        B. `-d`
        C. `-S`
        D. `-s`

6. The `adduser` command is a symbolic link to which command in Fedora 28?

        A. `adduser`
        B. `add-user`
        C. `user-mod`
        D. `user-add`

7. Which option with the `chage` command will print out the account expiration settings?

        A. `-a`
        B. `-l`
        C. `-c`
        D. `-d`

8. Which code with the `passwd --status` command indicates that the account is locked?

        A. `P`
        B. `A`
        C. `L`
        D. `N`

9. Which option with the `groupmod` command specifies a primary group for a user?

        A. `-g`
        B. `-G`
        C. `-A`
        D. `-b`

10. Which command is used to change a group's password?

> A. adduser
> B. groupedit
> C. groupmod
> D. grouppasswd

Further reading

- This site gives useful information: /etc/skel: https://unix.stackexchange. com
- This site gives useful information about user account creation: http://www. linfo.org
- This site gives useful information about various groups: http://www. linuxguide.it

13
Automating Tasks

In the previous chapter, we covered a wide array of techniques for managing user and group accounts. First, we investigated the various directories from which the new user's home directories are populated. Next, we dealt with user account creation. In addition to this, we looked at the various configuration files where the user passwords are kept. Finally, our focus was on the groups. We covered the steps for creating a group, as well as adding, removing, and assigning a password to a group.

In this chapter, our focus switches to automation, particularly automating tasks. We will cover the scheduling of tasks using various methods. We often work with various tasks on a daily basis, rather than having to run the tasks manually and repetitively over a period of time; it's good practice to implement some type of additional automation, and we will be looking at permissions regarding execution of tasks.

In this chapter, we will be covering the following topics:

- The at, atq, and atrm commands
- The crontab file and anacron command
- Permissions for tasks using configuration files

Managing automation using the at, atq, and atrm commands

In this section, we will cover some common methods for automating various type of tasks within a Linux system. First, we will cover the at command. Next, we will work with handling queues using the atq command. Finally, we will finish off this section with the technique used for removing jobs, using the atrm command.

The at command

The `at` command schedules a task to run at a fixed time; it runs once. You can schedule a simple task such as appending some output to a file or a complex task such as backing up a database. The basic syntax for starting the `at` utility is as follows:

```
at <time>
```

We can see the `at` command in action using our Fedora 28 system. Here, we simply type `at` without specifying an option:

```
[root@localhost philip]# at
Garbled time
[root@localhost philip]#
```

Based on the preceding command, without specifying a time, the `at` utility will return `Garbled time`. Here is how we specify the time:

```
[root@localhost philip]# at 18:10
warning: commands will be executed using /bin/sh
at>
```

Based on the preceding output, as soon as we enter a date (in this case we entered a time in the format of HH:MM) it launches the `at` utility and we are presented with a `warning: commands will be executed using /bin/sh` warning; this tells us which shell the `at` utility is going to use when it is executed. From here, we can type any command that we would like to run at the specified time. An example might be this:

```
[root@localhost philip]# at 18:10
warning: commands will be executed using /bin/sh
at> ls -l > /home/philip/Documents/schedule
at>
```

It may seem that nothing has changed; for the changes to be saved we would have to tell the `at` utility that we have finished entering our commands. This is done using the *Ctrl + D* combination:

```
[root@localhost philip]# at 18:10
warning: commands will be executed using /bin/sh
at> ls -l > /home/philip/Documents/schedule
at> <EOT>
job 1 at Tue Sep  4 18:10:00 2018
[root@localhost philip]#
```

Based on the preceding output, the at utility has scheduled a task to run at 18:10 from the present time. Another way to schedule a task with the at utility is to specify the time in the 12-hour format. Here is how we accomplish this:

```
[root@localhost philip]# at 9:00 PM
warning: commands will be executed using /bin/sh
at> date > /home/philip/Documents/date_schedule
at> <EOT>
job 2 at Tue Sep  4 21:00:00 2018
[root@localhost philip]#
```

Awesome! Based on the preceding output, we have specified the time using a 12-hour format by tagging PM. This tells the at utility to execute the job at 9:00 PM from the current time. Also, we can specify the time using a keyword. For instance, we can say tomorrow, noon tomorrow, next week, next monday, fri, to name a few. Here is how this would look:

```
[root@localhost philip]# at next monday
warning: commands will be executed using /bin/sh
at> ls -l /etc > /home/philip/Documents/ls_schedule
at> <EOT>
job 4 at Mon Sep 10 09:11:00 2018
[root@localhost philip]#
```

Great! Based on the preceding output, the at utility has used the current date to calculate when it will be executed. Also, <EOT> is the result of pressing *Ctrl + D*. Another way to specify when to run the at utility is to use a combination of keywords. We could, for example, specify now + 4 weeks, now + 6 years, now + 25 minutes, and so on. Here is how this looks:

```
[root@localhost philip]# at now + 15 minutes
warning: commands will be executed using /bin/sh
at> ls -a /var/log > /home/philip/Documents/lsa_schedule
at> <EOT>
job 5 at Thu Sep  6 09:32:00 2018
[root@localhost philip]# date
Thu Sep  6 09:19:25 EDT 2018
[root@localhost philip]#
```

Excellent! Based on the preceding output, we can see that the at utility uses the current date and time to base its calculations. Also, we can specify the year to see its calculation too:

```
[root@localhost philip]# at now + 25 years
warning: commands will be executed using /bin/sh
at> systemctl status sshd.service >
/home/philip/Documents/ssh_25yrs_schedule
```

```
at> <EOT>
job 7 at Sun Sep  6 09:25:00 2043
[root@localhost philip]#
```

Great job! Based on the preceding output, the at utility is going to run this task 25 years from the present time. We can see a list of some common options that can be passed with the at utility; we pass the -help option:

```
[root@localhost philip]# at -help
Usage: at [-V] [-q x] [-f file] [-mMlbv] timespec ...
       at [-V] [-q x] [-f file] [-mMlbv] -t time
       at -c job ...
       atq [-V] [-q x]
       at [ -rd ] job ...
       atrm [-V] job ...
       batch
[root@localhost philip]#
Awesome job!
```

The atq command

Thus far, we have been creating a number of tasks to be executed using the at utility. It would be nice to keep a track of what is scheduled to run using the at command; the atq command does just that. To see how this works, we can run the atq command:

```
[root@localhost philip]# atq
4               Mon Sep 10 09:11:00 2018 a root
7               Sun Sep  6 09:25:00 2043 a root
[root@localhost philip]#
```

Based on the preceding output, we have two jobs listed to be run by the at utility. When we run the atq command as the root user, all jobs are listed to be run by the at command; this is different when we run the at command as a standard user. Only the user jobs will be listed. Here is how this would look:

```
[root@localhost philip]# exit
exit
[philip@localhost ~]$ atq
[philip@localhost ~]$
```

Based on the preceding output, the user is unaware of the jobs that the root user has scheduled using the `at` command. Also, we can view the queue using the `at` command; we pass the `-l` option:

```
[root@localhost philip]# at -l
4               Mon Sep 10 09:11:00 2018 a root
7               Sun Sep  6 09:25:00 2043 a root
[root@localhost philip]#
```

Awesome! Based on the preceding command, we can see that the output is identical to that of the `atq` command. This is due to the fact that the `-l` option used with the `at` command is simply an alias of the `atq` command.

The atrm command

It's nice to have the ability to schedule jobs to be run using the `at` utility. However, we need some form of control over the jobs scheduled. If we've decided to cancel a job, we can use the `atrm` command. The `atrm` command is used for canceling a job before it is executed by the `at` utility. For instance, we schedule a reboot using the `at` utility:

```
[root@localhost philip]# at now + 5 minutes
warning: commands will be executed using /bin/sh
at> reboot
at> <EOT>
job 8 at Thu Sep  6 10:06:00 2018
[root@localhost philip]# date
Thu Sep  6 10:01:21 EDT 2018
[root@localhost philip]#
```

Based on the preceding command, we have specified to reboot the system in five minutes using the `at` command. Now, if for some reason we want to cancel this job, we can use the `atrm` command. We can do this as follows:

```
[root@localhost philip]# atq
4               Mon Sep 10 09:11:00 2018 a root
8               Thu Sep  6 10:06:00 2018 a root
7               Sun Sep  6 09:25:00 2043 a root
[root@localhost philip]# atrm 8
[root@localhost philip]# atq
4               Mon Sep 10 09:11:00 2018 a root
7               Sun Sep  6 09:25:00 2043 a root
[root@localhost philip]#
```

Great! Based on the preceding command, we used the `atq` command to list the scheduled jobs; we then used the `at rm` command and specified the job ID to remove it. Also, we can remove a job using the `at` utility; to do so, we pass the `-r` or `-d` option:

```
[root@localhost philip]# atq
4               Mon Sep 10 09:11:00 2018 a root
7               Sun Sep  6 09:25:00 2043 a root
[root@localhost philip]# at -r 4
[root@localhost philip]# atq
7               Sun Sep  6 09:25:00 2043 a root
[root@localhost philip]#
```

Great! Based on the preceding output, we can see that the job with ID 4 was removed using the `-r` option of the `at` command. The `-d` option of the `at` command works in the same way:

```
[root@localhost philip]# atq
7               Sun Sep  6 09:25:00 2043 a root
[root@localhost philip]#
[root@localhost philip]# at -d 7
[root@localhost philip]# atq
[root@localhost philip]#
Excellent!
```

Managing automation using cron, crontab, and anacron

In this section, we will cover some techniques for managing tasks that normally require being run more than once. First, we will begin with the various `cron` directories. Next, we will work with `crontab`. Finally, we will then cover `anacron`. The highlight will be the fact that they are not a replacement for each other, but rather they play key roles in managing tasks within a Linux system.

Cron

As we saw earlier, the `at` utility only runs a task once. There are times when we need to run a task multiple times. It is cumbersome having to be present to type a task with the `at` utility each time we want to execute a given job. For instance, backups are one of the most common tasks that most Linux admins are responsible for carrying out.

In light of these circumstances, we can use the `cron` utility, more specifically the `/etc/cron.*` directories; we place our task, which we would like to be run. The jobs could be run hourly, daily, or monthly. Cron uses the `crond` daemon. In Ubuntu, the `cron` daemon is called `cron` or `cron.service`, whereas in Fedora 28, the `cron` daemon is called `crond` or `crond.service`. We can check the status of the `cron` daemon on Ubuntu as follows:

```
root@philip-virtual-machine:/home/philip# systemctl status crond
Unit crond.service could not be found.
root@philip-virtual-machine:/home/philip# systemctl status cron
cron.service - Regular background program processing daemon
   Loaded: loaded (/lib/systemd/system/cron.service; enabled; vendor
preset: enabled)
   Active: active (running) since Thu 2018-09-06 10:58:35 EDT; 10min ago
     Docs: man:cron(8)
 Main PID: 608 (cron)
    Tasks: 1 (limit: 4636)
   CGroup: /system.slice/cron.service
           └─608 /usr/sbin/cron -f
root@philip-virtual-machine:/home/philip#
```

Based on the preceding output, the `cron` daemon called `cron.service`. Let's check in Fedora 28 for the `cron` daemon:

```
[root@localhost philip]# systemctl status cron
Unit cron.service could not be found.
[root@localhost philip]# systemctl status crond
crond.service - Command Scheduler
   Loaded: loaded (/usr/lib/systemd/system/crond.service; enabled; vendor
preset: enabled)
   Active: active (running) since Tue 2018-09-04 08:56:09 EDT; 2 days ago
 Main PID: 867 (crond)
    Tasks: 1 (limit: 2331)
   Memory: 3.3M
   CGroup: /system.slice/crond.service
           └─867 /usr/sbin/crond -n
[root@localhost philip]#
```

Great! As can be seen in Fedora 28, the cron service is called `crond.service`. Next, let's take a look at the `cron` directories:

```
root@philip-virtual-machine:/home/philip# ls -l /etc/cron.hourly/
total 0
root@philip-virtual-machine:/home/philip#
```

Based on the preceding output, there are no tasks scheduled to be run every hour. However, we will place a number of tasks in the /etc/cron.daily directory:

```
root@philip-virtual-machine:/home/philip# ls -l /etc/cron.daily/
total 52
-rwxr-xr-x 1 root root  311 May 29  2017 0anacron
-rwxr-xr-x 1 root root  376 Nov 20  2017 apport
-rwxr-xr-x 1 root root 1478 Apr 20 06:08 apt-compat
-rwxr-xr-x 1 root root  355 Dec 29  2017 bsdmainutils
-rwxr-xr-x 1 root root  384 Dec 12  2012 cracklib-runtime
-rwxr-xr-x 1 root root 1176 Nov  2  2017 dpkg
-rwxr-xr-x 1 root root  372 Aug 21  2017 logrotate
-rwxr-xr-x 1 root root 1065 Apr  7 06:39 man-db
-rwxr-xr-x 1 root root  538 Mar  1  2018 mlocate
-rwxr-xr-x 1 root root  249 Jan 25  2018 passwd
-rwxr-xr-x 1 root root 3477 Feb 20  2018 popularity-contest
-rwxr-xr-x 1 root root  246 Mar 21 13:20 ubuntu-advantage-tools
-rwxr-xr-x 1 root root  214 Jul 12  2013 update-notifier-common
root@philip-virtual-machine:/home/philip#
```

Based on the preceding output, there are a number of tasks, such as passwd, dpkg, mlocate, to name a few, which are scheduled to run daily. Likewise, we can look inside /etc/cron.monthly:

```
root@philip-virtual-machine:/home/philip# ls -al /etc/cron.monthly/
total 24
drwxr-xr-x   2 root root  4096 Apr 26 14:23 .
drwxr-xr-x 124 root root 12288 Sep  6 10:58 ..
-rwxr-xr-x   1 root root   313 May 29  2017 0anacron
-rw-r--r--   1 root root   102 Nov 16  2017 .placeholder
root@philip-virtual-machine:/home/philip#
```

Awesome! We can take a deeper look at one of the scheduled tasks. Let's look at the /etc/cron.daily/passwd task:

```
root@philip-virtual-machine:/home/philip# cat /etc/cron.daily/passwd
#!/bin/sh
cd /var/backups || exit 0
for FILE in passwd group shadow gshadow; do
        test -f /etc/$FILE                 || continue
        cmp -s $FILE.bak /etc/$FILE      && continue
        cp -p /etc/$FILE $FILE.bak && chmod 600 $FILE.bak
done
root@philip-virtual-machine:/home/philip#
```

Based on the preceding output, we can see the task is written as a script.

Crontab

As we've just seen, we can place our tasks in their respective /etc/cron.* directory. This is then executed every hour, every day, or on a monthly basis. However, we can get even more flexibility; instead of placing our scripts in the /etc/cron.* directory, we can place our script inside crontab itself. We can explore the /etc/crontab file as follows:

```
root@philip-virtual-machine:/home/philip# cat /etc/crontab
# /etc/crontab: system-wide crontab
# Unlike any other crontab you don't have to run the `crontab'
# command to install the new version when you edit this file
# and files in /etc/cron.d. These files also have username fields,
# that none of the other crontabs do.
SHELL=/bin/sh
PATH=/usr/local/sbin:/usr/local/bin:/sbin:/bin:/usr/sbin:/usr/bin
# m h dom mon dow user              command
17 *        * * *       root    cd / && run-parts --report /etc/cron.hourly
25 6        * * *       root        test -x /usr/sbin/anacron || ( cd / &&
run-parts --report /etc/cron.daily )
47 6        * * 7       root        test -x /usr/sbin/anacron || ( cd / &&
run-parts --report /etc/cron.weekly )
52 6        1 * *       root        test -x /usr/sbin/anacron || ( cd / &&
run-parts --report /etc/cron.monthly )
root@philip-virtual-machine:/home/philip#
```

Excellent! In the preceding output, we can see that the scripts we have covered are found in the last part; they are executed by crontab. We can add our own entry inside crontab. We pass the -e option with crontab; this means to enter edit mode:

```
root@philip-virtual-machine:/home/philip# crontab -e
Select an editor.  To change later, run 'select-editor'.
/bin/nano      <---- easiest
/usr/bin/vim.tiny
/bin/ed
Choose 1-3 [1]:
```

Now we have to specify which editor to use; we will accept the default:

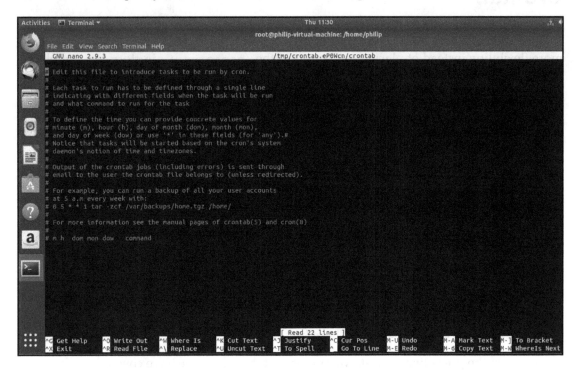

Awesome! Based on the preceding screenshot, we have some guidelines on how to define an entry. Let's define our own entry:

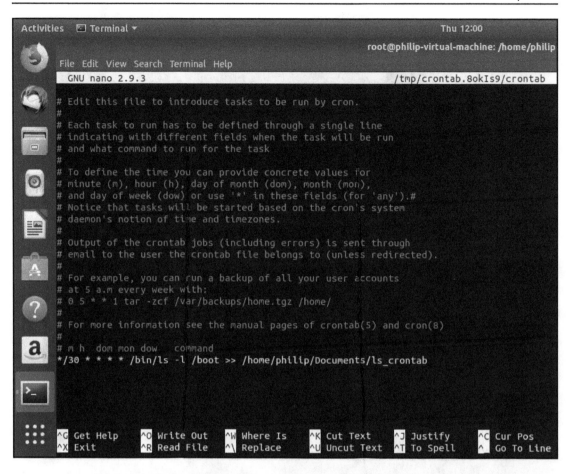

Based on the preceding screenshot, we have defined our entry to be run every half of a minute, every day; the ls command will be run against the /boot directory, and this will then append its output and save it to /home/philip/Documents/ls_crontab. The syntax for defining the time is as follows:

```
0/30        minute
*           hour
*           day of month
*           month
*           hour
```

Once we've finished creating our entry, we need to write our changes; we're using the nano editor so we press *Ctrl + O* to write the changes:

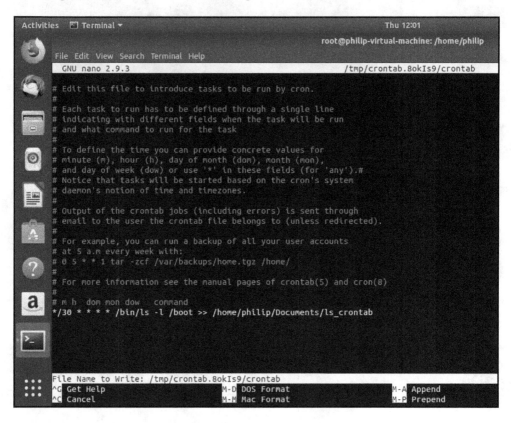

Now, the `crontab` file will be generated for the user as follows:

```
crontab: installing new crontab
root@philip-virtual-machine:/home/philip#
Awesome! Now, we can pass the "-l" option with the crontab command :
root@philip-virtual-machine:/home/philip# crontab -l
# Output of the crontab jobs (including errors) is sent through
# email to the user the crontab file belongs to (unless redirected).
# For example, you can run a backup of all your user accounts
# at 5 a.m every week with:
# 0 5 * * 1 tar -zcf /var/backups/home.tgz /home/
# For more information see the manual pages of crontab(5) and cron(8)
# m h  dom mon dow    command
*/30 * * * * ls -l /boot >> /home/philip/Documents/ls_crontab
root@philip-virtual-machine:/home/philip#
```

Based on the preceding output, we can see our entry at the bottom. Once 30 minutes have elapsed, our file will be generated, and we can see the output:

```
root@philip-virtual-machine:/home/philip# cat Documents/ls_crontab
total 66752
-rw-r--r-- 1 root root  1536934 Apr 24 00:56 abi-4.15.0-20-generic
-rw-r--r-- 1 root root   216807 Apr 24 00:56 config-4.15.0-20-generic
drwxr-xr-x 5 root root     4096 Sep  6 10:30 grub
-rw-r--r-- 1 root root 53739884 Sep  6 10:45 initrd.img-4.15.0-20-generic
-rw-r--r-- 1 root root   182704 Jan 28  2016 memtest86+.bin
-rw-r--r-- 1 root root   184380 Jan 28  2016 memtest86+.elf
-rw-r--r-- 1 root root   184840 Jan 28  2016 memtest86+_multiboot.bin
-rw-r--r-- 1 root root        0 Apr 24 00:56 retpoline-4.15.0-20-generic
-rw------- 1 root root  4038188 Apr 24 00:56 System.map-4.15.0-20-generic
-rw-r--r-- 1 root root  8249080 Apr 26 14:40 vmlinuz-4.15.0-20-generic
root@philip-virtual-machine:/home/philip#
root@philip-virtual-machine:/home/philip# date
Thu Sep  6 12:00:05 EDT 2018
root@philip-virtual-machine:/home/philip#
```

Awesome, we will wait another 30 minutes, and we will see the output appended:

```
root@philip-virtual-machine:/home/philip# date
Thu Sep  6 12:30:18 EDT 2018
root@philip-virtual-machine:/home/philip# cat Documents/ls_crontab
total 66752
-rw-r--r-- 1 root root  1536934 Apr 24 00:56 abi-4.15.0-20-generic
-rw-r--r-- 1 root root   216807 Apr 24 00:56 config-4.15.0-20-generic
drwxr-xr-x 5 root root     4096 Sep  6 10:30 grub
-rw-r--r-- 1 root root 53739884 Sep  6 10:45 initrd.img-4.15.0-20-generic
-rw-r--r-- 1 root root   182704 Jan 28  2016 memtest86+.bin
-rw-r--r-- 1 root root   184380 Jan 28  2016 memtest86+.elf
-rw-r--r-- 1 root root   184840 Jan 28  2016 memtest86+_multiboot.bin
-rw-r--r-- 1 root root        0 Apr 24 00:56 retpoline-4.15.0-20-generic
-rw------- 1 root root  4038188 Apr 24 00:56 System.map-4.15.0-20-generic
-rw-r--r-- 1 root root  8249080 Apr 26 14:40 vmlinuz-4.15.0-20-generic
total 66752
-rw-r--r-- 1 root root  1536934 Apr 24 00:56 abi-4.15.0-20-generic
-rw-r--r-- 1 root root   216807 Apr 24 00:56 config-4.15.0-20-generic
drwxr-xr-x 5 root root     4096 Sep  6 10:30 grub
-rw-r--r-- 1 root root 53739884 Sep  6 10:45 initrd.img-4.15.0-20-generic
-rw-r--r-- 1 root root   182704 Jan 28  2016 memtest86+.bin
-rw-r--r-- 1 root root   184380 Jan 28  2016 memtest86+.elf
-rw-r--r-- 1 root root   184840 Jan 28  2016 memtest86+_multiboot.bin
-rw-r--r-- 1 root root        0 Apr 24 00:56 retpoline-4.15.0-20-generic
-rw------- 1 root root  4038188 Apr 24 00:56 System.map-4.15.0-20-generic
-rw-r--r-- 1 root root  8249080 Apr 26 14:40 vmlinuz-4.15.0-20-generic
root@philip-virtual-machine:/home/philip#
```

Excellent! Note that a standard user would not see the `crontab` job for the root user:

```
philip@philip-virtual-machine:~$ crontab -l
no crontab for philip
philip@philip-virtual-machine:~$
```

However, the root user can see entries for any user by passing the -u option:

```
root@philip-virtual-machine:/home/philip# crontab -u philip -l
no crontab for philip
root@philip-virtual-machine:/home/philip#
```

Awesome!

Anacron

Interestingly, Anacron is not meant as a replacement for `cron`, but instead it's intended to be used in scenarios where the environment involves the system being off some of the time. Furthermore, Anacron does not expect the system to be on at all times. For instance, laptops are shut down from time to time. Another distinct feature of Anacron is the fact that the duration is defined in days or monthly and not hours or minutes. If you have a job to be executed at a certain time and the system is off, rest assured when the system is powered up Anacron will execute the job. We can take a look at the `anacrontab` file:

```
root@philip-virtual-machine:/home/philip# cat /etc/anacrontab
# /etc/anacrontab: configuration file for anacron
# See anacron(8) and anacrontab(5) for details.
SHELL=/bin/sh
PATH=/usr/local/sbin:/usr/local/bin:/sbin:/bin:/usr/sbin:/usr/bin
HOME=/root
LOGNAME=root
# These replace cron's entries
1               5                       cron.daily              run-parts --report
/etc/cron.daily
7               10                      cron.weekly     run-parts --report
/etc/cron.weekly
@monthly        15                      cron.monthly    run-parts --report
/etc/cron.monthly
root@philip-virtual-machine:/home/philip#
```

Based on the preceding output, we can see some `cron` entries inside the `anacrontab` file. We can see that `anacron` compliments `cron` and it does not replace `cron`. The way we read an entry in the `anacrontab` file is as follows:

```
1
=Daily, other
possible values are
7 = weekly,
@daily, @monthly
5
=Delay in minutes
cron.daily
= Job ID
run-parts --report /etc/cron.daily
= Command
```

We can get information on the jobs in the `/var/spool/anacron` directory:

```
root@philip-virtual-machine:/home/philip# ls -l /var/spool/anacron/
total 12
-rw------- 1 root root 9 Sep  6 10:44 cron.daily
-rw------- 1 root root 9 Sep  6 10:53 cron.monthly
-rw------- 1 root root 9 Sep  6 10:48 cron.weekly
root@philip-virtual-machine:/home/philip#
```

Awesome! We can look inside one of these files and see the last time the job was run:

```
root@philip-virtual-machine:/home/philip# cat /var/spool/anacron/cron.daily
20180906
root@philip-virtual-machine:/home/philip#
```

Great! Based on the preceding output, we can see the timestamp when the job was executed. To see the jobs which `anacron` is handling in foreground, we can use the `-d` option with `anacron`:

```
root@philip-virtual-machine:/home/philip# anacron -d
Anacron 2.3 started on 2018-09-06
Normal exit (0 jobs run)
root@philip-virtual-machine:/home/philip#
```

Based on the preceding output, currently there are no jobs being executed. We can create an entry by editing the /etc/anacrontab file:

```
root@philip-virtual-machine:/home/philip# cat /etc/anacrontab
# /etc/anacrontab: configuration file for anacron
# See anacron(8) and anacrontab(5) for details.
SHELL=/bin/sh
PATH=/usr/local/sbin:/usr/local/bin:/sbin:/bin:/usr/sbin:/usr/bin
HOME=/root
LOGNAME=root
# These replace cron's entries
1               5               cron.daily          run-parts --report
/etc/cron.daily
7               10              cron.weekly       run-parts --report
/etc/cron.weekly
@monthly        15              cron.monthly     run-parts --report
/etc/cron.monthly
1               10              test                /bin/ls -l /boot >
/home/philip/Documents/ls_anacron
root@philip-virtual-machine:/home/philip#
Excellent! Now, can check the /var/spool/anacrontab:
root@philip-virtual-machine:/home/philip# ls -l /var/spool/anacron/
total 12
-rw------- 1 root root 9 Sep  6 10:44 cron.daily
-rw------- 1 root root 9 Sep  6 10:53 cron.monthly
-rw------- 1 root root 9 Sep  6 10:48 cron.weekly
-rw------- 1 root root 0 Sep  6 13:47 test
root@philip-virtual-machine:/home/philip#
```

Based on the preceding output, we now see a new entry for our custom entry. We can look inside the file:

```
root@philip-virtual-machine:/home/philip# cat /var/spool/anacron/test
root@philip-virtual-machine:/home/philip#
```

Based on the preceding output, the file is empty because the job has not yet been run. We can text for a syntax error in the anacrontab file by passing the -T option with anacron:

```
root@philip-virtual-machine:/home/philip# anacron -T
root@philip-virtual-machine:/home/philip#
```

Based on the preceding output, no syntax error was found. We can update the timestamp for the jobs without running the jobs by using the -u option:

```
root@philip-virtual-machine:/home/philip# anacron -u
root@philip-virtual-machine:/home/philip#
```

We didn't see any output because the timestamps were updated in the background. We can add the −d option, and we will see what is happening in the foreground:

```
root@philip-virtual-machine:/home/philip# anacron -d -u
Updated timestamp for job `cron.daily' to 2018-09-06
Updated timestamp for job `cron.weekly' to 2018-09-06
Updated timestamp for job `test' to 2018-09-06
Updated timestamp for job `cron.monthly' to 2018-09-06
root@philip-virtual-machine:/home/philip#
```

Awesome! We can execute the job immediately by passing the −f option with anacron:

```
root@philip-virtual-machine:/home/philip# anacron -d -f
Anacron 2.3 started on 2018-09-06
Will run job `cron.daily' in 5 min.
Will run job `cron.weekly' in 10 min.
Will run job `test' in 10 min.
Will run job `cron.monthly' in 15 min.
^C
root@philip-virtual-machine:/home/philip#
```

Based on the preceding output, anacron is attempting to execute the jobs. However, it has to wait until the delay has elapsed for each job. Here is where the power of −n shines; it will ignore the delay set:

```
root@philip-virtual-machine:/home/philip# anacron -d -f -n
Anacron 2.3 started on 2018-09-06
Will run job `cron.daily'
Will run job `cron.weekly'
Will run job `test'
Will run job `cron.monthly'
Jobs will be executed sequentially
Job `cron.daily' started
Job `cron.daily' terminated
Job `cron.weekly' started
Job `cron.weekly' terminated (mailing output)
anacron: Can't find sendmail at /usr/sbin/sendmail, not mailing output
Job `test' started
Job `test' terminated (exit status: 1) (mailing output)
anacron: Can't find sendmail at /usr/sbin/sendmail, not mailing output
Job `cron.monthly' started
Job `cron.monthly' terminated
Normal exit (4 jobs run)
root@philip-virtual-machine:/home/philip#
```

Excellent! Now, we can check the `/home/philip/Documents` for the `ls_anacron` file:

```
root@philip-virtual-machine:/home/philip# ls -l /home/philip/Documents/
total 4
-rw-r--r-- 1 root root    0 Sep  6 14:11 ls_anacron
-rw-r--r-- 1 root root 3405 Sep  6 14:00 ls_crontab
root@philip-virtual-machine:/home/philip#
```

Great! We can look inside the `ls_anacron` file:

```
root@philip-virtual-machine:/home/philip# cat
/home/philip/Documents/ls_anacron
abi-4.15.0-20-generic
config-4.15.0-20-generic
grub
initrd.img-4.15.0-20-generic
memtest86+.bin
memtest86+.elf
memtest86+_multiboot.bin
retpoline-4.15.0-20-generic
System.map-4.15.0-20-generic
vmlinuz-4.15.0-20-generic
root@philip-virtual-machine:/home/philip#
```

Perfect!

Permissions for tasks using configuration files

We can restrict access to the `at` and `cron` utilities using `/etc/at.allow`, `/etc/at.deny`, `/etc/cron.allow` and `/etc/cron.deny`. If the files don't exist then we can create them; the `/etc/at.allow` and `/etc/cron.allow` files are sufficient. For the `/etc/at.allow` file, we do the following:

```
root@philip-virtual-machine:/home/philip# cat /etc/at.allow
cat: /etc/at.alow: No such file or directory
root@philip-virtual-machine:/home/philip# cat /etc/cron.allow
cat: /etc/cron.allow: No such file or directory
We can use an editor and create the file and store the usernames, one
username per line:
root@philip-virtual-machine:/home/philip# cat /etc/at.allow
philip
harry
teddy
```

```
root@philip-virtual-machine:/home/philip#
root@philip-virtual-machine:/home/philip# cat /etc/cron.allow
philip
harry
teddy
root@philip-virtual-machine:/home/philip#
```

Awesome! Now, only these users will be allowed to execute jobs using at or cron.

Summary

In this chapter, we dealt with automation at the command line. We touched on the at utility, focusing on creating a job that runs once. Next, our focus was the usage of the atq utility and how it displays all scheduled jobs that the at utility will run. Also, we saw how to leverage an option with the at utility to enable us to view the job queue. Following this, we looked at the atrm utility, the primary focus being the ability to remove a scheduled job. In addition to this, we also saw the possibility of stopping a job by using the at command and passing an option. We then covered cron , focusing on the various cron directories; each plays a vital role in terms of automating tasks. Next, we worked with crontab; we saw the breakdown of the syntax, and we then created a custom entry in crontab. Following this, we worked with anacron. We saw the use case of anacron and how it complements cron. We then created our own custom entry and executed the jobs in order to gain a better understanding of anacron. Finally, we looked at restrictions in terms of automation; primarily, we looked at restricting access to the at and cron utilities.

In the next chapter, our focus will be on time management, particularly, maintaining the system time and performing logging, both local and remote. The next chapter is of utmost importance to anyone working within a networking environment who deals with monitoring on a daily basis. I invite you to come and join me for another exciting chapter.

Questions

1. What will be the output if no option is passed with the at command?

   A. Invalid syntax
   B. Garbled time
   C. No output
   D. None of the above

2. Which is a valid `at` command?

    A. `at 9:00 AM next next`
    B. `at 9:00 AM tonite tonite`
    C. `at 9:00 AM next Monday`
    D. None of the above

3. What does `<EOT>` mean in the `at` utility?

    A. End of Time
    B. *Ctrl+ D* was pressed
    C. *Ctrl + X* was pressed
    D. None of the above

4. Which option prints a queue using the `at` command?

    A. `-a`
    B. `-c`
    C. `-d`
    D. `-l`

5. Which option removes a job using the `at` command?

    A. `-a`
    B. `-c`
    C. `-a`
    D. `-r`

6. Which other command can be used to print the job queue created with the `at` command?

    A. `atrm`
    B. `atc`
    C. `atq`
    D. `atr`

7. Which option runs a job every minute using `crontab`?

    A. `1/30 * * * *`
    B. `*/20 * * * *`
    C. `* * * * *`
    D. `* * * * 1`

8. Which option is used to open `crontab` and start making changes?

        A. `-a`
        B. `-e`
        C. `-b`
        D. `-c`

9. Which word can represent 7 in anacron?

        A. `@daily`
        B. `@monthly`
        C. `@weekly`
        D. `@sunday`

10. Which option forces `anacron` to run jobs before their schedule?

        A. `-f`
        B. `-e`
        C. `-c`
        D. `-a`

Further reading

- This site gives useful information about the `at` utility: `https://linuxconfig.org`
- This site gives useful information about `cron` : `https://code.tutsplus.com`
- This site gives useful information about `anacron` : `https://linux.101hacks.com`

14
Maintaining System Time and Logging

In the previous chapter, we dealt with automation at the command line. We touched on the `at`, `atq`, and `atrm` commands. Following this, we worked with the various `cron` directories, and then we covered the `crontab` utility. Additionally, we covered `anacron`. Finally, we looked at restrictions in terms of automation.

In this chapter, our focus is on maintaining the system time and performing logging. First, we will cover configuration of the system time, synchronizing time over a network. Then our attention will be on the various log files. Finally, we will perform remote logging between separate Linux systems.

We will cover the following topics in this chapter:

- Date configuration
- Setting up local system logging
- Configure remote logging

Date configuration

In most Linux environments, it's critical to have the systems synchronized with the correct time. We can expose the current date using the `date` command. We can view the system date and time by simply running the following command:

```
root@philip-virtual-machine:/home/philip# date
Thu Sep  6 16:25:56 EDT 2018
root@philip-virtual-machine:/home/philip#
```

Based on the preceding output, we can see the current date. It is also possible to set the date and time using the date command. To be able to specify the date in the string format, we pass the -s option:

```
philip@philip-virtual-machine:~$ date -s "19 Dec 2020 12:00:00"
date: cannot set date: Operation not permitted
Sat Dec 19 12:00:00 EST 2020
philip@philip-virtual-machine:~$
```

Based on the preceding output, we have hit a roadblock; this is because we need root privileges in order to change the date. Let's try again, this time as root:

```
root@philip-virtual-machine:/home/philip# date -s "19 Dec 2020 12:00:00"
Sat Dec 19 12:00:00 EST 2020
root@philip-virtual-machine:/home/philip# date
Fri Sep  7 09:51:24 EDT 2018
root@philip-virtual-machine:/home/philip#
```

Wow! What happened? Well, here is the deal: the system is configured to auto-sync its time. This can be verified by using another powerful command: the timedatectl command. We can run the timedatectl command to view the current sync settings:

```
root@philip-virtual-machine:/home/philip# timedatectl
                Local time: Fri 2018-09-07 09:57:49 EDT
            Universal time: Fri 2018-09-07 13:57:49 UTC
                  RTC time: Fri 2018-09-07 13:57:49
                 Time zone: America/New_York (EDT, -0400)
 System clock synchronized: yes
systemd-timesyncd.service active: yes
           RTC in local TZ: no
root@philip-virtual-machine:/home/philip#
```

Awesome! Based on the preceding output, the systemd-timesyncd.service active: yes section indicates that the system is indeed currently set to synchronized. Also, we can pass the status option, and this will return similar results:

```
root@philip-virtual-machine:/home/philip# timedatectl status
                Local time: Fri 2018-09-07 10:02:38 EDT
            Universal time: Fri 2018-09-07 14:02:38 UTC
                  RTC time: Fri 2018-09-07 14:02:38
                 Time zone: America/New_York (EDT, -0400)
 System clock synchronized: yes
systemd-timesyncd.service active: yes
           RTC in local TZ: no
root@philip-virtual-machine:/home/philip#
```

Awesome! We can manually set the time, but first we will need to disable the auto-sync by passing the `set-ntp` option with the `timedatectl` command:

```
root@philip-virtual-machine:/home/philip# timedatectl set-ntp false
root@philip-virtual-machine:/home/philip#
root@philip-virtual-machine:/home/philip# timedatectl status
              Local time: Fri 2018-09-07 10:04:27 EDT
          Universal time: Fri 2018-09-07 14:04:27 UTC
                RTC time: Fri 2018-09-07 14:04:27
               Time zone: America/New_York (EDT, -0400)
 System clock synchronized: yes
systemd-timesyncd.service active: no
             RTC in local TZ: no
root@philip-virtual-machine:/home/philip#
```

Great job! Based on the preceding command, we can now see the `systemd-timesyncd.service active: no` section was changed to `no`. We can now try to change the date once again using the `date` command:

```
root@philip-virtual-machine:/home/philip# date
Fri Sep  7 10:06:28 EDT 2018
root@philip-virtual-machine:/home/philip# date -s "19 Dec 2020 12:00:00"
Sat Dec 19 12:00:00 EST 2020
root@philip-virtual-machine:/home/philip# date
Sat Dec 19 12:00:01 EST 2020
root@philip-virtual-machine:/home/philip#
```

Excellent! The command has been executed successfully and changed the current date. We can also use numerical values to represent the month as follows:

```
root@philip-virtual-machine:/home/philip# date -s "20240101 13:00:00"
Mon Jan  1 13:00:00 EST 2024
root@philip-virtual-machine:/home/philip# date
Mon Jan  1 13:00:08 EST 2024
root@philip-virtual-machine:/home/philip#
```

Based on the preceding output, we can see the date and time changed to reflect the new settings. In addition to this, it is possible to separate the date using hyphens as follows:

```
root@philip-virtual-machine:/home/philip# date -s "2000-10-05 07:00:00"
Thu Oct  5 07:00:00 EDT 2000
root@philip-virtual-machine:/home/philip# date
Thu Oct  5 07:00:02 EDT 2000
root@philip-virtual-machine:/home/philip#
```

Awesome! We can also set the time using regular expressions. We can use `+%T` to set the time:

```
root@philip-virtual-machine:/home/philip# date
Thu Oct  5 03:06:43 EDT 2000
root@philip-virtual-machine:/home/philip#
root@philip-virtual-machine:/home/philip# date +%T -s "20:00:00"
20:00:00
root@philip-virtual-machine:/home/philip# date
Thu Oct  5 20:00:03 EDT 2000
root@philip-virtual-machine:/home/philip#
```

It is also possible to change only the hour using the `date` command; we pass the `+%H` option:

```
root@philip-virtual-machine:/home/philip# date +%H -s "4"
04
root@philip-virtual-machine:/home/philip# date
Thu Oct  5 04:00:03 EDT 2000
root@philip-virtual-machine:/home/philip#
```

Excellent! It is also possible to change the date and time using the `timedatectl` command. We can change the date by passing the `set-time` option:

```
root@philip-virtual-machine:/home/philip# timedatectl set-time 10:00:00
root@philip-virtual-machine:/home/philip# date
Thu Oct  5 10:00:02 EDT 2000
root@philip-virtual-machine:/home/philip# timedatectl
      Local time: Thu 2000-10-05 10:00:06 EDT
  Universal time: Thu 2000-10-05 14:00:06 UTC
        RTC time: Thu 2000-10-05 14:00:06
       Time zone: America/New_York (EDT, -0400)
       System clock synchronized: no
systemd-timesyncd.service active: no
                 RTC in local TZ: no
root@philip-virtual-machine:/home/philip#
```

Awesome! It is also possible to set the date alone by passing the `set-time` option:

```
root@philip-virtual-machine:/home/philip# timedatectl set-time 2019-03-01
root@philip-virtual-machine:/home/philip# date
Fri Mar  1 00:00:02 EST 2019
root@philip-virtual-machine:/home/philip#
```

Based on the preceding output, the date was changed, but notice the time was changed too. We can fix this by combining the date and time:

```
root@philip-virtual-machine:/home/philip# timedatectl set-time '2019-03-01
10:00:00'
root@philip-virtual-machine:/home/philip# date
Fri Mar  1 10:00:01 EST 2019
root@philip-virtual-machine:/home/philip#
```

Excellent! We can also change the time zone using the timedatectl command; we can view the available time zones by passing the list-timezones option:

```
root@philip-virtual-machine:/home/philip# timedatectl list-timezones
Africa/Abidjan
Africa/Accra
Africa/Addis_Ababa
Africa/Algiers
Africa/Asmara
Africa/Bamako
Africa/Bangui
America/Guayaquil
America/Guyana
root@philip-virtual-machine:/home/philip#
```

Some output has been omitted for brevity. We change the time zone by passing the set-timezone option:

```
root@philip-virtual-machine:/home/philip# timedatectl
              Local time: Fri 2019-03-01 10:15:43 EST
          Universal time: Fri 2019-03-01 15:15:43 UTC
                RTC time: Fri 2019-03-01 15:15:43
               Time zone: America/New_York (EST, -0500)
 System clock synchronized: no
systemd-timesyncd.service active: no
             RTC in local TZ: no
root@philip-virtual-machine:/home/philip# timedatectl set-timezone
America/Guyana
root@philip-virtual-machine:/home/philip# timedatectl
         Local time: Fri 2019-03-01 11:15:59 -04
     Universal time: Fri 2019-03-01 15:15:59 UTC
           RTC time: Fri 2019-03-01 15:16:00
          Time zone: America/Guyana (-04, -0400)
       System clock synchronized: no
systemd-timesyncd.service active: no
            RTC in local TZ: no
root@philip-virtual-machine:/home/philip#
```

Awesome! We've successfully changed the time zone. The time zone information is stored in the /etc/timezone and /etc/localtime files. It's a symbolic link to /usr/share/zoneinfo/<timezone>; <timezone> is whatever we specified:

```
root@philip-virtual-machine:/home/philip# ls -l /etc/localtime
lrwxrwxrwx 1 root root 36 Mar  1 11:15 /etc/localtime ->
../usr/share/zoneinfo/America/Guyana
root@philip-virtual-machine:/home/philip#
root@philip-virtual-machine:/home/philip# cat /etc/timezone
America/Guyana
root@philip-virtual-machine:/home/philip#
```

Excellent! Based on the preceding output, we can see /etc/timezone and /etc/localtime were updated to the specified time zone.

The tzselect command

The tzselect command can be used to change the time zone of a system. When we launch the tzselect command, it will ask a series of questions in an interactive mode. This can be illustrated by the following:

```
root@philip-virtual-machine:/home/philip# tzselect
Please identify a location so that time zone rules can be set correctly.
Please select a continent, ocean, "coord", or "TZ".
 1) Africa
 2) Americas
 3) Antarctica
 4) Asia
 5) Atlantic Ocean
 6) Australia
 7) Europe]
 8) Indian Ocean
 9) Pacific Ocean
10) coord - I want to use geographical coordinates.
11) TZ - I want to specify the time zone using the Posix TZ format.
#?
```

Based on the preceding output, we then need to type a number that represents the continent:

```
#? 2
Please select a country whose clocks agree with yours.
 1) Anguilla            19) Dominican Republic  37) Peru
 2) Antigua & Barbuda 20) Ecuador              38) Puerto Rico
 3) Argentina           21) El Salvador         39) St Barthelemy
 4) Aruba               22) French Guiana       40) St Kitts & Nevis
 5) Bahamas             23) Greenland           41) St Lucia
 6) Barbados            24) Grenada             42) St Maarten (Dutch)
 7) Belize              25) Guadeloupe          43) St Martin (French)
 8) Bolivia             26) Guatemala           44) St Pierre & Miquelon
 9) Brazil              27) Guyana              45) St Vincent
#?
```

Some output has been omitted for brevity. We then have to specify the country:

```
The following information has been given:
                Guyana
Therefore TZ='America/Guyana' will be used.
Selected time is now:    Fri Mar  1 11:27:49 -04 2019.
Universal Time is now:   Fri Mar  1 15:27:49 UTC 2019.
Is the above information OK?
1) Yes
2) No
#?
```

Based on the preceding output, we then need to confirm the information:

```
#? 1
You can make this change permanent for yourself by appending the line
                TZ='America/Guyana'; export TZ
to the file '.profile' in your home directory; then log out and log in
again.
Here is that TZ value again, this time on standard output so that you
can use the /usr/bin/tzselect command in shell scripts:
America/Guyana
root@philip-virtual-machine:/home/philip#
```

We need to append the `TZ='America/Guyana'; export TZ` line inside `.profile` of the current user's home directory; the user then needs to log out and back in again for the changes to take effect permanently. Of course, we have already made our changes permanent by using the previous command: the `timedatectl` command.

The tzconfig command

The tzconfig command is an older method for changing the time zone in a system. It is actually not available; instead, it points you to the tzdata command in Ubuntu.

This can be illustrated by running the tzconfig command:

```
root@philip-virtual-machine:/home/philip# tzconfig
WARNING: the tzconfig command is deprecated, please use:
  dpkg-reconfigure tzdata
root@philip-virtual-machine:/home/philip#
```

Based on the preceding command, we need to run the dpkg-reconfigure tzdata command; this will launch an interactive dialog:

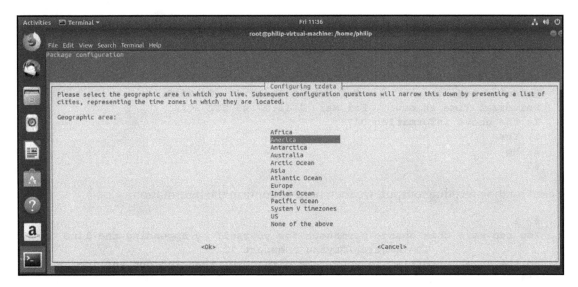

Now we need to scroll using the keyboard; you then press *Enter* to select the desired continent. You will then be presented with this:

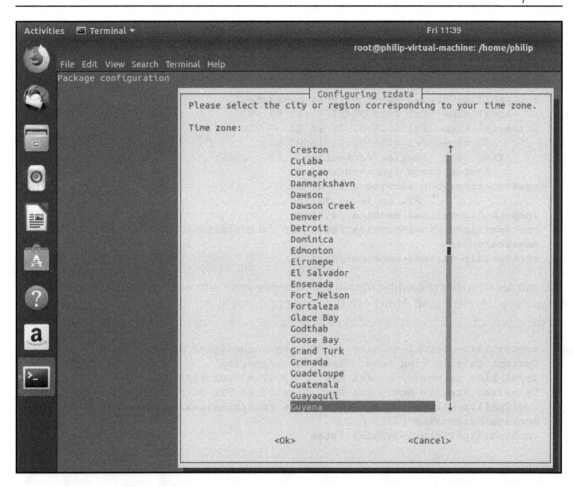

Based on the preceding output, you then scroll to your desired country and press the *Enter* key; this would then use the country's time zone which you highlighted:

```
root@philip-virtual-machine:/home/philip# dpkg-reconfigure tzdata
Current default time zone: 'America/Guyana'
Local time is now: Fri Mar 1 11:40:31 -04 2019.
Universal Time is now: Fri Mar 1 15:40:31 UTC 2019.
root@philip-virtual-machine:/home/philip#
```

Excellent! Another way to change the time zone is to manually remove /etc/localtime and create a symbolic link pointing to the desired time zone inside /usr/share/zoneinfo. Here is how this looks:

```
root@philip-virtual-machine:/etc# unlink localtime
root@philip-virtual-machine:/etc# ln -s
```

```
/usr/share/zoneinfo/America/Paramaribo localtime
root@philip-virtual-machine:/etc# ll /etc/localtime
lrwxrwxrwx 1 root root 38 Mar  1 13:01 /etc/localtime ->
/usr/share/zoneinfo/America/Paramaribo
root@philip-virtual-machine:/etc#
root@philip-virtual-machine:/etc# timedatectl
     Local time: Fri 2019-03-01 13:03:57 -03
 Universal time: Fri 2019-03-01 16:03:57 UTC
       RTC time: Fri 2019-03-01 16:03:57
      Time zone: America/Paramaribo (-03, -0300)
      System clock synchronized: no
systemd-timesyncd.service active: no
               RTC in local TZ: no
root@philip-virtual-machine:/etc#
root@philip-virtual-machine:/etc# cat /etc/timezone
America/Guyana
root@philip-virtual-machine:/etc#
```

We can see from the preceding output that the time zone info was updated in the timedetectl command. However, it was not updated in /etc/timezone. In order to update /etc/timezone, we need to run the dpkg-reconfigure tzdata command:

```
root@philip-virtual-machine:/etc# dpkg-reconfigure tzdata
Current default time zone: 'America/Paramaribo'
Local time is now:      Fri Mar  1 13:07:43 -03 2019.
Universal Time is now:  Fri Mar  1 16:07:43 UTC 2019.
root@philip-virtual-machine:/etc# cat /etc/timezone
America/Paramaribo
root@philip-virtual-machine:/etc#
```

Awesome!

The hwclock command

There is another clock; namely, the clock that runs even when the system is powered off; this is the hardware clock. We can view the time of the hardware clock as follows:

```
root@philip-virtual-machine:/etc# date
Fri Mar  1 13:11:49 -03 2019
root@philip-virtual-machine:/etc# hwclock
2019-03-01 13:11:51.634343-0300
root@philip-virtual-machine:/etc#
```

We can see from the preceding output that the date and time are relatively close. We can set the hardware clock to sync with the system time as follows:

```
root@philip-virtual-machine:/etc# hwclock --systohc
root@philip-virtual-machine:/etc# date
Fri Mar  1 12:17:04 -04 2019
root@philip-virtual-machine:/etc# hwclock
2019-03-01 12:17:06.556082-0400
root@philip-virtual-machine:/etc#
```

It is also possible to configure the system time to sync with the hardware clock. We do this as follows:

```
root@philip-virtual-machine:/etc# hwclock --hctosys
root@philip-virtual-machine:/etc# date
Fri Mar  1 12:18:52 -04 2019
root@philip-virtual-machine:/etc# hwclock
2019-03-01 12:18:54.571552-0400
root@philip-virtual-machine:/etc#
```

The hardware clock takes its settings from /etc/adjtime as can be seen below:

```
root@philip-virtual-machine:/etc# cat /etc/adjtime
0.000000 1551457021 0.000000
1551457021
UTC
root@philip-virtual-machine:/etc#
```

There is also the hardware clock; we can view the hardware clock using the hwclock command. If we are using UTC time, we can pass the --utc option with the hwclock command:

```
root@philip-virtual-machine:/home/philip# hwclock -r --utc
2018-09-06 16:30:27.493714-0400
root@philip-virtual-machine:/home/philip#
```

As the preceding command shows, the date of the hardware clock is presented in UTU. In addition to this, we can also use the --show option to display similar results:

```
root@philip-virtual-machine:/home/philip# hwclock --show --utc
2018-09-06 16:31:43.025628-0400
root@philip-virtual-machine:/home/philip#
```

Awesome!

Setting up local system logging

Within a Linux environment, it is critical to have logs that can be used to identify potential bottlenecks within the system. Fortunately, we have logging turned on by default. There are different types of log file available for inspection; primarily, the /var/log directory contains various log files, each geared to different aspects of the system. We can take a look at the /var/log directory:

```
root@philip-virtual-machine:/etc# cd /var
```

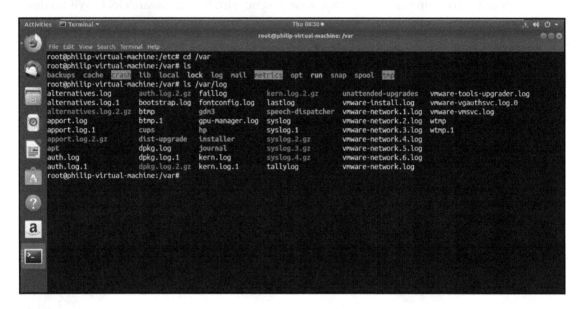

From the preceding output, right off the bat, there is the /var/log/syslog file. This contains pertinent information about the functioning of the system. We can view the /var/log/syslog file as follows:

```
root@philip-virtual-machine:/var# ll /var/log/syslog
-rw-r----- 1 syslog adm 48664 Mar 1 15:38 /var/log/syslog
root@philip-virtual-machine:/var# tail -f /var/log/syslog
Mar  1 14:31:52 philip-virtual-machine snapd[725]: 2019/03/01
14:31:52.052401 autorefresh.go:327: Cannot prepare auto-refresh change:
cannot refresh snap-declaration for "core": Get
https://api.snapcraft.io/api/v1/snaps/assertions/snap-declaration/16/99T7MU
1RhtI3U0QFg15mXXESAiSwt776?max-format=2: net/http: request canceled while
waiting for connection (Client.Timeout exceeded while awaiting headers)
Mar  1 14:31:52 philip-virtual-machine snapd[725]: 2019/03/01
14:31:52.053013 stateengine.go:101: state ensure error: cannot refresh
snap-declaration for "core": Get
```

```
https://api.snapcraft.io/api/v1/snaps/assertions/snap-declaration/16/99T7MU
1RhtI3U0QFg15mXXESAiSwt776?max-format=2: net/http: request canceled while
waiting for connection (Client.Timeout exceeded while awaiting headers)
Mar  1 14:38:03 philip-virtual-machine gnome-shell[1576]: Object
Gdm.UserVerifierProxy (0x560080fc4cd0), has been already deallocated -
impossible to access to it. This might be caused by the fact that the
object has been destroyed from C code using something such as destroy(),
dispose(), or remove() vfuncs
^C
root@philip-virtual-machine:/var#
```

Some output has been omitted for brevity. We've used the `tail` command with the `-f`
option; this will print out the most recent logs as they are generated inside the
`/var/log/syslog` file. Another useful log file is `/var/log/auth.log`. This displays
various authentication messages. We can view the `/var/log/auth.log` file as follows:

```
root@philip-virtual-machine:/var# tail -f /var/log/auth.log
Mar  1 13:17:01 philip-virtual-machine CRON[7162]: pam_unix(cron:session):
session closed for user root
Mar  1 13:30:01 philip-virtual-machine CRON[7167]: pam_unix(cron:session):
session opened for user root by (uid=0)
Mar  1 13:30:01 philip-virtual-machine CRON[7167]: pam_unix(cron:session):
session closed for user rootMar  1 14:00:01 philip-virtual-machine
CRON[7178]: pam_unix(cron:session): session opened for user root by (uid=0)
Mar  1 14:00:01 philip-virtual-machine CRON[7178]: pam_unix(cron:session):
session closed for user root
Mar  1 14:17:01 philip-virtual-machine CRON[7184]: pam_unix(cron:session):
session opened for user
 ^C
root@philip-virtual-machine:/var#
```

Awesome! In the preceding output, we can see various logs pertaining to the root user.
Also, if someone is trying to break into the system, those login attempts will be present
here, too:

```
root@philip-virtual-machine:/var/log# tail -f /var/log/auth.log
Mar  4 10:39:04 philip-virtual-machine sshd[26259]: Failed password for
invalid user tom from 172.16.175.129 port 39010 ssh2
Mar  4 10:39:04 philip-virtual-machine sshd[26259]: Connection closed by
invalid user tom 172.16.175.129 port 39010 [preauth]
Mar  4 10:39:04 philip-virtual-machine sshd[26259]: PAM 2 more
authentication failures; logname= uid=0 euid=0 tty=ssh ruser=
rhost=172.16.175.129
Mar  4 10:39:09 philip-virtual-machine sshd[26261]: Invalid user harry from
172.16.175.129 port 39012
Mar  4 10:39:10 philip-virtual-machine sshd[26261]: pam_unix(sshd:auth):
check pass; user unknown
```

```
Mar  4 10:39:10 philip-virtual-machine sshd[26261]: pam_unix(sshd:auth):
authentication failure; logname= uid=0 euid=0 tty=ssh ruser=
rhost=172.16.175.129
Mar  4 10:39:12 philip-virtual-machine sshd[26261]: Failed password for
invalid user harry from 172.16.175.129 port 39012 ssh2
Mar  4 10:39:13 philip-virtual-machine sshd[26261]: pam_unix(sshd:auth):
check pass; user unknown
Mar  4 10:39:15 philip-virtual-machine sshd[26261]: Failed password for
invalid user harry from 172.16.175.129 port 39012 ssh2
Mar  4 10:39:16 philip-virtual-machine sshd[26261]: pam_unix(sshd:auth):
check pass; user unknown
Mar  4 10:39:18 philip-virtual-machine sshd[26261]: Failed password for
invalid user harry from 172.16.175.129 port 39012 ssh2
Mar  4 10:39:18 philip-virtual-machine sshd[26261]: Connection closed by
invalid user harry 172.16.175.129 port 39012 [preauth]
Mar  4 10:39:18 philip-virtual-machine sshd[26261]: PAM 2 more
authentication failures; logname= uid=0 euid=0 tty=ssh ruser=
rhost=172.16.175.129
```

Excellent! We can see authentication messages regarding users trying to log in to the system. Another useful log file is /var/log/kern.log. This file contains various messages related to the kernel during boot up. We can take a look at this file:

```
root@philip-virtual-machine:/var/log# tail -f /var/log/kern.log
Mar 1 15:40:32 philip-virtual-machine kernel: [106182.510455] hrtimer:
interrupt took 7528791 ns
Mar 2 04:58:37 philip-virtual-machine kernel: [154065.757609] sched: RT
throttling activated
Mar 4 10:07:45 philip-virtual-machine kernel: [345414.648164] IPv6:
ADDRCONF(NETDEV_UP): ens33: link is not ready
Mar 4 10:07:45 philip-virtual-machine kernel: [345414.653620] IPv6:
ADDRCONF(NETDEV_UP): ens33: link is not ready
Mar 4 10:07:45 philip-virtual-machine kernel: [345414.655942] e1000: ens33
NIC Link is Up 1000 Mbps Full Duplex, Flow Control: None
Mar 4 10:07:45 philip-virtual-machine kernel: [345414.656712] IPv6:
ADDRCONF(NETDEV_CHANGE): ens33: link becomes ready
^C
root@philip-virtual-machine:/var/log#
```

In the preceding file, we can see logs pertaining to interrupts and networking. Over on the Fedora 28 system, when we check the /var/log file, we will notice that there is no /var/log/syslog file:

```
[root@localhost philip]# ls /var/log
anaconda          dnf.log               hawkey.log            pluto
vmware-network.7.log
audit             dnf.log-20180805      hawkey.log-20180805   ppp    vmware-
network.8.log
```

```
blivet-gui        dnf.log-20180812      hawkey.log-20180812   README vmware-
network.9.log
boot.log          dnf.log-20180827      hawkey.log-20180827   samba   vmware-
network.log
btmp              dnf.log-20180904      hawkey.log-20180904   speech-
dispatcher        vmware-vgauthsvc.log.0
btmp-20180904     dnf.rpm.log           httpd                 sssd
vmware-vmsvc.log
chrony            dnf.rpm.log-20180805  journal               tallylog
wtmp
cups              dnf.rpm.log-20180812  kdm.log               vmware-
network.1.log  Xorg.0.log
dnf.librepo.log   dnf.rpm.log-20180827  kdm.log-20180904      vmware-
network.2.log  Xorg.0.log.old
dnf.librepo.log-20180805  dnf.rpm.log-20180904  lastlog
vmware-network.3.log
dnf.librepo.log-20180812  firewalld             libvirt
vmware-network.4.log
dnf.librepo.log-20180827  gdm                   lightdm
vmware-network.5.log
dnf.librepo.log-20180904  glusterfs             mariadb
vmware-network.6.log
[root@localhost philip]#
```

Based on the preceding output, Fedora 28 is using systemd. This has replaced /var/log/messages and /var/log/syslog with journal. This in turn is implemented inside the journald daemon. We can view the logs using the journalctl command. To view all of the log files, we can simply type journalctl without any options:

```
root@localhost philip]# journalctl
-- Logs begin at Tue 2018-07-31 10:57:23 EDT, end at Fri 2018-09-07
15:51:56 EDT. --
Jul 31 10:57:23 localhost.localdomain kernel: Linux version
4.16.3-301.fc28.x86_64 (mockbuild@bkernel02.phx2.fedoraprojec>
Jul 31 10:57:23 localhost.localdomain kernel: Command line:
BOOT_IMAGE=/vmlinuz-4.16.3-301.fc28.x86_64 root=/dev/mapper/f>
Jul 31 10:57:23 localhost.localdomain kernel: Disabled fast string
operations
Jul 31 10:57:23 localhost.localdomain kernel: x86/fpu: Supporting XSAVE
feature 0x001: 'x87 floating point registers'
Jul 31 10:57:23 localhost.localdomain kernel: x86/fpu: Supporting XSAVE
feature 0x002: 'SSE registers'
Jul 31 10:57:23 localhost.localdomain kernel: x86/fpu: Enabled xstate
features 0x3, context size is 576 bytes, using 'sta>
Jul 31 10:57:23 localhost.localdomain kernel: e820: BIOS-provided physical
RAM map:
Jul 31 10:57:23 localhost.localdomain kernel: BIOS-e820: [mem
```

```
0x0000000000000000-0x000000000009ebff] usable
Jul 31 10:57:23 localhost.localdomain kernel: BIOS-e820: [mem
0x000000000009ec00-0x000000000009ffff] reserved
Jul 31 10:57:23 localhost.localdomain kernel: BIOS-e820: [mem
0x00000000000dc000-0x00000000000fffff] reserved
 [root@localhost philip]#
```

Some output has been omitted for brevity. There are a number of log messages. We can filter what we would like to be displayed. For instance, to view the logs since the most recent system boot, we can pass the -b option:

```
[root@localhost philip]# journalctl -b
-- Logs begin at Tue 2018-07-31 10:57:23 EDT, end at Fri 2018-09-07
15:52:26 EDT. --
Sep 04 08:55:38 localhost.localdomain kernel: Linux version
4.16.3-301.fc28.x86_64 (mockbuild@bkernel02.phx2.fedoraprojec>
Sep 04 08:55:38 localhost.localdomain kernel: Command line:
BOOT_IMAGE=/vmlinuz-4.16.3-301.fc28.x86_64 root=/dev/mapper/f>
Sep 04 08:55:38 localhost.localdomain kernel: Disabled fast string
operations
Sep 04 08:55:38 localhost.localdomain kernel: x86/fpu: Supporting XSAVE
feature 0x001: 'x87 floating point registers'
Sep 04 08:55:38 localhost.localdomain kernel: x86/fpu: Supporting XSAVE
feature 0x002: 'SSE registers'
Sep 04 08:55:38 localhost.localdomain kernel: x86/fpu: Enabled xstate
features 0x3, context size is 576 bytes, using 'sta>
Sep 04 08:55:38 localhost.localdomain kernel: e820: BIOS-provided physical
RAM map:
Sep 04 08:55:38 localhost.localdomain kernel: BIOS-e820: [mem
0x0000000000000000-0x000000000009ebff] usable
[root@localhost philip]#
```

In the preceding output, we see quite a number of messages. We can even display logs with timestamps in UTC by passing the --utc option:

```
[root@localhost philip]# journalctl -b --utc
-- Logs begin at Tue 2018-07-31 14:57:23 UTC, end at Fri 2018-09-07
19:52:26 UTC. --
Sep 04 12:55:38 localhost.localdomain kernel: Linux version
4.16.3-301.fc28.x86_64 (mockbuild@bkernel02.phx2.fedoraprojec>
Sep 04 12:55:38 localhost.localdomain kernel: Command line:
BOOT_IMAGE=/vmlinuz-4.16.3-301.fc28.x86_64 root=/dev/mapper/f>
Sep 04 12:55:38 localhost.localdomain kernel: Disabled fast string
operations
Sep 04 12:55:38 localhost.localdomain kernel: x86/fpu: Supporting XSAVE
feature 0x001: 'x87 floating point registers'
[root@localhost philip]#
```

Excellent! Based on the preceding output, the very first line, `-- Logs begin at Tue 2018-07-31 14:57:23 UTC, end at Fri 2018-09-07 19:52:26 UTC. --`, indicates that the timestamps are in UTC. The `journalctl` file also stores information inside `/var/log/journal` as the following shows:

```
[root@localhost philip]# ls /var/log/journal/
30012ff3b6d648a09e33e4927d140504
[root@localhost philip]#
```

We can even dive deeper and see more log files under `/var/journal/30012ff3b6d648a09e33e4927d140504`, as follows:

```
[root@localhost philip]# ls
/var/log/journal/30012ff3b6d648a09e33e4927d140504/
system@000572748a062ca4-7a3da8346cf70fb7.journal~
system@0005746b23e241ef-7ed07e858f3a6f48.journal~
system@0005746c7d7bed2f-80a58e1cfa65a3dd.journal~
system@0005750b2d37139f-3ddba79811cf1357.journal~
system@123e7dba3db2484697ae1cc5bfff550d-0000000000000001-0005750b2cb5f7d4.j
ournal
system.journal
user-1000@000572749f063152-ae4ff154ee396e12.journal~
user-1000@4e535b252cc04ea69811c152632aafcd-0000000000000907-000572749f062b7
4.journal
user-1000.journal
[root@localhost philip]#
```

Excellent! We can expose this information using `journalctl`. For instance, we can view a log pertaining to previous boots; this can be viewed by passing the `--list-boots` option:

```
[root@localhost philip]# journalctl --utc --list-boots
-6 6d6ff5ab30284bbe8da4c97e54298944 Tue 2018-07-31 14:57:23 UTC—Tue
2018-07-31 20:17:06 UTC
-5 a7a23120abff44c8bca6807f1711c1c2 Thu 2018-08-02 14:22:09 UTC—Sun
2018-08-12 14:18:21 UTC
-4 905ba9f3c37d46b69920466e9a93a67d Mon 2018-08-27 13:59:47 UTC—Mon
2018-08-27 15:06:04 UTC
-3 e4d2ad4c25df41a2b905fdcb8cfae312 Mon 2018-08-27 15:06:18 UTC—Mon
2018-08-27 15:37:50 UTC
-2 ae1c87d6ea6842da91eb4a1cba331ead Mon 2018-08-27 15:38:18 UTC—Mon
2018-08-27 20:22:15 UTC
-1 7cfc215cb74149748fe717b688630bd3 Mon 2018-08-27 20:22:33 UTC—Wed
2018-08-29 12:50:59 UTC
 0 d3cb4fafa63a41f99bd3cc4da0b74d1d Tue 2018-09-04 12:55:38 UTC—Fri
2018-09-07 19:59:02 UTC
[root@localhost philip]#
```

Based on the preceding output, we can see seven files that contain boot information; we can view any of these files by passing the offset of the file. The offset of each file is the value in the first column. Let's take a look at the −6 offset:

```
[root@localhost philip]# journalctl -b -6 --utc
-- Logs begin at Tue 2018-07-31 14:57:23 UTC, end at Fri 2018-09-07
20:01:02 UTC. --
Jul 31 14:57:23 localhost.localdomain kernel: Linux version
4.16.3-301.fc28.x86_64 (mockbuild@bkernel02.phx2.fedoraprojec>
Jul 31 14:57:23 localhost.localdomain kernel: Command line:
BOOT_IMAGE=/vmlinuz-4.16.3-301.fc28.x86_64 root=/dev/mapper/f>
Jul 31 14:57:23 localhost.localdomain kernel: Disabled fast string
operations
Jul 31 14:57:23 localhost.localdomain kernel: x86/fpu: Supporting XSAVE
feature 0x001: 'x87 floating point registers'
Jul 31 14:57:23 localhost.localdomain kernel: x86/fpu: Supporting XSAVE
feature 0x002: 'SSE registers'
Jul 31 14:57:23 localhost.localdomain kernel: x86/fpu: Enabled xstate
features 0x3, context size is 576 bytes, using 'sta>
Jul 31 14:57:23 localhost.localdomain kernel: e820: BIOS-provided physical
RAM map:
 [root@localhost philip]#
```

Some output has been omitted for brevity. We can look at /etc/systemd/journald.conf:

```
[root@localhost philip]# cat /etc/systemd/journald.conf
[Journal]
#Storage=auto
#Compress=yes
#Seal=yes
#SplitMode=uid
#SyncIntervalSec=5m
#RateLimitIntervalSec=30s
#RateLimitBurst=1000
#SystemMaxUse=
#SystemKeepFree=
#SystemMaxFileSize=
#SystemMaxFiles=100
#RuntimeMaxUse=
#RuntimeKeepFree=
#RuntimeMaxFileSize=
#RuntimeMaxFiles=100
#MaxRetentionSec=
#MaxFileSec=1month
#ForwardToSyslog=no
#ForwardToKMsg=no
#ForwardToConsole=no
```

```
#ForwardToWall=yes
#TTYPath=/dev/console
#MaxLevelStore=debug
#MaxLevelSyslog=debug
#MaxLevelKMsg=notice
#MaxLevelConsole=info
#MaxLevelWall=emerg
#LineMax=48K
[root@localhost philip]#
```

Some output has been omitted for brevity. Based on the preceding output, all of the settings are at their defaults; # indicates a comment. We can specify a date from which we would like to view the log information by passing the --since option:

```
root@localhost philip]# journalctl --since today --utc
-- Logs begin at Tue 2018-07-31 14:57:23 UTC, end at Fri 2018-09-07
20:01:02 UTC. --
Sep 07 04:00:58 localhost.localdomain systemd[1]: Started Update a database
for mlocate.
Sep 07 04:00:58 localhost.localdomain audit[1]: SERVICE_START pid=1 uid=0
auid=4294967295 ses=4294967295 subj=system_u:sy>
Sep 07 04:00:58 localhost.localdomain systemd[1]: Starting update of the
root trust anchor for DNSSEC validation in unbou>
Sep 07 04:00:59 localhost.localdomain systemd[1]: Started update of the
root trust anchor for DNSSEC validation in unboun>
Sep 07 04:00:59 localhost.localdomain audit[1]: SERVICE_START pid=1 uid=0
auid=4294967295 ses=4294967295 subj=system_u:sy>
Sep 07 04:00:59 localhost.localdomain audit[1]: SERVICE_STOP pid=1 uid=0
auid=4294967295 ses=4294967295 subj=system_u:sys>
Sep 07 04:01:01 localhost.localdomain CROND[13532]: (root) CMD (run-parts
/etc/cron.hourly)
Sep 07 04:01:01 localhost.localdomain run-parts[13535]: (/etc/cron.hourly)
starting 0anacron
Sep 07 04:01:01 localhost.localdomain run-parts[13543]: (/etc/cron.hourly)
finished 0anacron
Sep 07 04:01:01 localhost.localdomain anacron[13541]: Anacron started on
2018-09-07
Sep 07 04:01:01 localhost.localdomain anacron[13541]: Normal exit (0 jobs
run)
Sep 07 04:01:19 localhost.localdomain audit[1]: SERVICE_STOP pid=1 uid=0
auid=4294967295 ses=4294967295 subj=system_u:sys>
Sep 07 04:05:16 localhost.localdomain dhclient[1011]: DHCPREQUEST on ens33
to 172.16.175.254 port 67 (xid=0x1269bc29)
[root@localhost philip]#
```

Awesome! Some output has been omitted for brevity. Also, we can specify the date in numbers:

```
[root@localhost philip]# journalctl --since "2018-09-07 15:00:00"
-- Logs begin at Tue 2018-07-31 10:57:23 EDT, end at Fri 2018-09-07
16:11:54 EDT. --
Sep 07 15:01:01 localhost.localdomain CROND[16031]: (root) CMD (run-parts
/etc/cron.hourly)
Sep 07 15:01:01 localhost.localdomain run-parts[16034]: (/etc/cron.hourly)
starting 0anacron
Sep 07 15:01:01 localhost.localdomain run-parts[16040]: (/etc/cron.hourly)
finished 0anacron
Sep 07 15:09:56 localhost.localdomain dhclient[1011]: DHCPREQUEST on ens33
to 172.16.175.254 port 67 (xid=0x1269bc29)
Sep 07 15:09:56 localhost.localdomain dhclient[1011]: DHCPACK from
172.16.175.254 (xid=0x1269bc29)
Sep 07 15:09:56 localhost.localdomain NetworkManager[833]: <info>
[1536347396.3834] dhcp4 (ens33):    address 172.16.175.>
Sep 07 15:09:56 localhost.localdomain NetworkManager[833]: <info>
[1536347396.3842] dhcp4 (ens33):    plen 24 (255.255.25>
Sep 07 15:09:56 localhost.localdomain NetworkManager[833]: <info>
[1536347396.3845] dhcp4 (ens33):    gateway 172.16.175.2
[root@localhost philip]#
```

Some output has been omitted for brevity. However, we can see information pertaining to networking. Similarly, we can view authentication information inside `/var/log/audit/audit.log`. Here is an excerpt of this file:

Great job! From the excerpt, we can see login attempts coming into the Fedora system. Also, we can leverage the `journalctl` command to display the authentication information. We can pass the `-u` option and specify which service we're looking for:

```
[root@localhost philip]# journalctl -u sshd.service
-- Logs begin at Tue 2018-07-31 10:57:23 EDT, end at Mon 2018-09-10
12:06:49 EDT. --
Sep 10 12:05:28 localhost.localdomain sshd[27585]: Invalid user ted from
172.16.175.132 port 37406
Sep 10 12:05:29 localhost.localdomain sshd[27585]: pam_unix(sshd:auth):
check pass; user unknown
Sep 10 12:05:29 localhost.localdomain sshd[27585]: pam_unix(sshd:auth):
authentication failure; logname= uid=0 euid=0 tty>
Sep 10 12:05:31 localhost.localdomain sshd[27585]: Failed password for
invalid user ted from 172.16.175.132 port 37406 ss>
Sep 10 12:05:32 localhost.localdomain sshd[27585]: pam_unix(sshd:auth):
check pass; user unknown
Sep 10 12:05:34 localhost.localdomain sshd[27585]: Failed password for
invalid user ted from 172.16.175.132 port 37406 ss>
Sep 10 12:05:54 localhost.localdomain sshd[27585]: pam_unix(sshd:auth):
check pass; user unknown
Sep 10 12:05:56 localhost.localdomain sshd[27585]: Failed password for
invalid user ted from 172.16.175.132 port 37406 ss>
Sep 10 12:05:56 localhost.localdomain sshd[27585]: Connection closed by
invalid user ted 172.16.175.132 port 37406 [preau>
Sep 10 12:05:56 localhost.localdomain sshd[27585]: PAM 2 more
authentication failures; logname= uid=0 euid=0 tty=ssh ruse>
[root@localhost philip]#
```

From this, we can see the effectiveness of the `journalctl` utility.

Configure remote logging

It's always good to view the local system's log files, but what about managing remote logs? Well, it is possible to configure a Linux system to perform remote logging. We have to install (if not already installed) the logging software. For this demonstration, we'll use the Fedora 28 as the logging client and the Ubuntu 18 system as the logging server. Also, we will use `rsyslog` as the logging software. By default, it's already installed in the Ubuntu 18 system. However, over on Fedora 28, we will have to install the `rsyslog` software. First, let's install the `rsyslog` software in Fedora 28. We use the `dnf` command, illustrated as follows:

```
[root@localhost philip]# dnf search rsyslog
Last metadata expiration check: 1:38:20 ago on Mon 10 Sep 2018 10:41:18 AM
```

```
EDT.
========================================== Name Exactly Matched: rsyslog
==========================================
rsyslog.x86_64 : Enhanced system logging and kernel message trapping daemon
========================================== Summary & Name Matched:
rsyslog ==========================================
rsyslog-mysql.x86_64 : MySQL support for rsyslog
rsyslog-hiredis.x86_64 : Redis support for rsyslog
rsyslog-doc.noarch : HTML documentation for rsyslog
[root@localhost philip]#
```

Some output has been omitted for brevity. We've found the rsyslog package. Next, we will pass the install option in order to install the rsyslog package:

```
[root@localhost philip]# dnf install rsyslog.x86_64
Last metadata expiration check: 2:42:37 ago on Mon 10 Sep 2018 10:41:18 AM
EDT.
Dependencies resolved.
================================================================================
==========================================
 Package                     Arch                    Version
Repository                 Size
================================================================================
==========================================
Installing:
 rsyslog                     x86_64                  8.37.0-1.fc28
updates                    697 k
Installing dependencies:
 libestr                     x86_64                  0.1.9-10.fc28
fedora                      26 k
 libfastjson                 x86_64                  0.99.8-2.fc28
fedora                      36 k
Transaction Summary
================================================================================
==========================================
Install  3 Packages
Total download size: 759 k
Installed size: 2.2 M
Is this ok [y/N]: y
Installed:
  rsyslog.x86_64 8.37.0-1.fc28              libestr.x86_64 0.1.9-10.fc28
libfastjson.x86_64 0.99.8-2.fc28
Complete!
[root@localhost philip]#
```

Once again, some output has been omitted for brevity. We have successfully installed the
`rsyslog` package. Now, we need to edit `/etc/rsyslog.conf` in a text editor, such as vi or
nano; we need to specify the remote logging server IP address. Here is how we do that:

```
[root@localhost philip]# cat /etc/rsyslog.conf
# rsyslog configuration file
# For more information see /usr/share/doc/rsyslog-*/rsyslog_conf.html
# or latest version online at http://www.rsyslog.com/doc/rsyslog_conf.html
# If you experience problems, see
http://www.rsyslog.com/doc/troubleshoot.html
#queue.maxdiskspace="1g"           # 1gb space limit (use as much as
possible)
#queue.saveonshutdown="on"         # save messages to disk on shutdown
#queue.type="LinkedList"           # run asynchronously
#action.resumeRetryCount="-1"      # infinite retries if host is down
# # Remote Logging (we use TCP for reliable delivery)
# # remote_host is: name/ip, e.g. 192.168.0.1, port optional e.g. 10514
#Target="remote_host" Port="XXX" Protocol="tcp")
*.*            @172.16.175.132:514
[root@localhost philip]#
```

Excellent! Some output has been omitted for brevity. In the preceding output, we added the
last entry `*.*        @172.16.175.132:514`. This is informing the local system to send all
log facilities the `*.` messages with all the `.*` severity to the `172.16.175.132` remote
system using the UDP protocol and the `514` port number. We can also be more specific; for
instance, we can only send emergency messages from every facility by specifying the
`emerg` keyword:

```
[root@localhost philip]# cat /etc/rsyslog.conf
# rsyslog configuration file
#queue.maxdiskspace="1g"           # 1gb space limit (use as much as
possible)
#queue.saveonshutdown="on"         # save messages to disk on shutdown
#queue.type="LinkedList"           # run asynchronously
#action.resumeRetryCount="-1"      # infinite retries if host is down
# # Remote Logging (we use TCP for reliable delivery)
# # remote_host is: name/ip, e.g. 192.168.0.1, port optional e.g. 10514
#Target="remote_host" Port="XXX" Protocol="tcp")
*.emerg                @172.16.175.132:514
[root@localhost philip]#
```

Every facility with emergency messages will be sent to the remote server via UDP. Up to this point, we've been using UDP to send the logs, but it is also possible to send the logs using TCP. In order to use TCP as transport, we need to add another @ in front of the first @. We're going to change the message type from `emerg` to `info` and use TCP as the transport protocol, as follows:

```
[root@localhost philip]# cat /etc/rsyslog.conf
# rsyslog configuration file
 #queue.saveonshutdown="on"        # save messages to disk on shutdown
#queue.type="LinkedList"          # run asynchronously
#action.resumeRetryCount="-1"     # infinite retries if host is down
# # Remote Logging (we use TCP for reliable delivery)
# # remote_host is: name/ip, e.g. 192.168.0.1, port optional e.g. 10514
#Target="remote_host" Port="XXX" Protocol="tcp")
*.info      @@172.16.175.132:514
[root@localhost philip]#
```

Awesome! Some output has been omitted for brevity. Now, the last step is to restart the `rsyslog` daemon so that the new changes can take effect. We use the `systemctl` command, as in the following, to restart the `rsyslog` daemon:

Now we can see that the `rsyslog` daemon is running. Note at the bottom of the `systemctl` status, there are some logs about connecting to `172/16.175.132`. This is because we have not configured the remote server to accept the logs coming from the Fedora system. Now we will head over to the Ubuntu system, edit `/etc/rsyslog.conf` and add the following:

```
root@philip-virtual-machine:/var/log# cat /etc/rsyslog.conf
# provides UDP syslog reception
#module(load="imudp")
#input(type="imudp" port="514")
# provides TCP syslog reception
module(load="imtcp")
input(type="imtcp" port="514")
root@philip-virtual-machine:/var/log#
```

Excellent! Some output has been omitted for brevity. We've taken off the comments in the TCP section. The last step is to restart the `rsyslog` daemon; this can be done using the `systemctl` command as the following screenshot shows:

We can see the `rsyslog` daemon running without error. Now to test, we will check `/var/log/syslog` for logs from the Fedora logging client. We can use another powerful command to generate a test log: the `logger` command. The following is how we use the `logger` command.

On the Fedora 28 `rsyslog` client, we issue the following:

```
[root@localhost philip]# logger This is the Fedora Logging client
172.16.175.129
[root@localhost philip]# logger This is another Logging test from the
```

```
Fedora client 172.16.175.129
[root@localhost philip]#
```

Over on the Ubuntu 18 `rsyslog` server we will see the following:

```
root@philip-virtual-machine:/home/philip# tail -f /var/log/syslog
Sep 10 14:20:46 localhost dbus-daemon[720]: [system] Successfully activated
service 'net.reactivated.Fprint'
Sep 10 14:20:46 localhost systemd[1]: Started Fingerprint Authentication
Daemon.
Sep 10 14:20:50 localhost kscreenlocker_greet[58309]: QObject::disconnect:
No such signal QObject::screenChanged(QScreen*)
Sep 10 14:22:25 localhost philip[58396]: This is the Fedora Logging client
172.16.175.129
Sep 10 14:23:04 localhost philip[58403]: This is another Logging test from
the Fedora client 172.16.175.129
^C
root@philip-virtual-machine:/home/philip#
```

Awesome! We can see that the `rsyslog` client is indeed sending the logs across the network to the Ubuntu 18 `rsyslog` server.

Summary

In this chapter, the main focus was on the maintenance of the system's time and logging. In particular, we looked at ways in which we can manipulate the system time; we worked extensively with the `date` and `timedatectl` commands. Additionally, we touched on regular expressions for changing the date. Furthermore, we worked with the hardware clock; we saw ways to sync the system clock with the hardware clock and vice versa. Moving on, we worked with logging; we explored the common log files. The `/var/log/syslog` file was explored in the Ubuntu environment, whereas the `journalctl` command was used extensively in Fedora 28 for viewing the logs. Finally, we worked with remote logging; we installed the `rsyslog` package in the Fedora 28 and configured it as a `rsyslog` client. We then went over to Ubuntu 18 and configured its `/etc/rsyslog.conf` file to accept remote logs and use TCP as its transport protocol. We then generated test logs over on our Fedora system and verified that we received the logs over on our Ubuntu `rsyslog` server.

In the next chapter, we dive into the world of the Internet Protocol. We will touch on the various IPv4 addresses and IPv6 addresses. Also, we will cover subnetting an IPv4 address and the ways of cutting down on the lengthy IPv6 address. Finally, we will look at some of the well-known protocols.

Questions

1. Which option is used to set the date using the `date` command?

    A. `-s`
    B. `-S`
    C. `-t`
    D. `-u`

2. Which option is used to turn off the sync in the `timedatectl` command?

    A. `--set-ntp`
    B. `--set-sync`
    C. `set-ntp`
    D. `set-sync`

3. Which regular expression is used to set only the time with the `date` command?

    A. `-$%t`
    B. `+$T`
    C. `-$t`
    D. `+%T`

4. Which option is used to set the time using the `timedatectl` command?

    A. `set-time`
    B. `set-clock`
    C. `set-sync`
    D. `--set-zone`

5. Which file is generated from `/usr/share/zoneinfo/<zone>`?

    A. `/etc/synczone`
    B. `/etc/timedate`
    C. `/etc/clock`
    D. `/etc/localtime`

6. Which command replaces the `tzconfig` command in newer Ubuntu distributions?

    A. `tztime`
    B. `tzdata`
    C. `tzzone`
    D. `tzclock`

7. Which command is used for setting the time zone?

    A. `tzsync`
    B. `tzselect`
    C. `tzdate`
    D. `tztime`

8. Which option with the `journalctl` command lists logs for a particular daemon?

    A. `-a`
    B. `-e`
    C. `-b`
    D. `-u`

9. Which protocol is being used when we have `*.*  @@1.2.3.4` inside `/etc/rsyslog.conf`?

    A. ICMP
    B. UDP
    C. ECHO
    D. TCP

10. Which command can be used to send a test message as part of the verification that the `rsyslog` client is communicating with the `rsyslog` server?

    A. `send-message`
    B. `nc`
    C. `logger`
    D. `logrotate`

Further reading

- This site gives useful information regarding logs: `https://www.digitalocean.com/community/tutorials/how-to-view-and-configure-linux-logs-on-ubuntu-and-centos`
- This site gives useful information about clocks: `https://www.systutorials.com/docs/linux/man/n-clock/`
- This site gives useful information about logging: `http://freelinuxtutorials.com/tutorials/configure-centralized-syslog-server-in-linux-setup-syslog-clients-on-different-platforms/`

15
Fundamentals of Internet Protocol

In the last chapter, the focus was on maintaining the system's time and logging. Particularly, we touched on ways in which we could manipulate the system. Next, we worked with logging and explored the common log files. Finally, we worked with remote. We then generated test logs over on our Fedora system and verified that we received the logs over on our Ubuntu `rsyslog` server.

In this chapter, the focus is on **Internet Protocol** (**IP**). We will start off with IPv4, looking at the address structure and the various IPv4 addresses commonly used in today's environment. We will then move on to subnetting an IPv4 address, determining the network and host portion of an IPv4 address. This is then followed up with IPv6. We look at the structure of an IPv6 address and some well-known IPv6 addresses. Then we focus on ways in which we can reduce the lengthy IPv6 address. Finally, our focus is on the protocols. We will cover some well-known protocols and their respective port numbers.

We will be covering the following topics:

- IPv4 addressing
- IPv6 addressing
- Well-known protocols

IPv4 addressing

IP version 4 is the fourth version of IP. It plays a vital role in the internet as we know it. By far, IPv4 is the most commonly used protocol for addressing various devices within a network and out on the internet. Another interesting fact about IP is that it's not connection-oriented as is the case for TCP; instead, IP is connectionless.

An IPv4 address is 32 bits or 4-bytes in length. We calculate the addresses in base 2; this gives us 2^32, which equals 4,294,967,296 addresses. It may seem as though there are plenty of IPv4 addresses; however, the reality differs. In fact, there is currently an IPv4 shortage. An IPv4 address is represented in dotted decimal format. An example of an IPv4 address is as follows:

```
192.168.1.1
```

Here, we can see that an IPv4 address is indeed represented in a dotted decimal format. The dots . act as separators between the address. The numbers can be anywhere between 0 and 255 inclusive. Each portion of an IPv4 address is known as an octet; thus, the four numbers make up four octets. There are various types of IPv4 addresses available in today's environment; particularly within a **local area network** (**LAN**). You may see one of the following:

- `10.0.0.0/8`
- `172.16.0.0/12`
- `192.16.0.0/16`

The addresses may look familiar. These three addresses can be further explained by the RFC 1918; this specifies certain addresses that are to be used within a private network, such as a LAN.

We have five classes of address space; the first four classes are commonly used in various types of environment. These are classes of addresses:

Class A	0-127
Class B	128-191
Class C	192-223
Class D	224-239
Class E	240-255

Here, the number range represents the place holder in the first octet. We can break down an IPv4 address in order to gain a better understanding. We will use the first octet as reference. First, we will build a table. Every octet of an IPv4 address represents 1 byte; 1 byte = 8 bits. We can then use this information to form our table:

7	6	5	4	3	2	1	0	= 8 bit positions
128	64	32	16	18	4	2	1	= 255

Awesome! Based on this, the reason we counted from 7 to 0 is because we always start at 0 when calculating a value for an octet inside an IPv4 address and we move from right to left when adding. Now, the way we got the value was by putting 2^x, where x = the last character to the right. So it would be as follows:

7	6	5	4	3	2	1	0	= 8-bit position
1	1	1	1	1	1	1	1	= 1 means that the bit is turned on
2^	2^	2^	2^	2^	2^	2^	2^	= base 2
128	6	32	16	8	4	2	1	= Result of base 2 for each bit position

Using all of the values inside the 8 bits, we get *128+64+32+16+8+4+2+1 = 255*.

Based on this, we now see how the table is built using base 2 for calculation. Hence, at any given time, only values between 0-255, including the 0 and 255, are legal values.

Class A

The Class A address space, 0-127, looks at the only leading bit position (position 7 because we count from 0 to 7) in the first octet; this is known as the most significant bit position. The 127 address space is reserved; this is known as the loopback address space. Hence, we are only using the values 0-126. Moreover, the 0 is actually reserved for network use (more on this later when we cover subnetting). For now, the way we calculate the first values for a Class A address is as follows:

7	6	5	4	3	2	1	0	= 8 bit position
128	64	32	16	8	4	2	1	= 255
0	0	0	0	0	0	0	0	= 0-127

Based on this, we have all eight bits turned off in the first octet. This, therefore, gives us the Class A address space which is between 0-126 in first octet, 0 being reserved and 127 being the loopback space. Hence, the real usable IPv4 addresses in the first octet are 1-126. This is then followed by the three remaining octets being all zeros. So the Class A address space would be as follows:

- Class A `0-126.0.0.0/8`, where the leading bit is 0 in the 8th bit position
- Class A reserved address space `127.0.0.0/8`
- Class A **Automatic Private IP Addressing (APIPA)** `169.0.0.0/8` reserved

Based on this, we are given a maximum of up to 126 networks that we can define. The remaining three octets of the Class A address 0.0.0 makes up the host portion; each octet is made up of eight bits. A host is any device that can be assigned an IPv4 address(s). The maximum number of hosts allowed in a Class A address is 16,777,214 hosts per network defined. The host portion is the result of 2^3 octets (eight bits per octet x 3 =24 bits) – 2 = 1677216-2 = 16,777,214 hosts per Class A network.

Class B

In the Class B address spaces, 128-191, look at the leading bits position 7 and 6 (remember that we start counting from 0, moving from left to right). The first most significant bit, position 7, is turned on in binary. This is set to 1 and the second most significant bit, position 6, is set to 0. This can be seen using the table that we created earlier:

7	6	5	4	3	2	1	0	= 8 bit position
128	64	32	16	8	4	2	1	= 255
1	0	0	0	0	0	0	0	= 128

Based on this, the most significant bit is turned on and the second most significant bit is turned off. This gives us the address space of 128-191, where the 128 is reserved for network use and the 191 is reserved as the broadcast address. We will discuss broadcast addresses later in this chapter when we cover subnetting. In a Class B address space, the first 16 bits are reserved for network use; however, two bits are reserved. This would then give us 2^{14} = 16,384 networks per Class B address. This can be illustrated as follows:

7	6	5	4	3	2	1	0	= 8 bit position
128	64	32	16	8	4	2	1	= 255
1	0	0	0	0	0	0	0	= 128

We have to skip the first two bits, positions 7 and 6; this then gives us 2^{14} = 1,63,864 networks.

Based on this, we see the maximum amount of the networks available but we don't see the maximum amount of hosts. Well, the way we calculate the hosts for a Class B address is to use the last two octets for the hosts; we would do 2^2 octets (eight bits per octets x 2 = 16 bits)—two bits for network and broadcast = 65,536 -2 = 65,534 hosts per Class B network.

Class C

The Class C address space, 192-223, takes the first three most significant bits into consideration; namely, positions 7,6, and 5. The first two most significant bits are turned on; they are set to 1 in binary. The third bit, position 5 in binary, is turned off; this is set to 0. The first 24 bits are reserved for network use in a Class C address space. We can then construct our table using this information. This is how the table would look:

7	6	5	4	3	2	1	0	= 8 bit position
128	64	32	16	8	4	2	1	= 255
1	1	0	0	0	0	0	0	= 128+64=>192

Based on this, we can then see that the Class C address space starts at 192 and ends at 223. The 192 is reserved for the network and the 223 is reserved as the broadcast. We can then calculate the number of networks by using 2^21 = 2,097,152 networks. This can be represented in the following table:

7	6	5	4	3	2	1	0	= 8 bit position
128	64	32	16	8	4	2	1	= 255
1	1	0	0	0	0	0	0	= first 3 bits total 192

24 bits are reserved for Class C, 24 bits—three most significant bits = 21 then 2^{21} bits = 2,097,152 networks.

The last octet .0 (eight bits) is reserved for the host addresses. This then means 2^1 octet (8 bits)—2 bits for network and broadcast = 256 - 2 = 254 hosts per Class C address.

Class D

The Class D, 224-239, address space is reserved for multicast use. The first three most significant bits are turned on; they are set to 1. The fourth most significant bit is set to 0. The Class D address space is not used for IP addressing, as is the case in the previous classes of address. Instead, the Class D address space is used to assign an IP address to a multicast group. The hosts then are part of a group that in turn shares a group address. The following table illustrates the bits that are used for the Class D address space:

7	6	5	4	3	2	1	0	= 8 bit position
128	64	32	16	8	4	2	1	= 255
1	1	1	0	0	0	0	0	= total 224

Based on this, the Class D address space starts at 224.0.0.0 and ends at 239.255.255.255.

Class E

The Class E, 240-255, address space is reserved for future use. As such, it is not implemented as is the previous address space. The first four most significant bits are turned on; they are set to 1. The only address that is used in a Class E is the 255.255.255.255; this is what is known as the all broadcast address. The following table illustrates the bits that are used for the Class E address space:

7	6	5	4	3	2	1	0	= 8 bit position
128	64	32	16	8	4	2	1	= 255
1	1	1	1	0	0	0	0	= total 240

Based on this, the Class E address space starts at 240.0.0.0 and ends at 255.255.255.255, where 255.255.255.255 is reserved for the all broadcast address.

Subnet masks

We've just covered the various classes of IPv4 address spaces, but there are times when using those classes of address space might not be appropriate. The fact of the matter is that Class A, B, and C are classful address spaces if we use the default subnet mask for those classes of IPs. For instance, a Class A uses a subnet mask of 255.0.0.0. But wait, what is a subnet mask? To begin with, a subnet mask identifies the network portion and the host portion of a given IP address. This includes both IPv4 and IPv6. A subnet mask enables us to easily find out the network address for a given IP address. A subnet mask is often written in dotted decimal format. However, it is possible to represent a subnet mask in a slash notation; namely, the CIDR notation. Classless Inter Domain Routing, or CIDR for short, represents a subnet mask by appending the number of network bits in a slash format to an IP address. For a Class A address, a subnet mask will be as follows:

```
255.0.0.0
```

Based on this, the `255.0.0.0` value means that all of the bits in the first octets are turned on; they are set to 1. We can present this using the table that we created earlier:

7	6	5	4	3	2	1	0	= bit position
128	64	32	16	8	4	2	1	= 2^ bit position
1	1	1	1	1	1	1	1	= bits turned on

128+64+32+16+8+4+2+1 = 255 bits

Based on this, the value of 255 is derived from the sum of all eight bits being turned on. Adding to this, the subnet mask can also be represented in binary format. Using the Class A address, the subnet mask could be written as follows:

- **Class A subnet mask in decimal**: `255.0.0.0`
- **Class A subnet mask in binary**: `11111111.00000000.00000000.00000000`

Awesome! Now, we can see that a subnet mask can be represented in either decimal format using values between 0-255 or in binary format using values of either 0 or 1. Furthermore, it is possible to represent a subnet mask in CIDR notation. We would represent a Class A address in CIDR format using the following:

- **Class A subnet mask in decimal**: `255.0.0.0`
- **Class A subnet mask in binary**: `11111111.00000000.00000000.00000000`
- **Class A subnet mask in CIDR**: `/8`

Based on this, the `/8` means that eight bits are turned on for the network portion of an address.

Using a Class B address, we would represent a Class B address in the following format using the dotted decimal format:

`255.255.0.0`

Based on this, the value `255.255.0.0` means that all of the bits in the first and second octets are turned on and set to 1. We can present this using the table that we created earlier:

First octet:

7	6	5	4	3	2	1	0	= bit position
128	64	32	16	8	4	2	1	= 2^ bit position
1	1	1	1	1	1	1	1	= bits turned on

128+64+32+16+8+4+2+1 = 255 bits

Second octet:

7	6	5	4	3	2	1	0	= bit position
128	64	32	16	8	4	2	1	= 2^ bit position
1	1	1	1	1	1	1	1	= bits turned on

128+64+32+16+8+4+2+1 = 255 bits

Based on this, the value of `255.255.0.0` is derived from the sum of all 16 bits being turned on. Adding to this, the subnet mask can also be represented in binary format. Using the Class B address, the subnet mask could be written as follows:

- **Class B subnet mask in decimal**: `255.255.0.0`
- **Class B subnet mask in binary**: `11111111.11111111.00000000.00000000`

Awesome! Now, we can see that a subnet mask can be represented in either decimal format using values between 0-255 or in binary format using values of either 0 or 1. Furthermore, it is possible to represent a subnet mask in a CIDR notation. We would represent a Class B address in CIDR format using the following:

- **Class B subnet mask in decimal**: `255.255.0.0`
- **Class B subnet mask in binary**: `11111111.11111111.00000000.00000000`
- **Class B subnet mask in CIDR**: `/16`

Based on this, the `/16` means that 16 bits are turned on for the network portion of an address.

Using a Class C address, we would represent a Class C address in the following format using the dotted decimal format:

```
255.255.255.0
```

Based on this, the `255.255.255.0` value means that all of the bits in the first and second octets are turned on; they are set to `1`. We can present this using the table that we created earlier.

First octet:

7	6	5	4	3	2	1	0	= bit position
128	64	32	16	8	4	2	1	= 2^ bit position
1	1	1	1	1	1	1	1	= bits turned on

128+64+32+16+8+4+2+1 = 255 bits

Second octet:

7	6	5	4	3	2	1	0	= bit position
128	64	32	16	8	4	2	1	= 2^ bit position
1	1	1	1	1	1	1	1	= bits turned on

128+64+32+16+8+4+2+1 = 255 bits

Third octet:

7	6	5	4	3	2	1	0	= bit position
128	64	32	16	8	4	2	1	= 2^ bit position
1	1	1	1	1	1	1	1	= bits turned on

128+64+32+16+8+4+2+1 = 255 bits

Based on this, the value of 255.255.255.0 is derived from the sum of all 24 bits being turned on. Adding to this, the subnet mask can also be represented in binary format. Using the Class C address, the subnet mask could be written as the following:

- **Class C subnet mask in decimal**: 255.255.255.0
- **Class C subnet mask in binary**: 11111111.11111111.11111111.00000000

Awesome! Now, we can see that a subnet mask can be represented in either decimal format using values between 0-255 or in binary format using values of either 0 or 1. Furthermore, it is possible to represent a subnet mask in CIDR notation. We would represent a Class C address in CIDR format using the following:

- **Class C subnet mask in decimal**: 255.255.255.0
- **Class C subnet mask in binary**: 11111111.11111111.11111111.00000000
- **Class C subnet mask in CIDR**: /24

Based on this, the /24 means that 24 bits are turned on for the network portion of an address.

Subnetting

As we've just seen with Classes A, B, and C, their subnet masks are /8, /16, and /24, respectively, using CIDR notation. In most environments today, these default subnet masks are known as classful, meaning if we use these subnet masks as they are, we would not be able to perform any sort of traffic engineering. This becomes an issue when we want to control the broadcast domain. We should try to minimize the broadcast to a given room, office, or department. This ensures that in the event of any type of network broadcast, the entire network does not start to experience latency. We can leverage subnetting in order to overcome the limitation of classful networks. For instance, let's pick a Class C IP address:

```
192.168.0.0/24
```

Based on this, we can have up to 254 hosts per network address. We might be in a situation where we only have eight systems that require IP connectivity. This would mean that we are losing those remaining IP addresses because we've used a default Class C subnet. The requirement in this scenario is to have eight IP addresses and not to waste the remaining IPs. We can achieve this requirement by subnetting. Subnetting is made possible by borrowing bits from the host portion. Let's write out the subnet mask for the given IP address:

```
192.168.0.0/24 Network
```

- **Subnet mask in decimal**: 255.255.255.0
- **Subnet mask in binary**: 11111111.11111111.11111111.00000000

Based on this, the first 24 bits are turned on. We can subnet this address in order to gain more control over our IP address space. We want eight IPs. The way we borrow bits is by taking them from the host bits. We can use our table for assistance:

7	6	5	4	3	2	1	0	= bit position
128	64	32	16	8	4	2	1	= 2^ bit position
1	1	1	1	0	0	0	0	= 4 bits borrowed

Based on the preceding table, let's refer to the following points:

- 2^4 bits = 16 network networks can be created
- 2^4 -2 = 14 hosts per network

Based on this, we've borrowed four bits from the host portion of the network; this enables us to create four smaller subnets/networks. Each network created would then have 14 hosts per network. This allows us to save on the amount of IPs being lost as opposed to using a standard Class C /24 network. So, we've borrowed four bits for the network portion. How would we represent this in decimal and CIDR notation? Well, the way we represent the newly created subnet is through a process of adding the network bits. This can by illustrated in the following table:

7	6	5	4	3	2	1	0	= bit position
128	64	32	16	8	4	2	1	= 2^ bit position
1	1	1	1	0	0	0	0	= 4 bits

128+64+32+16 = 240

Let's refer to the following subnets:

- Old subnet in decimal = 255.255.255.0
- Old subnet in CIDR = /24
- New subnet in decimal = 255.255.255.240
- New subnet in CIDR = /28
- Network address = 192.168.0.0/28

Based on this, we can see the new subnet mask in both decimal and CIDR notation. The next step would be to identify the usable subnets/networks using this new subnet mask. We can calculate the usable subnets by using the following table:

7	6	5	4	3	2	1	0	= bit position
128	64	32	16	8	4	2	1	= 2^ bit position
1	1	1	1	0	0	0	0	= 4 bits

The networks are incremented by the bit position's base 2 value:

- **First network**: 192.168.0.0/28
- **Second network**: 192.168.0.16/28
- **Third network**: 192.168.0.32/28
- **Fourth network**: 192.168.0.48/28
- **Till sixteen network**: 192.168.0.240/28

Based on this, we can see that the fourth octet is where the increments are taking place. In particular, for a /28, the subnets are incremented by 16; this is due to the fact that the fourth bit position is 16 when the calculated 2^4 bit position = 16. The last step would be to identify the usable IPs that can be assigned to hosts within the network. We will use the following as a breakdown:

- **First subnet/network**: 192.168.0.0/28
- **First usable IP address**: 192.168.0.1/28
- **Last usable IP address**: 192.168.0.14/28
- **Broadcast IP address**: 192.168.0.15/28
- **Second subnet/network**: 192.168.0.16/28

Based on this, we see that two IPs are not usable. They are what we've been taking into consideration when we were calculating the hosts IPs. Similarly, we can get the usable IPs for the second subnet 192.168.0.16/28, by using the following breakdown:

- **Second subnet/network**: 192.168.0.16/28
- **First usable IP address**: 192.168.0.17/28
- **Last usable IP address**: 192.168.0.30/28
- **Broadcast IP address**: 192.168.0.31/28
- **Third subnet/network**: 192.168.0.32/28

Awesome! Based on this, we can see a pattern; we always end up with 14 usable IP addresses. Also, we can subnet a Class B address and make use of host bits to better manage our network. Let's use the following Class B address:

```
172.16.0.0/16
Subnet mask:255.255.0.0
```

Based on this, we have over 65,000 host IPs per network; this is not ideal in most environments. For instance, we want to subnet this IP in order to have 500 host IPs. This can be achieved by borrowing some host bits from the hosts portion of the address. We can use the following breakdown to assist us:

```
255.255.0.0
11111111.11111111.00000000.00000000 =/16 bits being used
```

The way we calculate the host is by moving from right to left.

Fourth octet:

7	6	5	4	3	2	1	0	= bit position
128	64	32	16	8	4	2	1	= 2^ bit position
1	1	1	1	1	1	1	1	= 8 bits total 255

$2^8 = 255-2 = 254$ hosts per network.

Third octet:

7	6	5	4	3	2	1	0	= bit position
128	64	32	16	8	4	2	1	= 2^ bit position
0	0	0	0	0	0	0	1	= 9 bit turned on

$2^9 = 512 - 2 = 510$ hosts per network.

Awesome! Based on this, it will take nine bits in order to achieve the requirements. This then would mean that we will have to borrow eight bits from the third octets to meet the requirements. We can break this down by using the following:

```
255.255.0.0
11111111.11111111.11111110.00000000 =/23 bits being used.
```

7	6	5	4	3	2	1	0	= bit position
128	64	32	16	8	4	2	1	= 2^ bit position
1	1	1	1	1	1	1	0	= 7 bit turned on

```
Eight bits in first octet + eight bits in second octet + seven bits in
third octet =23 bits
The sum of the bits turned on in the third octet 128+64+32+16+8+4+2 =254
The new subnet mask in decimal = 255.255.254.0
```

Based on these calculations, the new network would be written as follows:

```
172.16.0.0/23
The total number of subnets = 2 ^ 7 = 128 subnets created
The total number of hosts per subnet/network =2^9 - 2 = 512 -2 = 510 hosts
per subnet/network
Subnets = 172.16.0.0/23 , 172.16.2.0/23, 172.16.4.0/23, 172.16.6.0/23 -
172.16.254.0/23
```

Based on this, we have the total subnet and hosts per subnets. Now, we need to calculate the usable IP addresses per subnet. This can be done using the following breakdown:

- **First subnet/network**: 172.16.0.0/23
- **First usable IP**: 172.16.0.1/23
- **Last usable IP**: 172.16.2.254/23
- **Broadcast IP**: 172.16.2.255
- **Second subnet/network**: 172.16.2.0/23

Based on this, we can see the usable IP addresses; 172.16.2.255 is a valid IP using a /23 subnet. Also, 172.16.1.0/23 is also a valid IP address. In some operating systems, such as Windows, if you try to assign either of these two IPs, you may encounter an error. However, in Linux, everything is fair game. We increment the subnets by 2 because that is where the last network bit position ends.

We can even subnet a Class A address. For instance, let's say we want to create 100 subnets out of a single class A address. We will use the following:

```
10.0.0.0/8
255.0.0.0
```

We can do this using the table we created earlier.

Second octet:

7	6	5	4	3	2	1	0	= bit position
128	64	32	16	8	4	2	1	= 2^ bit position
1	1	1	1	1	1	1	0	= 7 bit turned on

Awesome! Based on this, we can quickly derive that we would need to borrow seven bits from the second octet in order to create 100 subnets. In fact, we will have 128 subnets. This is because we're calculating 2^7 bits in the second octet. We can then write out our subnets in the following format:

```
11111111.11111110.00000000.00000000
Subnet 255.254.0.0 /15
Subnets 10.0.0.0/15, 10.2.0.0/15, 10.4.0.0/15, 10.6.0.0/15 - 10.254.0.0/15
```

Excellent! It's that easy to subnet a Class A. Now we need to calculate the total hosts per subnet. We can use the following for this:

```
Subnet in binary
11111111.11111110.00000000.00000000
Network bits are represented by n
```

```
Host bits are represented by h
nnnnnnnn.nnnnnnnh.hhhhhhhh.hhhhhhhh
2^17 -2 = 131072 - 2 = 131070 hosts per subnet/network
```

Based on this, we can see that we garner quite a number of hosts per subnet using a /15. We can use the following in order to derive the usable IPs per subnet:

- **First subnet/network**: 10.0.0.0/15
- **First usable IP**: 10.0.0.1/15
- **Last usable IP**: 10.2.255.254/15
- **Broadcast IP**: 10.2.255.255
- **Second subnet/network**: 10.2.0.0/15

Excellent! The easiest way to calculate either of the subnets is to always multiply the network bits by 2. For calculating the total hosts, always multiply the hosts bits by 2 and then minus 2 for the network and broadcast address.

IPv6 addressing

Internet Protocol version 6 (IPv6) was developed by the **Internet Engineering Task Force (IETF)**. The IPv6 address was meant to address the shortage of IPv4 addresses. IPv4 has been completely exhausted, and companies are now willing to trade their IPv4 block of addresses for huge sums of money. An IPv6 address is 128 bits or 16 bytes in length. This gives us 2^128 of IPv6 addresses. An IPv6 address is represented in hexadecimal format. There are three types of IPv6 address.

Unicast

A unicast address specifies an identifier for a single interface on a device similar to an IPv4 address. Using IPv6, it's likely that all IPv6 traffic will be mostly unicast based.

Multicast

The concept of an IPv6 multicast address is similar to that of an IPv4 address. Packets are sent to an IPv6 multicast address and receivers that are part of a multicast group would receive the multicast packet.

Anycast

This address type was introduced in IPv6. The concept of anycast works by multiple devices being assigned the same anycast IPv6 address. When a sender sends a packet to an anycast IPv6 address, the anycast packet is routed via a routing protocol to the nearest host from the sender.

Here is an example of an IPv6 address:

```
2001:0db8:0000:0000:0000:ff00:0042:8329
```

Based on this, we can see that an IPv6 address is made up of eight sets of 16-bit or 2-byte values separated by colons. This is how we derive 128 bits or 16 bytes in length. It may seem lengthy to write an IPv6 address, but we can use a few methods to make an IPv6 address a bit smaller.

Removing leading zeros

We can remove the leading zeros from an IPv6 address, thus making it more readable:

```
2001:0db8:0000:0000:0000:ff00:0042:8329
2001:db8:0:0:0:ff00:42:8329
```

Awesome! Based on this, we made the IPv6 address much more presentable. But wait, we can also make it even smaller by using the technique described next.

Removing consecutive zeros

We can remove zeros that are contiguous in an IPv6 address and replace the zeros with a double colon. This can only be done once:

```
2001:db8::ff0:42:8329
```

Great! As we can see, the IPv6 address is now much more readable. Also, when entering an IPv6 address in a browser, we would do the following:

```
http://[ 2001:db8::ff0:42:8329]/
```

Based on this, we would enclose an IPv6 address in square brackets. There are some special types of unicast IPv6 address that are worth mentioning:

- **Global unicast addresses**: These addresses begin with `2000::/3`, as specified in RFC 4291. They are publicly routable addresses that are similar to public IPv4 addresses.
- **Link-local addresses**: These addresses begin with `fe80::/10`; they are only valid on the local physical link.
- **Site-local addresses**: These addresses begin with `fec::/10`; they are valid only within a single site. They have been discouraged by the RFC body.
- **Unique-local addresses**: These addresses begin with `fc00::/7`; they are meant to be routed within a set of cooperating sites. There were meant to replace the site-local addresses. An interesting feature of the unique-local addresses is the fact that they reduce the risk of address conflict.

There are some special IPv6 addresses similar to IPv4. Here are some reserved IPv6 addresses:

`2000::/3`	Global Unicast
`::/128`	Unspecified address
`::/0`	Default route
`::1/128`	Loopback address
`FF00::/8`	Multicast addresses

Awesome! In terms of identifying the subnet, we would have to dissect the following IPv6 address:

`2001:db8:0000:0000:0000:ff0:42:8329`

We can break down the IP address using the following method:

Global routing prefix	Subnet	Host ID
`2001:db8:0000:`	`0000:`	`0000:ff0:42:8329`
48 bits or 3bytes	16 bits or 2bytes	64 bits or 8 bytes

Based on this, the global routing prefix consists of 48 bits. The subnet is made of the next 16 bits. The host identifier is made up of the last 64 bits.

Well-known protocols

There are a number of well-known protocols that we use in our environment that we need to be aware of. For starters, when we browse the internet, we are in fact use the HTTP protocol in order to view a web page. Additionally, when we are copying a file from a server and providing authentication; in the backend, we are using some type of FTP protocol. Likewise, when we type out a URL, we are in fact using DNS for name resolution. As we can see, we are using a number of protocols in our environments. Some well-known protocols and their respective port numbers are described next.

TCP

Transmission Control Protocol (**TCP**) is a connection-oriented protocol that offers a number of services, including error checking and sequencing, to name a few. It operates at layer 4 of the OSI model, the transport layer.

HTTP

The **Hyper Text Transfer Protocol** (**HTTP**) serves up web pages on demand; it's the protocol for data communication via URLs on the internet. It uses port 80 for communication. Moreover, it rides on top of TCP.

HTTPS

The **Hyper Text Transfer Protocol Secure** (**HTTPS**) offers secure communications for URLs on the internet. It uses port 443 for communication. Moreover, its communication uses **Transport Layer Security** (**TLS**). It rides on top of TCP.

FTP

The **File Transfer Protocol** (**FTP**), is used for transferring files between a client and a server. This could be locally within a LAN or via the internet. With FTP support authentication, however, all transmissions are sent in clear text; there is no security builtin. FTP uses TCP port 20 for data traffic and port 21 for command traffic.

UDP

The **User Datagram Protocol** (**UDP**) is a connectionless protocol that offers speed but does not do any sort of error checking. It operates at layer 4 of the OSI model, the transport layer.

DNS

The **Domain Name System** (**DNS**) provides the means for translating IP addresses into user-friendly names that users can relate to. It usually uses UDP port 53 but also uses TCP port 53 whenever a request or response is larger than a single packet.

TFTP

Trivial File Transfer Protocol (**TFTP**) is used for transferring data at a fast rate. No authentication methods are supported; also, there is no error checking. TFTP uses UDP port 69.

ICMP

The **Internet Control Message Protocol** (**ICMP**) is another protocol used in the networking environment. It is usually used for troubleshooting by sending messages between various networking devices on a LAN or via the internet. There is also ICMPv6, which is used for IPv6. ICMP uses IP protocol 1, whereas ICMPv6 uses IP protocol 58.

Summary

In this chapter, we took took quite an in-depth look into the world of IPv4, and IPv6. In addition to this, we covered subnet masks and ways to identify a subnet mask. Next, we covered subnetting. We worked through a few examples and illustrated the techniques to derive the required number of hosts and also the required number of subnets. Finally, we worked with well-known protocols. We covered some of the most widely-used protocols and their port numbers.

In the next chapter, we will move on to network configuration and troubleshooting. We will work on the Linux boxes, assigning IPv4 addresses and also IPv6 addresses, looking at various ways of troubleshooting network connectivity.

Questions

1. Which address is a Class A address?

   A. 192.0.0.1
   B. 172.0.0.1
   C. 10.0.0.1
   D.None of the above

2. Which address is a Class C address?

   A. 128.0.0.1
   B. 100.0.0.2
   C. 192.168.0.1
   D. None of the above

3. Which address is known as an IPv4 loopback address?

   A. 127.0.0.1
   B. 169.0.0.1
   C. 172.16.0.1
   D. 192.1.1.1

4. Which address is an APIPA address?

   A. 169.0.0.1
   B. 172.16.0.1
   C. 10.1.1.1
   D. 192.168.1.1

5. Which address is a class B address?

   A. 128.0.0.1
   B. 10.11.1.1
   C. 127.0.0.1
   D. 223.0.0.1

6. What does a IPv6 multicast address start with?

   A. `fc0e::/8`
   B. `fce::/7`
   C. `ff00::/8`
   D. `fd0:/9`

7. Which address is an IPv6 default route?

   A. `::1/0`
   B. `::/0`
   C. `01A:00000000:00000000:00000000:00000000::9`
   D. `::1/128`

8. Which address is an IPv6 loopback address?

   A. `::0/1`
   B. `::0/0`
   C. `::1/128`
   D. `::128/128`

9. What does a link-local address start with?

   A. `ff00::/8`
   B. `fc00::/10`
   C. `fcd00::128`
   D. `fe80::/10`

10. Which port does HTTP use?

   A. TCP 10
   B. UDP 80
   C. TCP 80
   D. UDP 69

Further reading

- This site gives useful information about the IP: `https://tools.ietf.org`
- This site gives useful information about subnetting: `https://www.quora.com`
- This site gives useful information about IPv6: `https://www.ipv6.com`

16
Network Configuration and Troubleshooting

In the last chapter, we took quite an in-depth look into the world of Internet Protocol version 4 (or IPv4), and Internet Protocol version 6 or (IPv6). In addition to this, we then covered subnet masks, followed by subnetting. Finally, we worked with well-known protocols. We covered some of the most widely used protocols and their port numbers.

In this chapter, our focus moves into the configuration of IPv4 and IPv6. First, we will work with ways of configuring an IPv4 address along with its subnet mask. Next, we will look at the routing table in a Linux system; particularly looking at configuring a static route, and ending with a default route configuration. This is followed with the configuration of an IPv6 address inside a Linux system; followed by the routing table for IPv6. This is then followed by configuring an IPv6 route, ending with the configuration of a default route for IPv6. After this, our focus switches to the configuration of DNS; particularly, configuring DNS IP addresses pointing to DNS servers within a Linux environment. Finally, this chapter concludes with network troubleshooting; we look at various command-line tools that we can use in order to aid us in troubleshooting a potential connection-related issue.

In this chapter, we will cover the following topics:

- IPv4 configuration
- IPv6 configuration
- Client-side DNS
- Network troubleshooting

IPv4 configuration

There are various ways of configuring an IPv4 address within a Linux system. First, we can use a GUI utility to perform IPv4 configuration. Let's look at our Ubuntu 18 system.

We can select the network icon, then select the drop-down arrow and select **Wired Settings**, as shown in the following screenshot:

Awesome! Based on what we can see in the previous example, when we select **Wired Settings**, it will open up the **Settings** dialog box; after this, we should select the gear icon. This would then open network settings. In order to configure the IPv4 settings, we would select the **IPv4** tab, as shown in the following screenshot:

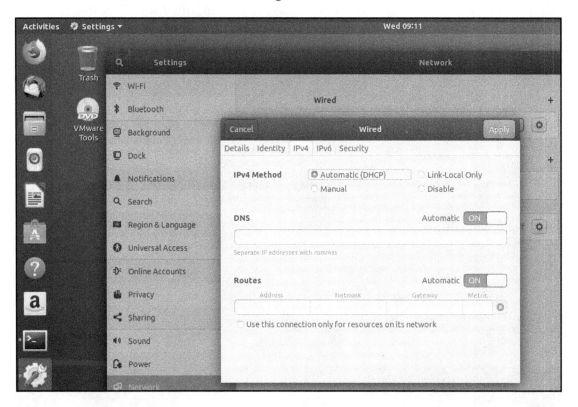

Based on the previous example, we can see that the default method for the IPv4 addressing is **Automatic (DHCP)**; this means that the system is going to acquire its IPv4 addressing information via a server on the network that is configured to issue IPv4, addressing information dynamically. For the purpose of demonstration, we want to assign our IPv4 address using the **Manual** method. After we have selected **Manual**, an **Addresses** field will appear, allowing us to enter the IPv4 addressing information, as can be seen in the following screenshot:

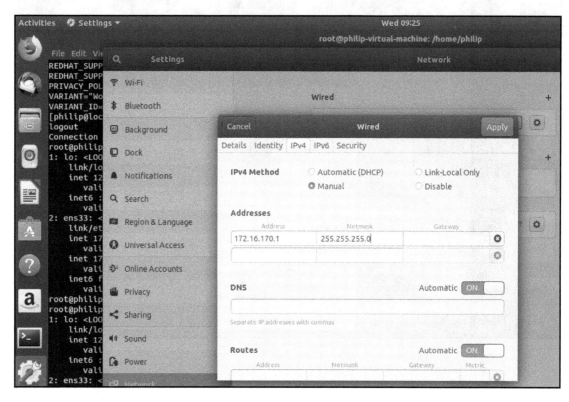

Excellent! Based on the previous screenshot, we can see that we are given the opportunity to enter the IPv4 information. We've entered an IPv4 address; additionally, we will see a text box titled **Netmask**, this is another name for a subnet mask. Once we have finished entering the IPv4 address information, we would then select the **Apply** button. An important thing to keep in mind is the fact that we're allowed to configure multiple IPv4 addresses on an interface. We can simply click inside the text box in the second row and enter an IPv4 address of our choice, as seen in the following screenshot:

Based on what we have seen in the previous example, as we enter the second IPv4 address, another text box should appear in the third row; this would happen again if we were to enter an IPv4 address in the third row. Once we're satisfied with our configuration, we should then select the **Apply** button in order to save our changes. Another way to manage the IPv4 addressing is through the shell; we can add and remove IPv4 addresses using various commands at the command prompt.

The ifconfig command

The ifconfig command can be used to manage IPv4 addressing information at the command line. We can run the ifconfig command without any options and it will display only active interfaces, as seen in the following command:

```
root@philip-virtual-machine:/home/philip# ifconfig
Command 'ifconfig' not found, but can be installed with:
apt install net-tools
root@philip-virtual-machine:/home/philip#
```

Based on what we have found in the preceding command, we see that the ifconfig utility is not installed in Ubuntu 18 by default; this can easily be remedied by running either the apt or apt-get command, as shown in the following example:

```
root@philip-virtual-machine:/home/philip# apt install net-tools
Reading package lists... Done
Building dependency tree
Reading state information... Done
The following NEW packages will be installed:
  net-tools
Setting up net-tools (1.60+git20161116.90da8a0-1ubuntu1) ...
root@philip-virtual-machine:/home/philip#
```

Some output has been omitted for brevity. Now we can run the ifconfig command once again, as shown in the following command:

```
root@philip-virtual-machine:/home/philip# ifconfig
ens33: flags=4163<UP,BROADCAST,RUNNING,MULTICAST>  mtu 1500
        inet 172.16.175.132  netmask 255.255.255.0  broadcast
172.16.175.255
        inet6 fe80::d5a6:db57:33f4:7285  prefixlen 64  scopeid 0x20<link>
        ether 00:0c:29:32:fc:d5  txqueuelen 1000  (Ethernet)
        RX packets 75738  bytes 57194615 (57.1 MB)
        RX errors 0  dropped 0  overruns 0  frame 0
        TX packets 35446  bytes 3084763 (3.0 MB)
        TX errors 0  dropped 0 overruns 0  carrier 0  collisions 0
lo: flags=73<UP,LOOPBACK,RUNNING>  mtu 65536
        inet 127.0.0.1  netmask 255.0.0.0
        inet6 ::1  prefixlen 128  scopeid 0x10<host>
        loop  txqueuelen 1000  (Local Loopback)
        RX packets 17102  bytes 1274792 (1.2 MB)
        RX errors 0  dropped 0  overruns 0  frame 0
        TX packets 17102  bytes 1274792 (1.2 MB)
        TX errors 0  dropped 0 overruns 0  carrier 0  collisions 0
root@philip-virtual-machine:/home/philip#
```

Awesome! Based on what we have found in the preceding code, we can see that we get a wealth of information; particularly, that the IPv4 addressing is located in the `inet` section. We can filter through to display only the IPv4 addressing information, as shown in the following code:

```
root@philip-virtual-machine:/home/philip# ifconfig | grep inet
        inet 172.16.175.132  netmask 255.255.255.0  broadcast
172.16.175.255
        inet6 fe80::d5a6:db57:33f4:7285  prefixlen 64  scopeid 0x20<link>
        inet 127.0.0.1  netmask 255.0.0.0
        inet6 ::1  prefixlen 128  scopeid 0x10<host>
root@philip-virtual-machine:/home/philip#
```

Based on the previous code, we can see the IPv4 addressing information in addition to some IPv6. We had previously configured two more IPv4 addresses; however, they're not displayed because, by default, only the primary IPv4 address will be displayed. We will see in the next command how we can easily view those additional IPv4 addresses. In addition to viewing only active interfaces, we can also view inactive interfaces. We would therefore pass the `-a` option, as shown in the following code:

```
root@philip-virtual-machine:/home/philip# ifconfig -a
ens33: flags=4163<UP,BROADCAST,RUNNING,MULTICAST>  mtu 1500
        inet 172.16.175.132  netmask 255.255.255.0  broadcast
172.16.175.255
        inet6 fe80::d5a6:db57:33f4:7285  prefixlen 64  scopeid 0x20<link>
        ether 00:0c:29:32:fc:d5  txqueuelen 1000  (Ethernet)
        RX packets 75817  bytes 57204880 (57.2 MB)
        RX errors 0  dropped 0  overruns 0  frame 0
        TX packets 35485  bytes 3087793 (3.0 MB)
        TX errors 0  dropped 0 overruns 0  carrier 0  collisions 0
lo: flags=73<UP,LOOPBACK,RUNNING>  mtu 65536
        inet 127.0.0.1  netmask 255.0.0.0
        inet6 ::1  prefixlen 128  scopeid 0x10<host>
        loop  txqueuelen 1000  (Local Loopback)
        RX packets 17110  bytes 1275456 (1.2 MB)
        RX errors 0  dropped 0  overruns 0  frame 0
        TX packets 17110  bytes 1275456 (1.2 MB)
        TX errors 0  dropped 0 overruns 0  carrier 0  collisions 0
root@philip-virtual-machine:/home/philip#
```

Based on what we can see in the previous example, only one physical interface is on this system so the output is the same as running the `ifconfig` command without any option. Furthermore, we can choose which interface we want to be displayed using the `ifconfig` command; we would specify the interface as shown in the following code:

```
root@philip-virtual-machine:/home/philip# ifconfig ens33
```

```
ens33: flags=4163<UP,BROADCAST,RUNNING,MULTICAST>  mtu 1500
        inet 172.16.175.132  netmask 255.255.255.0  broadcast
172.16.175.255
        inet6 fe80::d5a6:db57:33f4:7285  prefixlen 64  scopeid 0x20<link>
        ether 00:0c:29:32:fc:d5  txqueuelen 1000  (Ethernet)
        RX packets 75825  bytes 57205574 (57.2 MB)
        RX errors 0  dropped 0  overruns 0  frame 0
        TX packets 35493  bytes 3088408 (3.0 MB)
   TX errors 0 dropped 0 overruns 0 carrier 0 collisions 0
root@philip-virtual-machine:/home/philip#
```

Awesome! This is useful in situations where the system may have a lot of interfaces and you're only interested in a particular interface. We can assign an IPv4 address using the `ifconfig` command; we would simply pass the interface and the IPv4 address, as shown in the following code:

```
root@philip-virtual-machine:/home/philip# ifconfig ens33 172.10.1.1
root@philip-virtual-machine:/home/philip# ifconfig ens33
ens33: flags=4163<UP,BROADCAST,RUNNING,MULTICAST>  mtu 1500
        inet 172.10.1.1  netmask 255.255.0.0  broadcast 172.10.255.255
        inet6 fe80::d5a6:db57:33f4:7285  prefixlen 64  scopeid 0x20<link>
        ether 00:0c:29:32:fc:d5  txqueuelen 1000  (Ethernet)
        RX packets 76407  bytes 57564515 (57.5 MB)
        RX errors 0  dropped 0  overruns 0  frame 0
        TX packets 35550  bytes 3099266 (3.0 MB)
        TX errors 0  dropped 0 overruns 0  carrier 0  collisions 0
root@philip-virtual-machine:/home/philip#
```

Based on what we have found in the preceding code, we can see that the primary IPv4 address has been changed to the IPv4 address we specified. So what if we did not want to remove the previous IPv4 address? We can satisfy this requirement by creating an alias interface; it's merely a logical interface. We would then assign the second IPv4 address onto the alias interface. Here is how we would accomplish this:

```
root@philip-virtual-machine:/home/philip# ifconfig ens33 172.16.175.132/24
root@philip-virtual-machine:/home/philip# ifconfig ens33:0 172.10.1.1
root@philip-virtual-machine:/home/philip# ifconfig ens33
ens33: flags=4163<UP,BROADCAST,RUNNING,MULTICAST>  mtu 1500
        inet 172.16.175.132  netmask 255.255.255.0  broadcast
172.16.175.255
        inet6 fe80::d5a6:db57:33f4:7285  prefixlen 64  scopeid 0x20<link>
        ether 00:0c:29:32:fc:d5  txqueuelen 1000  (Ethernet)
        RX packets 76902  bytes 57781395 (57.7 MB)
        RX errors 0  dropped 0  overruns 0  frame 0
        TX packets 35579  bytes 3104505 (3.1 MB)
        TX errors 0  dropped 0 overruns 0  carrier 0  collisions 0
root@philip-virtual-machine:/home/philip# ifconfig ens33:0
```

```
ens33:0: flags=4163<UP,BROADCAST,RUNNING,MULTICAST>  mtu 1500
        inet 172.10.1.1  netmask 255.255.0.0  broadcast 172.10.255.255
        ether 00:0c:29:32:fc:d5  txqueuelen 1000  (Ethernet)
root@philip-virtual-machine:/home/philip#
```

Excellent! Based on that, we can now see that we've got the original IPv4 on the physical interface in addition to the creation of an alias interface that has the secondary IPv4 address. A point to note is the fact that when we specified the IPv4 address for the alias interface, we did not specify any subnet mask. The system auto-detected the subnet mask based on the first octet; the subnet mask was set to a Class B subnet mask of 255.255.0.0 or /16. We can remedy this by either removing the IPv4 address and then adding the IPv4 address with the subnet mask in CIDR notation, as shown in the following code:

```
root@philip-virtual-machine:/home/philip# ifconfig ens33:0 down
root@philip-virtual-machine:/home/philip# ifconfig ens33:0
ens33:0: flags=4163<UP,BROADCAST,RUNNING,MULTICAST>  mtu 1500
        ether 00:0c:29:32:fc:d5  txqueuelen 1000  (Ethernet)
root@philip-virtual-machine:/home/philip# ifconfig ens33:0 172.10.1.1/23
root@philip-virtual-machine:/home/philip# ifconfig ens33:0
ens33:0: flags=4163<UP,BROADCAST,RUNNING,MULTICAST>  mtu 1500
        inet 172.10.1.1  netmask 255.255.254.0  broadcast 172.10.1.255
        ether 00:0c:29:32:fc:d5  txqueuelen 1000  (Ethernet)
root@philip-virtual-machine:/home/philip#
```

Great job! Based on what we have found in the preceding code, in order to remove the IPv4 address, we could disable the interface by typing down. We should then add the IPv4 address with the subnet mask in CIDR notation. Added to this, the broadcast address was set for us and the system calculated the broadcast address based on the subnet mask. However, we can set the broadcast using the ifconfig command, and thus we would pass the broadcast option, as shown in the following example:

```
root@philip-virtual-machine:/home/philip# ifconfig ens33:0 broadcast
172.10.20.255
root@philip-virtual-machine:/home/philip# ifconfig ens33:0
ens33:0: flags=4163<UP,BROADCAST,RUNNING,MULTICAST>  mtu 1500
        inet 172.10.0.1  netmask 255.255.254.0  broadcast 172.10.20.255
        ether 00:0c:29:32:fc:d5  txqueuelen 1000  (Ethernet)
root@philip-virtual-machine:/home/philip#
```

Based on what we have found in the preceding code, we can see that the broadcast address was changed using the address that we supplied. Let's fix this by changing it back to its correct broadcast address, as shown in the following example:

```
root@philip-virtual-machine:/home/philip# ifconfig ens33:0 broadcast
172.10.1.255
root@philip-virtual-machine:/home/philip# ifconfig ens33:0
```

```
ens33:0: flags=4163<UP,BROADCAST,RUNNING,MULTICAST>  mtu 1500
        inet 172.10.0.1  netmask 255.255.254.0  broadcast 172.10.1.255
        ether 00:0c:29:32:fc:d5  txqueuelen 1000   (Ethernet)
root@philip-virtual-machine:/home/philip#
```

Another way to remove the IPv4 address is to pass the `del` option with the `ifconfig` command, as shown in the following example:

```
root@philip-virtual-machine:/home/philip# ifconfig ens33:0 del 172.10.0.1
root@philip-virtual-machine:/home/philip# ifconfig ens33:0
ens33:0: flags=4163<UP,BROADCAST,RUNNING,MULTICAST>  mtu 1500
        ether 00:0c:29:32:fc:d5  txqueuelen 1000   (Ethernet)
root@philip-virtual-machine:/home/philip#
```

Awesome! In the previous example, we saw that the IPv4 address was removed successfully. When we've finished working with the alias, we can remove its configuration by passing the `down` option as seen in the following code:

```
root@philip-virtual-machine:/home/philip# ifconfig ens33:0 down
root@philip-virtual-machine:/home/philip# ifconfig -a
ens33: flags=4163<UP,BROADCAST,RUNNING,MULTICAST>  mtu 1500
        inet 172.16.175.132  netmask 255.255.255.0  broadcast 172.16.175.255
        inet6 fe80::d5a6:db57:33f4:7285  prefixlen 64  scopeid 0x20<link>
        ether 00:0c:29:32:fc:d5  txqueuelen 1000   (Ethernet)
        RX packets 77475  bytes 57962754 (57.9 MB)
        RX errors 0  dropped 0  overruns 0  frame 0
        TX packets 35781  bytes 3140240 (3.1 MB)
        TX errors 0  dropped 0 overruns 0  carrier 0  collisions 0
lo: flags=73<UP,LOOPBACK,RUNNING>  mtu 65536
        inet 127.0.0.1  netmask 255.0.0.0
        inet6 ::1  prefixlen 128  scopeid 0x10<host>
        loop  txqueuelen 1000   (Local Loopback)
        RX packets 17311  bytes 1289908 (1.2 MB)
        RX errors 0  dropped 0  overruns 0  frame 0
        TX packets 17311  bytes 1289908 (1.2 MB)
        TX errors 0  dropped 0 overruns 0  carrier 0  collisions 0
root@philip-virtual-machine:/home/philip#
```

Excellent! Looking at the previous example, we can see that the interface is no longer recognized with the `ifconfig` command.

The ifup command

The `ifup` command is used to bring up or enable an interface. The interface is then able to send and receive packets.

However, only interfaces that are listed in /etc/network/interfaces are recognized by the ifup command. Let's shut down the ens33 interface and use the ifup command to bring back up the ens33 interface. Here is how we would do this:

```
root@philip-virtual-machine:/home/philip# ifconfig ens33 down
root@philip-virtual-machine:/home/philip# ifup ens33
Unknown interface ens33
root@philip-virtual-machine:/home/philip# cat /etc/network/interfaces
# interfaces(5) file used by ifup(8) and ifdown(8)
auto lo
iface lo inet loopback
root@philip-virtual-machine:/home/philip#
```

Based on what we have seen in the previous example, the ifup does not recognize the ens33 interface. This is due to the fact that the ens33 interface is not listed in the /etc/network/interfaces. We can add this entry and then it will work with the ifup command. This can be seen in the following example:

```
root@philip-virtual-machine:/home/philip# cat /etc/network/interfaces
# interfaces(5) file used by ifup(8) and ifdown(8)
auto lo
iface lo inet loopback
auto ens33
iface ens33 inet manual
root@philip-virtual-machine:/home/philip# ifup ens33
root@philip-virtual-machine:/home/philip# ifconfig
ens33: flags=4163<UP,BROADCAST,RUNNING,MULTICAST>  mtu 1500
        inet 172.16.170.1  netmask 255.255.255.0  broadcast 172.16.170.255
        inet6 fe80::d5a6:db57:33f4:7285  prefixlen 64  scopeid 0x20<link>
        ether 00:0c:29:32:fc:d5  txqueuelen 1000  (Ethernet)
        RX packets 77776  bytes 58152478 (58.1 MB)
        RX errors 0  dropped 0  overruns 0  frame 0
        TX packets 35893  bytes 3155908 (3.1 MB)
        TX errors 0  dropped 0 overruns 0  carrier 0  collisions 0
lo: flags=73<UP,LOOPBACK,RUNNING>  mtu 65536
        inet 127.0.0.1  netmask 255.0.0.0
        inet6 ::1  prefixlen 128  scopeid 0x10<host>
        loop  txqueuelen 1000  (Local Loopback)
        RX packets 17323  bytes 1290784 (1.2 MB)
        RX errors 0  dropped 0  overruns 0  frame 0
        TX packets 17323  bytes 1290784 (1.2 MB)
        TX errors 0  dropped 0 overruns 0  carrier 0  collisions 0
root@philip-virtual-machine:/home/philip#
```

Excellent! Based on what we have seen in the previous example, the `ifup` command has successfully brought up the `ens33` interface. Moreover, the IPv4 address that was assigned was the IPv4 address that we configured via the GUI network settings. In Ubuntu 18, by default all of the network settings are handled by the network-manager service; whenever we make a change via the command prompt, if the system is restarted or the network-manager service is restarted, then all of changes via the Command Prompt are lost and only changes that reside in the `network-manager.service` are used. To work around this we would stop the `network-manger.service` and then disable the network-manager service. Be aware that doing this could leave your system without connectivity if you don't save the changes for your network settings in the `/etc/network/interfaces` (these include the IP, subnet mask default gateway, DNS and IPs) for the Ubuntu 18 system.

Do not stop the `network-manager.service` unless you're sure that you've saved the network configuration in the `/etc/network/interfaces` file.

The ifdown command

The `ifdown` command can be used to bring down or disable an interface; again, only interfaces that are listed in the `/etc/network/interfaces` are recognized. Let's bring down the `ens33` interface using the `ifdown` command, as seen in the following code:

```
root@philip-virtual-machine:/home/philip# ifdown ens33
root@philip-virtual-machine:/home/philip# ifconfig
lo: flags=73<UP,LOOPBACK,RUNNING>  mtu 65536
        inet 127.0.0.1  netmask 255.0.0.0
        inet6 ::1  prefixlen 128  scopeid 0x10<host>
        loop  txqueuelen 1000  (Local Loopback)
        RX packets 17323  bytes 1290784 (1.2 MB)
       RX errors 0  dropped 0  overruns 0  frame 0
        TX packets 17323  bytes 1290784 (1.2 MB)
        TX errors 0  dropped 0 overruns 0  carrier 0  collisions 0
root@philip-virtual-machine:/home/philip#
```

Awesome! In the previous example, the `ifdown` command successfully brought down the `ens33` interface due to the fact that we added the `ens33` interface inside the `/etc/network/interfaces` file.

The ip command

The `ip` command is far more scalable than the `ifconfig` command. For instance, we can view all of the secondary IPv4 addresses that are configured on every interface with the ip command. Without any option, the `ip` command will display the options that can be used; this can be seen in the following example:

```
root@philip-virtual-machine:/home/philip# ip
Usage: ip [ OPTIONS ] OBJECT { COMMAND | help }
       ip [ -force ] -batch filename
where  OBJECT := { link | address | addrlabel | route | rule | neigh |
ntable |
tunnel | tuntap | maddress | mroute | mrule | monitor | xfrm |
netns | l2tp | fou | macsec | tcp_metrics | token | netconf | ila |
vrf | sr }
OPTIONS := { -V[ersion] | -s[tatistics] | -d[etails] | -r[esolve] |
-h[uman-readable] | -iec |
-f[amily] { inet | inet6 | ipx | dnet | mpls | bridge | link } |
-4 | -6 | -I | -D | -B | -0 |
-l[oops] { maximum-addr-flush-attempts } | -br[ief] |
-o[neline] | -t[imestamp] | -ts[hort] | -b[atch] [filename] |
-rc[vbuf] [size] | -n[etns] name | -a[ll] | -c[olor]}
root@philip-virtual-machine:/home/philip#
```

Based on the previous example, we can see a number of options that can be passed; one such option is the a option. This displays all of the addressing information, as seen in the following code:

```
root@philip-virtual-machine:/home/philip# ip a
1: lo: <LOOPBACK,UP,LOWER_UP> mtu 65536 qdisc noqueue state UNKNOWN group
default qlen 1000
    link/loopback 00:00:00:00:00:00 brd 00:00:00:00:00:00
    inet 127.0.0.1/8 scope host lo
       valid_lft forever preferred_lft forever
    inet6 ::1/128 scope host
       valid_lft forever preferred_lft forever
2: ens33: <BROADCAST,MULTICAST,UP,LOWER_UP> mtu 1500 qdisc fq_codel state
UP group default qlen 1000
    link/ether 00:0c:29:32:fc:d5 brd ff:ff:ff:ff:ff:ff
    inet 172.16.170.1/24 brd 172.16.170.255 scope global noprefixroute
ens33
        valid_lft forever preferred_lft forever
    inet 172.16.30.1/24 brd 172.16.30.255 scope global noprefixroute ens33
       valid_lft forever preferred_lft forever
root@philip-virtual-machine:/home/philip#
```

Looking at the previous example, we can immediately see multiple IPv4 addresses for the `ens33` interface. We can add an IPv4 address using the `ip` command. Here, we would pass the `add` option, as can be seen in the following code:

```
root@philip-virtual-machine:/home/philip# ip a add 172.16.20.2/24 dev ens33
root@philip-virtual-machine:/home/philip# ip a | grep ens33
2: ens33: <BROADCAST,MULTICAST,UP,LOWER_UP> mtu 1500 qdisc fq_codel state
UP group default qlen 1000
    inet 172.16.170.1/24 brd 172.16.170.255 scope global noprefixroute
ens33
    inet 172.16.30.1/24 brd 172.16.30.255 scope global noprefixroute ens33
    inet 172.16.20.2/24 scope global ens33
root@philip-virtual-machine:/home/philip#
```

Excellent! So now we can see that the IPv4 address has been added. Similarly, we can remove the IPv4 address; we would pass the `del` option, as can be seen in the following code:

```
root@philip-virtual-machine:/home/philip# ip a del 172.16.20.2/24 dev ens33
root@philip-virtual-machine:/home/philip# ip a show ens33
2: ens33: <BROADCAST,MULTICAST,UP,LOWER_UP> mtu 1500 qdisc fq_codel state
UP group default qlen 1000
    link/ether 00:0c:29:32:fc:d5 brd ff:ff:ff:ff:ff:ff
    inet 172.16.170.1/24 brd 172.16.170.255 scope global noprefixroute
ens33
        valid_lft forever preferred_lft forever
    inet 172.16.30.1/24 brd 172.16.30.255 scope global noprefixroute ens33
        valid_lft forever preferred_lft forever
root@philip-virtual-machine:/home/philip#
```

Based on that, we can see that the IPv4 address that we specified with the `del` option has been removed. Also, we used `show` option, which enabled us to specify the interface that we're interested in seeing. It is also possible to specify a broadcast address similar to the `ifconfig` command. To do this, we would pass either the `brd` or `broadcast` option, as shown in the following example:

```
root@philip-virtual-machine:/home/philip# ip a add 172.16.20.2/22 brd
255.255.252.0 dev ens33
root@philip-virtual-machine:/home/philip# ip a show ens33
2: ens33: <BROADCAST,MULTICAST,UP,LOWER_UP> mtu 1500 qdisc fq_codel state
UP group default qlen 1000
    link/ether 00:0c:29:32:fc:d5 brd ff:ff:ff:ff:ff:ff
    inet 172.16.170.1/24 brd 172.16.170.255 scope global noprefixroute
ens33
        valid_lft forever preferred_lft forever
    inet 172.16.30.1/24 brd 172.16.30.255 scope global noprefixroute ens33
```

```
        valid_lft forever preferred_lft forever
    inet 172.16.20.2/22 brd 255.255.252.0 scope global ens33
        valid_lft forever preferred_lft forever
root@philip-virtual-machine:/home/philip#
```

Excellent! Based on the previous example, we can see that the broadcast address has been assigned for the IPv4 address. In addition to this, it possible to shut down or enable an interface with the `ip` command. To do this, we would pass the `link` option of the `ip` command, as can be seen in the following code:

```
root@philip-virtual-machine:/home/philip# ip link set dev ens33 down
root@philip-virtual-machine:/home/philip# ip a show ens33 | grep DOWN
2: ens33: <BROADCAST,MULTICAST> mtu 1500 qdisc fq_codel state DOWN group
default qlen 1000
root@philip-virtual-machine:/home/philip#
```

By looking at the previous example, we can see that the link has been brought down. Similarly, we can bring up an interface by passing the `up` option, as seen in the following code:

```
root@philip-virtual-machine:/home/philip# ip link set dev ens33 up
root@philip-virtual-machine:/home/philip# ip a show ens33 | grep UP
2: ens33: <BROADCAST,MULTICAST,UP,LOWER_UP> mtu 1500 qdisc fq_codel state
UP group default qlen 1000
root@philip-virtual-machine:/home/philip#
```

Awesome! Based on the previous example, we can see that the interface was brought back up. We can also work with an alias using the IP command. For this, we would pass the `a` or `add` option with the `ip` command. This can be seen in the following code:

```
root@philip-virtual-machine:/home/philip# ip a a 172.50.5.1/24 brd + dev
ens33 label ens33:1
root@philip-virtual-machine:/home/philip# ip a show ens33
2: ens33: <BROADCAST,MULTICAST,UP,LOWER_UP> mtu 1500 qdisc fq_codel state
UP group default qlen 1000
    link/ether 00:0c:29:32:fc:d5 brd ff:ff:ff:ff:ff:ff
    inet 172.16.170.1/24 brd 172.16.170.255 scope global noprefixroute
ens33
        valid_lft forever preferred_lft forever
    inet 172.16.30.1/24 brd 172.16.30.255 scope global noprefixroute ens33
        valid_lft forever preferred_lft forever
    inet 172.50.5.1/24 brd 172.50.5.255 scope global ens33:1
        valid_lft forever preferred_lft forever
    inet6 fe80::d5a6:db57:33f4:7285/64 scope link noprefixroute
        valid_lft forever preferred_lft forever
root@philip-virtual-machine:/home/philip#
root@philip-virtual-machine:/home/philip# ifconfig
```

```
ens33: flags=4163<UP,BROADCAST,RUNNING,MULTICAST>  mtu 1500
        inet 172.16.170.1  netmask 255.255.255.0  broadcast 172.16.170.255
        inet6 fe80::d5a6:db57:33f4:7285  prefixlen 64  scopeid 0x20<link>
        ether 00:0c:29:32:fc:d5  txqueuelen 1000  (Ethernet)
        RX packets 79421  bytes 58846078 (58.8 MB)
        RX errors 0  dropped 1  overruns 0  frame 0
       TX packets 36124  bytes 3191485 (3.1 MB)
        TX errors 0  dropped 0 overruns 0  carrier 0  collisions 0
ens33:1: flags=4163<UP,BROADCAST,RUNNING,MULTICAST>  mtu 1500
        inet 172.50.5.1  netmask 255.255.255.0  broadcast 172.50.5.255
        ether 00:0c:29:32:fc:d5  txqueuelen 1000  (Ethernet)
        TX errors 0  dropped 0 overruns 0  carrier 0  collisions 0
root@philip-virtual-machine:/home/philip#
```

Awesome! Based on the previous example, we can see the alias being listed under `ens33` with the `ip` command. However, when we use the `ifconfig` command, we see the `ens33:1` listed as a separate logical interface. Once we've finished using the alias, we can remove the alias by passing the `del` option with the `ip` command, as shown in the following example:

```
root@philip-virtual-machine:/home/philip# ip a del 172.50.5.1/24 brd + dev
ens33 label ens33:1
root@philip-virtual-machine:/home/philip# ip a show ens33
2: ens33: <BROADCAST,MULTICAST,UP,LOWER_UP> mtu 1500 qdisc fq_codel state
UP group default qlen 1000
    link/ether 00:0c:29:32:fc:d5 brd ff:ff:ff:ff:ff:ff
    inet 172.16.170.1/24 brd 172.16.170.255 scope global noprefixroute
ens33
       valid_lft forever preferred_lft forever
    inet 172.16.30.1/24 brd 172.16.30.255 scope global noprefixroute ens33
       valid_lft forever preferred_lft forever
    inet6 fe80::d5a6:db57:33f4:7285/64 scope link noprefixroute
       valid_lft forever preferred_lft forever
root@philip-virtual-machine:/home/philip# ifconfig
ens33: flags=4163<UP,BROADCAST,RUNNING,MULTICAST>  mtu 1500
        inet 172.16.170.1  netmask 255.255.255.0  broadcast 172.16.170.255
        inet6 fe80::d5a6:db57:33f4:7285  prefixlen 64  scopeid 0x20<link>
        ether 00:0c:29:32:fc:d5  txqueuelen 1000  (Ethernet)
root@philip-virtual-machine:/home/philip#
```

Some output has been omitted for brevity. Based the previous example, we can see that the alias interface has been removed. In environments where the network is using VLANs or Virtual LANs, it is possible to create sub-interfaces that can map to a VLAN, effectively making the Linux system able to handle VLAN traffic that is tagged. You would need to configure the network switch to tag the traffic, which will then send the traffic inside the VLAN to the Linux system. The link between the Linux system and the switch is then treated as a `trunk` port because it can send multiple VLANs across its physical link, and the Linux system can handle the traffic because it is aware of the VLANs that we create. We would use the `ip link` with the `add` option. Here is how we would create a sub-interface and map it to a VLAN:

```
root@philip-virtual-machine:/home/philip# ip link add link ens33 name
ens33.100 type vlan id 100
root@philip-virtual-machine:/home/philip# ip a | grep ens
2: ens33: <BROADCAST,MULTICAST,UP,LOWER_UP> mtu 1500 qdisc fq_codel state
UP group default qlen 1000
    inet 172.16.170.1/24 brd 172.16.170.255 scope global noprefixroute
ens33
    inet 172.16.30.1/24 brd 172.16.30.255 scope global noprefixroute ens33
3: ens33.100@ens33: <BROADCAST,MULTICAST> mtu 1500 qdisc noop state DOWN
group default qlen 1000
root@philip-virtual-machine:/home/philip#
```

Excellent! Based on what we have seen in the previous example, the interface was created and is being treated as a separate interface. To check this out, we can assign an IPv4 address just as we would a physical interface, as shown in the following example:

```
root@philip-virtual-machine:/home/philip# ip a a 172.16.5.5/24 dev
ens33.100
root@philip-virtual-machine:/home/philip# ip a | grep ens
2: ens33: <BROADCAST,MULTICAST,UP,LOWER_UP> mtu 1500 qdisc fq_codel state
UP group default qlen 1000
    inet 172.16.170.1/24 brd 172.16.170.255 scope global noprefixroute
ens33
    inet 172.16.30.1/24 brd 172.16.30.255 scope global noprefixroute ens33
3: ens33.100@ens33: <BROADCAST,MULTICAST> mtu 1500 qdisc noop state DOWN
group default qlen 1000
    inet 172.16.5.5/24 scope global ens33.100
root@philip-virtual-machine:/home/philip#
```

Awesome! The last step would be to bring up the interface. To do this, we would pass the `up` option to the `ip link` command, as shown in the following code:

```
root@philip-virtual-machine:/home/philip# ip link set dev ens33.100 up
root@philip-virtual-machine:/home/philip# ip a | grep ens
2: ens33: <BROADCAST,MULTICAST,UP,LOWER_UP> mtu 1500 qdisc fq_codel state
```

```
UP group default qlen 1000
    inet 172.16.170.1/24 brd 172.16.170.255 scope global noprefixroute
ens33
    inet 172.16.30.1/24 brd 172.16.30.255 scope global noprefixroute ens33
3: ens33.100@ens33: <BROADCAST,MULTICAST,UP,LOWER_UP> mtu 1500 qdisc
noqueue state UP group default qlen 1000
    inet 172.16.5.5/24 scope global ens33.100
root@philip-virtual-machine:/home/philip#
```

Based on the previous example, we can see that the sub-interface that maps to VLAN 100 is now up. We can make add and remove IP address information similarly to that of a physical interface. When we've finished working with the sub-interface, we can remove it by passing the `del` option to the `ip link` command, as shown in the following example:

```
root@philip-virtual-machine:/home/philip# ip link del ens33.100
root@philip-virtual-machine:/home/philip# ip a | grep ens
2: ens33: <BROADCAST,MULTICAST,UP,LOWER_UP> mtu 1500 qdisc fq_codel state
UP group default qlen 1000
    inet 172.16.170.1/24 brd 172.16.170.255 scope global noprefixroute
ens33
    inet 172.16.30.1/24 brd 172.16.30.255 scope global noprefixroute ens33
root@philip-virtual-machine:/home/philip#
```

Wonderful! Looking at that example, we can see that the sub-interface is no longer present. Another useful purpose of the `ip` command is the ability to view the statistics of an interface. We would pass the `-s` and the `ls` option with the `ip link` command, as shown in the following code:

```
root@philip-virtual-machine:/home/philip# ip -s link ls ens33
2: ens33: <BROADCAST,MULTICAST,UP,LOWER_UP> mtu 1500 qdisc fq_codel state
UP mode DEFAULT group default qlen 1000
    link/ether 00:0c:29:32:fc:d5 brd ff:ff:ff:ff:ff:ff
    RX: bytes  packets  errors  dropped overrun mcast
    58851742   79482    0       1       0       0
    TX: bytes  packets  errors  dropped carrier collsns
    3199078    36174    0       0       0       0
root@philip-virtual-machine:/home/philip#
```

Based on the previous example, we can see statistics regarding packets received and transmitted; we can even see frame, missed, and CRC errors by adding another `-s` option to the current command, as shown in the following code:

```
root@philip-virtual-machine:/home/philip# ip -s -s link ls ens33
2: ens33: <BROADCAST,MULTICAST,UP,LOWER_UP> mtu 1500 qdisc fq_codel state
UP mode DEFAULT group default qlen 1000
    link/ether 00:0c:29:32:fc:d5 brd ff:ff:ff:ff:ff:ff
    RX: bytes  packets  errors  dropped overrun mcast
```

```
    58852018    79485      0          1         0         0
  RX errors:   length      crc      frame      fifo     missed
                0          0          0         0         0
    TX: bytes   packets   errors   dropped  carrier  collsns
    3199078     36174      0          0         0         0
  TX errors:   aborted    fifo     window heartbeat transns
                0          0          0         0         20
root@philip-virtual-machine:/home/philip#
```

Excellent! Based on the previous example, we can see counters pertaining to CRC, frames, and so on.

Configuring IPv4 routing

So far, we've been assigning IPv4 addressing information but we've not specified any type of routing information. We can view the current routing table by using a number of commands. For instance, we can use the `route` command to display the routing table, as shown in the following example:

```
root@philip-virtual-machine:/home/philip# route
Kernel IP routing table
Destination     Gateway          Genmask          Flags Metric Ref    Use
Iface
link-local      0.0.0.0          255.255.0.0      U     1000   0      0
ens33
172.16.30.0     0.0.0.0          255.255.255.0    U     100    0      0
ens33
172.16.170.0    0.0.0.0          255.255.255.0    U     100    0      0
ens33
root@philip-virtual-machine:/home/philip#
```

Based on what we have seen in the previous example, only connected routes that map to the configured IPv4 addresses are displayed. It is also possible to display the routing table using the `ip` command. Here, we would pass the `route` option, as shown in the following command:

```
root@philip-virtual-machine:/home/philip# ip route
169.254.0.0/16 dev ens33 scope link metric 1000
172.16.30.0/24 dev ens33 proto kernel scope link src 172.16.30.1 metric 100
172.16.170.0/24 dev ens33 proto kernel scope link src 172.16.170.1 metric
100
root@philip-virtual-machine:/home/philip#
```

Based on the previous example, we can see similar information to that of the route command. Another command that can be used to print the routing table is the netstat command. To do this, we would pass the -r option, as shown in the following example:

```
root@philip-virtual-machine:/home/philip# netstat -r
Kernel IP routing table
Destination     Gateway          Genmask          Flags   MSS Window  irtt
Iface
link-local      0.0.0.0          255.255.0.0      U         0 0         0
ens33
172.16.30.0     0.0.0.0          255.255.255.0    U         0 0         0
ens33
172.16.170.0    0.0.0.0          255.255.255.0    U         0 0         0
ens33
root@philip-virtual-machine:/home/philip#
```

Great job! In the previous example, the routing table has been printed once again. We have not configured a default route; a default route is used for reaching hosts who are not on the same subnet, or who reside outside of the LAN. We will use the ip route command with the add and default options to define a default route. The following example shows how this would look:

```
root@philip-virtual-machine:/home/philip# ip route add default via
172.16.175.1
root@philip-virtual-machine:/home/philip# ip route | grep def
default via 172.16.175.1 dev ens33
root@philip-virtual-machine:/home/philip#
root@philip-virtual-machine:/home/philip# route  | grep UG
default         _gateway         0.0.0.0            UG   0       0         0
ens33
root@philip-virtual-machine:/home/philip#
```

Awesome! Based on the previous example, we can see that a default route has been added. When we ran the route command, we saw the word _gateway instead of the IPv4 address; we can pass the -n option to view the numerical value of the default gateway. The following example demonstrates this:

```
root@philip-virtual-machine:/home/philip# route -n | grep UG
0.0.0.0         172.16.175.1     0.0.0.0            UG   0       0         0
ens33
root@philip-virtual-machine:/home/philip#
```

Excellent! We can also create a static route by specifying the subnet that we are trying to reach. Here is how we would accomplish this:

```
root@philip-virtual-machine:/home/philip# ip route add 10.20.0.0/24 via
172.16.30.1
root@philip-virtual-machine:/home/philip# ip route | grep via
default via 172.16.175.1 dev ens33
10.20.0.0/24 via 172.16.30.1 dev ens33
root@philip-virtual-machine:/home/philip#
root@philip-virtual-machine:/home/philip# route -n | grep UG
0.0.0.0         172.16.175.1    0.0.0.0         UG    0    0    0
ens33
10.20.0.0       172.16.30.1     255.255.255.0   UG    0    0    0
ens33
root@philip-virtual-machine:/home/philip#
```

Excellent! Based on the previous example, we can now see the static route added for the `10.20.0.0/24` subnet via `172.16.30.1`. When we no longer desire a route, we can remove it using the `ip route` command with the `del` option, as shown in the following command:

```
root@philip-virtual-machine:/home/philip# ip route del 10.20.0.0/24 via
172.16.30.1
root@philip-virtual-machine:/home/philip# ip route | grep via
default via 172.16.175.1 dev ens33
root@philip-virtual-machine:/home/philip# route -n | grep UG
0.0.0.0         172.16.175.1    0.0.0.0         UG    0    0    0
ens33
root@philip-virtual-machine:/home/philip#
```

As we can see in the previous example, the static route for `10.20.0.0/24` is no longer present in our routing table.

IPv6 configuration

We can configure IPv6 addressing information in a similar way to that used for IPv4. To view only IPv6 addresses, we can use the `ip` command and pass the `-6` option, as shown in the following command:

```
root@philip-virtual-machine:/home/philip# ip -6 a
1: lo: <LOOPBACK,UP,LOWER_UP> mtu 65536 state UNKNOWN qlen 1000
    inet6 ::1/128 scope host
        valid_lft forever preferred_lft forever
2: ens33: <BROADCAST,MULTICAST,UP,LOWER_UP> mtu 1500 state UP qlen 1000
```

```
        inet6 fe80::d5a6:db57:33f4:7285/64 scope link noprefixroute
           valid_lft forever preferred_lft forever
root@philip-virtual-machine:/home/philip#
```

Based on the previous example, we can see only IPv6 information, particularly the link-local address, which starts with `fe80`. We can add an IPv6 address using the `ip` command. We would add an IPv6 address in the following way:

```
root@philip-virtual-machine:/home/philip# ip -6 a a 2001:0db8:0:f101::1/64
dev ens33
root@philip-virtual-machine:/home/philip# ip -6 a show ens33
2: ens33: <BROADCAST,MULTICAST,UP,LOWER_UP> mtu 1500 state UP qlen 1000
    inet6 2001:db8:0:f101::1/64 scope global
        valid_lft forever preferred_lft forever
    inet6 fe80::d5a6:db57:33f4:7285/64 scope link noprefixroute
        valid_lft forever preferred_lft forever
root@philip-virtual-machine:/home/philip#
```

Excellent! In the previous example, we can see that the IPv6 address was assigned to the `ens33` interface. Also, we could use the `ifconfig` command to display the IPv6 addressing information, as shown in the following example:

```
root@philip-virtual-machine:/home/philip# ifconfig | egrep 'ens|inet6'
ens33: flags=4163<UP,BROADCAST,RUNNING,MULTICAST>  mtu 1500
        inet6 2001:db8:0:f101::1  prefixlen 64  scopeid 0x0<global>
        inet6 fe80::d5a6:db57:33f4:7285  prefixlen 64  scopeid 0x20<link>
        inet6 ::1  prefixlen 128  scopeid 0x10<host>
root@philip-virtual-machine:/home/philip#
```

Looking at the previous example, we can see the IPv6 information in the `inet6` section. It is also possible to configure multiple IPv6 addresses. For this, we would simply use the `ip` with `-6` command, as shown in the following command:

```
root@philip-virtual-machine:/home/philip# ip -6 a a 2001:0db8:0:f102::2/64
dev ens33
root@philip-virtual-machine:/home/philip# ip -6 a show ens33
2: ens33: <BROADCAST,MULTICAST,UP,LOWER_UP> mtu 1500 state UP qlen 1000
    inet6 2001:db8:0:f102::2/64 scope global
        valid_lft forever preferred_lft forever
    inet6 2001:db8:0:f101::1/64 scope global
        valid_lft forever preferred_lft forever
    inet6 fe80::d5a6:db57:33f4:7285/64 scope link noprefixroute
        valid_lft forever preferred_lft forever
root@philip-virtual-machine:/home/philip#
```

Based on that example, we can see that the second IPv6 address has been added. When we no longer need an IPv6 address, we can pass the `del` option with the `ip` command, as shown in the following example:

```
root@philip-virtual-machine:/home/philip# ip -6 a del
2001:0db8:0:f102::2/64 dev ens33
root@philip-virtual-machine:/home/philip# ip -6 a show ens33
2: ens33: <BROADCAST,MULTICAST,UP,LOWER_UP> mtu 1500 state UP qlen 1000
    inet6 2001:db8:0:f101::1/64 scope global
        valid_lft forever preferred_lft forever
    inet6 fe80::d5a6:db57:33f4:7285/64 scope link noprefixroute
        valid_lft forever preferred_lft forever
root@philip-virtual-machine:/home/philip#
```

Excellent! In the previous example, the IPv6 address was removed, which we specified with the `del` option.

Configuring IPv6 routing

We've looked at the IPv4 routing table but there is also an IPv6 routing table. We can use the same `ip route` command with the `-6` option, as shown in the following example:

```
root@philip-virtual-machine:/home/philip# ip -6 route
2001:db8:0:f101::/64 dev ens33 proto kernel metric 256 pref medium
fe80::/64 dev ens33 proto kernel metric 100 pref medium
fe80::/64 dev ens33 proto kernel metric 256 pref medium
root@philip-virtual-machine:/home/philip#
```

As we have seen in the previous example, only the IPv6 routing information is being displayed. There is currently no default gateway configured for IPv6 in this system. We can fix this by using the `ip route` command and passing the `-6` and `add` options, as shown in the following example:

```
root@philip-virtual-machine:/home/philip# ip -6 route add ::/0 via
2001:db8:0:f101::2
root@philip-virtual-machine:/home/philip# ip -6 route
2001:db8:0:f101::/64 dev ens33 proto kernel metric 256 pref medium
fe80::/64 dev ens33 proto kernel metric 100 pref medium
fe80::/64 dev ens33 proto kernel metric 256 pref medium
default via 2001:db8:0:f101::2 dev ens33 metric 1024 pref medium
root@philip-virtual-machine:/home/philip#
```

Awesome! In the previous example, we can see that a default route was added for IPv6. We can also see the IPv6 routing information using the route command. For this, we would pass the -6 option, as shown in the next example:

```
root@philip-virtual-machine:/home/philip# route -6 | grep UG
[::]/0                          _gateway              UG    1024 1      0
ens33
root@philip-virtual-machine:/home/philip#
root@philip-virtual-machine:/home/philip# route -6 -n | grep UG
::/0                    2001:db8:0:f101::2            UG    1024 1      0
ens33
root@philip-virtual-machine:/home/philip#
```

Based on the previous example, we can see the IPv6 address of the default gateway. It is also possible to configure a static route for an IPv6 subnet, which is on a different IPv6 subnet, or outside the LAN. Here is how we would add a static route for an IPv6 subnet:

```
root@philip-virtual-machine:/home/philip# ip -6 route add
2001:db8:2222:1::/64 via 2001:db8:0:f101::2
root@philip-virtual-machine:/home/philip# ip -6 route | grep via
2001:db8:2222:1::/64 via 2001:db8:0:f101::2 dev ens33 metric 1024 pref
medium
default via 2001:db8:0:f101::2 dev ens33 metric 1024 pref medium
root@philip-virtual-machine:/home/philip# route -6 | grep UG
2001:db8:2222:1::/64            _gateway              UG    1024 1      0
ens33
[::]/0                          _gateway              UG    1024 1      0
ens33
root@philip-virtual-machine:/home/philip# route -6 -n | grep UG
2001:db8:2222:1::/64    2001:db8:0:f101::2            UG    1024 1      0
ens33
::/0                    2001:db8:0:f101::2            UG    1024 1      0
ens33
root@philip-virtual-machine:/home/philip#
```

Great job! In the previous example, you can see that we've added a static route for an IPv6 subnet. Similarly, we can remove a static route for an IPv6 subnet by passing the `del` option with the `ip route` command, as shown in the following example:

```
root@philip-virtual-machine:/home/philip# ip -6 route del
2001:db8:2222:1::/64 via 2001:db8:0:f101::2
root@philip-virtual-machine:/home/philip# route -6 -n | grep UG
::/0                            2001:db8:0:f101::2        UG    1024 1      0
ens33
root@philip-virtual-machine:/home/philip#
```

Excellent!

Client-side DNS

Up to this point, we've been assigning various IPv4 and IPv6 addressing information but this does not mean that we can browse the internet. For that, we will need to configure the DNS information; particularly, we need to tell the Linux system which DNS server to use when attempting to venture out to the internet. As we've seen earlier in this chapter, there are various text boxes that we can fill out for IPv4, IPv6, gateway and DNS information using a GUI utility. Here, we will look at configuring the DNS information at the command prompt; particularly the `/etc/resolv.conf` file. Here is the content of the `/etc/resolv.conf` file:

```
root@philip-virtual-machine:/home/philip# cat /etc/resolv.conf
# This file is managed by man:systemd-resolved(8). Do not edit.
nameserver 127.0.0.53
root@philip-virtual-machine:/home/philip#
```

Some output has been omitted for brevity. As can be seen in the previous example, the format for defining DNS server in Ubuntu 18 is as follows:

```
nameserver <DNS IP>
```

Based on that code, we can specify our DNS server IPs in this file. Let's see if we can browse the internet, as shown in the following screenshot:

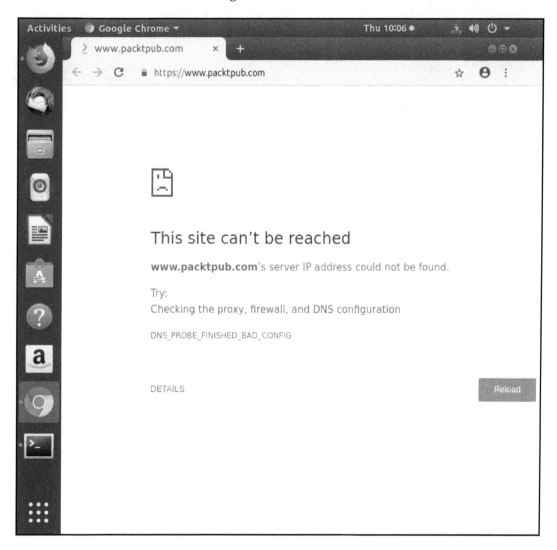

Based on what we have seen in the previous example, we're unable to reach out to the internet. Let's put in a DNS server's IP address inside /etc/resolv.conf by using an editor such as vi or nano; the following entry is what we want to put in:

```
root@philip-virtual-machine:/home/philip# cat /etc/resolv.conf | grep name
nameserver 8.8.8.8
root@philip-virtual-machine:/home/philip#
```

As we have seen in the previous example, we've added a DNS entry. Now, when we refresh the page, we will see the content start to populate the page as shown in the following screenshot:

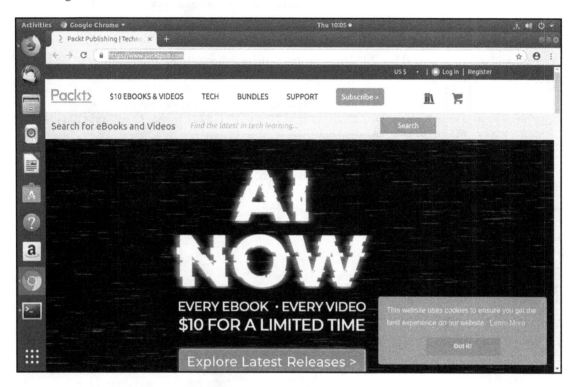

Excellent! We can also create local DNS entries for local name resolution inside the /etc/hosts file. Here is the content of the /etc/hosts file:

```
root@philip-virtual-machine:/home/philip# cat /etc/hosts
127.0.0.1               localhost
127.0.1.1               philip-virtual-machine
# The following lines are desirable for IPv6 capable hosts
::1     ip6-localhost ip6-loopback
fe00::0 ip6-localnet
ff00::0 ip6-mcastprefix
ff02::1 ip6-allnodes
ff02::2 ip6-allrouters
root@philip-virtual-machine:/home/philip#
```

We could edit this file and add an entry for the Fedora 28 system using a text editor such as vi or nano. Here is an example of sample entry:

```
root@philip-virtual-machine:/home/philip# cat /etc/hosts | grep Fed
172.16.175.129  Fedora28
root@philip-virtual-machine:/home/philip#
```

Awesome! Now we would be able to meet the Fedora 28 system by using either its IP address or its name, as shown in the following example:

```
root@philip-virtual-machine:/home/philip# ssh philip@Fedora28
The authenticity of host 'fedora28 (172.16.175.129)' can't be established.
ECDSA key fingerprint is
SHA256:DqRh+J43GfuMKC0i+QHkMU+V2MpephHZqSYANA362hg.
Are you sure you want to continue connecting (yes/no)? yes
Warning: Permanently added 'fedora28' (ECDSA) to the list of known hosts.
philip@fedora28's password:
root@philip-virtual-machine:/home/philip#
```

Excellent!

Network troubleshooting

We can use a number of tools to aid us in troubleshooting a network connection issue, ranging from GUI utilities to command-line tools. Our focus will be troubleshooting using the command-line tools available to us.

The ping command

The `ping` utility uses the ICMP protocol to send out requests and receive replies. We can use the ping utility to test for basic reachability between systems locally or out on the internet. The basic syntax for the ping utility is:

```
ping  <DNS name or IPv4>
```

Based on what we have seen in the previous example, we can now try out the `ping` utility, as shown in the following example:

```
root@philip-virtual-machine:/home/philip# ping Fedora28
PING Fedora28 (172.16.175.129) 56(84) bytes of data.
64 bytes from Fedora28 (172.16.175.129): icmp_seq=1 ttl=64 time=0.299 ms
64 bytes from Fedora28 (172.16.175.129): icmp_seq=2 ttl=64 time=0.341 ms
64 bytes from Fedora28 (172.16.175.129): icmp_seq=3 ttl=64 time=0.733 ms
```

```
64 bytes from Fedora28 (172.16.175.129): icmp_seq=4 ttl=64 time=0.957 ms
64 bytes from Fedora28 (172.16.175.129): icmp_seq=5 ttl=64 time=0.224 ms
^C
--- Fedora28 ping statistics ---
6 packets transmitted, 6 received, 0% packet loss, time 5064ms
rtt min/avg/max/mdev = 0.224/0.564/0.957/0.287 ms
root@philip-virtual-machine:/home/philip#
```

As we have seen in the previous example, the `ping` utility will run until it is stopped by the user using *CTRL + C*; this is different in a Windows environment, where only four ICMP echo request/replies are seen.

The ping6 command

It is also possible to test for potential connectivity issues for IPv6. We would use the `ping6` command for this; the syntax for the `ping6` command is as follows:

```
ping6   <DNS name or IPv6>
```

Based on what we have seen in the previous example, we would simply need to specify either the DNS name or IPv6 address of the target system. Here is how we use the `ping6` command:

```
root@philip-virtual-machine:/home/philip# ping6 2001:db8:0:f101::3
PING 2001:db8:0:f101::3(2001:db8:0:f101::3) 56 data bytes
64 bytes from 2001:db8:0:f101::3: icmp_seq=1 ttl=64 time=0.355 ms
64 bytes from 2001:db8:0:f101::3: icmp_seq=2 ttl=64 time=0.289 ms
64 bytes from 2001:db8:0:f101::3: icmp_seq=3 ttl=64 time=0.222 ms
64 bytes from 2001:db8:0:f101::3: icmp_seq=4 ttl=64 time=0.596 ms
^C
--- 2001:db8:0:f101::3 ping statistics ---
4 packets transmitted, 4 received, 0% packet loss, time 3052ms
rtt min/avg/max/mdev = 0.222/0.365/0.596/0.142 ms
root@philip-virtual-machine:/home/philip#
```

Awesome!

The traceroute command

We can use the `traceroute` command to test for potential connectivity issues. The `traceroute` command displays each device that is on the path of the destination system; each device is considered as a `hop`. The basic syntax for the `traceroute` is as follows:

```
traceroute <DNS name or IPv4>
```

You can see that we simply need to specify either the DNS name or IPv4 address of the target system. This is shown in the following example:

```
root@philip-virtual-machine:/home/philip# traceroute Fedora28
Command 'traceroute' not found, but can be installed with:
apt install inetutils-traceroute
apt install traceroute
root@philip-virtual-machine:/home/philip# apt install inetutils-traceroute
update-alternatives: using /usr/bin/inetutils-traceroute to provide
/usr/bin/traceroute (traceroute) in auto mode
Processing triggers for man-db (2.8.3-2) ...
root@philip-virtual-machine:/home/philip#
```

As we have seen in the previous example, the `traceroute` utility is not installed by default in Ubuntu 18; we quickly remedied this by installing the `inetutils-traceroute` package. Now let's try to run the `traceroute` command once again, as shown in the following example:

```
root@philip-virtual-machine:/home/philip# traceroute Fedora28
traceroute to Fedora28 (172.16.175.129), 64 hops max
 1 172.16.175.129 0.199ms 0.199ms 0.251ms
root@philip-virtual-machine:/home/philip#
```

Awesome! Based on the previous example, we can see that the device is one hop away from the Ubuntu system.

The traceroute6 command

It is also possible to test for a potential bottleneck between systems for IPv6 using the `traceroute6` command. The basic syntax for the `traceroute6` command is as follows:

```
traceroute6  <DNS name or IPv6>
```

Based on what we have seen in the previous example, we would simply specify either the DNS name or IPv6 address of the target system. The following example shows how we would use the `traceroute6` command:

```
root@philip-virtual-machine:/home/philip# traceroute6 2001:db8:0:f101::2
traceroute to 2001:db8:0:f101::2 (2001:db8:0:f101::2) from
2001:db8:0:f101::1, 30 hops max, 24 byte packets
sendto: Invalid argument
 1 traceroute: wrote 2001:db8:0:f101::2 24 chars, ret=-1
^C
root@philip-virtual-machine:/home/philip#
```

So we can see that the `traceroute6` command works in a similar way to that of the `traceroute` command.

The netstat command

We can use the `netstat` command to troubleshoot a number of different issues. We've seen earlier in this chapter, when we covered routing, that we needed to pass the `-r` option to view the routing table. Well, we can also use the `netstat` command to view active connections. This is especially useful in server environments when we are running various programs utilizing various ports; these ports could be either TCP or UDP ports. We can pass the `-n` option, which shows numerical address(s); the `-t` option, which shows TCP connections; the `-l`, which shows what sockets are listening; and the `-p` option, which shows the program ID and program name. These options work well together when trying to narrow down your TCP ports. Here is how this would look for TCP:

Excellent! Looking at the previous example, we can see a number of programs running, including `dns`, `sshd`, `ryslogd`, to name a few. Similarly, we can view UDP connections; we would pass the `nulp` options. The `-u` means UDP, as shown in the following example:

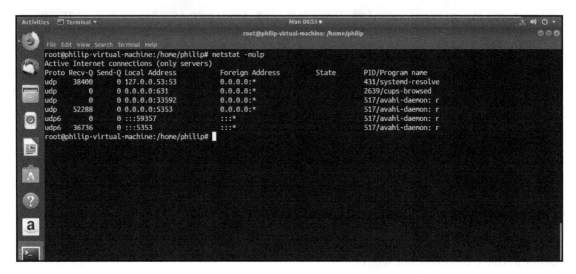

Excellent! Looking at the previous example, we can see quite a few services listening for connection, the `systemd-resolve` (port 53) being one of them.

The tracepath command

The `tracepath` command is another method for testing potential bottlenecks between systems. It works in a similar way to the `traceroute` command. The basic syntax for the `tracepath` command is as follows:

```
tracepath <DNS name or IPv4>
```

Based on what we have seen in the previous example, we would simply need to specify either the DNS name or IPv4 address in order to use the `tracepath` command. This is shown in the following command:

```
root@philip-virtual-machine:/home/philip# tracepath Fedora28
 1?: [LOCALHOST]                pmtu 1500
 1:  Fedora28                   0.309ms reached
 1:  Fedora28                   0.201ms reached
     Resume: pmtu 1500 hops 1 back 1
root@philip-virtual-machine:/home/philip#
```

In the previous example, the `pmtu` or `Path MTU` is shown in addition to number of hop(s) to the destination device.

The tracepath -6 command

Similarly to the `tracepath` command, `tracepath` with the `-6` option is another method for testing potential bottlenecks between systems using IPv6 addressing. The basic syntax for the `tracepath` with the `-6` option is as follows:

```
tracepath -6 <DNS name or IPv6>
```

Based on what we have seen in the previous example, we would simply need to specify either the DNS name or IPv6 address in order to use `tracepath` with the `-6` option. This is shown in the following example:

```
root@philip-virtual-machine:/home/philip# tracepath -6 2001:db8:0:f101::3
 1?: [LOCALHOST]                        0.012ms pmtu 1500
 1:  2001:db8:0:f101::3                             0.384ms reached
 1:  2001:db8:0:f101::3                             0.352ms reached
     Resume: pmtu 1500 hops 1 back 1
root@philip-virtual-machine:/home/philip#
```

Excellent! Based on what we have seen in the previous example, we can see that the `tracepath` with the `-6` option works in a similar way to the `tracepath` command for IPv4.

The nmap command

The Network Mapper, or nmap, can also troubleshoot potential connection issues by using the `nmap` command; this command scans a given system and displays services and their respective port numbers that are open for the system specified with the `nmap` command.

The basic syntax for the `nmap` command is as follows:

```
nmap <option>  <IP of destination>
```

Based on what we have seen in the previous example, we would specify the option and the IP of the destination system that we are troubleshooting as shown in the following example:

```
root@Linuxplus:/home/philip# nmap -A -T4 172.16.175.129
Nmap scan report for Fedora28 (172.16.175.129)
Host is up (0.00066s latency).
Not shown: 845 closed ports, 154 filtered ports
PORT   STATE SERVICE VERSION
22/tcp open  ssh       OpenSSH 7.7 (protocol 2.0)
| ssh-hostkey:
|   2048 b8:02:f8:79:f4:d8:77:b4:26:de:70:93:e8:66:94:69 (RSA)
|   256 9b:e0:d1:33:3b:08:02:bf:fd:c6:48:c1:47:7d:9c:9e (ECDSA)
|_  256 cd:f8:47:d1:75:95:e3:59:f3:b6:c0:12:a0:8b:d1:0e (EdDSA)
MAC Address: 00:0C:29:04:35:BD (VMware)
Device type: general purpose
Running: Linux 3.X|4.X
OS CPE: cpe:/o:linux:linux_kernel:3 cpe:/o:linux:linux_kernel:4
OS details: Linux 3.10 - 4.8
Network Distance: 1 hop
TRACEROUTE
HOP RTT     ADDRESS
1   0.66 ms Fedora28 (172.16.175.129)
OS and Service detection performed. Please report any incorrect results at
https://nmap.org/submit/ .
Nmap done: 1 IP address (1 host up) scanned in 49.30 seconds
root@Linuxplus:/home/philip#
```

Excellent! Based on the previous example, we can see which service and their respective port number is running on the destination system. The -A option is used to display OS and version detection; the -T4 option is used for faster execution. You should seek permission from the owner or administrator of the destination system or network prior to running the `nmap` command; this is true especially in corporate environments where there are policies governing the use of a given network.

 Always seek permission before performing any kind of port scan in a network.

The dig command

So far, we've looked at ways of troubleshooting connectivity issues, but DNS issues could pose a risk too. We can use the `dig` utility to perform DNS lookups for a given domain. The basic syntax for the `dig` command is as follows:

```
dig <domain>
```

As you can see, we simply specify the domain that we want to perform a lookup against.

Here is how we would perform a simple lookup:

```
root@philip-virtual-machine:/home/philip# dig www.packtpub.com
; <<>> DiG 9.11.3-1ubuntu1-Ubuntu <<>> www.packtpub.com
;; global options: +cmd
;; Got answer:
;; ->>HEADER<<- opcode: QUERY, status: NOERROR, id: 39472
;; flags: qr rd ra; QUERY: 1, ANSWER: 2, AUTHORITY: 0, ADDITIONAL: 1
;; OPT PSEUDOSECTION:
; EDNS: version: 0, flags:; udp: 512
;; QUESTION SECTION:
;www.packtpub.com.                      IN        A
;; ANSWER SECTION:
www.packtpub.com.       14037     IN         CNAME
varnish.packtpub.com.
varnish.packtpub.com.   14049     IN         A         83.166.169.231
;; Query time: 77 msec
;; SERVER: 8.8.8.8#53(8.8.8.8)
;; WHEN: Wed Mar 06 16:21:23 -04 2019
;; MSG SIZE  rcvd: 83
root@philip-virtual-machine:/home/philip#
```

Excellent! Based on the previous example, we can see the DNS record for the given domain; in particular we can see the A records. The server that answered our query is `8.8.8.8`, which we configured in the `/etc/resolv.conf`. However, we can use a different DNS server by passing the @ with the `dig` command, as shown in the following example:

```
root@philip-virtual-machine:/home/philip# dig @8.8.4.4 packtpub.com
; <<>> DiG 9.11.3-1ubuntu1-Ubuntu <<>> @8.8.4.4 packtpub.com
; (1 server found)
;; global options: +cmd
;; Got answer:
;; ->>HEADER<<- opcode: QUERY, status: NOERROR, id: 16754
;; flags: qr rd ra; QUERY: 1, ANSWER: 1, AUTHORITY: 0, ADDITIONAL: 1
;; OPT PSEUDOSECTION:
; EDNS: version: 0, flags:; udp: 512
;; QUESTION SECTION:
```

```
;packtpub.com.                                          IN        A
;; ANSWER SECTION:
packtpub.com.                    21599    IN        A
83.166.169.231
;; Query time: 116 msec
;; SERVER: 8.8.4.4#53(8.8.4.4)
;; WHEN: Wed Mar 06 16:25:29 -04 2019
;; MSG SIZE  rcvd: 57
root@philip-virtual-machine:/home/philip#
```

As we can see from the previous example, we have specified a different DNS server to answer our query. Adding to this, we can also look for particular DNS information such as the name server or NS by passing NS with the dig command, as shown in the following example:

```
root@philip-virtual-machine:/home/philip# dig @8.8.4.4 packtpub.com NS
; <<>> DiG 9.11.3-1ubuntu1-Ubuntu <<>> @8.8.4.4 packtpub.com NS
; (1 server found)
;; global options: +cmd
;; Got answer:
;; ->>HEADER<<- opcode: QUERY, status: NOERROR, id: 40936
;; flags: qr rd ra; QUERY: 1, ANSWER: 4, AUTHORITY: 0, ADDITIONAL: 1
;; OPT PSEUDOSECTION:
; EDNS: version: 0, flags:; udp: 512
;; QUESTION SECTION:
;packtpub.com.                                          IN
NS
;; ANSWER SECTION:
packtpub.com.                    21599    IN        NS
dns2.easydns.net.
packtpub.com.                    21599    IN        NS
dns3.easydns.org.
packtpub.com.                    21599    IN        NS
dns4.easydns.info.
packtpub.com.                    21599    IN        NS
dns1.easydns.com.
;; Query time: 105 msec
;; SERVER: 8.8.4.4#53(8.8.4.4)
;; WHEN: Wed Mar 06 16:26:06 -04 2019
;; MSG SIZE  rcvd: 159
root@philip-virtual-machine:/home/philip#
```

Excellent! In the previous example, we can see the name servers for the given domain.

The whois command

It is also possible to gain information for a domain using the `whois` command. The basic syntax for the `whois` command is as follows:

```
whois <domain>
```

Thus we can simply pass a domain name with the `whois` command and get valuable information for a given domain, as shown in the following example:

```
root@Linuxplus:/home/philip# whois packtpub.com
   Domain Name: PACKTPUB.COM
   Registry Domain ID: 97706392_DOMAIN_COM-VRSN
   Registrar WHOIS Server: whois.easydns.com
   Registrar URL: http://www.easydns.com
   Updated Date: 2015-08-10T20:01:35Z
   Creation Date: 2003-05-09T14:34:02Z
  Registry Expiry Date: 2024-05-09T14:34:02Z
   Registrar: easyDNS Technologies, Inc.
   Registrar IANA ID: 469
   Registrar Abuse Contact Email:
   Registrar Abuse Contact Phone:
   Domain Status: clientTransferProhibited
https://icann.org/epp#clientTransferProhibited
   Domain Status: clientUpdateProhibited
https://icann.org/epp#clientUpdateProhibited
   Name Server: DNS1.EASYDNS.COM
   Name Server: DNS2.EASYDNS.NET
   Name Server: DNS3.EASYDNS.ORG
   Name Server: DNS4.EASYDNS.INFO
You have 20 lookups left today
root@Linuxplus:/home/philip#
```

Awesome! Some output has been omitted for brevity. The previous example shows that we are given a wealth of information for the given domain.

The hostname command

This command is simply used for setting or returning the DNS name of the system and the IP address of the system. The basic syntax is as follows:

```
hostname <options> <new hostname>
```

The example shows that, if we simply enter the `hostname` command, it will yield the following code:

```
root@philip-virtual-machine:/home/philip# hostname
philip-virtual-machine
root@philip-virtual-machine:/home/philip#
```

So, we can see the DNS name of the system. We can also pass the `-i` option to view the IP associated with the `hostname`, as shown in the following example:

```
root@philip-virtual-machine:/home/philip# hostname -i
127.0.1.1
root@philip-virtual-machine:/home/philip#
```

Excellent! Based on the previous example, we can see an IP from the loopback range of `127.0.0.0/8`. We can change the `hostname` by passing a new `hostname` value, as shown in the following code:

```
root@philip-virtual-machine:/home/philip# hostname Linuxplus
root@philip-virtual-machine:/home/philip# hostname
Linuxplus
root@philip-virtual-machine:/home/philip#
```

Using the previous example, we can see that the `hostname` command indicates that the `hostname` has been changed but it has not updated the prompt. We can exit out of root and sign back in and we will see the following changes:

```
root@philip-virtual-machine:/home/philip# exit
exit
philip@philip-virtual-machine:~$ sudo su
[sudo] password for philip:
root@Linuxplus:/home/philip#
```

Excellent! Now we can see that the hostname was changed to reflect the name that we specified. However, when we reboot the system the hostname will be set back to the value specified in the `/etc/hostname` file, as shown in the following example:

```
root@Linuxplus:/home/philip# cat /etc/hostname
philip-virtual-machine
root@Linuxplus:/home/philip#reboot
root@philip-virtual-machine:/home/philip# cat /etc/hostname
philip-virtual-machine
root@philip-virtual-machine:/home/philip# hostname Linuxplus
```

We can fix this by editing the `/etc/hostname` file using a text editor such as vi or nano and place the value as shown in the following code:

```
root@philip-virtual-machine:/home/philip#cat /etc/hostname
Linuxplus
root@philip-virtual-machine:/home/philip# reboot
root@Linuxplus:/home/philip#
```

Excellent!

Summary

In this chapter, we configured IPv4, IPv6 configuration, client-side DNS and network troubleshooting. First, we worked with IPv4, and we looked at various ways with which we would manage IPv4 addressing. Next, we covered IPv4 routing; we saw how we would add a default route in addition to adding static routes for subnets not directly connected. This was then followed with IPv6 configuration; we saw how we would manage our IPv6 infrastructure using various tools available via the command line. Following this, we looked at configuring routing for IPv6, particularly focusing on default routes and static routes for subnets not directly connected. Next, we covered client-side DNS. We looked at ways of configuring the DNS servers' IP addressing. We then tested our DNS configuration by browsing out to the internet. Finally, we covered network troubleshooting; we covered a number of tools available at the command line to assist us in troubleshooting potential network connectivity issues.

In the next chapter, we will focus on security; particularly host security, SSH, and encryption. The next chapter is critical because of the many security risks that exist in today's environments. I hope to see you in the next chapter.

Questions

1. Which option with the `ifconfig` command displays all interfaces active and inactive?

        A. `-s`
        B. `-d`
        C. `-A`
        D. `-a`

2. Which keyword is used with the `ip route` command when creating a gateway of last resort?

   A. `default`
   B. `0.0.0.0`
   C. `gateway`
   D. None of the above

3. Which protocol does `ping` use to send and receive messages between source and destination?

   A. FTP
   B. TFTP
   C. ICMP
   D. SSH.1.1

4. Which file holds the `hostname` value for the system?

   A. `/etc/hosts`
   B. `/etc/hostname`
   C. `/etc/hostname/hosts`
   D. `/var/log/hosts`

5. Which command performs a trace and outputs the hops along with the `pmtu` value?

   A. `traceroute`
   B. `trace`
   C. `tracepath`
   D. `tracert`

6. Which command performs a DNS query for a given domain?

   A. `ping`
   B. `traceroute`
   C. `dnsq`
   D. `dig`

7. Which command adds a default route for IPv6?

   A. `ip -6 route add default via 2001:db8:0:f101::2`
   B. `iproute add default via 2001:db8:0:f101::2`
   C. `ip-6 route add default via 2001:db8:0:f101::2`
   D. `ip -6 add default via 2001:db8:0:f101::2`

8. Which options with the netstat command displays the IP address and port numbers for UDP connections which are open, program ID, and program name?

   A. `-t`
   B. `-u`
   C. `-udp`
   D. `-ulp`

9. Which command is used for scanning a system in order to expose the services and their respective port numbers being used?

   A. `traceroute`
   B. `dig`
   C. `nmap`
   D. `ip`

10. Which command displays registry information for a given domain?

    A. `who`
    B. `whois`
    C. `whoami`
    D. `w`

Further reading

- This site gives useful information about configuring IPv4 and IPv6: `https://superuser.com`
- This site gives useful information about configuring client-side DNS: `https://unix.stackexchange.com`
- This site gives useful information about troubleshooting: `https://www.computernetworkingnotes.com`

17
Performing Administrative Security Tasks

In the last chapter, we covered IPv4, IPv6, client-side DNS, and network troubleshooting. We worked with IPv4 and discussed IPv4 routing, and then we did the same for IPv6. This led into client-side DNS and network troubleshooting; we covered a number of command-line tools that assist in troubleshooting potential network connectivity issues.

In this chapter, we will focus on security: host security, SSH, and encryption. First, we will cover host security; the `/etc/sudoers`, `/etc/hosts.allow`, and `/etc/.hosts.deny` files will be our main focus. Next, we will work with SSH. We will focus on the steps involved in setting up SSH, and the steps for generating a key. We will also look at logging in to a remote system using SSH. Additionally, we will work with the various SSH files that are available to us. Encryption will be our next focal point; we will look at ways to encrypt and decrypt files. This will be an important chapter, in terms of securing a Linux system.

We will cover the following topics in this chapter:

- Host security
- SSH
- Encryption

Host security

In Linux, we can perform a range of security tasks to safeguard our system. Up to this point in the book, we've been performing most of our administrative tasks as the root user. Can we perform some of these tasks as a regular user, instead? Well, we can use a regular user account and give it certain root privileges, without having to actually log in as the root user. This is made possible with the /etc/sudoers file. We'll work with the Fedora 28 system in this demo. If we try to view boot files inside /boot/grub2/, we will be presented with the following:

```
[philip@localhost ~]$ ls /boot/grub2/
ls: cannot open directory '/boot/grub2/': Permission denied
[philip@localhost ~]$
```

Based on the preceding information, the user does not have sufficient permission to view the contents of /boot/grub2; we have received a Permission denied message. Adding to this, if we try to make a change (such as adding an IP address), we will be presented with the following:

```
[philip@localhost ~]$ ip a s ens33
2: ens33: <BROADCAST,MULTICAST,UP,LOWER_UP> mtu 1500 qdisc fq_codel state
UP group default qlen 1000
    link/ether 00:0c:29:04:35:bd brd ff:ff:ff:ff:ff:ff
    inet 172.16.175.129/24 brd 172.16.175.255 scope global dynamic
noprefixroute ens33
       valid_lft 1700sec preferred_lft 1700sec
    inet 172.16.11.0/23 scope global ens33
       valid_lft forever preferred_lft forever
    inet6 2001:db8:0:f101::3/64 scope global
       valid_lft forever preferred_lft forever
    inet6 fe80::413:ea63:2e8a:5f2b/64 scope link noprefixroute
       valid_lft forever preferred_lft forever
[philip@localhost ~]$ ip a a 10.20.1.1/24 dev ens33
RTNETLINK answers: Operation not permitted
[philip@localhost ~]$
```

Based on the preceding information, we will execute the first command: the IP command, with the a and s options (a for address, s for show)—but when we attempt to add an IP address, we get an Operation not permitted message. The message will vary, depending on what you're trying to view, as this is a case with the ls command, as opposed to making a change in the demo later.

The su command

One technique to work around the standard user permission problem is to use the `su` command; `su` means **substitute user**. The basic syntax of the `su` command is as follows:

```
su <option>
```

Based on the preceding command, we can also use the `su` command without using any options, as seen in the following command:

```
[philip@localhost ~]$ su
Password:
[root@localhost philip]#
```

Awesome! When we use the `su` command without any options, it prompts us for the root password, and then logs us in as the root user. However, this might not be ideal, due to security concerns. A better approach would be for us to execute a command, but not stay signed in as the root user; this can be accomplished by passing the `-l` option, which expects the user account's name, and the `-c` option, which expects the command. The following command shows how we can use the `su` command to effectively display the contents of the `/boot/grub2/` directory, and, at the same time, stay logged in as the standard user:

```
[philip@localhost ~]$ su -l root -c 'ls /boot/grub2/'
Password:
device.map  fonts  grub.cfg  grubenv  i386-pc  locale  themes
[philip@localhost ~]$
```

Excellent! The contents of the `/boot/grub2/` directory will now be displayed. However, the contents will be displayed without any color (other than white); we can pass the `--color` option to instruct the `ls` command to display colors, just like if we were logged in as the root user. This is shown as follows:

Awesome! We can see the difference when we omit the `--color` option, as opposed to including it with the `ls` command. Also, when the command has intervening spaces, we have to enclose the entire command with a single quote (`'`). Another useful option is the `-s` option; this tells the `su` command to use the specified shell provided by the user, as indicated by the following screenshot:

```
[philip@localhost ~]$ su -l root -c 'ls /boot/grub2/'
Password:
device.map  fonts  grub.cfg  grubenv  i386-pc  locale  themes
[philip@localhost ~]$ su -l root -c 'ls /boot/grub2/' -s /usr/bin/sh
Password:
device.map  fonts  grub.cfg  grubenv  i386-pc  locale  themes
[philip@localhost ~]$
```

Wonderful! When we used the `-s` option and specified the shell (in our case, `/usr/sbin/sh`), we did not to specify the `--color` option with the `ls` command.

Another way to use the `su` command is to pass the `-` option, which implies the root user, as follows:

```
[philip@localhost ~]$ su - -c 'ls /boot/grub2/' -s /usr/bin/sh
Password:
device.map  fonts  grub.cfg  grubenv  i386-pc  locale  themes
[philip@localhost ~]$
```

Perfect! The contents are displayed, and we did not specify the login `root`. We can see a list of shells that are available by looking inside of the `/etc/shells` file, as follows:

```
[philip@localhost ~]$ cat /etc/shells
/bin/sh
/bin/bash
/sbin/nologin
/usr/bin/sh
/usr/bin/bash
/usr/sbin/nologin
/usr/bin/tmux
/bin/tmux
[philip@localhost ~]$
```

Awesome! We can see the various shells that can be used with the -s option of the su command. So far, we've only viewed content with the su command, but we can also make changes with it. The following command shows how we can make a change using the su command:

```
[philip@localhost ~]$ su - -c 'ip a a 172.20.1.1/24 dev ens33'
Password:
[philip@localhost ~]$ ip a s ens33 | grep inet
    inet 172.16.175.129/24 brd 172.16.175.255 scope global dynamic
noprefixroute ens33
    inet 172.16.11.0/23 scope global ens33
    inet 172.20.1.1/24 scope global ens33
    inet6 2001:db8:0:f101::3/64 scope global
    inet6 fe80::413:ea63:2e8a:5f2b/64 scope link noprefixroute
[philip@localhost ~]$
```

Excellent! The IP address was added successfully.

A major drawback when using the su command is that every user has to know the root password in order to execute it.

The sudo command

The sudo command solves the dilemma of standard users needing the root password, as long as the user's account resides in the /etc/sudoers configuration file. The basic syntax of the sudo command is as follows:

```
sudo <command>
```

Along with the preceding command, we simply specify the command that we would like to execute, which would normally require root privileges. Let's try the sudo command as follows:

```
[philip@localhost ~]$ sudo ls /boot/grub2/
[sudo] password for philip:
device.map  fonts  grub.cfg  grubenv  i386-pc  locale  themes
[philip@localhost ~]$
```

Excellent! When we executed the `sudo` command and passed the command that required root privileges, we were prompted for the password of the standard user, not the root user. Afterwards, we can pass another command with the `sudo` command, and we won't be prompted for our password, as you can see in the following code snippet:

```
[philip@localhost ~]$ sudo ip a a 192.168.5.5/24 dev ens33
[philip@localhost ~]$ ip a | grep inet
    inet 127.0.0.1/8 scope host lo
    inet6 ::1/128 scope host
    inet 172.16.175.129/24 brd 172.16.175.255 scope global dynamic
noprefixroute ens33
    inet 172.16.11.0/23 scope global ens33
    inet 172.20.1.1/24 scope global ens33
    inet 192.168.5.5/24 scope global ens33
    inet6 2001:db8:0:f101::3/64 scope global
    inet6 fe80::413:ea63:2e8a:5f2b/64 scope link noprefixroute
[philip@localhost ~]$
```

Awesome! The command executed successfully, without requiring the user's password. This is possible because there is a timeout setting that saves the user's password; after the time has elapsed, we will be prompted to enter the user's password again. However, this does not hold true in the event that the user opens another Terminal, as shown in the following screenshot:

Awesome! We can see that the timeout value does not affect a new Terminal, because the user was prompted to enter their password.

There may be times when we prefer to increase the timeout value, especially when we're going to be working for a long period of time. Rest assured; we can increase the timeout value by searching for env_reset inside of the /etc/sudoers file and appending the timestamp_timeout option alongside it. The contents of the /etc/sudoers file are as follows:

```
## Sudoers allows particular users to run various commands as
## the root user, without needing the root password.
## This file must be edited with the 'visudo' command.
## Host Aliases
## Groups of machines. You may prefer to use hostnames (perhaps using
## wildcards for entire domains) or IP addresses instead.
# Host_Alias     FILESERVERS = fs1, fs2
# Host_Alias     MAILSERVERS = smtp, smtp2
## User Aliases
## These aren't often necessary, as you can use regular groups
## (ie, from files, LDAP, NIS, etc) in this file - just use %groupname
## rather than USERALIAS
# User_Alias ADMINS = jsmith, mikem
## Command Aliases
## These are groups of related commands...
## Networking
# Cmnd_Alias NETWORKING = /sbin/route, /sbin/ifconfig, /bin/ping,
/sbin/dhclient, /usr/bin/net, /sbin/iptables, /usr/bin/rfcomm,
/usr/bin/wvdial, /sbin/iwconfig, /sbin/mii-tool
## Installation and management of software
Defaults      env_reset
Defaults      env_keep =  "COLORS DISPLAY HOSTNAME HISTSIZE KDEDIR LS_COLORS"
## Allow root to run any commands anywhere
root       ALL=(ALL)            ALL
## Allows people in group wheel to run all commands
%wheel                ALL=(ALL)                ALL
## Same thing without a password
# %wheel              ALL=(ALL)            NOPASSWD: ALL
#includedir /etc/sudoers.d
[philip@localhost ~]$
```

In the preceding code, some output has been omitted for brevity. There are a number of options that we can change. For instance, to increase the timeout value, we can edit /etc/sudoers using the visudo editor; it is highly recommended to not use any editor other than visudo, as follows:

```
[philip@localhost ~]$ sudo cat /etc/sudoers | grep env_reset
Defaults      env_reset,timestamp_timeout=60
[philip@localhost ~]$
```

Excellent! We've added `timestamp_timeout=60`; this tells `sudo` to save the user's password for 60 minutes. Another useful option to set is to see the output as we type the user's password; it is possible to display asterisks (*) for each key typed by the user. This is made possible by appending the `pwfeedback` option alongside the `env_reset` option, as follows:

```
[philip@localhost ~]$ sudo cat /etc/sudoers | grep env_reset
Defaults     env_reset,timestamp_timeout=60,pwfeedback
[philip@localhost ~]$
```

Based on the preceding command, when the user first tries to use the `sudo` command, the password will be represented with asterisks, as follows:

```
[philip@localhost ~]$ sudo ls /boot/grub2/
[sudo] password for philip: *******
device.map  fonts  grub.cfg  grubenv  i386-pc  locale  themes
[philip@localhost ~]$
```

Excellent! We can now see asterisks that represent the typed password.

When we add a new user, the new user will not automatically be added to the /etc/sudoers file. We have to add the user manually, as follows:

```
[philip@localhost ~]$ sudo useradd teddy
[philip@localhost ~]$ sudo passwd teddy
Changing password for user teddy.
New password:
BAD PASSWORD: The password fails the dictionary check - it is based on a
dictionary word
Retype new password:
passwd: all authentication tokens updated successfully.
[philip@localhost ~]$
```

Now, we can switch users, either by logging out and back in on the computer, or by using the `su` command, as follows:

```
[philip@localhost ~]$ su teddy
Password:
[teddy@localhost philip]$
```

We've successfully logged in as the new user; now, when we try to issue the `sudo` command, the results will be as follows:

```
[teddy@localhost philip]$ sudo ls /boot/grub2/
We trust you have received the usual lecture from the local System
Administrator. It usually boils down to these three things:
    #1) Respect the privacy of others.
```

```
    #2) Think before you type.
    #3) With great power comes great responsibility.
[sudo] password for teddy:
teddy is not in the sudoers file.  This incident will be reported.
[teddy@localhost philip]$
```

We're given a notification message, but when we enter the new user's password, we get the dreaded `teddy is not in the sudoers file` message, along with, `This incident will be reported`. This basically tells us that we have to add the new user to the /etc/sudoer file. This can be done in a number of ways; one way, which may be the simplest, is to add the new user to the `wheel` group. The `wheel` group can execute all commands, as can be seen in the /etc/sudoer file:

```
[philip@localhost ~]$ sudo cat /etc/sudoers | grep wheel
## Allows people in group wheel to run all commands
%wheel                  ALL=(ALL)               ALL
# %wheel                ALL=(ALL)               NOPASSWD: ALL
[philip@localhost ~]$
```

As you can see, the `wheel` group exists, with full access; we can use the `usermod` command and pass the -a and -G options (a for appends, G for group), as follows:

```
[philip@localhost ~]$ usermod -aG wheel teddy
usermod: Permission denied.
usermod: cannot lock /etc/passwd; try again later.
[philip@localhost ~]$
```

We will need root privileges to modify another user's properties. For this, we can use the `sudo` command, as follows:

```
[philip@localhost ~]$ sudo usermod -aG wheel teddy
[philip@localhost ~]$ su teddy
Password:
  [teddy@localhost philip]$ sudo ls /boot/grub2/
[sudo] password for teddy:
device.map  fonts  grub.cfg  grubenv  i386-pc  locale  themes
[teddy@localhost philip]$
```

Excellent! The new user is now capable of using the `sudo` command. Let's examine the syntax for adding an entry inside of /etc/sudoer, as follows:

```
[teddy@localhost philip]$ sudo cat /etc/sudoers | grep %
%wheel                  ALL=(ALL)               ALL
[teddy@localhost philip]$
Based on the above, the syntax for an entry is as follows:
<user/group> <system/ALL> = <effective user/ALL> <command(s)>
```

We can define an entry for one particular user or group (we have to put a % in front of a group's name); we can then specify which system we want the entry for, which user we want to allow to execute the commands, and, finally, the actual commands. Let's give this a try; we will remove the `wheel` group from the new user and create an entry for the new user, as follows:

```
[philip@localhost ~]$ sudo usermod -G "" teddy
[philip@localhost ~]$ groups teddy
teddy : teddy
[philip@localhost ~]$ sudo cat /etc/sudoers | grep teddy
teddy ALL=(ALL) /usr/sbin/ls
[philip@localhost ~]$
```

Wonderful! We've restricted the new user to executing only the `ls` and `cat` commands; this can be proven as follows:

```
[philip@localhost ~]$ su teddy
Password:
[teddy@localhost philip]$ sudo ls /boot/grub2/
device.map  fonts  grub.cfg  grubenv  i386-pc  locale  themes
[teddy@localhost philip]$ sudo cat /etc/resolv.conf
Sorry, user teddy is not allowed to execute '/usr/bin/cat /etc/resolv.conf'
as root on localhost.localdomain.
[teddy@localhost philip]$
```

Excellent! The new user can only use the `ls` command with root privileges, and is unable to make any other changes with the `sudo` command. Additionally, we can grant the new user the ability to execute as many commands as we specify, as follows:

```
[philip@localhost ~]$ sudo cat /etc/sudoers | grep teddy
teddy     ALL=(ALL)              /usr/bin/ls,          /usr/bin/cat
[philip@localhost ~]$
[teddy@localhost philip]$ sudo ls /boot/grub2/
device.map  fonts  grub.cfg  grubenv  i386-pc  locale  themes
[teddy@localhost philip]$ sudo cat /etc/resolv.conf
# Generated by NetworkManager
nameserver 8.8.8.8
[teddy@localhost philip]$
[teddy@localhost philip]$ sudo ip a a 172.16.20.1/24 dev ens33
Sorry, user teddy is not allowed to execute '/usr/sbin/ip a a
172.16.20.1/24 dev ens33' as root on localhost.localdomain.
[teddy@localhost philip]$
```

Awesome! We added the `cat` command for the new user, making it possible for the new user to execute the `cat` command with root privileges. The thing to remember when placing multiple commands alongside each other, is that you have to place tabs by pressing the *Tab* key between the commands. Another option that we can use with the `sudo` command is the `-l` option; this lists the privileges of the current user, as follows:

```
[philip@localhost ~]$ sudo -l
Matching Defaults entries for philip on localhost:
    !visiblepw, env_reset, timestamp_timeout=60, pwfeedback,
env_keep="COLORS DISPLAY HOSTNAME HISTSIZE KDEDIR LS_COLORS",
env_keep+="MAIL PS1 PS2
    QTDIR USERNAME LANG LC_ADDRESS LC_CTYPE", env_keep+="LC_COLLATE
LC_IDENTIFICATION LC_MEASUREMENT LC_MESSAGES", env_keep+="LC_MONETARY
LC_NAME
    LC_NUMERIC LC_PAPER LC_TELEPHONE", env_keep+="LC_TIME LC_ALL LANGUAGE
LINGUAS _XKB_CHARSET XAUTHORITY",
secure_path=/usr/local/sbin\:/usr/local/bin\:/usr/sbin\:/usr/bin\:/sbin\:/b
in
User philip may run the following commands on localhost:
    (ALL) ALL
[philip@localhost ~]$
```

As you can see, the user `philip` can run all of the commands with the `sudo` command. However, if we run the `sudo` command with `-l` for the other user, `teddy`, we will see that user's access, as follows:

```
[teddy@localhost philip]$ sudo -l
[sudo] password for teddy:
Matching Defaults entries for teddy on localhost:
    !visiblepw, env_reset, timestamp_timeout=60, pwfeedback,
env_keep="COLORS DISPLAY HOSTNAME HISTSIZE KDEDIR LS_COLORS",
env_keep+="MAIL PS1 PS2
    QTDIR USERNAME LANG LC_ADDRESS LC_CTYPE", env_keep+="LC_COLLATE
LC_IDENTIFICATION LC_MEASUREMENT LC_MESSAGES", env_keep+="LC_MONETARY
LC_NAME
    LC_NUMERIC LC_PAPER LC_TELEPHONE", env_keep+="LC_TIME LC_ALL LANGUAGE
LINGUAS _XKB_CHARSET XAUTHORITY",
secure_path=/usr/local/sbin\:/usr/local/bin\:/usr/sbin\:/usr/bin\:/sbin\:/b
in
User teddy may run the following commands on localhost:
    (ALL) /usr/bin/ls, /usr/bin/cat
[teddy@localhost philip]$
```

Awesome! We can only see two commands that `teddy` can execute with root privileges. It is also possible to pass the username with the –u option and specify which command is to be executed with `sudo`, as follows:

```
[philip@localhost ~]$ sudo -u teddy cat /etc/resolv.conf
# Generated by NetworkManager
nameserver 8.8.8.8
[philip@localhost ~]$ sudo -u teddy ip a a 10.10.10.10/24 dev ens33
RTNETLINK answers: Operation not permitted
[philip@localhost ~]$
```

Excellent! Another useful option is –v, which resets the authentication timeout for the user, as follows:

```
[philip@localhost ~]$ sudo -v
[philip@localhost ~]$
```

Similarly, it is possible to kill the authentication session immediately by passing the –k option with `sudo`, as follows:

```
[philip@localhost ~]$ sudo -k
[philip@localhost ~]$ sudo ls /boot/grub2/
[sudo] password for philip:
device.map  fonts  grub.cfg  grubenv  i386-pc  locale  themes
[philip@localhost ~]$
```

Awesome! In the preceding code, the user had to provide their password when they attempted to execute the `sudo` command with the –k option.

So far, we've been providing the user's password the first time we execute `sudo`; it is possible to run `sudo` without entering a password. We add the NOPASSWD option in the entry that we added for the new user, as follows:

```
[philip@localhost ~]$ sudo cat /etc/sudoers | grep teddy
teddy    ALL=(ALL)            NOPASSWD:/usr/bin/ls,
/usr/bin/cat
[philip@localhost ~]$
[philip@localhost ~]$ su teddy
Password:
[teddy@localhost philip]$ sudo cat /etc/resolv.conf
# Generated by NetworkManager
nameserver 8.8.8.8
[teddy@localhost philip]$ sudo ls /boot/grub2/
device.map  fonts  grub.cfg  grubenv  i386-pc  locale  themes
[teddy@localhost philip]$
```

Wonderful! Whenever the user `teddy` tries to execute the `sudo` command, they will no longer be prompted for their password.

TCP wrappers

We can add another layer of security within a Linux system by using TCP wrappers. **TCP wrappers** filter traffic as it enters the system. TCP wrappers check the traffic against two files: `/etc/hosts.allow` and `/etc/hosts.deny`. The rules are applied with a top-down approach, meaning that the first rule is always applied before all other rules. We can view the contents of `/etc/hosts.allow` as follows:

```
[philip@localhost ~]$ cat /etc/hosts.allow
#
# hosts.allow   This file contains access rules which are used to
# allow or deny connections to network services that
# either use the tcp_wrappers library or that have been
# started through a tcp_wrappers-enabled xinetd.
# See 'man 5 hosts_options' and 'man 5 hosts_access'
# for information on rule syntax.
# See 'man tcpd' for information on tcp_wrappers
#
[philip@localhost ~]$
```

The file only contains comments that start with #. The basic syntax for creating a rule is as follows:

```
<daemon>:          <client list> [:<option>: <option>:...]
```

We can add a rule using a text editor, such as vi or nano, as follows:

```
[philip@localhost ~]$ sudo cat /etc/hosts.allow
#
vsftpd:                  172.16.175.
[philip@localhost ~]$
```

In the preceding command, we added a rule for `vsftpd`; this is a secure version of FTP. We then specified the client list—the subnet `172.16.175.`. The `.` means that any IP addresses within that subnet will be able to access the `vsftpd`. Another way to define the rule is to specify a domain, as follows:

```
[philip@localhost ~]$ sudo cat /etc/hosts.allow
#
vsftpd:                  .packtpub.com
[philip@localhost ~]$
```

Excellent! Anyone from within .packtpub.com will be able to access the vsftpd on the local system. Adding to this, we can use the keyword ALL inside a rule; this matches everything, and it can be placed in the daemon or in the client list section, as follows:

```
[philip@localhost ~]$ sudo cat /etc/hosts.allow
vsftpd:                     .packtpub.com
in.telnetd:         ALL
[philip@localhost ~]$
```

Awesome! Everyone can access the Telnet Service on the local system. It is also possible to execute another command, by passing the spawn option. This is useful when we want to log who is attempting to access a given service on the local system. We use the spawn option as follows:

```
[philip@localhost ~]$ sudo cat /etc/hosts.allow
vsftpd:                     .packtpub.com: spawn /bin/echo `/bin/date` from
%h>>/var/log/vsftp.log : allow
in.telnetd:         ALL
[philip@localhost ~]$
```

Excellent! The spawn option creates a message containing the current date (/bin/date), which is then appended with the hostname (%h) of the system attempting to access the vsftpd; this then gets appended inside of /var/log/vsftp.log. We can then take a look at the /etc/hosts.deny file, as follows:

```
[philip@localhost ~]$ sudo cat /etc/hosts.deny
# hosts.deny   This file contains access rules which are used to
#              deny connections to network services that either use
#              the tcp_wrappers library or that have been
#              The rules in this file can also be set up in
#              /etc/hosts.allow with a 'deny' option instead.
#              See 'man 5 hosts_options' and 'man 5 hosts_access'
#              for information on rule syntax.
#              See 'man tcpd' for information on tcp_wrappers
  [philip@localhost ~]$
```

In the preceding command, /etc/hosts.deny only contains comments (#). It is recommended that you deny everything in this file, as follows:

```
[philip@localhost ~]$ sudo cat /etc/hosts.deny
ALL:ALL
[philip@localhost ~]$
```

Awesome! We've specified `ALL:ALL:`, to deny everything except the rules that are listed in `/etc/hosts.allow`.

SSH

We mainly use SSH for the purpose of securely logging into a remote system. Most Linux distributions come with the SSH package, by default. In order to verify whether SSH is currently running, we use the `systemctl` command; we pass the `status` option, as follows:

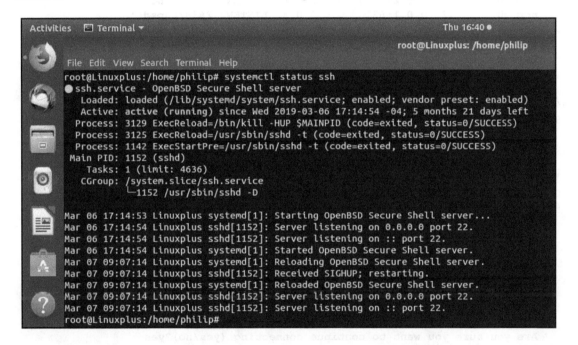

The SSH daemon `ssh.service` is currently running (particularly, the Secure Shell server). Another method that we can use to verify that the SSH service is running is the `netstat` command; we pass the `ntlp` options (n for display port numbers, t for TCP protocol, l for currently listening, and p for program ID/program name), as follows:

```
root@Linuxplus:/home/philip# netstat -ntlp
Active Internet connections (only servers)
Proto Recv-Q Send-Q Local Address Foreign Address State        PID/Program
name
tcp  0   0  0.0.0.0:514      0.0.0.0:*   LISTEN   519/rsyslogd
tcp  0   0  127.0.0.53:53    0.0.0.0:*   LISTEN   431/systemd-resolve
tcp  0   0  0.0.0.0:22       0.0.0.0:*   LISTEN   1152/sshd
tcp  0   0  127.0.0.1:631    0.0.0.0:*   LISTEN   2638/cupsd
tcp6 0   0  :::514           :::*        LISTEN   519/rsyslogd
tcp6 0   0  :::22            :::*        LISTEN   1152/sshd
tcp6 0   0  ::1:631          :::*        LISTEN   2638/cupsd
root@Linuxplus:/home/philip#
```

As you can see, the SSH server daemon is currently running on TCP port 22. The basic syntax for establishing a connection to a remote system is as follows:

```
ssh <remote system>
```

We can simply run the `ssh` command and pass only the remote system; we will use the `ssh` command from the Fedora 28 system and try to connect to the Ubuntu 18 system, as follows:

```
[philip@localhost ~]$ ssh 172.16.175.130
The authenticity of host '172.16.175.130 (172.16.175.130)' can't be
established.
ECDSA key fingerprint is
SHA256:SfI3vfS3yRRWSGN2jgAG7K5aQc65c/zVt/1z+D8mQBQ.
ECDSA key fingerprint is
MD5:a2:03:c5:38:b3:83:88:fa:85:b5:5f:e6:91:eb:87:c1.
Are you sure you want to continue connecting (yes/no)?yes
Warning: Permanently added '172.16.175.130' (ECDSA) to the list of known
hosts.
philip@172.16.175.130's password:
Welcome to Ubuntu 18.04 LTS (GNU/Linux 4.15.0-20-generic x86_64)
 * Documentation:  https://help.ubuntu.com
 * Management:     https://landscape.canonical.com
 * Support:        https://ubuntu.com/advantage
Ubuntu comes with ABSOLUTELY NO WARRANTY, to the extent permitted by
applicable law.
philip@Linuxplus:~$
```

In the preceding command, some output has been omitted for brevity. If you specify the command without any options, the SSH program uses the current user, `philip`, and a fingerprint identifying the server is presented. This added the user `philip` to `~/.ssh/known_hosts` in the Fedora 28 system. We can take a look at the file, as follows:

```
[philip@localhost ~]$ cat .ssh/known_hosts
172.16.175.130 ecdsa-sha2-nistp256
AAAAE2VjZHNhLXNoYTItbmlzdHAyNTYAAAAIbmlzdHAyNTYAAABBBPhEHNo6YSOE+ZZ9vHVmQqB
PFQd8WtAUFoGYAJe3VPQJlhjhc9bxy+vwsetQiEIKTyMgnfrOC7LNbhxxmJ4IX8w=
[philip@localhost ~]$
```

Awesome! We have Ubuntu's system information inside of `~/.ssh/known_hosts` for the user `philip` on the Fedora 28 system. It is also possible to use a different username with the `ssh` command; we specify the `-l` option, as follows:

```
[philip@localhost ~]$ ssh -l hacker 172.16.175.130
hacker@172.16.175.130's password:
Welcome to Ubuntu 18.04 LTS (GNU/Linux 4.15.0-20-generic x86_64)
$ exit
Connection to 172.16.175.130 closed.
[philip@localhost ~]$
```

We were able to log in using a different user, via SSH. Also, notice that we were presented with the earlier message identifying the server's fingerprint. This is because the information was previously stored in `~/.ssh/known_hosts`. If we were to remove the contents using a text editor, such as vi or nano, we would be presented with the identity message again, as follows:

```
[philip@localhost ~]$ cat .ssh/known_hosts
[philip@localhost ~]$
[philip@localhost ~]$ ssh -l hacker 172.16.175.130
The authenticity of host '172.16.175.130 (172.16.175.130)' can't be
established.
ECDSA key fingerprint is
SHA256:SfI3vfS3yRRWSGN2jgAG7K5aQc65c/zVt/lz+D8mQBQ.
ECDSA key fingerprint is
MD5:a2:03:c5:38:b3:83:88:fa:85:b5:5f:e6:91:eb:87:c1.
Are you sure you want to continue connecting (yes/no)? yes
Warning: Permanently added '172.16.175.130' (ECDSA) to the list of known
hosts.
hacker@172.16.175.130's password:
Welcome to Ubuntu 18.04 LTS (GNU/Linux 4.15.0-20-generic x86_64)
[philip@localhost ~]$
```

Excellent! We removed the contents, and we were once again presented with the identity message.

So far, we've been prompted to enter a password every time that we've attempted to start an SSH session. However, it is possible to bypass the password prompt and log in to the system without any hindrance. We use SSH keys to authenticate; this is known as **key-based authentication**. Key-based authentication involves the creation of a pair of keys: a private key and a public key. The private key is stored on the client's system, and the public key is stored on the destination system(s). Specifically, we generate an SSH key using the ssh-keygen command on the destination system. Next, we copy over the client system; we use the ssh-copy-id command to copy the keys. When you first connect using key-based authentication, the servers transmit a message, using the public key, over to the client's system, which can then be interpreted using the private key, which resides on the client's system.

Let's generate the SSH keys using the ssh-keygen command on the client system from where we need to log in; it will be the Fedora 28 system, as follows:

```
[philip@localhost ~]$ ssh-keygen
Generating public/private rsa key pair.
Enter file in which to save the key (/home/philip/.ssh/id_rsa):
```

By default, the algorithm is rsa, and the location to store the key pair is inside of the current user's home directory (~/.ssh/id_rsa). We accept the defaults and press *Enter*, as follows:

```
[philip@localhost ~]$ ssh-keygen
Generating public/private rsa key pair.
Enter file in which to save the key (/home/philip/.ssh/id_rsa):
Enter passphrase (empty for no passphrase):
Enter same passphrase again:
```

We have to specify a passphrase; we will use a super secret passphrase, and then press *Enter*, as follows:

```
[philip@localhost ~]$ ssh-keygen
Generating public/private rsa key pair.
Enter file in which to save the key (/home/philip/.ssh/id_rsa):
Enter passphrase (empty for no passphrase):
Enter same passphrase again:
Your identification has been saved in /home/philip/.ssh/id_rsa.
Your public key has been saved in /home/philip/.ssh/id_rsa.pub.
The key fingerprint is:
SHA256:BwdFiHu2iEyvnnXhnY+1tNpZmlaZZdL1Zugwda9PJ7g
philip@localhost.localdomain
```

```
The key's randomart image is:
+---[RSA 2048]----+
|          ..+o      |
|           . ..      . o|
|           ..  .   . ++|
|        . . oo   o o O|
|      o o +S..   = X |
|        o o..+ .. B o|
|        .. o o oo.+.|
|      .o .    *EB  .|
|      .o      ooO    |
+----[SHA256]-----+
[philip@localhost ~]$
```

Excellent! The key was generated using a 2,048-bit key size. Now, we can run the `ls`
command on the user's home directory and look inside of ~/.ssh, as follows:

```
[philip@localhost ~]$ ls -a .ssh
.  ..  id_rsa  id_rsa.pub  known_hosts
[philip@localhost ~]$
```

Wonderful! Apart from the known_hosts file, which we covered earlier, we now have two
additional files: id_rsa (this is the private key) and id_rsa.pub (this is the public key).
We can look at the contents by using the cat command:

```
[philip@localhost ~]$ cat ~/.ssh/id_rsa.pub
ssh-rsa
AAAAB3NzaC1yc2EAAAADAQABAAABAQDNvsCDZaUs6mra1W+c1QnQ9cMeUqW0c/4IF8DThVK0Bi4
CPnQApafJZrOyeQeJbLxORCJf+YLkE+DWREwJw0EU21PkiZeij0DEI1spqToo6BkKDPfXXC135O
QxSUXER1AhGQQpVSbEJLy0WZsbs6iAy4ohmKcCWeEdHLz/3p0VUyd3NHvXaLsyno/Qa2ZOBOOZg
wUeHUA/p0zykUff7M4kIyGYatt1/vYKDH+UOC5fyB/nLtvrq7P1Mr1fMGyEjtc7nFDEHz4VeAP1
iUItKEzsyrqEH/KbAa3/ZeSoSfaFxoKvEtSKF5tnICyVp6uiUTNfi/cN74dmiDfG+vtcF0nt
philip@localhost.localdomain
[philip@localhost ~]$
```

Awesome! The next step is to copy the public key from the client's system to the destination
server, using the `ssh-copy id` command; in our case, the server is the Ubuntu system.
Before we run the `ssh-copy-id` command, let's check the ~/.ssh directory on the Ubuntu
system, as follows:

```
philip@Linuxplus:~$ ls -a ~/.ssh
.  ..
philip@Linuxplus:~$
```

As you can see, ~/.ssh is currently empty. Now, let's execute the ssh-copy-id command on the client system, as follows:

```
[philip@localhost ~]$ ssh-copy-id philip@172.16.175.130
/usr/bin/ssh-copy-id: INFO: Source of key(s) to be installed:
"/home/philip/.ssh/id_rsa.pub"
/usr/bin/ssh-copy-id: INFO: attempting to log in with the new key(s), to
filter out any that are already installed
/usr/bin/ssh-copy-id: INFO: 1 key(s) remain to be installed -- if you are
prompted now it is to install the new keys
philip@172.16.175.130's password:
Number of key(s) added: 1
Now try logging into the machine, with:   "ssh 'philip@172.16.175.130'"
and check to make sure that only the key(s) you wanted were added.
[philip@localhost ~]$
```

Excellent! The public key ~/.ssh/id_rsa.pub was securely transferred to the server's system. Now, let's check the ~/.ssh directory on the Ubuntu system again, as follows:

```
philip@Linuxplus:~$ ls -a ~/.ssh
.  ..  authorized_keys
philip@Linuxplus:~$
```

Awesome! We now have an authorized_keys file, located in the ~/.ssh directory. We can use the cat command to verify that the public key is indeed the same as the public key on the client's system, as follows:

```
philip@Linuxplus:~$ cat ~/.ssh/authorized_keys
ssh-rsa
AAAAB3NzaC1yc2EAAAADAQABAAABAQDNvsCDZaUs6mralW+c1QnQ9cMeUqW0c/4IF8DThVK0Bi4
CPnQApafJZrOyeQeJbLxORCJf+YLkE+DWREwJw0EU21PkiZeij0DEI1spqToo6BkKDPfXXC135O
QxSUXER1AhGQQpVSbEJLy0WZsbs6iAy4ohmKcCWeEdHLz/3p0VUyd3NHvXaLsyno/Qa2ZOBOOZg
wUeHUA/p0zykUff7M4kIyGYatt1/vYKDH+UOC5fyB/nLtvrq7P1MrlfMGyEjtc7nFDEHz4VeAP1
iUItKEzsyrqEH/KbAa3/ZeSoSfaFxoKvEtSKF5tnICyVp6uiUTNfi/cN74dmiDfG+vtcF0nt
philip@localhost.localdomain
philip@Linuxplus:~$
```

Excellent! The last step is to run the ssh command on the client system (Fedora 28) and verify that we are able to log in to the server (Ubuntu 18) without using a password, as follows:

```
[philip@localhost ~]$ ssh 172.16.175.130
Enter passphrase for key '/home/philip/.ssh/id_rsa':
Welcome to Ubuntu 18.04 LTS (GNU/Linux 4.15.0-20-generic x86_64)
Last login: Thu Sep 13 16:47:50 2018 from 172.16.175.129
philip@Linuxplus:~$
```

In the preceding code, we were asked for the `passphrase`, not the user's password. Furthermore, it's possible to store the `passphrase` inside of an agent, which will allow us to log in seamlessly in the future, without having to provide the passphrase each time that we attempt to log in. This is possible by using the `ssh-agent` and `ssh-add` commands. The `ssh agent` command stores the `passphrase`. After using that we would use the `ssh-add` command. This creates what is known as a **single sign-on** (**SSO**). The following code snippet shows how we use the `ssh-add` command:

```
[philip@localhost ~]$ ssh-agent
SSH_AUTH_SOCK=/tmp/ssh-qLovqqH69q1D/agent.79449; export SSH_AUTH_SOCK;
SSH_AGENT_PID=79450; export SSH_AGENT_PID;
echo Agent pid 79450;
  [philip@localhost ~]$
```

Excellent! We started the `ssh agent`, which created the necessary variables and started the process. Next, we will run the `ssh-add` command with the `-l` option; this will list all of the identities that the `ssh agent` is aware of, as follows:

```
[philip@localhost ~]$ ssh-add -l
The agent has no identities.
[philip@localhost ~]$
```

As you can see in the preceding command, there are no identities known by the agent; we will now add the identity that we created earlier, by using the `ssh-add` command without any options, as follows:

```
[philip@localhost ~]$ ssh-add
Enter passphrase for /home/philip/.ssh/id_rsa:
Identity added: /home/philip/.ssh/id_rsa (/home/philip/.ssh/id_rsa)
[philip@localhost ~]$ ssh-add -l
2048 SHA256:BwdFiHu2iEyvnnXhnY+1tNpZmlaZZdL1Zugwda9PJ7g
/home/philip/.ssh/id_rsa (RSA)
[philip@localhost ~]$
```

Wonderful! You can now see the identity for the private key that we generated earlier. Now, we will try to initiate an SSH session, as follows:

```
[philip@localhost ~]$ ssh 172.16.175.130
Welcome to Ubuntu 18.04 LTS (GNU/Linux 4.15.0-20-generic x86_64)
Last login: Fri Sep 14 10:06:44 2018 from 172.16.175.129
philip@Linuxplus:~$ exit
[philip@localhost ~]$
```

Excellent! We successfully logged in, without having to enter the user's password or the `passphrase`. The SSH configuration is stored in `/etc/ssh/ssh_config`:

```
philip@localhost ~]$ cat /etc/ssh/ssh_config
# $OpenBSD: ssh_config,v 1.33 2017/05/07 23:12:57 djm Exp $
# IdentityFile ~/.ssh/id_dsa
# IdentityFile ~/.ssh/id_ecdsa
# IdentityFile ~/.ssh/id_ed25519
# Port 22
# Protocol 2
#    Ciphers aes128-ctr,aes192-ctr,aes256-ctr,aes128-cbc,3des-cbc
#    MACs hmac-md5,hmac-sha1,umac-64@openssh.com
#    EscapeChar ~
#    Tunnel no
#    TunnelDevice any:any
# To modify the system-wide ssh configuration, create a  *.conf  file under
#  /etc/ssh/ssh_config.d/  which will be automatically included below
Include /etc/ssh/ssh_config.d/*.conf
[philip@localhost ~]$
```

In the preceding code, some output has been omitted for brevity. All of the settings are using their defaults.

Another location where the `known_hosts` are kept is `/etc/ssh/known_hosts`; this allows administrators to add the identities of all servers inside of a LAN. This method prevents the identity message from appearing every time a new user attempts to initiate an SSH session to a server. We can copy the contents of `~./ssh/known_hosts` to `/etc/ssh/known_hosts`, and, if we try to log in as another user, we won't see the identity message:

```
[philip@localhost ~]$ cat ~/.ssh/known_hosts
172.16.175.130 ecdsa-sha2-nistp256
AAAAE2VjZHNhLXNoYTItbmlzdHAyNTYAAAAIbmlzdHAyNTYAAABBBPhEHNo6YSOE+ZZ9vHVmQqB
PFQd8WtAUFoGYAJe3VPQJlhjhc9bxy+vwsetQiEIKTyMgnfrOC7LNbhxxmJ4IX8w=
[philip@localhost ~]$ cat /etc/ssh/ssh_known_hosts
172.16.175.130 ecdsa-sha2-nistp256
AAAAE2VjZHNhLXNoYTItbmlzdHAyNTYAAAAIbmlzdHAyNTYAAABBBPhEHNo6YSOE+ZZ9vHVmQqB
PFQd8WtAUFoGYAJe3VPQJlhjhc9bxy+vwsetQiEIKTyMgnfrOC7LNbhxxmJ4IX8w=
[philip@localhost ~]$
  [philip@localhost ~]$ ssh hacker@172.16.175.130
hacker@172.16.175.130's password:
Welcome to Ubuntu 18.04 LTS (GNU/Linux 4.15.0-20-generic x86_64)
$ exit
Connection to 172.16.175.130 closed.
[philip@localhost ~]$ ssh teddy@172.16.175.130
teddy@172.16.175.130's password:
[philip@localhost ~]$
```

Excellent. Neither of the users were presented with the identity message. Note that they were prompted for their respective passwords, because we only set up key-based authentication for the `philip` user; we have to generate the keys for each of the users.

Encryption

In today's environment, it's critical to safeguard our data. We can use various methods of encryption; in our environment, we will use the **GNU Privacy Guard** (**GnuPG**, or **GPG**) for encrypting and decrypting our files and folders. We will use the `gpg` command when working with encryption and decryption.

First, we will encrypt a file using the most basic form, **symmetric encryption**; this uses a password. The following command shows how we can perform symmetric encryption using the `gpg` command, with either the `-c` or `--symmetric` option:

```
[philip@localhost ~]$ cd Documents/
[philip@localhost Documents]$ ls
date_schedule  lsa_schedule  ls.txt  schedule  ssh  STDERR.txt
STDIN_STDOUT  STDIN_STDOUT.txt  TestFile1  The_Tee_command.txt
[philip@localhost Documents]$ gpg -c The_Tee_command.txt
Enter passphrase:
```

We have to enter a password/passphrase, then reenter it, as follows:

```
[philip@localhost Documents]$ gpg -c The_Tee_command.txt
Repeat passphrase:
[philip@localhost Documents]$
[philip@localhost Documents]$ ls -l | grep The
-rw-r--r--. 1 root    root    370 Aug  7 14:53 The_Tee_command.txt
-rw-rw-r--. 1 philip philip 307 Sep 14 11:01 The_Tee_command.txt.gpg
[philip@localhost Documents]$
```

Awesome! A new file was created, with a `.gpg` extension; this is the encrypted file. We can try to view the contents by using the `cat` command:

```
[philip@localhost Documents]$ cat The_Tee_command.txt.gpg
```

The content is encrypted, and we can now remove the original content and leave the encrypted content, as follows:

```
[philip@localhost Documents]$ rm The_Tee_command.txt
rm: remove write-protected regular file 'The_Tee_command.txt'? yes
[philip@localhost Documents]$ ls -l | grep The
-rw-rw-r--. 1 philip philip 307 Sep 14 11:01 The_Tee_command.txt.gpg
[philip@localhost Documents]$
```

Now, only the encrypted file remains. We can decrypt this file by passing the −d option, as follows:

```
[philip@localhost Documents]$ gpg -d The_Tee_command.txt.gpg
gpg: AES encrypted data
Enter passphrase:
```

We must provide the passphrase in order to decrypt the file, as follows:

```
[philip@localhost Documents]$ gpg -d The_Tee_command.txt.gpg
gpg: AES encrypted data
Enter passphrase:
gpg: AES encrypted data
gpg: encrypted with 1 passphrase
#
# hosts.allow This file contains access rules which are used to
#             allow or deny connections to network services that
#             either use the tcp_wrappers library or that have been
#             started through a tcp_wrappers-enabled xinetd.
#
#             See 'man 5 hosts_options' and 'man 5 hosts_access'
#             for information on rule syntax.
#             See 'man tcpd' for information on tcp_wrappers
#
[philip@localhost Documents]$ ls -l | grep The
-rw-rw-r--. 1 philip philip 307 Sep 14 11:01 The_Tee_command.txt.gpg
[philip@localhost Documents]$
```

Excellent! The contents of the file are displayed, but, as we can see, when we ran the ls command, we still only had the encrypted file, and no new file was generated. Rest assured; we can pass the −o option to save the output to a file, as follows:

```
[philip@localhost Documents]$ gpg -o The_Tee_command.txt -d
The_Tee_command.txt.gpg
gpg: AES encrypted data
gpg: encrypted with 1 passphrase
[philip@localhost Documents]$ ls -l | grep The
-rw-rw-r--. 1 philip philip 370 Sep 14 11:10 The_Tee_command.txt
-rw-rw-r--. 1 philip philip 307 Sep 14 11:01 The_Tee_command.txt.gpg
[philip@localhost Documents]$
```

Awesome! Now we have both the encrypted and the unencrypted file.

We can also encrypt and decrypt by using private/public key pairs. First, we have to generate the key pairs by using gpg with the `--gen-key` option, as follows:

```
[philip@localhost Documents]$ gpg --gen-key
gpg (GnuPG) 1.4.22; Copyright (C) 2015 Free Software Foundation, Inc.
This is free software: you are free to change and redistribute it.
There is NO WARRANTY, to the extent permitted by law.
Please select what kind of key you want:
    (1) RSA and RSA (default)
    (2) DSA and Elgamal
    (3) DSA (sign only)
    (4) RSA (sign only)
Your selection?
```

We have to choose the type of key, that is option `(1) RSA and RSA default`; we will accept the default, as follows:

```
RSA keys may be between 1024 and 4096 bits long.
```

We also have to specify the size of the key, the default being `2048`; we will choose `4096`, because a longer key is much more secure:

```
What keysize do you want? (2048) 4096
Requested keysize is 4096 bits
Please specify how long the key should be valid.
        0 = key does not expire
      <n> = key expires in n days
      <n>w = key expires in n weeks
      <n>m = key expires in n months
      <n>y = key expires in n years
Key is valid for? (0) 1y
```

We also have to specify when the key will expire; the default is `0`, which means that it will never expire. We will choose `1y`, which means that it will expire in one year:

```
Key expires at Sat 14 Sep 2019 11:15:50 AM EDT
Is this correct? (y/N) y
You need a user ID to identify your key; the software constructs the user
ID
from the Real Name, Comment and Email Address in this form:
    "Heinrich Heine (Der Dichter) <heinrichh@duesseldorf.de>"
Real name: Philip Inshanally
```

Then, we have to confirm the expiration date and specify the `Real Name`; we will fill in the information as follows:

```
Email address: pinshanally@gmail.com
Comment: It's always good to help others
You selected this USER-ID:
    "Philip Inshanally (It's always good to help others)
<pinshanally@gmail.com>"
Change (N)ame, (C)omment, (E)mail or (O)kay/(Q)uit?
```

We now have to confirm by typing O, as follows:

```
Change (N)ame, (C)omment, (E)mail or (O)kay/(Q)uit? O
You need a Passphrase to protect your secret key.
Repeat passphrase:
```

We also have to protect our secret keys, as follows:

```
We need to generate a lot of random bytes. It is a good idea to perform
some other action (type on the keyboard, move the mouse, utilize the
disks) during the prime generation; this gives the random number
generator a better chance to gain enough entropy.
.+++++
...+++++
We need to generate a lot of random bytes. It is a good idea to perform
some other action (type on the keyboard, move the mouse, utilize the
disks) during the prime generation; this gives the random number
generator a better chance to gain enough entropy.
...............+++++
...+++++
gpg: key 73941CF4 marked as ultimately trusted
public and secret key created and signed.
gpg: checking the trustdb
gpg: 3 marginal(s) needed, 1 complete(s) needed, PGP trust model
gpg: depth: 0  valid:   1  signed:   0  trust: 0-, 0q, 0n, 0m, 0f, 1u
gpg: next trustdb check due at 2019-09-14
pub   4096R/73941CF4 2018-09-14 [expires: 2019-09-14]
      Key fingerprint = 3C24 9577 0081 C03B 4D88  2D34 60E4 B83C 7394 1CF4
uid                  Philip Inshanally (It's always good to help others)
<pinshanally@gmail.com>
sub   4096R/B29CE2BA 2018-09-14 [expires: 2019-09-14]
[philip@localhost Documents]$
```

Excellent! We have successfully generated our key pairs; we can verify this by passing the --list-keys option with the gpg command, as follows:

```
[philip@localhost Documents]$ gpg --list-keys
/home/philip/.gnupg/pubring.gpg
-----------------------------
pub    4096R/73941CF4 2018-09-14 [expires: 2019-09-14]
uid                    Philip Inshanally (It's always good to help others)
<pinshanally@gmail.com>
sub    4096R/B29CE2BA 2018-09-14 [expires: 2019-09-14]
[philip@localhost Documents]$
```

Wonderful! As you can see, our public key information is in
/home/philip/.gnupg/pubring.gpg:

```
[philip@localhost Documents]$ ls -a ~/.gnupg/
.  ..  gpg.conf  pubring.gpg  pubring.gpg~  random_seed  secring.gpg
trustdb.gpg
[philip@localhost Documents]$
```

We can now see our public key information. Next, we will check for our private key information; we will pass the --list-secret-keys option with the gpg command, as follows:

```
[philip@localhost Documents]$ gpg --list-secret-keys
/home/philip/.gnupg/secring.gpg
-----------------------------
sec    4096R/73941CF4 2018-09-14 [expires: 2019-09-14]
uid                    Philip Inshanally (It's always good to help others)
<pinshanally@gmail.com>
ssb    4096R/B29CE2BA 2018-09-14
[philip@localhost Documents]$
```

Excellent! We can see information pertaining to the private key; namely, that the private key is in /home/philip/.gnupg/secring.gpg, as follows:

```
[philip@localhost Documents]$ ls -a ~/.gnupg/
.  ..  gpg.conf  pubring.gpg  pubring.gpg~  random_seed  secring.gpg
trustdb.gpg
[philip@localhost Documents]$
```

Awesome! We can now encrypt by using the public key that we just created, passing the -r option with the gpg command, as follows:

```
[philip@localhost Documents]$ gpg -e The_Tee_command.txt
You did not specify a user ID. (you may use "-r")
Current recipients:
```

```
Enter the user ID.  End with an empty line: pinshanally@gmail.com
Current recipients:
4096R/B29CE2BA 2018-09-14 "Philip Inshanally (It's always good to help
others) <pinshanally@gmail.com>"
Enter the user ID.  End with an empty line:
File `The_Tee_command.txt.gpg' exists. Overwrite? (y/N) y
[philip@localhost Documents]$ ls
date_schedule  ls.txt    ssh         STDIN_STDOUT       TestFile1
The_Tee_command.txt.gpg
lsa_schedule   schedule  STDERR.txt  STDIN_STDOUT.txt  The_Tee_command.txt
[philip@localhost Documents]$
```

We did not specify a user ID with the command, so we were prompted to specify the user ID; we then pressed *Enter* to move to the second line, `Enter the user ID`. It is important to end with an empty line: `""`, we simply pressed *Enter* to generate an empty line. Following this, we have to confirm whether we want to overwrite the file that was encrypted earlier, when we performed symmetric encryption. We can also specify the `user ID` with the `-r` option. Let's give this a try:

```
[philip@localhost Documents]$ rm The_Tee_command.txt.gpg
[philip@localhost Documents]$ gpg -e -r pinshanally@gmail.com
The_Tee_command.txt
[philip@localhost Documents]$ ls -l | grep The
-rw-rw-r--. 1 philip philip 370 Sep 14 11:10 The_Tee_command.txt
-rw-rw-r--. 1 philip philip 827 Sep 14 11:34 The_Tee_command.txt.gpg
[philip@localhost Documents]$
```

Excellent! We weren't prompted to enter the `user ID`, because we specified it using the `-r` option. In order to decrypt the file, we pass the `-d` option, as follows:

```
[philip@localhost Documents]$ gpg -d The_Tee_command.txt.gpg
You need a passphrase to unlock the secret key for
user: "Philip Inshanally (It's always good to help others)
<pinshanally@gmail.com>"
4096-bit RSA key, ID B29CE2BA, created 2018-09-14 (main key ID 73941CF4)
Enter passphrase:
user: "Philip Inshanally (It's always good to help others)
<pinshanally@gmail.com>"
4096-bit RSA key, ID B29CE2BA, created 2018-09-14 (main key ID 73941CF4)
gpg: encrypted with 4096-bit RSA key, ID B29CE2BA, created 2018-09-14
      "Philip Inshanally (It's always good to help
others) <pinshanally@gmail.com>"
# hosts.allow     This file contains access rules which are used to
#                 allow or deny connections to network services that
#                 either use the tcp_wrappers library or that have been
#                 started through a tcp_wrappers-enabled xinetd.
#
```

```
#              See 'man 5 hosts_options' and 'man 5 hosts_access'
#                 for information on rule syntax.
#                 See 'man tcpd' for information on tcp_wrappers
[philip@localhost Documents]$
```

In the preceding code, we ran into the same problem that we did during symmetric decryption; the displayed content is not saved. We can solve this quickly by passing the -o option:

```
[philip@localhost Documents]$ ls -l | grep The
-rw-rw-r--. 1 philip philip 370 Sep 14 11:10 The_Tee_command.txt
-rw-rw-r--. 1 philip philip 827 Sep 14 11:34 The_Tee_command.txt.gpg
[philip@localhost Documents]$ rm The_Tee_command.txt
[philip@localhost Documents]$ gpg -o The_Tee_command.txt -d
The_Tee_command.txt.gpg
You need a passphrase to unlock the secret key for
user: "Philip Inshanally (It's always good to help others)
<pinshanally@gmail.com>"
4096-bit RSA key, ID B29CE2BA, created 2018-09-14 (main key ID 73941CF4)
Enter passphrase:
gpg: encrypted with 4096-bit RSA key, ID B29CE2BA, created 2018-09-14
      "Philip Inshanally (It's always good to help others)
<pinshanally@gmail.com>"
[philip@localhost Documents]$ ls -l | grep The
-rw-rw-r--. 1 philip philip 370 Sep 14 11:39 The_Tee_command.txt
-rw-rw-r--. 1 philip philip 827 Sep 14 11:34 The_Tee_command.txt.gpg
[philip@localhost Documents]$
```

Excellent! The file was decrypted successfully.

It is also possible to edit a key; we pass the --edit-key option with the gpg command, as follows:

```
[philip@localhost Documents]$ gpg --edit-key pinshanally@gmail.com
gpg (GnuPG) 1.4.22; Copyright (C) 2015 Free Software Foundation, Inc.
This is free software: you are free to change and redistribute it.
There is NO WARRANTY, to the extent permitted by law.
Secret key is available.
pub  4096R/73941CF4  created: 2018-09-14  expires: 2019-09-14  usage: SC
                     trust: ultimate      validity: ultimate
sub  4096R/B29CE2BA  created: 2018-09-14  expires: 2019-09-14  usage: E
[ultimate] (1). Philip Inshanally (It's always good to help
others)<pinshanally@gmail.com>
gpg>
```

In the preceding command, we can make a number of changes. For instance, if we want to disable the key, we can type `disable`, as follows:

```
gpg> disable
gpg> list
pub   4096R/73941CF4  created: 2018-09-14  expires: 2019-09-14  usage: SC
                      trust: ultimate      validity: ultimate
*** This key has been disabled
sub   4096R/B29CE2BA  created: 2018-09-14  expires: 2019-09-14  usage: E
[ultimate] (1). Philip Inshanally (It's always good to help others)
<pinshanally@gmail.com>
Please note that the shown key validity is not necessarily correct
unless you restart the program.
gpg>
```

In the preceding command, we changed the `*** This key has been disabled` key; let's see the effect of this by saving and exiting, as follows:

```
gpg> save
Key not changed so no update needed.
[philip@localhost Documents]$ rm The_Tee_command.txt.gpg
[philip@localhost Documents]$
[philip@localhost Documents]$ gpg -e -r pinshanally@gmail.com
The_Tee_command.txt
gpg: pinshanally@gmail.com: skipped: public key not found
gpg: The_Tee_command.txt: encryption failed: public key not found
[philip@localhost Documents]$
```

When we try to use the key to encrypt the file, we are given an error. We can fix this quickly by changing `disable` to `enable` inside of the `gpg` console, as follows:

```
philip@localhost Documents]$ gpg --edit-key pinshanally@gmail.com
gpg (GnuPG) 1.4.22; Copyright (C) 2015 Free Software Foundation, Inc.
This is free software: you are free to change and redistribute it.
There is NO WARRANTY, to the extent permitted by law.
Secret key is available.
pub   4096R/73941CF4  created: 2018-09-14  expires: 2019-09-14  usage: SC
                      trust: ultimate      validity: ultimate
*** This key has been disabled
sub   4096R/B29CE2BA  created: 2018-09-14  expires: 2019-09-14  usage: E
[ultimate] (1). Philip Inshanally (It's always good to help others)
<pinshanally@gmail.com>
gpg> enable
gpg> list
pub   4096R/73941CF4  created: 2018-09-14  expires: 2019-09-14  usage: SC
                      trust: ultimate      validity: ultimate
sub   4096R/B29CE2BA  created: 2018-09-14  expires: 2019-09-14  usage: E
[ultimate] (1). Philip Inshanally (It's always good to help others)
```

```
<pinshanally@gmail.com>
Please note that the shown key validity is not necessarily correct
unless you restart the program.
gpg> save
Key not changed so no update needed.
[philip@localhost Documents]$
[philip@localhost Documents]$ gpg -e -r pinshanally@gmail.com
The_Tee_command.txt
gpg: checking the trustdb
gpg: 3 marginal(s) needed, 1 complete(s) needed, PGP trust model
gpg: depth: 0  valid:   1  signed:   0  trust: 0-, 0q, 0n, 0m, 0f, 1u
gpg: next trustdb check due at 2019-09-14
[philip@localhost Documents]$ ls -l | grep The
-rw-rw-r--. 1 philip philip 370 Sep 14 11:54 The_Tee_command.txt
-rw-rw-r--. 1 philip philip 827 Sep 14 11:55 The_Tee_command.txt.gpg
[philip@localhost Documents]$
```

Excellent!

Summary

In this chapter, we covered a wide array of security features that are available to us in the Linux environment. First, we covered accessing commands with root privileges; particularly, we looked at the su and sudo commands. We then moved on to TCP wrappers, focusing on the /etc/hosts.allow and /etc/hosts.deny files. We looked at how the two files can complement each other by allowing access via the /etc/hosts.allow file and denying everything in the /etc/hosts.deny file.

Next, we covered SSH; we looked at setting up SSH access between a client and a server, allowing for a seamless login without entering a password, and we covered using a passphrase. We then cached the passphrase, so that the user would not have to enter a passphrase when logging into the server. Finally, we covered encryption in depth. We focused on symmetric encryption, which involves a passphrase; we then took it up a notch by working with key pairs in encryption. We finished by looking at how we can edit key properties.

In the next (and final) chapter, we will finish the book by focusing on shell scripting and SQL data management. It is crucial to acquire some shell scripting and SQL management skills while working in a Linux environment.

Questions

1. Which of the following commands can launch another command each time a rule is activated in /etc/hosts.allow?

    A. ALL
    B. deny
    C. spawn
    D. log

2. What does su stand for?

    A. Superuser
    B. Substitute user
    C. Switch user
    D. None of the above

3. Which of the following users' password is requested when we use the su command without any options?

    A. Root user
    B. Current user
    C. SSH passphrase
    D. None of the above

4. Which of the following options allows for a command to be executed without logging in, using the su command?

    A. -a
    B. -c
    C. -d
    D. -l

5. Which of the following symbols has to be in front of a group when being declared in /etc/sudoers?

    A. -
    B. ^
    C. -$
    D. %

6. Which of the following commands is used to create an SSH key pair?

      A. `ssh-keygen`
      B. `ssh-key-gen`
      C. `ssh-create-key`
      D. `ssh-key`

7. Which of the following commands is used to add an identity to the SSH agent?

      A. `ssh-add`
      B. `ssh-agent`
      C. `ssh.service`
      D. `ssh-daemon`

8. Which of the following commands copies over the SSH public key securely?

      A. `ssh-copy`
      B. `ssh-copy-id`
      C. `ssh-cp`
      D. `ssh-id-copy`

9. Which of the following options is used to encrypt a file with the `gpg` command?

      A. `-d`
      B. `-e`
      C. `-r`
      D. `-a`

10. Which of the following options is used to provide the identity with the `gpg` command?

      A. `-f`
      B. `-e`
      C. `-r`
      D. `-a`

Further reading

- The following site provides useful information about `sudo`: `https://www.computerhope.com/unix/sudo.htm`
- The following site provides useful information about SSH: `https://www.ssh.com`
- The following site provides useful information about encryption: `http://linuxaria.com`

18
Shell Scripting and SQL Data Management

In the last chapter, we covered a wide array of security features that are available in the Linux environment. First, we discussed executing commands with root privileges. We then moved on to TCP wrappers, focusing on the `/etc/hosts.allow` and `/etc/hosts.deny` files. Next, we covered SSH; we looked at setting up SSH access between a client and a server. Finally, we covered encryption in depth.

In this chapter, the final chapter of this book, we will be covering the basics of shell scripting and SQL management. First, we will look at the syntax for writing a shell script; this will be followed by writing scripts with various loops, such as the `for` and `while` loops. Next, we will cover writing shell scripts using `if` statements. Finally, we will finish this chapter (and book) by covering the basics of SQL management.

We will cover the following topics in this chapter:

- Shell scripting
- SQL data management

Shell scripting

In this section, we will cover shell scripting, starting with the basics and moving on to writing scripts using loops and `if` statements.

The following topics will be covered in this section:

- The basics of shell scripting
- Writing scripts using `for` loops
- Writing scripts using `while` loops
- Writing scripts using `if` statements

The basics of shell scripting

On the command line, we often work with a series of the same commands on a regular basis. It would be ideal to somehow bundle those commands and simplify the process, executing a single command or script to accomplish an overall objective that would take longer if we had to type out a single command repetitively. This is where shell scripting shines. We can place our commands, regardless of how long they may be, into a single file; give it an appropriate name; and execute the script as needed. The following code shows the basic syntax for creating a shell script:

```
#! /bin/sh
```

The preceding command is the first line in the script; it is used to define the shell interpreter. The first characters, `#!`, are often known as shebang, sha-bang, hashbang, pound-bang, or hash-pling. The `/bin/sh` object defines which interpreter should be used for this script; in this case, it's the Shell Command Language (`sh`). Another popular interpreter that you are bound to see is the following:

```
#!/bin/bash
```

This is similar to the previous declaration, in that we have `#!`, which indicates that we are going to define the shell interpreter to use; in this case, we're using the Bourne Again Shell, or Bash. This shell offers more extensions than the regular `sh` shell; in fact, most newer Linux distributions are ported with Bash as a defacto shell. We can easily identify which shell is in play by issuing the following command in the Terminal:

```
[philip@localhost Documents]$ echo $SHELL
/bin/bash
[philip@localhost Documents]$
```

Awesome! The environment variable, SHELL, stores the current shell; the value returned indicates that we are running the bash shell. Another way to identify the shell is as follows:

```
[philip@localhost Documents]$ echo $0
bash
[philip@localhost Documents]$
```

Excellent! The bash shell is being used. Also, we can use the ps command to display the current shell, as follows:

```
[philip@localhost Documents]$ ps
   PID TTY          TIME CMD
 74972 pts/1     00:00:03 bash
 75678 pts/1     00:00:39 dnf
 92796 pts/1     00:00:00 ps
[philip@localhost Documents]$
```

Awesome! For our purposes, we will be using #!/bin/bash for written scripts. To begin writing your very first script, open a text editor, such as vi or nano, and enter the following:

```
philip@localhost Documents]$ vi myFirstScript.sh
```

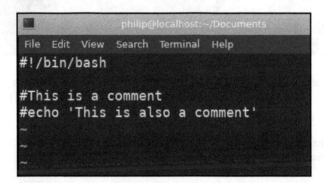

Excellent! We have our declaration in the first line; we've defined the /bin/bash shell. Next, we have two lines that begin with a # symbol. Any line (other than the first line at the top) is referred to as a comment. That being said, the last two lines are comments. We can prove this by saving our script; we can use :wq, which will save and exit our script, as follows:

```
[philip@localhost Documents]$ cat myFirstScript.sh
#!/bin/bash
#This is a comment
#echo 'This is also a comment'
[philip@localhost Documents]$
```

In the preceding code snippet, we can see the contents of our script. The next step is to make our script executable; in order to run a script, it has to be executable. We can do this with the chmod command, as follows:

```
date_schedule  ls.txt      ssh           STDIN_STDOUT      TestFile1           The_Tee_command.txt.gpg
lsa_schedule   schedule  STDERR.txt  STDIN_STDOUT.txt  The_Tee_command.txt
[philip@localhost Documents]$ vi myFirstScript.sh
[philip@localhost Documents]$ vi myFirstScript.sh
[philip@localhost Documents]$ cat myFirstScript.sh
#!/bin/bash

#This is a comment
#echo 'This is also a comment'
[philip@localhost Documents]$ ls
date_schedule  ls.txt              schedule  STDERR.txt      STDIN_STDOUT.txt  The_Tee_command.txt
lsa_schedule   myFirstScript.sh  ssh           STDIN_STDOUT  TestFile1           The_Tee_command.txt.gpg
[philip@localhost Documents]$ ls -l myFirstScript.sh
-rw-rw-r--. 1 philip philip 63 Sep 17 09:45 myFirstScript.sh
[philip@localhost Documents]$ chmod +x myFirstScript.sh
[philip@localhost Documents]$ ls -l myFirstScript.sh
-rwxrwxr-x. 1 philip philip 63 Sep 17 09:45 myFirstScript.sh
[philip@localhost Documents]$
[philip@localhost Documents]$
[philip@localhost Documents]$
[philip@localhost Documents]$
[philip@localhost Documents]$
[philip@localhost Documents]$
[philip@localhost Documents]$
```

Excellent! We've used +x, which turns on the execute bit for the user, group, and others; also, the script's name has been changed to the color green, to indicate that the file is now executable. In order to run this script, we use the following commands:

```
[philip@localhost Documents]$ ./myFirstScript.sh
[philip@localhost Documents]$
```

Awesome! The script was executed; however, the contents were not displayed. This is due to the fact that we've only defined comments so far; we have not defined anything else inside of our script. Let's make our script display a short message. Open the script using either vi or nano, and enter the following:

```
[philip@localhost Documents]$ cat myFirstScript.sh
#!/bin/bash
#This is a comment
#echo 'This is also a comment'
echo 'Hello world'
[philip@localhost Documents]$
```

Awesome! We've added our first command to be executed: the echo command. This will simply respond with whatever is passed, as follows:

```
[philip@localhost Documents]$ ./myFirstScript.sh
Hello world
[philip@localhost Documents]$
```

Excellent! We've successfully written our very first script. Let's add another command, to illustrate the effectiveness of scripting; we'll add the date command, which will provide the date whenever we execute our script, as follows:

```
[philip@localhost Documents]$ cat myFirstScript.sh
#!/bin/bash
#This is a comment
#echo 'This is also a comment'
echo 'Hello world'
date
[philip@localhost Documents]$ ./myFirstScript.sh
Hello world
Mon Sep 17 10:04:48 EDT 2018
[philip@localhost Documents]$
```

Wonderful! We now have two commands that are executed every time our script runs. In addition to sending output to the display, we can carry out other tasks. For instance, we can create an archive file. Let's create a .tar file of the /home/philip/Downloads directory for illustration, as follows:

```
[philip@localhost Documents]$ cat myFirstScript.sh
#!/bin/bash
#This is a comment
#echo 'This is also a comment'
echo 'Hello world'
date
tar -cvf mytar.tar /home/philip/Downloads
[philip@localhost Documents]$
```

In the preceding code, we used the tar command to create an archive of the /home/philip/Downloads directory. Now, we can run the script to see the results, as follows:

```
[philip@localhost Documents]$ ./myFirstScript.sh
Hello world
Mon Sep 17 10:35:37 EDT 2018
tar: Removing leading `/' from member names
/home/philip/Downloads/
/home/philip/Downloads/home/
/home/philip/Downloads/home/philip/
```

```
/home/philip/Downloads/home/philip/Downloads/
/home/philip/Downloads/home/philip/Downloads/song.mp3
[philip@localhost Documents]$ ls  | grep tar
mytar.tar
[philip@localhost Documents]$
```

Excellent! Our script was successful, and an archive was created with the `.tar` extension. Additionally, we can create a script that takes input from the user, using the `read` command. Let's create another script and name it `input.sh`, using vi or nano, as follows:

```
[philip@localhost Documents]$ ls -l input.sh
-rw-rw-r--. 1 philip philip 75 Sep 17 10:42 input.sh
[philip@localhost Documents]$ cat input.sh
#!/bin/bash

echo 'Whats your name?'
read name
echo 'your name is $name'
[philip@localhost Documents]$ chmod +x input.sh
[philip@localhost Documents]$
```

Awesome! We've created an `input.sh` script; we've used the `read` command to store the input from the user. The value stored in the name is called a variable. It is displayed in the last line, by adding a `$` in front of the variable's name. The result of the script is shown as follows:

The prompt is paused until we enter something; we will enter a name and look at the results, as follows:

```
[philip@localhost Documents]$ ./input.sh
Whats your name?
Philip
your name is: Philip
[philip@localhost Documents]$
```

Excellent! The name that we entered was appended to the last line. Another way that we can define a variable is by using the following syntax:

```
<variable name> = <value>
```

In the preceding code, we give the variable a name, and then specify a value.

Let's create a new script named `myvar.sh`, using either vi or nano. The following code shows how we can define a variable using a new script:

```
[philip@localhost Documents]$ vi myvar.sh
[philip@localhost Documents]$ cat myvar.sh
#!/bin/bash


OUR_VAR="Philip Inshanally"

echo "The variable which we defined is $OUR_VAR"
[philip@localhost Documents]$ chmod +x myvar.sh
[philip@localhost Documents]$ ./myvar.sh
The variable which we defined is Philip Inshanally
[philip@localhost Documents]$
```

Awesome! We defined a variable, OUR_VAR, and we gave it the value, Philip Inshanally; this was then called inside of the echo command, by placing a $ symbol in front of the variable name. As you can see, there are various ways to define a variable. The variable value needs to be enclosed in parentheses whenever there is a space between the words. If there is only a single word, or numbers, you do not have to enclose the value in parentheses. Do not enclose a single word or a number in parentheses.

Writing scripts using for loops

It is possible to write out each command in a script line by line, which can be cumbersome at times. We can achieve the same objective by using loops, which execute based on an expression being met, generating the commands for us. The basic syntax of a `for` loop is as follows:

```
for             <condition>
do
                <command1>
                <command2>
                ...
                <commandN>
done
```

The first line defines a condition and, once the condition is met, we have a series of commands. To see this in action, let's create a script, called `myForLoop.sh`, using either vi or nano:

```
[philip@localhost Documents]$ vi myForLoop.sh
[philip@localhost Documents]$ chmod +x myForLoop.sh
[philip@localhost Documents]$ cat myForLoop.sh
#!/bin/bash
echo 'This script displays how a for loop works'
for o in {1..10}
do
                echo "The loop is running for the: $o time"
done
[philip@localhost Documents]$
```

Awesome! The line that begins with `for o in {1..10}` defines how many times we would like to execute the `for` loop; it will be executed 10 times. The command under the `do` section is the command that will be executed; the `$o` is the variable that was defined in the `for` section. The result will be as follows:

```
[philip@localhost Documents]$ ./myForLoop.sh
This script displays how a for loop works
The loop is running for the: 1 time
The loop is running for the: 2 time
The loop is running for the: 3 time
The loop is running for the: 4 time
The loop is running for the: 5 time
The loop is running for the: 6 time
The loop is running for the: 7 time
The loop is running for the: 8 time
The loop is running for the: 9 time
The loop is running for the: 10 time
[philip@localhost Documents]$
```

Excellent! This condition can also be written in the following format:

```
[philip@localhost Documents]$ cat myForLoop.sh
#!/bin/bash
echo 'This script displays how a for loop works'
#for o in {1..10}
for p in 1 2 3 4 5 6 7 8 9 10 11 12
do
                echo "The loop is running for the: $p time"
done
[philip@localhost Documents]$
 [philip@localhost Documents]$ ./myForLoop.sh
This script displays how a for loop works
The loop is running for the: 1 time
The loop is running for the: 2 time
The loop is running for the: 3 time
The loop is running for the: 4 time
The loop is running for the: 5 time
The loop is running for the: 6 time
The loop is running for the: 7 time
The loop is running for the: 8 time
The loop is running for the: 9 time
The loop is running for the: 10 time
The loop is running for the: 11 time
The loop is running for the: 12 time
[philip@localhost Documents]$
```

Awesome! We wrote the values, separated by spaces, and the script was successful. We can also specify the condition in three parts, similar to the C programming language, as follows:

```
[philip@localhost Documents]$ cat myForLoop.sh
#!/bin/bash


echo 'This script displays how a for loop works'


#for o in {1..10}
#for p in 1 2 3 4 5 6 7 8 9 10 11 12
for ((p=1; p<=6; p++))
do
 echo "The loop is running for the: $p time"
done
[philip@localhost Documents]$
 [philip@localhost Documents]$ ./myForLoop.sh
This script displays how a for loop works
The loop is running for the: 1 time
The loop is running for the: 2 time
The loop is running for the: 3 time
The loop is running for the: 4 time
The loop is running for the: 5 time
The loop is running for the: 6 time
[philip@localhost Documents]$
```

Excellent! In the preceding code, the `for ((p=1; p<=6; p++))` line defines a variable and assigns it a value of `p=1`; the `p<=6` checks for the condition, and the `p++` means to increment the value of the variable as long as the condition is met.

Writing scripts using the while loop

Another popular loop that can be used in scripting is the `while` loop. The basic syntax of a `while` loop is as follows:

```
while <condition>
do
                <command1>
                <command2>
                ...
                <commandN>
done
```

In the preceding code, we specify a condition, and, as long as the condition is met, the loop will be executed.

Create a script named `myWhile.sh`, using either vi or nano, as follows:

```
[philip@localhost Documents]$ vi myWhile.sh
[philip@localhost Documents]$ chmod +x myWhile.sh
[philip@localhost Documents]$ cat myWhile.sh
#!/bin/bash


d=1


while (( $d <= 8 ))
do
                echo "The number is $d times"
                d=$(( d+1 ))
done
[philip@localhost Documents]$
```

Excellent! First, we defined a variable, `d=1`, and we then specified a condition, `(( $d <= 8 ))`, which checks whether the variable, d, is less than or equal to 8; following this, we are using the `echo` command to provide the text, based on the condition. The last part, `d=$(( d+1 ))`, will increment the variable after each condition is met, as follows:

```
[philip@localhost Documents]$ ./myWhile.sh
The number is 1 times
The number is 2 times
The number is 3 times
The number is 4 times
The number is 5 times
The number is 6 times
The number is 7 times
The number is 8 times
[philip@localhost Documents]$
```

Awesome! Another technique that can be used for a condition is `:`, which is used after the `while` statement. `:` will always be `True`; this means that the loop will not end until we end the script, using *Ctrl + C*. Let's create another script, named `infinite.sh`, using either vi or nano, as follows:

```
[philip@localhost Documents]$ vi infinite.sh
[philip@localhost Documents]$ chmod +x infinite.sh
[philip@localhost Documents]$ cat infinite.sh
#!/bin/bash
while :
```

```
do
  echo "You can enter text and press Enter as many times (exit using
CTRL+c)"
  read someText
  echo "You typed $someText"
done
[philip@localhost Documents]$
```

A prompt will appear, allowing us to type anything; as soon as we press the *Enter* key, another message will be displayed, including whatever we typed. This will continue infinitely, until we exit the script using *Ctrl + C*, as follows:

```
[philip@localhost Documents]$ ./infinite.sh
You can enter text and press Enter as many times (exit using CTRL+c)
Hi
You typed Hi
You can enter text and press Enter as many times (exit using CTRL+c)
How are you?
You typed How are you?
You can enter text and press Enter as many times (exit using CTRL+c)
I can keep typing
You typed I can keep typing
You can enter text and press Enter as many times (exit using CTRL+c)
and typing
You typed and typing
You can enter text and press Enter as many times (exit using CTRL+c)
I can exit by using the keystroke as shown in the message above
You typed I can exit by using the keystroke as shown in the message above
You can enter text and press Enter as many times (exit using CTRL+c)
^C
[philip@localhost Documents]$
```

Awesome! The script did not quit until we used the *Ctrl + C* combination. Another way to illustrate the effectiveness of the `while` loop is to look for a string before the script exits. Create another script, named `whileString.sh`, using either vi or nano, as follows:

```
[philip@localhost Documents]$ vi whileString.sh
[philip@localhost Documents]$ chmod +x whileString.sh
[philip@localhost Documents]$ cat whileString.sh
#!/bin/bash
someString=begin
while [ "$someString" != "quit" ]
do
                echo "Enter some text (type quit to exit)"
                read someString
                echo "You entered: $someString"
done
[philip@localhost Documents]$
```

Awesome! We declared a variable, `someString=begin`; this can be any value that you choose. Next, we checked for a condition, `[ "$someString" != "quit" ]`, which looks for the `quit` string. As long as the string is not `quit`, the script will keep running infinitely, until we type `quit` or press *Ctrl + C*, which will exit the script, as follows:

```
[philip@localhost Documents]$ ./whileString.sh
Enter some text (type quit to exit)
Hi
You entered: Hi
Enter some text (type quit to exit)
my name is Philip
You entered: my name is Philip
Enter some text (type quit to exit)
How are you
You entered: How are you
Enter some text (type quit to exit)
quit
You entered: quit
[philip@localhost Documents]$
```

Excellent! We could keep entering text, and the script would continue to run, unless we entered quit or pressed *Ctrl + C*, which would exit the script.

Notice that we used square brackets ([]) to enclose the text; the script would not work with the regular parentheses (()) when testing for a string value.

Writing scripts using if statements

We can use `if` statements in scripting in order to test a condition. The basic syntax of an `if` statement is as follows:

```
if [some condition]; then
            execute something
fi
or
if [[some condition]]; then
            execute something
fi
```

We can create a simple `if` script using the preceding code as guidance. Sometimes, we may need to use double square brackets, which offer enhancements over the older, single-bracket style. Let's create a script named `myif.sh`, using vi or nano, as follows:

```
[philip@localhost Documents]$ vi myif.sh
[philip@localhost Documents]$ cat myif.sh
```

```
#!/bin/bash


echo "Welcome to our if statement script"
if [[ $1 == 4 ]]; then
                echo "You're very smart"
fi
echo "See you soon!"
[philip@localhost Documents]$ chmod +x myif.sh
[philip@localhost Documents]$ ./myif.sh
Welcome to our if statement script
See you soon!
[philip@localhost Documents]$
```

We used the echo command to display a welcome message; we then used if [[$1 == 4]]; then; this statement is checking for 4. The script executed, but we did not see the echo command inside of the if statement being executed. In order to see the message inside of the if statement, we have to type a value when we run our script, as follows:

```
[philip@localhost Documents]$ ./myif.sh 4
Welcome to our if statement script
You're very smart
See you soon!
[philip@localhost Documents]$
```

Wonderful; the statement inside of the if construct was executed, but, if we passed any value other than 4, we would see the following:

```
[philip@localhost Documents]$ ./myif.sh 3
Welcome to our if statement script
See you soon!
[philip@localhost Documents]$
```

The command inside of the if statement was not executed, due to the fact that the value that we passed is not equal to the value being checked against. We can add another bit to the if statement to handle an alternate response. For this, we can use the else clause. The following is the syntax of the else clause that is injected into the if statement:

```
if [[some condition]]; then
                execute something
else
                execute something else
fi
```

We can edit our my.sh script, using either vi or nano, and add an else clause to handle any alternate responses, as follows:

```
[philip@localhost Documents]$ vi myif.sh
[philip@localhost Documents]$ cat myif.sh
#!/bin/bash
echo "Welcome to our if statement script"
if [[ $1 == 4 ]]; then
                echo "You're very smart"
else
                echo " Better luck next time"
fi
echo "See you soon!"
[philip@localhost Documents]$
```

Awesome! We can run our script with the else clause injected; the result will be as follows:

```
[philip@localhost Documents]$ ./myif.sh 3
Welcome to our if statement script
Better luck next time
See you soon!
[philip@localhost Documents]$ ./myif.sh 2
Welcome to our if statement script
Better luck next time
See you soon!
[philip@localhost Documents]$ ./myif.sh 4
Welcome to our if statement script
You're very smart
See you soon!
[philip@localhost Documents]$
```

Excellent! We're shown a different message whenever the user enters a value other than 4. Furthermore, we can nest an if statement inside of another if statement. The basic syntax for nesting if statements is as follows:

```
if [[first condition]]; then
execute something
elif [[second condition]]; then
                execute something else
  elif [[third condition]]; then
                execute something else
else
                execute_a_last_resort_command
  fi
```

We can edit our `myif.sh` script, using either vi or nano, and add a second `elif` statement, as follows:

```
[philip@localhost Documents]$ cat myif.sh
#!/bin/bash
echo "Welcome to our if statement script"
if [[ $1 == 4 ]]; then
                echo "You're very smart"
elif [[ $1 == 2 ]]; then
                echo "You've got your elseif value correct!"
else
                echo "Reach for the sky"
fi
echo "See you soon!"
[philip@localhost Documents]$
```

We've added `elif [[ $1 == 2 ]]; then`, which checks for the value 2. Once this condition is met, a message will be displayed, as follows:

```
[philip@localhost Documents]$ ./myif.sh 2
Welcome to our if statement script
You've got your elseif value correct!
See you soon!
[philip@localhost Documents]$ ./myif.sh 3
Welcome to our if statement script
Reach for the sky
See you soon!
[philip@localhost Documents]$ ./myif.sh 4
Welcome to our if statement script
You're very smart
See you soon!
[philip@localhost Documents]$
```

Excellent! We can see that when we enter a value that matches the `elif` condition, the command under the `elif` condition is executed. Additionally, when we enter a value that does not match either the `if` or `elif` condition, a catch-all message is displayed.

It is also possible to test multiple conditions on a single `if` statement or `elif` statement. Let's edit our `myif.sh`, using vi or nano, as follows:

```
[philip@localhost Documents]$ cat myif.sh
#!/bin/bash
echo "Welcome to our if statement script"
if [[ $1 == 4 ]] || [[ $1 == 3 ]] ; then
                echo "You're very smart"
elif [[ $1 == 2 ]]; then
                echo "You've got your elseif value correct!"
```

```
        else
                    echo "Reach for the sky"
        fi
        echo "See you soon!"
        [philip@localhost Documents]$
```

In the preceding code, we've added a second condition in the if statement; namely, if [[
$1 == 4]] || [[$1 == 3]] ; then. The || means *or*. This checks for either
condition to be met, and the command will be executed under the if statement, as follows:

```
[philip@localhost Documents]$ ./myif.sh 4
Welcome to our if statement script
You're very smart
See you soon!
[philip@localhost Documents]$ ./myif.sh 3
Welcome to our if statement script
You're very smart
See you soon!
 [philip@localhost Documents]$
```

Excellent! Once either condition is met in the if clause, the command is executed under the
if clause. Additionally, there is the && command, used for comparing conditions; this
means that both conditions must be met. We can quickly edit our myif.sh script and add
in &&, as follows:

```
[philip@localhost Documents]$ cat myif.sh
#!/bin/bash
echo "Welcome to our if statement script"
if [[ $1 == 4 ]] || [[ $1 == 3 ]] ; then
                    echo "You're very smart"
elif [[ $1 == 2 ]] && [[ $1 != 1 ]] ; then
                    echo "You've got your elseif value correct!"
else
                    echo "Reach for the sky"
fi
echo "See you soon!"
[philip@localhost Documents]$
```

When the user enters 2, the elif condition will be met; this is due to the fact that both
conditions need to be true. If the user enters any value other than 2, the catch-all else
clause will be executed as follows:

```
[philip@localhost Documents]$ ./myif.sh 1
Welcome to our if statement script
Reach for the sky
See you soon!
[philip@localhost Documents]$ ./myif.sh 2
```

```
Welcome to our if statement script
You've got your elseif value correct!
See you soon!
[philip@localhost Documents]$
```

Excellent! Both conditions were met in the `elif` clause, resulting in the command being executed under the `elif` clause.

SQL data management

Structured Query Language (**SQL**) is a well-known language used for database manipulation. There are various versions of SQL. We will be working with an open standard of MySQL: the `mysql-community-server` package. First, we will need the MySQL YUM repository in our Fedora 28 system; we will use the `dnf` command, as follows:

```
[philip@localhost Documents]$ sudo dnf install
https://dev.mysql.com/get/mysql80-community-release-fc28-1.noarch.rpm
===============================================================================
==================================================
 Package        Arch  Version    Repository                Size
===============================================================================
==================================================
Installing:
mysql80-community-release     noarch  fc28-1        @commandline
30 k


Transaction Summary
===============================================================================
==================================================
Install  1 Package
Total size: 30 k
Installed size: 29 k
Is this ok [y/N]: y
Installed:
mysql80-community-release.noarch fc28-1
Complete!
[philip@localhost Documents]$
```

Awesome! The repository was successfully installed. Now, we will install the server, as follows:

```
[philip@localhost Documents]$ sudo dnf install mysql-community-server
MySQL 8.0 Community Server
302 kB/s | 215 kB      00:00
```

```
MySQL Connectors Community
32 kB/s |   15 kB      00:00
MySQL Tools Community
75 kB/s |   28 kB      00:00


Total download size: 359 M
Installed size: 1.6 G
Is this ok [y/N]: y
```

In the preceding code, some output has been omitted for brevity. The package is going to take up over 1 GB in space; the time it will take to download will vary, depending on your internet connection. The progress will look as follows:

After some time, we will see the following:

```
Installed:
  mysql-community-server.x86_64 8.0.12-1.fc28                  mecab.x86_64
0.996-2.fc28
  mysql-community-client.x86_64 8.0.12-1.fc28                  mysql-
community-common.x86_64 8.0.12-1.fc28
  mysql-community-libs.x86_64 8.0.12-1.fc28
Complete!
[philip@localhost Documents]$
```

Excellent! The next step is to enable the `mysqld` service; we will use the `systemctl` command, as follows:

```
[philip@localhost Documents]$ sudo systemctl start mysqld
[philip@localhost Documents]$ sudo systemctl enable mysqld
[philip@localhost Documents]$ systemctl status mysqld
```

```
                                    philip@localhost:~/Documents
File  Edit  View  Search  Terminal  Help
[philip@localhost Documents]$ sudo systemctl enable mysqld
[philip@localhost Documents]$ systemctl status mysqld
● mysqld.service - MySQL Server
   Loaded: loaded (/usr/lib/systemd/system/mysqld.service; enabled; vendor preset: disabled)
   Active: active (running) since Mon 2018-09-17 15:25:48 EDT; 23s ago
     Docs: man:mysqld(8)
           http://dev.mysql.com/doc/refman/en/using-systemd.html
 Main PID: 106707 (mysqld)
   Status: "SERVER_OPERATING"
    Tasks: 37 (limit: 2331)
   Memory: 493.9M
   CGroup: /system.slice/mysqld.service
           └─106707 /usr/sbin/mysqld

Sep 17 15:25:21 localhost.localdomain systemd[1]: Starting MySQL Server...
Sep 17 15:25:48 localhost.localdomain systemd[1]: Started MySQL Server.
[philip@localhost Documents]$
[philip@localhost Documents]$
[philip@localhost Documents]$
[philip@localhost Documents]$
```

Awesome! The `mysqld.service` was started successfully. During the installation, a random `root` password for the `mysql` server was generated; we have to look inside of the `/var/log/mysqld.log` file, as follows:

```
[philip@localhost Documents]$ grep 'A temporary password is generated for
root@localhost' /var/log/mysqld.log |tail -1
2018-09-17T19:25:35.229434Z 5 [Note] [MY-010454] [Server] A temporary
password is generated for root@localhost: #a7RCyoyzwOF
[philip@localhost Documents]$
```

The random password for the `root` of the `mysql` is #a7RCyoyzwOF. Finally, we should secure our `mysql` database. For this, we will use the `mysql_secure_installation` command, as follows:

```
[philip@localhost Documents]$ mysql_secure_installation
Securing the MySQL server deployment.
Enter password for user root:
The existing password for the user account root has expired. Please set a
new password.
New password:
```

First, we have to enter the random password; then, we have to set a new password, as follows:

```
New password:
Re-enter new password:
The 'validate_password' component is installed on the server.
The subsequent steps will run with the existing configuration
of the component.
Using existing password for root.
Estimated strength of the password: 100
Change the password for root ? ((Press y|Y for Yes, any other key for No)  :
```

The `validate_password` plugin is installed by default; this sets the password specifications. We will have to enter a password that is a combination that consists of at least one uppercase character, one lowercase character, one digit, and one special character. The total password length must be at least eight characters, as follows:

```
Do you wish to continue with the password provided?(Press y|Y for Yes, any
other key for No) : y
By default, a MySQL installation has an anonymous user,
allowing anyone to log into MySQL without having to have
a user account created for them. This is intended only for
testing, and to make the installation go a bit smoother.
You should remove them before moving into a production
environment.
Remove anonymous users? (Press y|Y for Yes, any other key for No) : y
```

By default, an anonymous user account is generated; we will select y to remove it and continue:

```
Normally, root should only be allowed to connect from
'localhost'. This ensures that someone cannot guess at
the root password from the network.
Disallow root login remotely? (Press y|Y for Yes, any other key for No)  :
```

We will allow the `root` user to log in remotely, so we will press a key, and this step will be skipped, as follows:

```
 ... skipping.
By default, MySQL comes with a database named 'test' that
anyone can access. This is also intended only for testing,
and should be removed before moving into a production
environment.
Remove test database and access to it? (Press y|Y for Yes, any other key
for No) : y
 - Dropping test database...
Success.
```

```
- Removing privileges on test database...
Success.
Reloading the privilege tables will ensure that all changes
made so far will take effect immediately.
Reload privilege tables now? (Press y|Y for Yes, any other key for No) : y
Success.
All done!
[philip@localhost Documents]$
```

mysql is now more secure than the default installation. We can now log in to the mysql
database using the mysql command, as follows:

```
[philip@localhost Documents]$ mysql -u root -p
Enter password:
Welcome to the MySQL monitor.  Commands end with ; or \g.
Your MySQL connection id is 21
Server version: 8.0.12 MySQL Community Server - GPL
Copyright (c) 2000, 2018, Oracle and/or its affiliates. All rights
reserved.
Oracle is a registered trademark of Oracle Corporation and/or its
affiliates. Other names may be trademarks of their respective
owners.
Type 'help;' or '\h' for help. Type '\c' to clear the current input
statement.
mysql>
```

Excellent! We will now create our first database; we will use the create database
command for this:

```
mysql> create database netaccess;
Query OK, 1 row affected (0.10 sec)
mysql>
```

Awesome! We will now create a user that can access our database; we will use the create
user command here:

```
mysql> create user 'philip'@'172.16.175.130' identified by 'password123';
ERROR 1819 (HY000): Your password does not satisfy the current policy
requirements
mysql>
```

In the preceding code, once again, the password requirements are not being met; we can
remedy this either by lowering the settings or removing the validate_password
components. We will remove the validate_password components as follows:

```
mysql> uninstall plugin validate_password;
ERROR 1305 (42000): PLUGIN validate_password does not exist
```

```
mysql> exit
Bye
[philip@localhost Documents]$ mysql -h localhost -u root -p
Enter password:
Welcome to the MySQL monitor.  Commands end with ; or \g.
Your MySQL connection id is 22
Server version: 8.0.12 MySQL Community Server - GPL
mysql> UNINSTALL COMPONENT 'file://component_validate_password';
Query OK, 0 rows affected (0.10 sec)
mysql> exit
Bye
[philip@localhost Documents]$
```

Excellent! We used the UNINSTALL COMPONENT command to remove
the component_validate_password. Now, we can log in as we did earlier and continue:

```
mysql> grant all on netaccess.* to 'philip'@'172.16.175.130';
Query OK, 0 rows affected (0.06 sec)
mysql>
```

Awesome! The last step is to reload the grant tables; we will use the flush command, as
follows:

```
mysql> flush privileges
    -> ;
Query OK, 0 rows affected (0.00 sec)
mysql>
```

Awesome! When we left off ;, the command was not executed. We always need to end
with a semicolon (;). Now, we can test over the network, from our Ubuntu system. We will
have to install the mysql-client on the Ubuntu 18 system, as follows:

```
philip@Linuxplus:~$ mysql
Command 'mysql' not found, but can be installed with:
sudo apt install mysql-client-core-5.7
sudo apt install mariadb-client-core-10.1
philip@Linuxplus:~$ sudo apt install mysql-client-core-5.7
[sudo] password for philip:
Reading package lists... Done
Building dependency tree
Setting up mysql-client-core-5.7 (5.7.23-0ubuntu0.18.04.1) ...
Processing triggers for libc-bin (2.27-3ubuntu1) ...
philip@Linuxplus:~$ mysql -h 172.16.175.129 -u philip -p
Enter password:
Welcome to the MySQL monitor.  Commands end with ; or \g.
Your MySQL connection id is 25
Server version: 8.0.12 MySQL Community Server - GPL
Copyright (c) 2000, 2018, Oracle and/or its affiliates. All rights
```

```
reserved.
Oracle is a registered trademark of Oracle Corporation and/or its
affiliates. Other names may be trademarks of their respective
owners.
Type 'help;' or '\h' for help. Type '\c' to clear the current input
statement.
mysql>
```

Excellent! We successfully connected the `mysql` server hosted on our Fedora 28 system over the network, using the Ubuntu 18 client. We can now use a variety of commands, such as the `show databases` command:

```
mysql> show databases;
+--------------------+
| Database |
+--------------------+
| information_schema |
| netaccess |
+--------------------+
2 rows in set (0.06 sec)
mysql>
```

Awesome! We can see two databases here: the one that we created earlier and an internal database. However, if we run this command as the root user, we will see all of the available databases as follows:

```
mysql> show databases;
+--------------------+
| Database           |
+--------------------+
| information_schema |
| mysql              |
| netaccess          |
| performance_schema |
| sys                |
+--------------------+
5 rows in set (0.00 sec)
mysql>
```

Excellent! Another way to view the databases is to use the `mysql` command with the `-e` option; this allows us to perform commands from the shell. The following code snippet shows how we can list the databases:

```
philip@Linuxplus:~$ mysql -h 172.16.175.129 -u philip -p -e "show
databases"
Enter password:
+--------------------+
```

```
| Database           |
+--------------------+
| information_schema |
| netaccess          |
+--------------------+
philip@Linuxplus:~$
```

Awesome! Following this, we can use the `use` command to switch to a given database. The following code shows how we can specify the database to use:

```
mysql> use netaccess;
Database changed
mysql>
```

We are now inside of the `netaccess` database. To begin using the databases, we have to first create a table; before we create a table, we need to know what type of table we would like to create. For instance, let's suppose that we want to create a table about public places; we will want to have a field for the name of the place. If we just create a table with the name of the place, it will not be that appealing; we will want to add other aspects, such as the service provided and the location, to name a couple. As you can see, a table can contain a variety of options. To start, we will use the fields mentioned in our example. For this, we're going to use the `create table` command, as follows:

```
mysql> create table Public_Places (name VARCHAR(20), location VARCHAR(30),
service_provided VARCHAR(30));
Query OK, 0 rows affected (9.44 sec)
mysql>
```

Excellent! We successfully created our first table. We can view the tables using the `show tables` command:

```
mysql> show tables;
+--------------------+
| Tables_in_netaccess |
+--------------------+
| Public_Places      |
+--------------------+
1 row in set (0.11 sec)
mysql>
```

We can see our table listed. We can view the fields that we created using the `describe` command. The following code shows how we can use the `describe` command:

```
mysql> describe Public_Places;
+------------------+-------------+------+-----+---------+-------+
| Field            | Type        | Null | Key | Default | Extra |
+------------------+-------------+------+-----+---------+-------+
| name             | varchar(20) | YES  |     | NULL    |       |
| location         | varchar(30) | YES  |     | NULL    |       |
| service_provided | varchar(30) | YES  |     | NULL    |       |
+------------------+-------------+------+-----+---------+-------+
3 rows in set (0.23 sec)
mysql>
```

Awesome! We can see the fields, along with their types; the `varchar` type length can be a value between 0 and 65,535. Currently, the table is empty, so we have to populate it.

The insert command

We can use the `insert` command to populate a table. The basic syntax is as follows:

```
insert into <table> <field(s)><value(s)>
```

We can add some information to the table that we created earlier, as follows:

```
mysql> insert into Public_Places values('Police Station', 'Capital City',
'serve and protect');
Query OK, 1 row affected (0.17 sec)
mysql>
```

Wonderful! We specified the values and passed them with the `insert` command, which stored the data in the table. Another way to insert data is to insert data in only some of the fields; we have to specify the field names to do selective insertion. The following code shows how we can insert data into some portions of the table:

```
mysql> insert into Public_Places (name, location) values('Telephone
Company', 'Georgetown');
Query OK, 1 row affected (0.16 sec)
mysql>
```

Awesome! We only inserted values for two fields (`name` and `location`). Another way to insert data is to use the `mysql` command with the `-e` option, as follows:

```
philip@Linuxplus:~$ mysql -h 172.16.175.129 -u philip -p -e "USE netaccess;
INSERT INTO Public_Places values ('Hospital' , 'Georgetown',
'healthcare');"
Enter password:
philip@Linuxplus:~$
```

Awesome! The data was successfully entered into the table.

The select command

So far, we've been adding contents to our table. However, we have not seen the values that we've added. We can use the `select` command to view the contents of a table, as follows:

```
mysql> select * from Public_Places;
+--------------------+--------------+--------------------+
| name               | location     | service_provided   |
+--------------------+--------------+--------------------+
| Police Station     | Capital City | serve and protect  |
| Telephone Company  | Georgetown   | NULL               |
| Hospital           | Georgetown   | healthcare         |
+--------------------+--------------+--------------------+
3 rows in set (0.00 sec)
mysql>
```

Excellent! We can see all of the values that we have entered so far in our table. Furthermore, we can perform selective searches by specifying the `where` clause, as follows:

```
mysql> select * from Public_Places where name='Telephone Company';
+--------------------+------------+------------------+
| name               | location   | service_provided |
+--------------------+------------+------------------+
| Telephone Company  | Georgetown | NULL             |
+--------------------+------------+------------------+
1 row in set (0.00 sec)
mysql>
```

Wonderful! We can also perform searches using the following methods:

```
mysql> select name, service_provided from Public_Places;
+--------------------+--------------------+
| name               | service_provided   |
+--------------------+--------------------+
| Police Station     | serve and protect  |
```

```
| Telephone Company | NULL               |
| Hospital          | healthcare         |
+-------------------+--------------------+
3 rows in set (0.00 sec)
mysql> select service_provided from Public_Places;
+--------------------+
| service_provided   |
+--------------------+
| serve and protect  |
| NULL               |
| healthcare         |
+--------------------+
3 rows in set (0.00 sec)
mysql>
```

Awesome!

The update command

We can use the update command to make changes to a table, as follows:

```
mysql> update Public_Places set service_provided='Telephones' where
name='Telephone Company';
Query OK, 1 row affected (0.05 sec)
Rows matched: 1  Changed: 1  Warnings: 0
mysql>
```

Excellent! We've filled in the data for the service_provided field of Telephone Company; this can be verified using the select command, as follows:

```
mysql> select * from Public_Places;
+-------------------+--------------+--------------------+
| name              | location     | service_provided   |
+-------------------+--------------+--------------------+
| Police Station    | Capital City | serve and protect  |
| Telephone Company | Georgetown   | Telephones         |
| Hospital          | Georgetown   | healthcare         |
+-------------------+--------------+--------------------+
3 rows in set (0.00 sec)
mysql>
```

We can see that the field for service_provided has been filled. Additionally, we can change the data using the update command, as follows:

```
mysql> update Public_Places set location='Kaieteur Falls' where
name='Hospital';
```

```
Query OK, 1 row affected (0.15 sec)
Rows matched: 1  Changed: 1  Warnings: 0
mysql> select * from Public_Places;
+--------------------+----------------+---------------------+
| name               | location       | service_provided    |
+--------------------+----------------+---------------------+
| Police Station     | Capital City   | serve and protect   |
| Telephone Company  | Georgetown     | Telephones          |
| Hospital           | Kaieteur Falls | healthcare          |
+--------------------+----------------+---------------------+
3 rows in set (0.00 sec)
mysql> update Public_Places set name='GPF' where name='Police Station';
Query OK, 1 row affected (0.16 sec) The dele
Rows matched: 1  Changed: 1  Warnings: 0
mysql> select * from Public_Places;
+--------------------+----------------+---------------------+
| name               | location       | service_provided    |
+--------------------+----------------+---------------------+
| GPF                | Capital City   | serve and protect   |
| Telephone Company  | Georgetown     | Telephones          |
| Hospital           | Kaieteur Falls | healthcare          |
+--------------------+----------------+---------------------+
3 rows in set (0.00 sec)
mysql>
```

Excellent!

The delete command

We can remove values from the fields of a table using the `delete` command, as follows:

```
mysql> delete from Public_Places where name='Hospital';
Query OK, 1 row affected (0.18 sec)
mysql> select * from Public_Places;
+--------------------+--------------+---------------------+
| name               | location     | service_provided    |
+--------------------+--------------+---------------------+
| GPF                | Capital City | serve and protect   |
| Telephone Company  | Georgetown   | Telephones          |
+--------------------+--------------+---------------------+
2 rows in set (0.01 sec)
mysql>
```

The field that was specified with the `delete` command was removed.

The from option

We can use the `from` option to specify which table to use; for instance, if we specify a non-existing table, we will see the following messages:

```
mysql> select * from myTable;
ERROR 1146 (42S02): Table 'netaccess.myTable' doesn't exist
mysql>
```

The table does not exist, so we have to enter the correct table when performing queries, using the `from` option.

The where condition

We can use the `where` condition when we want to perform some selective manipulation. We've used the `where` condition previously, with the `select`, `update`, and `delete` commands. As a refresher, we can use the `where` condition as follows:

```
mysql> select * from Public_Places where name='GPF';
+--------+--------------+--------------------+
| name   | location     | service_provided   |
+--------+--------------+--------------------+
| GPF    | Capital City | serve and protect  |
+--------+--------------+--------------------+
1 row in set (0.00 sec)
mysql>
```

Excellent! Only the results from the condition are displayed.

The group by option

We can use the `group by` option to provide results based on the criteria that we specify, as follows:

```
mysql> select name from Public_Places group by name;
+-------------------+
| name              |
+-------------------+
| GPF               |
| Telephone Company |
+-------------------+
2 rows in set (0.02 sec)
mysql>
```

Awesome! The results are grouped by the specified criteria. This is useful when we have tables that consist of numbers, for instance, customer ID, employee ID, and ordered, to name a few.

The order by option

We can use the `order by` option to sort the data in the table, in either an ascending or descending order. The following code shows how to use the `order by` option:

```
mysql> select * from Public_Places order by service_provided;
+--------------------+--------------+---------------------+
| name               | location     | service_provided    |
+--------------------+--------------+---------------------+
| GPF                | Capital City | serve and protect   |
| Telephone Company  | Georgetown   | Telephones          |
+--------------------+--------------+---------------------+
2 rows in set (0.02 sec)
mysql>
```

Based on the default, the data is sorted in an ascending order; however, we can display the results in a descending order by passing the `DESC` keyword, as follows:

```
mysql> select * from Public_Places order by service_provided DESC;
+--------------------+--------------+---------------------+
| name               | location     | service_provided    |
+--------------------+--------------+---------------------+
| Telephone Company  | Georgetown   | Telephones          |
| GPF                | Capital City | serve and protect   |
+--------------------+--------------+---------------------+
2 rows in set (0.00 sec)
mysql>
```

Excellent! The results are displayed in a descending order.

The join option

We can use a simple join by passing the `join` option; this can be used to combine rows from separate tables and to look at a common factor between the tables. I've created two tables, as follows:

```
mysql> select * from Cust;
+--------+----------------------+---------------------+
| custID | custName             | location            |
+--------+----------------------+---------------------+
```

```
|           1 | Philip Inshanally       | Georgetown, Guyana |
|           2 | Matthew Zach Inshanally | Georgetown, Guyana |
+----------+-------------------------+--------------------+
2 rows in set (0.03 sec)
mysql> select * from Purchase;
+----------+------------+------------+
| orderID  | purchaseID | orderDate  |
+----------+------------+------------+
|        2 |   20150202 |  201800902 |
|        1 |   10031984 |   20180310 |
+----------+------------+------------+
2 rows in set (0.00 sec)
mysql>
```

The columns that are identical are the first columns of each table; the `Cust` table refers to this as `custID`, whereas the `Purchase` table refers to this as ordered. Based on this, we can create a select query that will merge the two tables, as follows:

```
mysql> SELECT Purchase.orderID, Cust.custName, Purchase.orderDate FROM
Purchase INNER JOIN Cust ON Purchase.orderID=Cust.custID;
+----------+-------------------------+------------+
| orderID  | custName                | orderDate  |
+----------+-------------------------+------------+
|        1 | Philip Inshanally       |   20180310 |
|        2 | Matthew Zach Inshanally |  201800902 |
+----------+-------------------------+------------+
2 rows in set (0.01 sec)
mysql>
```

Excellent! We referenced the fields by placing the table's name in front of `Purchase.orderID, Cust.custName, Purchase.orderDate`; this defined how the table would be presented.

The next portion, `FROM Purchase INNER JOIN Cust ON Purchase.orderID=Cust.custID;`, established that the content would be coming from the `Purchase` table, and it would be joined by using the common column of `Purchase.orderID=Cust.custID`, hence producing the results containing data from both tables.

This is known as an inner join; it returns data that has matching values in both tables.

Summary

In this chapter, we looked at shell scripting and SQL management. First, we covered the basics of shell scripting. Next, we worked our way through writing scripts using `for` loops. This was followed by using the `while` loop. We finished off with `if` statements in scripts.

Next, we worked with SQL management. First, we installed the MySQL repository, and then we installed the community-server edition of MySQL. This was followed by securing our `mysql` server. Then, we dove into the creation of a database, followed by creating a table. We then started to manage the data in the table by using a variety of techniques; we finished by creating additional tables, in order to demonstrate inner joins.

I've had an awesome time compiling every chapter in this book. I'm confident that you will learn a lot from this as you move forward with your career. I want to thank you for choosing this book and making it a part of your collection. Until next time, this is Philip Inshanally, reminding you to always be grateful. I'll see you soon!

Questions

1. Which characters identify the start of the line where the interpreter is defined?

   A. `#$`
   B. `#@`
   C. `#!`
   D. `#^`

2. Which of the following environment variables store the current shell?

   A. `SHELL`
   B. `BASH`
   C. `SH`
   D. `TCSH`

3. Which of the following keywords ends a `for` loop?

    A. `do`
    B. `do loop`
    C. `done`
    D. `fi`

4. If a script resides in the present directory, what character needs to be placed in front of / in order to run the script?

    A. `.`
    B. `:`
    C. `;`
    D. "

5. Which of the following commands can create a variable to store the user's input?

    A. `execute`
    B. `pause`
    C. `write`
    D. `read`

6. Which of the following characters can be used to test two conditions and return TRUE if either condition is true?

    A. `&&`
    B. `||`
    C. `//`
    D. `==`

7. Which of the following characters are used as a wildcard when using the `select` command to perform a `mysql` query?

        A. +
        B. /
        C. *
        D. –

8. Which of the following options is used to check for a condition when using the `select` command?

        A. `from`
        B. `if`
        C. `where`
        D. `JOIN`

9. Which of the following commands would create a table using mysql?

        A. `create tables`
        B. `CREATE TABLE`
        C. `CREATE TABLES`
        D. `create TABLEs`

10. Which of the following commands can be used to change a value using `mysql`?

        A. `INSERT`
        B. `DELETE`
        C. `UPDATE`
        D. `JOIN`

Further reading

- The following site provides useful information about shell scripting: `https://www.shellscript.sh`
- The following site provides useful information about loops: `https://www.tutorialspoint.com`
- The following site provides useful information about mysql: `https://www.w3schools.com`

19
Mock Exam - 1

Questions

1. Which of the passwords listed below is considered secured?

   A. `password123`
   B. `t%h@)_14!*!`
   C. `12345678`
   D. `abcdefgh`

2. Which environment variable stores the current shell?

   A. SHELL
   B. BASH
   C. SH
   D. TCSH

3. Which mount point hold system configuration files?

   A. `/boot`
   B. `/home`
   C. `/etc`
   D. `/var`

4. Which command is used to update GRUB2 in Ubuntu?

> A. `update-grub2`
> B. `make-grub`
> C. `update-grub-gfxpayload`
> D. `grub2-update`

Answer A

5. Which directory is the GRUB configuration files located in Ubuntu 18?

> A. `/boot/grub2/`
> B. `/var`
> C. `/etct/grub2/grub/`
> D. `/boot/grub/`

6. Which characters can be used to test 2 conditions and return TRUE if both conditions are true?

> A. `&&`
> B. `||`
> C. `//`
> D. `==`

7. Which character is used in front an equal sign = to ensure a condition is not TRUE in an if clause?

> A. `+`
> B. `!`
> C. `>`
> D. `<`

8. Which bit must be turned on in order for a script to be able to run?

    A. execute
    B. read
    C. write
    D. read and write

9. Which command can be used to modify permissions such as read, write & execute on a file?

    A. chown
    B. chmod
    C. file
    D. whois

10. Which value represents RWX permissions for a file?

    A. 5
    B. 4
    C. 7
    D. 1

11. Which value represents RW permissions for a file?

    A. 6
    B. 4
    C. 7
    D. 1

12. Which option can be used with the `mysql` command to enable the user to pass a command?

        A. `-a`
        B. `-e`
        C. `-c`
        D. `-b`

13. Which option with the `timedatectl` command can be used to display all the available timezones?

        A. `--list-timezones`
        B. `--list-time-zones`
        C. `list-timezones`
        D. `list-timezone`

14. Which character must be placed in front the H when setting the hour using the date command?

        A. `#`
        B. `@`
        C. `$`
        D. `%`

15. Which option is list used to query for a given package using the `rpm` command?

        A. `-a`
        B. `-q`
        C. `-e`
        D. `r`

16. Which command can be used to reconfigure a package in an Ubuntu system?

> A. `dpkg--update`
> B. `dpkg -r`
> C. `dpkg -e`
> D. `dpkg-reconfigure`

17. Which command can be used to change ownership for a file?

> A. `chmod`
> B. `chown`
> C. `chwn`
> D. `chmd`

18. Which keyword is used to sort in descending when performing a query in mysql?

> A. description
> B. DESC
> C. descending
> D. Descending

19. Which of the following command can be used to execute a job 5 minutes from the present?

> A. at now + 5 minutes
> B. at 5 minutes
> C. at tomorrow 5 minutes
> D. at next 5minutes

20. Which option with the at command can be used to print the job queue?

    A. -q
    B. -a
    C. -l
    D. -e

21. What is the name of the cron service in Fedora 28?

    A. crond.service
    B. cron.service
    C. cron-daemon.service
    D. crond.daemon.service

22. Which directory can we place a script if we would like to script to be executed every hour?

    A. /etc/crond.hourly
    B. /etc/cron.hourly/
    C. /etc/crond/hourly/jobs
    D. /etc/cron/hourly/

23. Which command should be used when editing the /etc/sudoers file?

    A. visudo
    B. visualdo
    C. nano
    D. vim.tiny

24. Which of the following timer values would enable a command to execute every 5 minutes?

        A. 0/5 * * * *
        B. * 5 * * *
        C. * * 5 * *
        D. * * * 5 *

25. Which option can be used to view the `crontab` file for the current user?

        A. -a
        B. -b
        C. -d
        D. -1

26. Which of the following timer values would enable a command to execute at 5:00 AM every day?

        A. 0/5 * * * *
        B. * 5 * * *
        C. * * 5 * *
        D. * * * 5 *

27. Which of the following statements is correct about the /proc/?

        A. Changes to files in /proc/ are not implemented in any way.
        B. The files in the /proc/ are meant to be used as comments
        C. Any change done in the /proc/ is implemented in real-time.
        D. Files within the /proc/ cannot be edited

28. Which character needs to b placed in front a variable in order to use it?

    A. #
    B. $
    C. !
    D. &

29. Which option can be used to set the system time from the hardware clock?

    A. `--hctosys`
    B. `--systohc`
    C. `--systohc`
    D. `--hctohc`

30. Which number can be used to restart a system using the `init` command?

    A. 1
    B. 0
    C. 6
    D. 2

31. Which option can be used to reboot a system using the `shutdown` command?

    A. `-a`
    B. `-s`
    C. `-c`
    D. `-r`

32. Which number can be used to enter rescue mode using the `init` command?

    A. 6
    B. 1
    C. 7
    D. 2

33. Which is the default runlevel on a CentOS 5 system using a SysV init system?

        A. 2
        B. 4
        C. 5
        D. 1

34. Which command can be used to display messages which were generated during boot up?

        A. `echo`
        B. `anacron`
        C. `message`
        D. `dmesg`

35. What is a common setting that is found in the BIOS?

        A. Boot options
        B. Kernel options
        C. initram options
        D. GRUB2 options

36. Which command can be used to display shared library information for a given command?

        A. `ldconfig`
        B. `ld`
        C. `ldd`
        D. `libconfig`

37. Which of the following defines the `/bin/sh` at the very starting of a shell script?

    A. `@!/bin/sh`
    B. `#!/bin/sh`
    C. `#%/bin/sh`
    D. `@#/bin/sh`

38. Which of the following is used to compare whether one condition is equivalent to another?

    A. `==`
    B. `!=`
    C. `=`
    D. `=!`

39. Which keyword is used to end an `if` statement?

    A. `if`
    B. `endif`
    C. `fi`
    D. `elif`

40. Which option is used to remove a package using the `rpm` command?

    A. `-e`
    B. `-a`
    C. `-r`
    D. `-d`

41. Which option is used to remove a package and its configuration files using the dpkg command?

       A. -R
       B. -r
       C. -p
       D. -P

42. Which command can be used to search for a package in a Debian distribution?

       A. apt-cache
       B. apt-get
       C. dpkg
       D. rpm

43. Which directory does apt uses for sources whenever installing a new package?

       A. /etc/apt/sources.d/sources.list
       B. /etc/apt/apt.sources.list
       C. /etc/apt/sources.list
       D. /etc/apt/list.sources

44. Which option can be used to display statistics about a package using the apt-cache command?

       A. statistics
       B. stats
       C. stat
       D. -s

45. Which character can be used to start a program in background?

      A. #
      B. !
      C. %
      D. &

46. Which of the following represents a default IPv6 route?

      A. `0:1:1:1:1:1:1:1/128`
      B. `::/0`
      C. `:0::/0`
      D. `:1::/0`

47. Which of the following port does FTP use for command traffic?

      A. TCP 21
      B. UDP 21
      C. ICMP 21
      D. HSRP 21

48. Which of the following represents a /23 in binary?

      A. `11111111.11111000.11111111.00000000`
      B. `11111110.00000000.00000001.00000000`
      C. `11111111.11111110.00000000.00000001`
      D. `11111111.11111111.11111110.00000000`

49. Which of the following represents a Classful B subnet mask?

      A. `255.255.255.128`
      B. `255.255.0.0`
      C. `255.254.255.0`
      D. `255.253.255.0`

50. Which option is used to view hidden files and directories using the ls command?

        A. -l
        B. -s
        C. -a
        D. -r

51. Which character is used to switch to the current user's home directory?

        A. ~
        B. `
        C. '
        D. !

52. Which option can be used to search for permissions using the find command?

        A. --permissions
        B. -perm
        C. --perms
        D. --view-permissions

53. Which command can be used to update the mlocate database?

        A. update-locate
        B. update-database
        C. updatedb
        D. updated

54. Which option can be used to ignore case when searching with the locate command?

        A. --ignore
        B. -i
        C. --no-case
        D. -c

55. Which option is used to display the total number of words using the wc command?

    A. -c
    B. -a
    C. -w
    D. -l

56. Which characters can be used when appending data to a file?

    A. >
    B. <
    C. <<
    D. >>

57. Which command can be used to display the output and simultaneously send the output to a file?

    A. tee
    B. cat
    C. echo
    D. pause

58. Which command can be used to change the niceness of a running program without having to stop and start the program?

    A. nice
    B. touch
    C. renice
    D. updatedb

59. Which command can be used to resume a paused job and place it n the background running?

    A. `bg`
    B. `fg`
    C. `gb`
    D. `gf`

60. Which file is usually used for storing alias?

    A. `.bash_logout`
    B. `.bash_history`
    C. `.bashrc`
    D. `.bash_login`

Answers

1. B	2. A	3.	4. C	5. A	6. D	7. A
8. A	9. B	10. C	11. A	12. B	13. C	14. D
15. B	16. D	17. B	18. B	19. A	20. B	21. A
22. B	23. A	24. A	25. D	26. B	27. C	28. B
29. A	30. C	31. D	32. B	33. C	34. D	35. A
36. C	37. B	38. A	39. C	40. C	41. A	42. D
43. A	44. C	45. B	46. D	47. B	48. A	49. D
50. B	51. C	52. A	53. B	54. C	55. B	56. C
57. D	58. A	59. C	60. A	61. C		

Mock Exam - 2

Questions

1. Which option can be used with the `netstat` command in order to display the routing table?

   A. `-s`
   B. `-a`
   C. `-r`
   D. `-d`

2. Which address family is the IP information located using either `ifconfig` or `ip a` command?

   A. `inet`
   B. `inet6`
   C. `int`
   D. `int6`

3. Which of the following is the correct method to shutdown an interface?

   A. `ifconfig down ens33`
   B. `ifconfig ens33 down`
   C. `ifconfig ens33 shutdown`
   D. `ifconfig shutdown ens33`

4. Which file does the `ifup` command checks whenever the command is issued?

      A. `/etc/network/sysconfig`
      B. `/etc/networking/interfaces`
      C. `/etc/network/interfaces`
      D. `/etc/sysconfig/network/interfaces`

5. Which of the following is the correct way to remove an IP using the `ip` command?

      A. `ip a del 10.10.10.1/24 dev ens33`
      B. `ip a 10.10.10.1/24 del dev ens33`
      C. `ip a 10.10.10.1/24 dev ens33 del`
      D. `ip del a 10.10.10.1/24 dev ens33`

6. What does the `*` represents in the output of the `fdisk -l` command?

      A. The device's partition is marked as unbootable
      B. The device's partition is marked as bootable
      C. The device's partition is marked as read-only
      D. The device's partition is inaccessible

7. Which option is used to change the partition type using the `fdisk` utility?

      A. l
      B. n
      C. l
      D. d

8. Which number type represents an NTFS partition using the `fdisk` utility?

      A. 7
      B. 8
      C. 6
      D. 5

9. Which option is used to change the size of a partition using the `parted` utility?

    A. `changesizepart`
    B. `sizechangepart`
    C. `resizepart`
    D. `sizeresizepart`

10. Which option can be used to display information such as the UUIDs of drives using the `lsblk` command?

    A. `-a`
    B. `-f`
    C. `-l`
    D. `-i`

11. Which option is used to display information in a human readable format using the `df` command?

    A. `-a`
    B. `-c`
    C. `-r`
    D. `-h`

12. Which of the following is the correct for defining a variable?

    A. `a=1`
    B. `a=Loop Free`
    C. `a= 1 2 3`
    D. `a=#1`

13. Which option is used to allow the user to define the user, uid, gid with the mount command?

   A. -v
   B. -t
   C. -u
   D. -o

14. Which command can be used to switch the display manager in a Fedora distribution?

   A. system-displaymanager
   B. system-switch-displaymanager
   C. switch-displaymanager
   D. system-switch-display

15. Which file can hold the default display manager in an Ubuntu distribution?

   A. /etc/X11/default-display-manager
   B. /etc/X11/display/default-manager
   C. /etc/X11/default-manager/display
   D. /etc/X11/default-display/manager

16. Which file holds the commands execute for a given user?

   A. ~/.bash_history
   B. /etc/.bash_history
   C. /var/bash/.bash_history
   D. /bash_history

17. Which option is used with the `useradd` command to display the defaults for a new user?

        A. -d
        B. -c
        C. -D
        D. -s

18. Which files holds the actual hashed passwords for all users?

        A. /etc/passwd
        B. /etc/shadow
        C. /etc/gshadow
        D. /etc/hidden/password

19. Which option is used to define a shell for a new user with the `useradd` command?

        A. -s
        B. -S
        C. -shell
        D. -Shell

20. Which option is used to define an expiration date for a user with the `chage` command?

        A. -e
        B. -l
        C. -a
        D. -E

21. Which option is used to display information regarding an account's current state using the `passwd` command?

        A. `-a`
        B. `--status`
        C. `-s`
        D. `--list-status`

22. Which letter indicates that an account's current state is unlocked with the `passwd` command?

        A. `U`
        B. `L`
        C. `P`
        D. `A`

23. Which option displays the date when the system booted up with the `who` command?

        A. `-a`
        B. `-c`
        C. `-r`
        D. `-e`

24. Which command displays users who have recently logged in?

        A. `which`
        B. `whois`
        C. `last`
        D. `recent`

25. Which command is used to create a group?

        A. `add-group`
        B. `groupadd`
        C. `add -G`
        D. `group -G`

26. Which option defines a user to use a group as its primary group?

        A. `-G`
        B. `--group`
        C. `--group-new`
        D. `-g`

27. Which option is used to display only TCP connection using the `netstat` command

        A. `-t`
        B. `-u`
        C. `-r`
        D. `-c`

28. Which port does HTTPS uses?

        A. `80`
        B. `21`
        C. `443`
        D. `69`

29. Which command handles the system log files in a Fedora 28 distribution?

        A. `log`
        B. `journalctl`
        C. `log.service`
        D. `logging.service`

30. Which classful range does `172.16.0.1` belong?

     A. Class B
     B. Class D
     C. Class A
     D. Class E

31. Which port does TFTP uses?

     A. `21`
     B. `53`
     C. `69`
     D. `443`

32. Which option prints the program ID and program name with the `netstat` command?

     A. `-r`
     B. `-a`
     C. `-l`
     D. `-p`

33. Which option is used to list only the targets with the `systemctl` command?

     A. `-t`
     B. `-r`
     C. `-type`
     D. `-M`

34. Which command can be used to generate a test log message?

     A. `log-test`
     B. `test-log`
     C. `logger`
     D. `log`

35. Which port does DNS uses?

        A. `139`
        B. `110`
        C. `143`
        D. `53`

36. Which option changes rsyslog to use TCP for reception?

        A. `module(load="tcp")`
        B. `module(load="imtcp")`
        C. `module("imtcp"=load)`
        D. `module("tcp"=load)`

37. Which of the following is the configuration file for rsyslog?

        A. `/etc/rsyslog.d/rsyslog.conf`
        B. `/etc/rsyslog/rsyslog.conf`
        C. `/etc/rsyslog.conf`
        D. `/etc/rsyslog.d/rsyslog.service`

38. Which of the following specifies only the informational messages should be sent to the rsyslog server?

        A. `*.info`
        B. `info.*`
        C. `*.message-type=informational`
        D. `message*.type=information`

39. Which configuration file should mount points be placed so that they are auto mounted upon system boot?

       A. `/etc/mounts.conf`
       B. `/etc/auto.mount.cfg`
       C. `/etc/fstab`
       D. `/etc/mn.conf`

40. Which of the follow mysql select statement is correct?

       A. `select * from netaccess where set=public_places`
       B. `select * from netaccess where custID='Philip'`
       C. `select * from netaccess where custID=Philip`
       D. `select * from netacces update set custID=Philip`

41. Which configuration file is the name servers defined?

       A. `/etc/hosts`
       B. `/etc/name.conf`
       C. `/etc/resolv.conf`
       D. `/etc/dig.conf`

42. Which of the following represents the link-local IPv6 range?

       A. `fe80::/10`
       B. `fd80::/7`
       C. `fc00::/7`
       D. `ff00::/10`

43. Which character is used when no password has been set for a group in the `/etc/gshadow`?

        A. #
        B. %
        C. !
        D. &

44. Which command is used to change a group ID of a given group?

        A. groupmod
        B. groupadd
        C. gidmod
        D. usermod

45. Which of the following is used to kill the sudo authentication timer immediately?

        A. -l
        B. -k
        C. -a
        D. -r

46. Which of the following is used to kill the sudo authentication timer immediately?

        A. -l
        B. -k
        C. -a
        D. -r

47. Which of the following must be placed in front of a group inside the `/etc/sudoers`?

    A. #
    B. @
    C. %
    D. &

48. Which option is used to display only a particular interface with the `ip a` command?

    A. s
    B. d
    C. v
    D. i

49. Which option is used to define a type using the `ip link` command?

    A. `--type`
    B. `type`
    C. `--link-type`
    D. `--type-id`

50. Which IP represents the local loopback address?

    A. `128.0.0.1`
    B. `192.168.0.1`
    C. `127.0.0.1`
    D. `127.0.0.0`

51. Which of the following represents a subnet mask of /28 in dotted decimal format?

> A. 255.255.255.240
> B. 255.255.252.240
> C. 255.255.254.240
> D. 255.255.253.240

52. Which of the following is correct for displaying statistics and other information like CRC counters using the `ip` command?

> A. `ip a -s link ls ens33`
> B. `ip a -a link ls ens33`
> C. `ip a -s -s link ens33`
> D. `ip a -a -s link ls ens33`

53. Which of the following MySQL select statement is correct for sorting the data in descending order?

> A. `select * from Public_Places order by service_provided;`
> B. `select * from Public_Places order by service_provided DESC;`
> C. `select * from Public_Places DESC order by service_provided;`
> D. `select DESC * from Public_Places order by service_provided;`

54. Which option displays the files owned by a package using the `dpkg` command?

> A. `-a`
> B. `-s`
> C. `-l`
> D. `-L`

55. Which is the first process started in a Linux distribution using SysV?

> A. SysV
> B. ps
> C. init
> D. systemd

56. If it exists, which file is a symbolic link to the /boot/grub/grub.conf?

> A. /boot/grub/grub2.cfg
> B. /boot/grub2/grub.cfg
> C. /boot/grub.d/menu.lst
> D. /boot/grub/menu.lst

57. Which directory would be used for adding a custom boot entry for GRUB2?

> A. /etc/default/grub
> B. /etc/grub.d/
> C. /etc/grub/default/custom
> D. /etc/default/grub-custom

58. What is the default partitioning scheme when performing an installation of CentOS7?

> A. ext4
> B. ext3
> C. LVM
> D. XFS

59. Which shell scripting keyword enables the user to test for another condition(s) if the condition(s) in the if clause were not met?

    A. `elif`
    B. `elseif`
    C. `else`
    D. `fi`

60. What shell scripting keyword defines the end of a while loop?

    A. `loop end`
    B. `fi`
    C. `else`
    D. `done`

Answers

1. C	2. A	3. B	4. C	5. A	6. B
7. C	8. A	9. C	10. B	11. D	12. A
13. D	14. B	15. A	16. A	17. C	18. B
19. A	20. D	21. B	22. C	23. A	24. C
25. B	26. D	27. A	28. C	29. B	30. A
31. C	32. D	33. A	34. C	35. D	36. B
37. C	38. A	39. C	40. B	41. C	42. A
43. C	44. A	45. B	46. B	47. C	48. A
49. B	50. C	51. A	52. C	53. B	54. D
55. C	56. D	57. B	58. C	59. A	60. A

Assessment

Chapter 1: Configuring the Hardware Settings

1. Answer is A: `/dev`
2. Answer is D: `cat /proc/cpuinfo`
3. Answer is C: `cat /proc/meminfo`
4. Answer is C: `free -h`
5. Answer is C: `mkswap`
6. Answer is D: `swapon`
7. Answer is B: `swapon`
8. Answer is B: `/dev/null`
9. Answer is D: `lsmod`
10. Answer is D: `modprobe`

Chapter 2: Booting the System

1. Answer is A: The boot sector
2. Answer is D: System V
3. Answer is C: `pstree`
4. Answer is B: `init`
5. Answer is D: `systemd`
6. Answer is C: `systemctl list-unit-files`
7. Answer is D: `dmesg`
8. Answer is C: `/boot/grub/`
9. Answer is A: `title`
10. Answer is C: `menuentry`
11. Answer is B: E

Chapter 3: Changing Runlevels and Boot Targets

1. Answer is B: 5
2. Answer is C: `runlevel`
3. Answer is D: `who -r`
4. Answer is B: The previous runlevel before it was changed to the current runlevel
5. Answer is D: `Single user`
6. Answer is B: `init`
7. Answer is C: `telinit`
8. Answer is A: `systemctl get-default`
9. Answer is C: `systemctl list-dependencies -type target`
10. Answer is B: `systemctl isolate multi-user.target`
11. Answer is A: `systemctl status multi-user.target`

Chapter 4: Designing a Hard Disk Layout

1. Answer is C: `fdisk - l /dev/sda`
2. Answer is D: n
3. Answer is B: a
4. Answer is A: l
5. Answer is B: n
6. Answer is D: w
7. Answer is B: `parted`
8. Answer is C: `print`
9. Answer is A: `mount /dev/sdb1`
10. Answer is A: `blkid`

Chapter 5: Installing a Linux Distribution

1. Answer is C: RAM
2. Answer is D: Try Ubuntu without installing
3. Answer is A: Install Ubuntu...
4. Answer is B: An active internet connection
5. Answer is A: Something else
6. Answer is C: Primary
7. Answer is B: To prevent the system from becoming unbootable by accidentally deleting files in `/boot`
8. Answer is B: I will configure partitioning
9. Answer is A: `grub-install`
10. Answer is D: `Minimal Install`

Chapter 6: Using Debian Package Management

1. Answer is B: `dpkg -l`
2. Answer is C: `dpkg-query -s`
3. Answer is A: `cat /var/log/dpkg.log`
4. Answer is A: `dpkg --get-selections`
5. Answer is D: `dpkg is -i`
6. Answer is C: `dpkg is -P`
7. Answer is B: `apt-get update`
8. Answer is B: `apt-cache search`
9. Answer is B: `apt-get purge`
10. Answer is C: `aptitude update`

Chapter 7: Using YUM Package Management

1. Answer is B: `yum list`
2. Answer is A: `yum makecache fast`
3. Answer is D: `yum provides`
4. Answer is A: `dpkg --get-selections`
5. Answer is B: `yum clean all`
6. Answer is A: `yum update`
7. Answer is B: `dnf repolist all`
8. Answer is A: `dnf check-update`
9. Answer is C: `rpm -qip`
10. Answer is B: `rpm --erase`

Chapter 8: Performing File Management

1. Answer is D: `/`
2. Answer is C: `cd`
3. Answer is B: `pwd`
4. Answer is A: `ls`
5. Answer is D: `-l`
6. Answer is C: `-a`
7. Answer is B: `rm`
8. Answer is C: `-empty -delete`
9. Answer is D: `updatedb`
10. Answer is D: `tee`

Chapter 9: Creating, Monitoring, Killing, and Restarting Processes

1. Answer is C: `ps`
2. Answer is C: `-e`
3. Answer is B: `--forest`
4. Answer is C: `-u`
5. Answer is B: `-l`
6. Answer is D: `9`
7. Answer is A: `-u`
8. Answer is C: `d`
9. Answer is D: `reload`
10. Answer is D: `/usr/lib/systemd/system`

Chapter 10: Modifying Process Execution

1. Answer is B: `l`
2. Answer is A: `NI`
3. Answer is D: `NI`
4. Answer is C: `20`
5. Answer is D: `-20`
6. Answer is B: `/lib/systemd/system`
7. Answer is A: `systemctl daemon-reload`
8. Answer is B: `PID`
9. Answer is A: `fg`
10. Answer is C: `bg`

Chapter 11: Displaying Managers

1. Answer is A: X Display Manager
2. Answer is B: /etc/X11/xdm
3. Answer is A: Xaccess
4. Answer is C: /etc/sysconfig/desktop
5. Answer is B: groupinstall
6. Answer is C: system-switch-displaymanager
7. Answer is A: Session Type
8. Answer is D: dpkg-reconfigure
9. Answer is C: /etc/X11/default-display-manager
10. Answer is B: ls -l /etc/systemd/system/display-manager.service

Chapter 12: Managing User and Group Accounts

1. Answer is D: /etc/skel/.bashrc
2. Answer is A: /etc.skel/.bash_logout
3. Answer is B: ~/.bash_history
4. Answer is C: -D
5. Answer is D: -s
6. Answer is D: user-add
7. Answer is B: -l
8. Answer is C: L
9. Answer is A: -g
10. Answer is C: groupmod

Chapter 13: Automating Tasks

1. Answer is B: Garbled time
2. Answer is C: At 9:00 AM next Monday
3. Answer is B: *CTRL + D* was pressed
4. Answer is D: `-l`
5. Answer is D: `-r`
6. Answer is C: `atq`
7. Answer is C: `*****`
8. Answer is B: `-e`
9. Answer is C: `@weekly`
10. Answer is A: `-f`

Chapter 14: Maintaining System Time and Logging

1. Answer is A: `-s`
2. Answer is C: `set-ntp`
3. Answer is D: `+%T`
4. Answer is A: `set-time`
5. Answer is D: `/etc/localtime`
6. Answer is B: `tzdata`
7. Answer is B: `tzselect`
8. Answer is D: `-u`
9. Answer is D: `TCP`
10. Answer is C: `logger`

Chapter 15: Fundamentals of Internet Protocol

1. Answer is C: `10.0.0.1`
2. Answer is C: `192.168.0.1`
3. Answer is A: `127.0.0.1`
4. Answer is A: `169.0.0.1`
5. Answer is A: `128.0.0.1`
6. Answer is C: `ff00::/8`
7. Answer is B: `::0/0`
8. Answer is C: `::1/128`
9. Answer is D: `fe80::/10`
10. Answer is C: `TCP 80`

Chapter 16: Network Configuration and Troubleshooting

1. Answer is D: `-a`
2. Answer is A: `default`
3. Answer is C: ICMP
4. Answer is B: `/etc/hostname`
5. Answer is C: `tracepath`
6. Answer is D: `dig`
7. Answer is A: `ip -6 route add default via 2001:db8:0:f101::2`
8. Answer is D: `-ulp`
9. Answer is C: `nmap`
10. Answer is B: `whois`

Chapter 17: Performing Administrative Security Tasks

1. Answer is C: `spawn`
2. Answer is B: `substitute user`
3. Answer is A: `root user`
4. Answer is B: `-c`
5. Answer is D: `%`
6. Answer is A: `ssh-keygen`
7. Answer is A: `ssh-add`
8. Answer is B: `ssh-copy-id`
9. Answer is B: `-e`
10. Answer is C: `-r`

Chapter 18: Shell Scripting and SQL Data Management

1. Answer is C: `#!`
2. Answer is A: `SHELL`
3. Answer is C: `done`
4. Answer is A: `.`
5. Answer is D: `read`
6. Answer is B: `||`
7. Answer is C: `*`
8. Answer is C: `where`
9. Answer is B: `CREATE TABLE`
10. Answer is C: `UPDATE`

Other Books You May Enjoy

If you enjoyed this book, you may be interested in these other books by Packt:

CompTIA A+ Certification Guide (220-901 and 220-902)
Matthew Bennett

ISBN: 978-1-78712-730-2

- Validate your skills and boost your career with CompTIA A+
- Learn all concepts raised by the A+ certification
- Understanding and installing CompTIA hardware required for CompTIA A+ 220-901.
- Install and configure an Operating System on a client/desktop, covering a range of mobile and network devices and platforms
- Learn how to secure a workstation and troubleshoot any security related issues

CompTIA Security+ Certification Guide
Ian Neil

ISBN: 978-1-78934-801-9

- Get to grips with security fundamentals from the CIA triad to Identify and Access Management
- Secure devices and applications that are used by your company
- Identify the different types of malware and virus and take appropriate actions to protect against them
- Protect your environment against social engineering and advance attacks
- Implement Public Key Infrastructure concepts
- Learn about secure coding techniques, quality control and testing
- Troubleshoot common security issues

Leave a review - let other readers know what you think

Please share your thoughts on this book with others by leaving a review on the site that you bought it from. If you purchased the book from Amazon, please leave us an honest review on this book's Amazon page. This is vital so that other potential readers can see and use your unbiased opinion to make purchasing decisions, we can understand what our customers think about our products, and our authors can see your feedback on the title that they have worked with Packt to create. It will only take a few minutes of your time, but is valuable to other potential customers, our authors, and Packt. Thank you!

Index

www.ingramcontent.com/pod-product-compliance
Lightning Source LLC
Chambersburg PA
CBHW060636060326
40690CB00020B/4419